HARPER'S TEAM

Harper's Team

Behind the Scenes in the Conservative Rise to Power

TOM FLANAGAN

Second Edition

McGill-Queen's University Press
Montreal & Kingston · London · Ithaca

© McGill-Queen's University Press 2009
ISBN 978-0-7735-3545-9

Legal deposit second quarter 2009
Bibliothèque nationale du Québec

Printed in Canada on acid-free that is 100% ancient forest free
(100% post-consummer recycled), processed chlorine free

First edition 2007, reprinted 2007

McGill-Queen's University Press acknowledges the support of the Canada
Council for the Arts for our publishing program. We also acknowledge
the financial support of the Government of Canada through the Book
Publishing Industry Development Program (BPIDP) for our publishing
activities.

Library and Archives Canada Cataloguing in Publication

Flanagan, Thomas, 1944–
    Harper's team: behind the scenes of the Conservative rise to power /
    Tom Flanagan. – 2nd ed.

    Includes bibliographical references and index.
    ISBN 978-0-7735-3545-9

    1. Conservative Party of Canada – History – 21st century. 2. Political
    campaigns – Canada. 3. Harper, Stephen, 1959–   . 4. Political leadership –
    Canada. 5. Canada – Politics and government – 1993–2006. I. Title.

    JL197.C75F48 2007   324.271'094   C2007-902741-5

This book was typeset by Interscript in 11/13.5 Sabon.

For the team

Contents

HARPER'S TEAM

Introduction

The years 2001–06 marked a tumultuous transition for Canadian conservatism. At the beginning of 2001, the newly minted Canadian Alliance started to fragment as its leader, Stockwell Day, got into serious trouble. Thirteen members left, most to join the Democratic Representative Caucus, which existed for some months in loose alliance with the Progressive Conservatives. Things seemed to be getting worse for the political right as now there were three conservative entities in Parliament, instead of two. Then in quick succession came:

- a leadership race for the Alliance, won by Stephen Harper in March 2002, promptly followed by the reintegration of the Democratic Representative Caucus into the Canadian Alliance;
- Joe Clark's resignation and a Progressive Conservative leadership race, won by Peter MacKay in May 2003;
- the merger of the two parties into the Conservative Party of Canada, approved in December 2003;
- a leadership race for the new party, won by Stephen Harper in March 2004;
- the general election of 28 June 2004, which brought Paul Martin down to a minority government;
- a failed Conservative attempt to force an election in May 2005; and
- the general election of 23 January 2006, which installed Stephen Harper in power with a minority government.

At the beginning of this five-year period, the pundits were openly sneering at conservatives, writing that they were hopelessly fragmented and that the Liberal Party would be in power for a generation. After Paul Martin concluded his decade-long campaign to push Jean Chrétien from power, most observers expected Martin to call a quick election and win the biggest majority in Canadian history. Martin himself spoke openly of winning two hundred seats in the next election.[1] He did call a quick election, but rather than win a huge majority he fell to a minority in 2004, lost power in 2006, and will soon be out of political life altogether.

What wrought this change? Partly it was a matter of the Liberals' corrupt practices catching up to them. Voters did not like what they learned about Adscam from the Auditor General and from the Gomery Commission, and they naturally looked for an alternative government. But conservatives could not have acceded to government without first creating the Conservative Party of Canada and building it into an organization capable of running a winning campaign.

I had the privilege of helping to reinvent the forces of conservatism. Almost by accident, I became Stephen Harper's chief organizer for the first four years of this transitional period. I managed his two leadership campaigns; I was his chief of staff for his first year as leader of the Canadian Alliance; I managed the Conservative national campaign in 2004; and I led much of the early organizational work behind the Conservative campaign of 2005–06. I stepped back in the spring of 2005 after I became convinced that Doug Finley would be at least as competent a campaign manager as I was, but I returned to work in the war room during the 2005–06 campaign. As the oldest guy on the team, who tried (not always successfully) to get a nap every afternoon, I helped channel the energy of the youngsters who took us over the top.

As far as I know, I'm the only political science professor, perhaps the only academic in Canadian history, who has had the opportunity to participate at this level in national campaigning (though my former student Ian Brodie, now chief of staff to Prime Minister Harper, is rapidly surpassing my experience). But I wasn't doing what you might expect an academic to do – researching, writing, strategizing, messaging. I was more like

Stephen Harper's business manager, devoting my time primarily to the less glamorous but essential tasks of raising money, hiring and supervising staff, leasing space, and contracting with pollsters, advertisers, graphic designers, printers, and telemarketers. I can't claim any credit for the strategies that Harper pursued on his way to 24 Sussex Drive. If I deserve credit for anything, it's for helping to make the new Conservative Party effective at wielding the tools of modern campaigning. In other words, I helped build the team – Harper's team.

The public spotlight is on the leader, and rightly so. A good political leader is like an outstanding athlete or entertainer – a person with a rare combination of talents. In order to succeed, a political leader must have intelligence, cunning, and toughness, as well as the ability to inspire confidence and loyalty in others. But, no matter how gifted the leader is, he can accomplish little – and indeed he won't last long – without a competent campaign team. When the leader gives a campaign speech on television, the public is looking at an individual but seeing a team effort. Behind the leader are the makeup artist and wardrobe adviser who make him look good, the speech coach and teleprompter operator who help him sound good, the policy adviser and speechwriter who craft the impressive lines, the pollster who researches the public's mood, the communications officers who set up the public appearance, the logistics people who maintain his schedule and get him to the event on time, the advance people who check the venue to make sure everything is working, the managers who hire all these people with their specialized skills, and the fundraisers who seek out the money to pay for everything.

I became a campaign organizer – a very odd role for a lifetime academic to take on. I had had some management experience at the University of Calgary as a department head and assistant to the president. I had also worked for twenty months for the Reform Party in the early 1990s, at first with the grandiose and inaccurate title "Director of Policy, Strategy, and Communications," then with the less pretentious and more accurate title "Director of Research." But I knew very little about campaigning. I had never worked in a campaign except at the humblest level – dropping leaflets door to door for my MP, Diane Ablonczy. Indeed, Stephen didn't recruit me initially to be his campaign manager. I was only supposed to help him put together a campaign team in the Canadian Alliance leadership race. But when the first team didn't work out, I offered to step in on an emergency basis and become the campaign manager. It was either that or Stephen might have abandoned his run for the leadership of the Canadian Alliance.

It is possible to manage something even if you don't know much about it. The trick is to put to work the knowledge of others. The knowledge is out there, even if it is dispersed.[2] Find people who have some understanding of the task, bring them together for discussion, let them bounce ideas off each other, and steer the discussion toward consensus. Once an agreement about action is reached, make sure that people do what they say they will – on time and within budget. If they can't deliver, find someone else. It's basically an exercise in team-building.

We were starting at the very beginning. There was no "Harper team" when Stephen decided to run for the leadership of the Canadian Alliance, because he had never put on a national campaign before. Of course, he had many friends from his local campaigns in Calgary West, his time as a Reform MP, and his days in the National Citizens Coalition; but a bunch of friends is not a team. Players have to be assigned to positions; they have to learn to work with their teammates and to take direction from the coach. And in this case, the team had to keep growing as the task became more daunting. Within three years, we went from trying to take over the Canadian Alliance to winning the leadership of the new Conservative Party to contesting with the Liberals for the privilege of governing Canada. It meant a continuous search for additional skills to fill the gaps that became apparent as we faced these new challenges, while maintaining a cohesive team loyal to the leader. We didn't complete the growth process until late summer 2005, when we filled the last holes and finally became able to confront the Liberals on more or less equal terms.

The only senior team members that I personally recruited were Ian and Vida Brodie; the others came through previous connections with Stephen or with other team members. My job was to integrate all these people coming from different places, to give them scope to make their unique contributions, and to keep them moving forward in spite of the serious reverses we suffered along the way. Our team's progress was anything but a Cinderella story of coming out of nowhere to win the championship. We had to disband our organization and start over in the first Harper leadership race in 2001–02; we lost the 2004 election when for a time it seemed winnable; we failed to force an election in spite of enormous effort in spring 2005. We finally won the 2006 election because we were good at one thing – correcting our previous mistakes.

While doing all this, I gained a new appreciation of campaigning. To be honest, I had never been particularly attracted to campaigning. I had regarded it as a necessary evil, a form of showmanship that you had to engage in before getting down to the serious business of governing. But after five years of almost nonstop campaigning and preparations for campaigning, I have a more informed view.

Campaigning is a kind of domesticated civil war, harnessed for the purpose of peacefully changing governments. Given the sorry record of political bloodshed over the centuries, it is no small achievement for democratic polities to have evolved this method of peaceful alternation in power. But the military spirit is still strong. They don't call it a "campaign" for nothing. Military terminology and metaphors abound throughout. Campaigners talk about the "war room," about the "air war" and the "ground war," about "carpet-bombing" the opposition, about "intel" and "ops." Maybe it's just playing at being soldiers, but it helps to justify the effort and intensity necessary for a successful campaign. Campaigning is a total commitment, dedicating every waking hour to defeating your opponents. You can't do it half-heartedly, any more than you can successfully conquer an enemy on the battlefield by fighting 9 AM to 5 PM, Monday through Friday.

Campaigning is also a form of persuasion. It's a collective action project to persuade large numbers of people to vote the same way at the same time. The study of persuasion should be an integral part of political science and not left to psychology or communications studies. Aristotle, the founder of political science, gave three great lecture series that his students later turned into books: one on ethics, the philosophy of right and wrong; one on politics, how government is and ought to be carried out; and one on rhetoric, how to persuade people to do things. Rhetoric, according to Aristotle, has three components: *ethos* (character), *pathos* (feeling), and *logos* (reason).[3] Political campaigning is a form of rhetoric that brings together *ethos*, *pathos*, and *logos* to motivate people to vote for your candidate. People don't vote just for ideas; they vote for potential governors whose character they can trust and who evoke emotions of loyalty and support.

Campaigning is an audition for government. In a modern state like Canada, governing means managing the activities of hundreds of thousands of public employees – setting a direction, evaluating performance and results, steering the ship if you will ("govern" is derived through Latin from the Greek word for steering a boat). Campaigning is like governing on a small scale. For a leader to put on a national campaign requires the effort of dozens or hundreds of paid staff and thousands of volunteers, carrying out a wide variety of tasks such as knocking on doors, making phone calls, placing ads on television, and organizing an extended tour of the leader and journalists around the country. If these tasks are not well done – if the tour doesn't run on time, if it doesn't attract good crowds to rallies, if the ads fail to impress, if candidates make gaffes and wander off message, if the campaign runs out of money or into debt – voters are entitled to wonder about the party's "ability to manage the infinitely more complex affairs of the federal government."[4] Governing entails another quantum leap in complexity beyond campaigning, so winning an election race is no guarantee of being able to govern competently. But a leader and team who can't put on a decent campaign are unlikely to be able to do a decent job of governing.

A campaign is all about "messaging." Speeches, leaflets, advertising, direct mail, and phone calls bombard voters with information and pleas for attention. But beyond all the overt messaging stands the campaign itself as a kind of meta-message about the leader. Harper's campaigns conveyed something about the essence of the man – that he was orderly and systematic, strategic in his thinking, and able to learn from experience. Canadians took his measure as they observed his campaigns, compared him to his rival Paul Martin, and eventually decided they could, at least on a trial basis, entrust him with the task of governing.

Campaigning, then, is not a frill. It is essential in democratic politics, and citizens should have information about how campaigns are funded, organized, and managed. This book is meant to give Canadians some of that information. Of course, I'm hardly the first to write on the subject. One or more journalists will usually produce a book about each general election (Paul Wells has done the honours for 2005–06).[5] A team of scholars organized from Carleton University publishes an edited book of essays about each federal election,[6] and Stephen Clarkson recently pulled together his contributions from that series into a book on Liberal Party campaigns (when he entitled it *The Big Red Machine*, he didn't know that's what the Hell's Angels are often called!).[7] The Canadian National Election Study team also publishes an analysis of each general election, based mainly on their tracking poll.[8] Also important are the historical books, such as John Duffy's *Fights of Our Lives*, which have narrated and analyzed some of the key campaigns in Canadian history.[9]

These books are all different from each other, but they have certain things in common. Written by external observers or historical researchers, they focus on strategy, messaging, advertising – those features of the campaign that are visible from the outside. In contrast, relatively little has been written from the inside about how Canadian political campaigns are organized, managed, and funded. John Laschinger's *Leaders and Lesser Mortals* is the main contribution of that type, written by someone who has spent most of his career actually organizing, managing, and raising money for campaigns.[10] Although I don't have Laschinger's experience as a campaign manager, this book resembles his in emphasizing the mechanics of campaigning, which are almost invisible to external observers. Coming fifteen years after his book, it also updates the description of campaign techniques, which have been heavily affected by the never-ending communications changes of the Information Age.

In one sense, campaigning hasn't changed much over the years or even centuries. *A Short Guide to Electioneering* – purportedly written by Cicero's brother in 63 BCE, when Cicero was planning to run for the consulship, the highest elected office in the Roman Republic – seems quite contemporary even after two millennia:

> Last of all, see that your whole campaign is full of show; that
> it is glorious and colourful, and pleasing to the people; that it
> has a fine appearance and dignity; furthermore, if it is by any
> means possible, see that your competitors are smeared with an
> evil reputation – which fits their characters – for crime, vice
> or bribery.[11]

Even if the essence of campaigning is timeless, the technology of
persuasion has been changing rapidly in recent years. One of the
most interesting parts of the Conservative campaign story is the
ceaseless struggle to put new technology to work – database and
predictive dialer, Internet and Blackberry, blogging and podcasting.

Harper's Team also helps document Canadian political history
at a time of rapid and important change. I can't pretend that the
book is history in the professional sense. It is based on my memories and my personal copies of documents, not on a comprehensive and impartial study of all sources. How could I aspire to
impartiality when I was so deeply involved on one side? But,
even though I couldn't see everything, I had a good seat at the table, so I think it's worth recounting what I saw and did.

That this book is organized mainly around my own perceptions and recollections creates obvious possibilities for error, because human memory is notoriously unreliable. Fortunately, I
was able to check facts in my own email archives, which are vo-
luminous and quite complete for the first Harper leadership
campaign and the election of 2005–06. All this material will be
donated to the University of Calgary Archives for the use of future researchers. I have also documented events as much as possible with references to media accounts, which helped to fill in
the gaps in my own archives. In addition, I have been able to
take advantage of the recent spate of books on Harper and the
Conservative Party by authors such as William Johnson, Lloyd
Mackey, Hugh Segal, Bob Plamondon, Don Martin, Paul Wells,
and Chantal Hébert.[12] Drawing on their accounts has helped to
discipline my own recollections and (I hope) prevented me from
giving in too much to the besetting temptation of writing memoirs – constructing a fantasy world in which the author was always right and everyone else was wrong.

As is true of all books, I could never have written it by myself. Sean Steel, Paul Willetts, Jane Arduini, and Gemma Collins printed and organized my massive email correspondence. Gemma also carried out invaluable internet research. Evan Wilson compiled the index. Several members of Team Harper saved me from many errors of fact and interpretation by reading and commenting upon the draft manuscript. And the Manning Centre for Building Democracy was kind enough to offer financial support for my research. Heartfelt thanks to all of you.

1
Prelude, 1991–2001

Like many people of an academic bent, I went through various phases of political belief when I was young. I thought of myself as a conservative, liberal, and social democrat at different times in my twenties and early thirties, until I encountered the works of Friedrich Hayek in 1977. Reading *The Constitution of Liberty* and, later, the three volumes of *Law, Legislation and Liberty* convinced me that Hayek was fundamentally right about his central concept of spontaneous order.[1]

In *Law, Legislation, and Liberty,* Hayek argued that society is a "spontaneous order," generating itself out of the transactions of individual human beings with each other. The capacity of society as an infinitely complex network of interaction to aggregate dispersed knowledge for the benefit of others depends crucially on respect for individual freedom, for individuals are in the best position to make choices based on their own limited knowledge. This insight leads to the standard tenets of economic conservatism, including the rule of law, smaller government, lower taxes, privatization, and deregulation. All of these have the effect of encouraging and allowing people to make choices for themselves rather than having choices made for them by government officials.

A less widely recognized aspect of Hayek's thought is his moral traditionalism. He saw the spontaneous order of society as a filter for separating the beneficial individual innovations out of what John Stuart Mill called the "experiments of living" that all of us conduct.[2] The results of the testing process are embodied in habits, traditions, customs, and conventions that can be followed without being rationally articulated. This aspect of Hayek's thinking dovetails nicely with Edmund Burke's famous praise of "prejudice" and gradual change.[3]

The great importance of Hayek is that he brought together two strands of conservatism – economic or fiscal conservatism, and social or moral conservatism – that often seem opposed to each other, particularly by those who claim to be "fiscally conservative but socially progressive." In my view, fiscal and social conservatives may emphasize different things, but they need each other because they have a common enemy – the hypertrophic welfare state, dominated by a soi-disant progressive elite, that wishes to remake society according to its own rationalistic vision.

My political views stabilized after studying Hayek, but I did not rush into political activism. I was fully occupied with a heavy academic agenda in the 1980s – editing the papers of Louis Riel, researching Metis land claims, studying Canadian human-rights commissions, and teaching courses on the application of game theory and evolutionary biology to political science. I gored a few sacred liberal cows in my academic publications, but I stayed out of real-world politics.

I wasn't too interested at first when Preston Manning founded the Reform Party. I regarded it as just another fringe movement, of which Alberta has seen so many. I was strongly in favour of free trade with the United States, so I voted Progressive Conservative in the federal election of 1988, even though I was rather disappointed with Brian Mulroney's first term in office. But, as the decade of the 1980s ended, I became even further disenchanted with the Progressive Conservatives, as deficit-spending remained stubbornly out of control and Mulroney seemed obsessed with meeting ever-escalating constitutional demands from Quebec.

In early 1990, Walter Van Halst, one of our graduate students, gave me a copy of the Reform Party's policy manual, known as the *Blue Book*. For the first time, I saw my own views reflected in those of a Canadian political party. Reform's mixture of market economics, direct democracy, decentralized federalism, and social conservatism was a perfect fit with my own thinking at the time. I learned later that the author of the *Blue* Book was Stephen Harper.

I first met Stephen Harper in late 1990 or early 1991. As chief policy officer of the Reform Party, he would sometimes come along with the leader, Preston Manning, to "egghead lunches" at the University of Calgary. These were brown-bag events, attended by a few staff members and graduate students from the Political Science department. Preston was looking for intellectual resources to strengthen the Reform Party as part of his plan to transform it from a volunteer organization to a professionally managed political party. Although Stephen was already well known as having, next to Preston, the sharpest mind in the Reform Party, he didn't say much at these meetings and I didn't really get to know him then.

Through these lunches, Preston and I got acquainted, and he invited me to become director of policy, strategy, and communication in Reform's Calgary office, effective 1 May 1991. I rarely saw Stephen Harper in the first months after I came to work because he had taken leave to finish his Master's thesis, which he was writing under the supervision of Frank Atkins in the department of economics at the University of Calgary.[4] It was a challenging piece of econometrics, an attempt to assess the importance of the so-called political business cycle in Canada, and it required time to run and interpret the various specifications of his multiple-regression model. Hence I didn't start to work much with Stephen until fall 1991. Nominally, he reported to me, but in practice he operated independently, given his status as chief policy officer and one of the founders of the Reform Party.

Our relationship was wary at first, but we got to know each other better in 1992. We both felt marginalized as Preston came to rely more and more on Rick Anderson as his principal adviser, and Cliff Fryers and Gordon Shaw as his main administrators. Increasingly cut off from making the main decisions, Stephen and I had time on our hands, and we would often sit in my office in the late afternoon, talking about Prestonian populism and where the Reform Party was going. I was fifteen years older than Stephen, nominally his superior, far better established in terms of professional reputation, but I found him persuasive, indeed almost mesmerizing. For one so young – thirty-three at the time – he combined a remarkably wide knowledge of politics with a keen strategic mind. When he got into a political discussion, his china-blue eyes became transfixing, and he could be passionately captivating and mordantly funny by turns. To those who know him well, the real Stephen Harper is very different from the unemotional image that he projects in public.

What attracted me most of all about Stephen was his strategic cast of mind. Politics is full of people who think they know where they want to go, but Stephen is one of those rare people who can actually figure out how to get there. Stephen also combines unusual mastery of both strategy – long-term thinking about how to achieve goals – and tactics – day-to-day political management. I wasn't yet thinking of him as a future prime minister, but I quickly became convinced that he would play a major role in the Canadian conservative movement.

Our relationship was cemented in autumn 1992, when we both disapproved of Preston's handling of the Charlottetown Accord and the subsequent referendum campaign. We thought at the time that his opposition to the Accord was lukewarm and that in conducting the campaign against it he strayed too much into tactics, such as calling it the "Mulroney Deal," rather than concentrating on what was wrong with it. I decided to resign from the employment of the Reform Party, effective the end of the year, but stayed on as an adviser at Preston's request. Were my concerns justified? I thought so at the time, but fifteen years later they look to me more like run-of-the-mill intra-party factionalism based on youth and inexperience.

Preston fired me as an adviser in summer 1993 after I told him I disapproved of his choice of Rick Anderson as campaign manager and would criticize it in public. I have never blamed Preston for firing me; really, I left him no choice. Anyway, by then I was more interested in writing *Waiting for the Wave* and quickly got started on it.[5] Stephen read the draft and made helpful comments, but he did not fully agree with my interpretation. I put a lot of stress in that book on Preston's populism and tried to trace his pattern of decision-making back to that root, whereas Stephen tended to see Preston's twists and turns as pragmatic attempts to get more votes for the Reform Party.

After Stephen was elected to Parliament in autumn 1993, we kept loosely in touch. I would sometimes attend consultative meetings that he would hold when he was back in Calgary. He once asked me to write a speech for him to deliver in the House of Commons about a posthumous pardon for Louis Riel.[6] But inevitably our paths started to diverge, and we talked less frequently. He was busy with his parliamentary work, while, after publishing *Waiting for the Wave* in 1995, I went back to some of my other research interests, such as Metis history and aboriginal land claims.

We came back together again, however, as a result of the "Winds of Change" conference held in Calgary in late May 1996.[7] It was organized by the noted Toronto author David Frum and the young Ezra Levant, then working in Toronto for the *National Post*, and chaired by Alberta Treasurer Stockwell Day. The purpose of the meeting was to "unite the right," which was split at the federal level between the Reform Party and the Progressive Conservatives. About a hundred politicians, writers, researchers, journalists, and political activists assembled in Calgary for two days of talks to hammer out a common approach to attaining unity. The attempt was doomed, however, because everyone there was associated either with the Reform Party or the provincial Progressive Conservative parties of Alberta and Ontario. The federal Progressive Conservatives boycotted the meeting and vetoed any further steps in the direction of unity or even cooperation. They just weren't interested at the time.

Stephen gave a magnificent talk to the Winds of Change audience, the gist of which was that conservatism in Canada had only been successful at the national level when it managed to bring together traditional Toryism, strong in Ontario and Atlantic Canada; grassroots populism, dominant in the West and parts of rural Ontario; and French-Canadian nationalism, the regnant worldview in Quebec. Stephen saw these three components of Canadian conservatism not just as essential voting blocs but also as complementary political cultures. He would later write that Reform's emphasis on principle had to be complemented by Tory virtues – a "respect for tradition, a penchant for incremental change, and a strong sense of honourable compromise."[8]

Brian Mulroney had reactivated the tripartite coalition temporarily, but he had overreached himself by bringing in Quebec separatists whose demands for constitutional change were difficult for the rest of the country to swallow. Mulroney's coalition then shattered into its three constituent elements, easily recognizable as the Reform Party, the Bloc Québécois, and the remnant Progressive Conservatives. It sounds like conventional wisdom today, but at the time no one had yet articulated this interpretation so clearly. I was so impressed that I called Stephen's wife Laureen later that weekend to say, "Stephen sounded like a prime minister today!" I wish my intuitions were always so accurate.

Indeed, history has endorsed Stephen's insight. Ten years after delivering that talk, he has become prime minister by doggedly pursuing the strategy of uniting the three separated parts of the conservative coalition – first winning the leadership of the Canadian Alliance (Western populism), then merging with the Progressive Conservatives (traditional Toryism), and finally making a breakthrough in Quebec in 2006 by winning ten seats.

I had been invited to speak at the Canadian Studies Centre at Harvard University in fall 1996, and I wanted to say something new. Stephen gave me permission to develop his short talk into a longer presentation, so I brought in a lot of historical material to bolster his thesis, taking a closer look at the successful Conservative coalitions of Macdonald, Borden, Bennett, Diefenbaker, and Mulroney, the factors that led to their formation, and the stresses that tore them apart. When Larry Solomon asked me if I would like to write something for his new magazine, *The Next City*, he accepted my suggestion that Stephen and I contribute a co-authored version of my Harvard presentation.

Larry, now with the *Financial Post*, is such an aggressive editor that he became almost a silent co-author of this essay. He wanted us to write more about electoral reform in particular and questions of democracy in general, while Stephen and I were primarily interested in trying to figure out how conservatism could come to power in Canada. Trying to mediate between Larry and Stephen, who is very particular about what goes out over his name, I wondered at times whether we would ever get this into print. It did appear, however, in January 1997, under Larry's title, "Our Benign Dictatorship: Can Canada Avoid a Second Century of Liberal Rule?"[9] Both the title and the cover illustration, showing Jean Chrétien in military uniform looking like Benito Mussolini or Francisco Franco, were echoed a few years later in Jeffrey Simpson's book, *The Friendly Dictatorship*.[10]

Stephen's position at this time was to advocate cooperation of parties rather than a merger. "A merger between Reform and the PCs, though still discussed, seems to us out of the question," we wrote. "Too many careers would be at stake. Political parties almost never merge in the true sense of the term, and the gap between today's opposition factions is simply too great."[11] We called rather for "limited cooperation ... leading to a system of sister parties."[12] We wanted the parties to divide up candidacies regionally, or to sponsor candidates jointly. That provided a segue to the discussion of electoral reform that Larry Solomon wanted, for electoral cooperation between parties is facilitated by an Australian-style preferential ballot or any of the numerous forms of proportional representation.

We were right about cooperation vs merger in the short term but not in the longer run, as shown when Stephen himself opted for a merger of the PCs and the Canadian Alliance in 2003. In the meantime, our article helped propel discussion of the whole issue in the media and in that sense was a predecessor of Preston Manning's United Alternative initiative, which he unveiled in 1998 after Reform failed to make an eastern breakthrough in the 1997 election. Preston, however, was aiming at creation of a new party, whereas we had advocated electoral cooperation of sister parties.[13]

In a revised version of the essay that we wrote for Bill Gairdner's edited book, *After Liberalism*, Stephen enlarged on another problem of the conservative movement, the tension between "neo-cons" and "theo-cons," or between fiscal and social conservatives. He saw this as a new incarnation of the divide between Burkean conservatives and classical liberals, which was prominent in the party systems of many nineteenth-century countries. But in his view, its significance was diminished by the twentieth-century rise of socialism and other radical left-wing ideologies, such as feminism and environmentalism. Against such opponents, Burkean conservatives and classical liberals had to realize that whatever separated them was less than what united them, namely a preference for small government, open markets, the rule of law, and opposition to governmental *dirigisme*. The tension between fiscal and social conservatives, though still real, would be manageable.[14] Stephen returned to this theme when he addressed Civitas in spring 2003:

> The truth is that strong economic and social conservatives are more often than not the same people, and not without reason. Except at the extremes of libertarianism and theocracy, the philosophical fusion has become deep and wide-spread. Social conservatives more often than not demand the government stop intervening in individual decisions, just as classical liberals often point to the religious roots of their focus on the individual.[15]

There were some hints here about how Stephen would conduct himself as a party leader. He told me after becoming leader of the Canadian Alliance that he always wanted to position himself in the middle of the party. There might be critics at either end (followers of Preston Manning and of Stockwell Day in the case of the Alliance), but they would have trouble ganging up on him if he placed himself between them. As leader both of the Alliance and the Conservative Party, Stephen has always tried to be in the middle of the party, to preserve a balance between different factions and tendencies – not just between fiscal and social conservatives but between populists and traditionalists and between Quebec nationalists and western followers of Diefenbaker's "One Nation" view.

Stephen resigned his seat in Parliament in January 1997. He had created an enviable reputation in the national media as perhaps the most thoughtful and knowledgeable member of the Reform caucus, and he had done important work on Quebec separatism as inter-governmental affairs critic, work which ultimately led to Jean Chrétien's Clarity Act. However, he had become pessimistic about the ability of the Reform Party to make an eastern breakthrough with Preston at the helm. He became vice-president and then president of the National Citizens Coalition, which had moved its national office from Toronto to Calgary. The NCC was a small organization compared to a national political party, but as president he had discretion to run it as he wished.

For the next few years, neither of us played any role in Reform Party affairs or the United Alternative. As a newspaper columnist, first for the *Globe and Mail* and then for the *National Post*, I would occasionally write op ed pieces about Reform and the United Alternative, but that was the sum of my political activity. Stephen flirted with running for the leadership of the federal Progressive Conservatives after Jean Charest resigned. Although he was courted by Conservative MPs Jim Jones and John Herron and Senator Gerry St Germain, he decided not to run, saying he didn't want to become an active opponent of Preston Manning.[16] When Joe Clark won the PC leadership in a race where David Orchard came second and Hugh Segal came third on the first ballot, it seemed that the movement to "unite the right" was further than ever from fruition, because all three were opposed to any serious dealings with Reform.

The United Alternative did achieve a partial success in 2000 when Reform morphed into the Canadian Alliance, though in fact most of the Tories recruited to the new party had been more active in provincial Progressive Conservative parties than in the federal PCs. Under Joe Clark's leadership, the federal Tories rejected all offers of merger and clung to Joe's "Highway 301" rule, which required them to run candidates in all ridings, thus precluding any form of cooperation with the Alliance except for the latter to fold its tent. When the Alliance held its leadership race, Stephen and I both believed that Preston Manning's leadership was played out. He endorsed Tom Long, while I gave $1,000 to Stockwell Day's campaign and did some favourable media commentary about him,[17] but neither of us was actively involved in the race. When Stock triumphed, I could boast that I had picked the winner, but Stephen was more acute than I in foreseeing that Stock would have problems managing Preston's party.

The election held in autumn 2000 was a disappointment for the Canadian Alliance. Under Day's leadership, it increased its vote share from 19 percent to 26 percent, and its seat total from sixty to sixty-six, but these gains were much less than hoped for at the beginning of the campaign. Also, the Alliance did not achieve any strategic objectives: electing two members in Ontario did not amount to a breakthrough; it failed to defeat any senior ministers, such as Anne McLellan in Edmonton or Ralph Goodale in Regina; it did not defeat Progressive Conservative Leader Joe Clark in Calgary; and it allowed the PCs to elect the minimum number of twelve members required to achieve official party status in the House of Commons.[18] All Alliance supporters were disappointed, but Stephen was particularly outraged over the way the Liberals had targeted Alberta in their campaign rhetoric and advertising. As Stephen Clarkson later described it,

> Advertisements across the country highlighted the role Stockwell Day had played in introducing legislation allowing a form of private health care in Alberta. One Liberal ad featured ordinary citizens-in-the-street in Alberta expressing apprehension about health care and the provincial government's controversial Bill 11, which was passed when Day was a member of the Alberta legislature.[19]

On 8 December 2000, Stephen published a column in the *National Post* complaining about the "shrewd and sinister Liberal attack plan" in the recent election. In response, he called for building "a stronger and much more autonomous Alberta. It is time to look at Quebec and to learn. What Albertans should take from this example is to become 'maîtres chez nous.'"[20]

Stephen wasn't just letting off steam; he wanted to develop a practical strategy to promote Alberta's autonomy, and he invited me to go to lunch to discuss the matter during the 2000 Christmas holidays. It was a miserably cold and snowy day, but we managed to get to a restaurant in a northwest Calgary shopping centre, where Stephen sketched out his idea for an "Alberta Agenda" – a set of policies that Alberta could pursue within the existing constitution to protect the province from Ottawa's manipulations. He asked me to draft something after consulting with like-minded academics and policy analysts in Calgary. Although I talked to some other people as well, I finally enlisted the following four, who were all keen to be part of the effort:

- Andy Crooks, a Calgary lawyer and president of the Canadian Taxpayers Federation;
- Ted Morton, a colleague of mine in the Political Science department of the University of Calgary, then a "Senator Elect" from Alberta, and a well-known critic of judicial activism;

- Rainer Knopff, another Political Science colleague, afterward associate vice-president of research at the University of Calgary, and frequent co-author with Ted Morton of books and articles on judicial activism;
- Ken Boessenkool, a professional economist, previously a staffer with the Reform Party in Ottawa and with Alberta's Ministry of Finance, where he had helped Stockwell Day bring in the so-called "flat tax," a single-rate provincial income tax.

We settled on five points to constitute the "Alberta Agenda":

1 Withdraw from the Canada Pension Plan to create an Alberta Pension Plan offering the same benefits at lower cost while giving Alberta control over the investment fund.
2 Collect our own revenue from personal income tax, as we already do for corporate income tax.
3 Start preparing to let the contract with the RCMP run out in 2012 and create an Alberta provincial police force.
4 Resume provincial responsibility for health care policy. If Ottawa objects to provincial policy, fight in the courts. If we lose, we can afford the financial penalties Ottawa might try to impose under the Canada Health Act.
5 Use Section 88 of the Supreme Court's decision in the Quebec Secession Reference to force Senate reform back onto the national agenda.[21]

We published our work in the form of an "Open Letter to Ralph Klein" in the National Post, 24 January 2001; this was easy to arrange because several of us were regular contributors to that newspaper. To reassure Premier Klein that we were not trying to blindside him, I called his office and sent him an advance copy of the column. Ralph Klein had been adventurous when he first became premier, but at this stage in his career he had accomplished his initial objectives and was now trying just not to rock the boat. To judge from subsequent statements, he had little sympathy for our "Alberta Agenda" and regarded it as an unwelcome intrusion in his bailiwick, especially with a provincial election expected for later that year. His irritation at being challenged in this way may help account for later actions undercutting Stephen's position as leader of the federal Conservative Party.

In trying to summarize the Alberta Agenda, we wrote: "It is imperative to take the initiative, to build firewalls around Alberta, to limit the extent to which an aggressive and hostile federal government can encroach upon legitimate provincial jurisdiction."[22] I still think "firewall," whether interpreted in the context of the building trades or computer software, is the perfect metaphor to express what we were trying to do through the Alberta Agenda, but the term proved to have talismanic connotations that none of us foresaw. We wanted our proposals to be called the "Alberta Agenda," but from the start they became known as the "Firewall." That evocative term gave them greater currency than they might otherwise have enjoyed, but some observers (most notably Preston Manning) preferred to emphasize the aggressive connotations of "fire" and the defensive connotations of "wall" in order to dismiss the whole idea without analyzing the merits of the various policy proposals.[23]

Publication of our open letter made it seem that Stephen Harper was interested in entering Alberta politics, and indeed the Alberta Agenda might have had the potential to become a winning program in provincial politics. It appealed immediately to a substantial minority of Alberta opinion; had a respected leader such as Stephen pushed it over a period of time, it could have become conventional wisdom in the province. Randy Thorsteinsen used it to build a platform for the Alberta Alliance, and Ted Morton drew heavily on it in his 2006 attempt to succeed Ralph Klein as leader of the provincial PCs. Ted didn't win that race, but he finished a strong second on the first ballot, higher than any observers were predicting at the outset, and was ultimately rewarded with a position in newly elected Premier Ed Stelmach's cabinet.

At the time, however, Stephen did not seem interested in getting into Alberta politics. His goal was more to use the provinces to block further expansion of the federal welfare state. He wanted to get the National Citizens Coalition to work up a similar proposal for Ontario, to try to push the two wealthiest provinces into a common front against Ottawa. He presented the

Alberta Agenda to me as a move in the federal political game, not a venture into Alberta politics.

In any case, the ground was already shifting under our feet while we were working on the Alberta Agenda. Stephen had always thought that he would have no chance of leading the Reform Party or the Canadian Alliance. He didn't think he could defeat Preston Manning; and even if Manning was gone he feared that Preston's followers would undermine his leadership because he had not been loyal enough to the founder of Reform. But that whole situation changed very quickly when Stockwell Day got into trouble as Alliance leader.

The knives were out, not only because the 2000 election results were disappointing but because the Alliance campaign had been hastily organized and Stock's own performance in the campaign had been uneven. Then, with his position already weakened, Stock's past came back with a vengeance. In 1999, when he was Minister of Finance in Alberta, he had publicly criticized a Red Deer lawyer and public school trustee, Lorne Goddard, who was defending a convicted pedophile accused of possessing child pornography. Stock wrote to the *Red Deer Advocate* that Goddard's (unsuccessful) defence of his client suggested "that he actually believes the pedophile has the right to possess child porn."[24] Goddard launched a libel suit for $600,000 in damages. With his legal defence paid for by the Alberta Risk Management Fund, Stock dug in to prepare for trial; but, as the legal bills mounted, the Alberta Government finally convinced him to settle out of court. On 16 January 2001, word got out that the settlement had cost Alberta taxpayers $800,000, and Stock had to endure weeks of remorseless criticism in the media.

His hold over the Alliance crumbled quickly in the next few months. Almost all senior staff in the Opposition Leader's Office and the party quit or were fired. In May, members started to resign or be suspended from the Alliance caucus – thirteen of them at the peak. Party fundraising tailed off badly. There were many other imbroglios, too many to mention. Not all of them were Stock's fault, but they all fed the impression of a leader who had lost control of his party. Under threat of a non-confidence vote at a caucus meeting scheduled for 17 July 2001, Stock promised to resign as leader ninety days before any scheduled leadership

vote. National Council then quickly announced there would be a
leadership race with the vote to be held 20 March 2002, about
nine months hence. Stock could continue as leader until 20 December 2001.[25]

Meanwhile a dozen of the Alliance MPs who had left caucus
formed themselves into the Democratic Representative Caucus
(DRC) and started merger talks with Joe Clark's Tories. This
group contained some of the most prominent Reformers, such as
Deborah Grey, Chuck Strahl, and Monte Solberg, most of whom
had close ties to Preston Manning. Although Preston himself remained enigmatically neutral,[26] several of his most senior staffers,
including Cliff Fryers, Rick Anderson, Ian Todd, and Morten
Paulsen, also got involved in the DRC, making it look like a Prestonian plot to bring Stock down. With supporters of Manning
and Day attacking each other in intemperate terms, it was a painful time for Alliance supporters. It looked as if the party would
tear itself apart and Joe Clark would pick up the pieces.

Stock's Calgary supporters, including Ezra Levant, Sean McKinsley, and Gerry Chipeur, were maneuvering frantically to preserve
some semblance of control. Stephen and I were invited to meet
with them and Ken Boessenkool and a couple of other people at
Gerry's house one night in June. We discussed various scenarios
for restoring order to the Canadian Alliance but couldn't come up
with anything workable. In reality, things had gone so far that
nothing but a leadership race offered any hope for the future.

Brokered by Ken Boessenkool, Stephen and Stock got together
briefly at a Stampede barbecue in July. Stephen said that he was
thinking about running for the leadership of the Alliance and
wanted to do so in a way that would preserve the Alliance from
disintegration while minimizing antagonism against Stock.[27]
Also, Stephen started quietly calling members of the Alliance
caucus and the DRC whom he knew from Reform days to see if
they would support his leadership bid.

News reports all summer raised questions about Stephen's potential candidacy, while the DRC schism, coupled with stories of
party debt and a drop to single-digit levels in national polls,[28]
made observers wonder about the future of the Alliance itself.
Ian McClelland, a former Alliance MP, was quoted in the *National Post* as saying, "The Canadian Alliance, in my opinion, as

a political vehicle capable of exerting leadership authority in the country, is over. It is finished. It is dead. There is no future." He hinted that perhaps Stephen was waiting for the situation to resolve itself before making any candidacy announcement.[29] Stephen quickly wrote a letter to the editor to distance himself from McClelland's views: "I do not believe that the credibility of conservatives in federal politics would be enhanced in any way by the destruction of the Canadian Alliance or the creation of yet another new political party."[30]

During this period, a lot of party faithful and friends threw their support behind Stephen. Link Byfield declared in his *Report Newsmagazine*, "Now is the time for Stephen Harper to come to the aid of the party."[31] The *Calgary Herald* echoed that if Harper sought the leadership "everything" would change, that his bid would "lend integrity" to the result of the race.[32] Barry Cooper and David Bercuson proclaimed in mock-Hegelian language that the Alliance's leadership problem was "pregnant with its own solution" and that the solution was Stephen Harper.[33] Michael Taube worried that Stephen, whom he called the Alliance's "best choice" and its "right knight," might not run.[34] Of course, there were also detractors. Jeffrey Simpson in the *Globe and Mail* said, "Don't do it," labelling Harper "too ideological to succeed in Canadian politics."[35] Warren Kinsella called the leadership of the Alliance "the worst job in Canada" and chastised Stephen for expressing interest in it.[36]

I wasn't involved in Harper's tentative leadership preparations until I was invited for late-afternoon drinks on 10 August at the 400 Club, a downtown Calgary business club that Stephen often used for political conversations. There I met Stephen and Ken Boessenkool, as well as John Weissenberger, a geologist who was a close friend of Stephen and had managed his 1993 campaign in Calgary West; George Koch, who had worked with Stephen and me in the Reform national office for much of 1992; Mark Kihn, western vice-president and chief fundraiser of the National Citizens Coalition; Eric Hughes, a university friend of Stephen who was now an accountant and CFO of a Calgary corporation; and Don Van Mierlo, whom I did not know and whose connection with the group I never quite understood. We talked about the political situation and whether Stephen should make a run for the Alliance leadership. Opinion was favourable, so we agreed to meet a few days later to discuss it further. In the meantime, Stephen put out a statement on Canada NewsWire on 13 August: "Stephen Harper has informed National Citizens Coalition Chairman Colin Brown that he intends to leave the presidency of the NCC no later than December 31st." He had been getting calls from Alliance and DRC MPs that they would join the PCs if he did not run, so his announcement was a quiet signal to Alliance partisans not to despair, that a rescue effort would be mounted.

My wife, Marianne, is an outstanding cook and loves to entertain as long as I do the dishes; so we met at our house on Saturday evening, 18 August, for chicken and potato salad. It was the same group that had met at the 400 Club, plus Stephen's brothers Robert and Grant, both of whom are accountants living in Calgary, and spouses to make it more of a social occasion. Again, the sentiment was in favour of launching a campaign, so we talked about what needed to be done – raising money, securing further caucus support, building an organization, renting space, getting phones installed, and so on. The general idea was that our group would act as a "Draft Harper" committee, not actually running the campaign but helping it get started.

All of us were busy people, with jobs and families to look after, but I knew I would have some free time because I was only scheduled to teach a half-load in the coming academic year. The teaching reduction was because of additional administrative responsibilities I was carrying, but I thought I could work around those. Also, I was older than anyone else in the group, so it seemed logical to exercise some leadership. When we neared the end of the evening and it still wasn't clear who would chair the Draft Harper Committee, I said to Stephen, "So, do you want me to be the chairman and John the vice-chairman?" Curiously, one of Stephen's greatest strengths is his decisiveness and strong will, yet he can be very subtle about communicating his administrative desires. I was as excited as a kid at Christmas, and I didn't sleep at all that night – the first of many sleepless nights over the next five years.

2

The Canadian Alliance Leadership
Campaign, 2001–2002

CAMPAIGN VISIBLE

After Stephen stepped down as president of the National Citizens Coalition in August and our "Draft Harper" website went live in September, speculation switched from "if" he would enter the race to "when."[1] His appearances at local Alliance functions were well received by attendees and well reported by local media.[2] Every time Stephen made a public speech, a rash of small cheques in the $50 to $150 range would show up in the Draft Harper mailbox. People seemed to find him compelling when they met him in person and heard what he had to say. These events were characterized by a fractured vision of the CA's future, with undeclared candidate Diane Ablonczy outlining her vision of uniting with Joe Clark's Tories and Stephen emphasizing that, as long as Clark was in power, no unification was feasible. Stephen noted at the Canadian Alliance BC regional conference in October that this was because "the Tory party under Joe Clark do not believe in any of the things that we believe in."[3]

On 30 November, the *National Post* ran a story quoting "a senior official on Mr. Harper's team ... who asked not to be named" as confirming that Stephen would be in the race officially within the week.[4] Shortly thereafter, we sent out a Draft Harper newsletter noting that this was "not unadjacent" to the truth.[5] Stephen formally declared his candidacy in Ottawa on 2 December 2001.

Our slogan for the campaign was "Getting It Right," so this was the title of his first speech and direct-mailing. Media coverage of the speech emphasized that as leader Stephen would not be interested in unification with the Joe Clark Tories, that he would not allow the religious right to hijack the party, and that the narrowly defined interests of certain minority groups would not dictate party policy.[6] The media response was largely favourable, but some reports worried that the unflinching stance Stephen took on merger with the PCs was going to hinder his bid and would bode badly for the future of the right in Canada.[7] For his part, Stephen was careful to specify that he was not opposed to cooperation with PCs, but that he did not think it would be beneficial or even possible as long as Joe Clark was the leader, given Clark's long and consistent record of opposition to cooperation on any terms except absorption into the Progressive Conservative Party.

On 12 December Alliance health critic Diane Ablonczy declared her interest in the leadership. Like Harper, Ablonczy was a founding member of the Reform Party. She framed herself immediately as a unity candidate and was critical of his standpoint, claiming it would guarantee defeat in the next election: "It's my opinion that [Mr. Harper's] approach would simply accept the fact that we would lose, that we would not win an election," she said in the National Post.[8] That same day Stockwell Day stepped down as Alliance party leader. The Ottawa Citizen declared the act "the least surprising resignation in Canadian political history."[9] He announced at the same time that he would be taking the holiday season to decide whether or not he would run again for his old job.[10]

Five days later, deputy leader Grant Hill announced his candidacy. A medical doctor by trade, Hill was a former Reform MP who, like Ablonczy, intended to present himself on a unity platform. His bid was supported by Monte Solberg as well as influential power brokers Peter White and Bob Dechert. Hill's campaign got off to a rocky start when his claim that a homosexual lifestyle was unhealthy, offered as a medical opinion, drew a torrent of criticism.[11]

Just before Christmas, Stephen wrote an article published in the National Post, restating his position on unity with the Progressive Conservatives. "While the Canadian Alliance and the Reform party before it twisted themselves into political pretzels to appease the Tories," he wrote, "Mr. Clark has shown he is not interested in combining forces on any terms but his own ... Yet Mr. Clark endorses nothing and proposes nothing."[12]

Day announced on 7 January 2002 that he would enter the leadership race. Observers expected the announcement, but some puzzled aloud as to his reasoning. Don Martin dubbed it a "masochistic decision to perpetuate the suffering,"[13] and Andrew Coyne wondered if it was a "vainglorious belief in a transcendental personal destiny."[14] Yet he certainly had supporters; a group of young Progressive Conservatives from Quebec quit their party the same day, throwing their support behind Stock.[15] Day's candidacy announcement brought the number of declared candidates to four. Five, if you count the cross-dressing drag queen Enza "Supermodel" Anderson, who made up in enthusiasm what s/he lacked in deposit money to qualify as an official candidate. Ultimately, Enza did not raise enough money in time for the 31 January deadline but did add levity to a few events where s/he showed up.

On the evening of 19 January 2002, Stephen gave his first major speech of the campaign in Montreal. The title, "Federalism and All Canadians," was in deliberate contrast to Pierre Trudeau's book *Federalism and the French Canadians*. Stephen emphasized, "I would prefer a vision of federalism that is pan-Canadian – federalism not just for French Quebecers, but federalism for all Canadians."[16] At the same time, the rest of the candidates attended an all-candidates debate in Chatham, Ontario. The media remarked that none of the candidates in attendance particularly shone and that the event lacked the "thrust-and-parry" that normally hallmarks a good debate.[17]

By the end of January, it was obvious that this had become a two-man race between Harper and Day. Eighteen MPs had publicly endorsed Stephen, while eleven had thrown their support behind Day. Ablonczy did not have any supporters, and Hill had only a handful, though they included some top-quality MPs such as Vic Toews and Monte Solberg.

At the first official all-candidates debate in Victoria, unity with the PCs was the hot topic. Both Hill and Ablonczy attacked Stephen's position, the latter most vehemently, suggesting that Stephen's approach would "take the party backward."[18] Stephen spoke of maintaining party principles and emphasized not surrendering the party to Joe Clark's Tories. One report observed that he "dominated the applause meter."[19]

In early February, Stephen delivered a speech entitled "The End of Moral Equivalence: Canada's National Security after September 11" in Calgary at the Alliance Policy Forum on National Security. He decried Liberal treatment of national defence, foreign affairs, immigration, and domestic security. He noted that the fault lay not in Liberal policy per se but in base ideology – "moral equivalence" as he dubbed it.[20] Reports lamented his "cold and charmless style" but lauded a candidate "who prefers a debate on industrial strategy to a photo-op."[21]

In the first week of February, both the Harper and Ablonczy campaigns were in Halifax for some wintry campaigning. Ablonczy hammered away at her pro-merger message to a sparse crowd, calling Stephen an ideologue and suggesting Day lacked the ability to "unite the right" in Canada.[22] A few days later, at Saint Mary's University, Stephen offered his "Canada has stopped digging, but it is still in a deep hole" speech. Excerpted the same day in the *National Post*, it questioned industrial policy, regional development schemes, and the functioning of equalization itself: "The incentives created by equalization make it more difficult for provincial governments to make decisions in the best economic interests of their population."[23]

Meanwhile the Day campaign held two rallies, one at Canada's largest Bible college and another at an evangelical Victory church. Neither event was posted on the public itinerary on the Day campaign website,[24] reinforcing concerns that Day was cultivating a base of religious conservatives that was too narrow to sustain the party as a whole.

On 20 February, five more Alliance MPs threw their support behind Stephen, bringing the total caucus endorsements for the Harper leadership to twenty-seven. A few days later, a national all-candidates debate aired on Global TV. In the month leading up to election day, media coverage focused again on the future of the Canadian Alliance itself. The *Hamilton Spectator* carried an endorsement of Stephen in the last week of February. "Harper is seen by many conservatives," wrote Michael Taube, "as the only leadership candidate with a sustained interest in the Alliance's past history and political future."[25] A few days later, the *Ottawa Citizen* echoed these words: "Mr. Harper understands the party's need to rebuild and consolidate, to rediscover its commitment to conservative ideas and to focus on selling these to Canadians."[26] Opinion was split as to which of the two men would emerge victorious. Political observer Chantal Hébert declared on 1 March that "The smart money is on Day"[27] but recanted on election day: "The sun might set on Day."[28] In the end, Harper took the leadership easily on the first ballot.

So much for the "campaign visible," i.e., how things would have looked to a moderately interested observer following the campaign in the media. Now let's go to the "campaign invisible," i.e., behind the scenes to see how Harper's victory was planned, organized, and executed.

INITIAL POSITION

We started from very far back to organize this campaign. We had no money except an initial donation of $20,000 from Scott Reid, the Alliance MP for Lanark-Carleton, who had worked as a Reform staffer when Stephen was a Reform MP. Stephen himself was no longer in Parliament; so, unlike all three of our eventual opponents, his campaign would have to pay for all office, staff, and travel costs. Indeed, he would have to forego a salary for seven months because he could not remain as president of the NCC if he entered the Alliance leadership race.

We did, however, have many assets in our group, not least that the members shared the same worldview, knew each other well, and had worked together on various projects in the past. John Weissenberger had managed Stephen's 1993 campaign in Calgary West and thus had an understanding of many practical aspects of campaigning. Mark Kihn was a capable fundraiser, and the NCC was prepared to give him latitude to raise money for the Harper campaign. George Koch was an experienced journalist who now worked in his wife's communications agency, making it easy for us to get pamphlets designed and printed. Ken Boessenkool was an economist who had worked for the Reform research department in 1994–96 as well as in Stockwell Day's leadership campaign in 2000. Eric Hughes had no campaign experience, but as an accountant he was prepared to manage our finances. Stephen's wife, Laureen, was a graphic artist who could help design buttons, posters, and newsletters. I had little firsthand knowledge of campaigning, but I had managerial experience from my years as a department head at the university, had worked for the Reform Party, and had many contacts in the conservative movement across the country. As a professor in the most conservative Political Science department in the country, I knew a number of graduate students, including Chris Matthews, Ray Novak, and Meredith McDonald, who were eager to get involved in the campaign and who had something to offer.

Harper's years as chief policy officer of the Reform Party and as a Reform MP meant that he was well regarded among the Western Canada and rural Ontario members who made up the bulk of the Alliance membership. We didn't know for sure what the rules of the leadership race would be, but we correctly assumed that the contest would be decided on the basis of one member, one vote, as in the 2000 leadership race. During Stephen's years in the Reform caucus, he had also developed ties with many caucus members as well as staffers, people who were now prepared to contribute not only their endorsement but also money, expertise, and volunteer labour to help make him leader of the Alliance.

Given all of that, our strategy was obvious – build on the Reform base, presenting Stephen as the inheritor of the Reform tradition and the saviour of the Canadian Alliance from disintegration and absorption into the Progressive Conservatives. Here is a memo I drafted in those early days, summarizing discussions of a preliminary SWOT (Strengths, Weaknesses, Opportunities, Threats) analysis and a subsequent strategy meeting with John Weissenberger, George Koch, Ken Boessenkool, and Mark Kihn:

DRAFT
Stephen Harper Leadership Campaign
Strategic Plan

Objectives
1. To elect Stephen Harper leader of the Canadian Alliance.
2. To identify the personnel that Stephen will use to gain control of the OLO, caucus, national council, national office of the party, and constituency associations. National council will require a side campaign of its own in early 2002.
3. To build a team that can fight further campaigns.

Assets

Stephen's main assets in this campaign are

1. His consistent, intelligent, articulate command of public policy issues.
2. His long experience in politics in general and the party in particular, including authorship of the Blue Book.
3. His ability to appeal to party members who have previously supported Manning, Day, or Long.

General Conception

The themes of Stephen's campaign will be to

1. Save the party from the disintegration with which it is threatened. This requires getting a wide range of endorsements before getting into the public phase of the campaign.
2. Rebuild it into a powerful force in Canadian politics. This means returning to a focus on policy rather than on public discussions of coalitions, mergers, and winning at all costs.

For those who are concerned with cooperation with the PCs, the answer is that Stephen is willing to cooperate from a position of strength. However, getting together with the Tories is *not* the purpose of the campaign.

Timetable

The campaign will unroll in three phases:

1. *August – September 2001. Getting ready*: behind the scenes, gathering endorsements and identifying workers. This is already underway and is going well. The main challenge is to get beyond listing supporters to create a formal organization by the end of September. We have to set a date to complete the organization chart and another date for a formal media launch.
2. *October-December 2001. Introducing Stephen to the party and the public*: attending local party functions, meeting with editorial boards of major newspapers, making major speeches on a few selected themes. This is the crucial period for establishing a favourable image for Stephen. We must

take care to showcase his strengths and shore up areas of perceived weaknesses:

- He can demonstrate his intelligence and mastery of policy by delivering speeches and appearing in the media.
- By visiting the standard conservative think tanks, he can show where his convictions lie.
- He can make some media appearances in French to demonstrate his ability to function in that language.
- To show he is not a loner, he should not appear alone. As much as possible, he should always be flanked by party notables who endorse him.
- He has to reach out to the social conservatives with an equivalent of Day's Kananaskis speech [Stock had spoken to the conservative discussion group Civitas during the 2000 Alliance leadership race].
- To show he is not a crypto-separatist, he should appear in Ontario, flanked by influential Ontarians, to discuss his constitutional agenda. Again, this calls for a major speech, as well as a visit to Queen's Park for photo ops with MPPs and ministers.

3. *January – March 2002. Getting out the vote:* participating in the official campaign debates, etc; intensive communication via telephone and direct mail. These activities are expensive, and the extent to which we can carry them out will depend upon the success of fundraising, which at this stage remains unknown. We will need later to prepare a detailed, week-by-week plan for this period.

We followed this plan more or less except for the parts about having Stephen visit Queen's Park and make frequent appearances flanked by party notables who had endorsed him. The flow of the campaign forced us to polarize somewhat against the social conservatives, but in the end that didn't matter. The biggest defect in the plan was that we didn't take enough account of the need to sell new memberships. We did a good job persuading existing members, but we had to scramble at the end not to be outdistanced by the Day campaign in renewing former members and bringing new members into the party.

EARLY STEPS

The first thing the core group did was to start making telephone calls around the country, looking for people who might be able to help Stephen's campaign. I called MPs whose support he had already obtained to see how they could help. I also called many party members and political activists whom I knew, personally contacting almost a hundred people in the first few weeks. It was a scattershot approach but probably necessary for someone like me, who lacked experience and did not already have a list of people to count on. MPs Scott Reid and James Rajotte were particularly helpful at this early stage, as was my former student Sean McKinsley, who had been deputy manager of Stockwell Day's leadership campaign. Sean explained to me many practical details of which I was unaware, because of my lack of experience.

One urgent practical necessity was to raise money beyond the initial $20,000 received from Scott Reid. I gave $2,000, and other members of the local committee chipped in with their own donations. Andy Crooks organized a luncheon fundraiser that gathered about $20,000 from Calgary businessmen; and Stephen's former employer, Colin Brown of the NCC, put on a similar event with a similar yield in Toronto. Gerry Maier, a retired Calgary oilman, also organized a productive reception for Stephen. Andy's fundraiser, because it was first, was a particular turning point. It built our confidence by demonstrating that people would get out their chequebooks for Stephen. Meanwhile, Eric Hughes applied for credit-card facilities from MasterCard, Visa, and American Express, which would be necessary when we got to the stage of mass fundraising through direct mail.

Stephen started making some trips, responding to invitations from supportive members of the caucus or friendly riding associations. His first "body man" and general all-purpose assistant was Chris Matthews, a graduate student of mine who was knowledgeable about campaigning and had done some work for the NCC.

We carried out a poll to check our intuition that Stephen had a decent shot at winning the Alliance leadership. We did not yet have access to the party's general membership list, but caucus supporters were able to get electronic copies of four riding lists –

Table 2.1
Four-Riding Poll Results, Fall 2001

Name	Score	Percentage Responding
Preston Manning	4.05	82
Stephen Harper	3.62	51
Diane Ablonczy	3.12	32
Monte Solberg	2.97	38
Stockwell Day	2.72	84
PC/DRC Coalition	2.56	78
Joe Clark	2.26	87

two in BC, one in Alberta, and one in Ontario – enough to give us an idea where we stood. Stephen and Stock were tied at 24 percent each, though the largest number of respondents said they were undecided. We thought that was encouraging for an undeclared candidate compared to the sitting party leader.

We obtained the results of table 2.1 when we asked for favourability ratings of a number of political figures (as well as the idea of cooperation between the Alliance and the PCs), on a scale from 1 to 5. Among our members, Preston Manning was well known and popular, while Joe Clark was well known and unpopular. Stephen's standing was second only to Preston's and well ahead of those who seemed like potential opponents at the time – Stockwell Day, Diane Ablonczy, and Monte Solberg. Stock, in particular, seemed to have little room to grow because his response percentage was the highest in the group of potential opponents, while his favourability rating was low.

These findings validated the strategy that we wanted to adopt for other reasons – polarize against Joe Clark. Don't attack merger or cooperation as such, but declare that cooperation with the PCs would be impossible as long as Joe was their leader. Never criticize Preston Manning; present Stephen as his legitimate heir from Reform days. And run with confidence, because our main opponent, Stockwell Day, had a relatively low approval score with no obvious way to recover from it, while other potential challengers were both less well known than Stephen and not as popular.

FALSE START

From the beginning, Stephen had wanted to build a professional, nationwide campaign organization as a means for taking control of the Alliance and making it a more effective campaign instrument in the next federal election. We thought we were moving in that direction when, in late September, we hired three people to fill senior positions in the campaign organization. The campaign manager was to be Brian Mulawka, who had managed campaigns for James Rajotte and others in Edmonton and was now president of First Past the Post, a small communications company. As Stephen's press secretary, we hired John Williamson, who was just coming off a stint on the editorial board of the *National Post*. Also from the Toronto area, we hired John Beishlag, who had worked on campaigns for both the Canadian Alliance and the Ontario Progressive Conservatives, as director of the field organization. The package also included Mark Spiro, another experienced Ontario activist, as a volunteer adviser and strategist. The paid people were backed up with other volunteers in Ottawa, Toronto, and Calgary. Overall, it was a young group of people, but experienced in running campaigns for parties of the right.

Our new organization did get some things accomplished in October. We brought most of the members to Calgary for a weekend SWOT analysis and planning session. Brian Mulawka's company put up a Draft Harper website, which signalled our intentions to the wider world. John Weissenberger and I were listed as co-chairs of a "Draft Harper" committee, which had no real existence except as a device to advertise that Stephen was seriously considering a run for Alliance leader. Consistent with our campaign strategy of capitalizing upon the Reform base, we put out an inexpensive little pamphlet – just a folded, photocopied page – entitled "Stephen Harper: True Reformer, True Conservative," emphasizing many familiar Reform policies. And we used an electronic list of those who had attended the Canadian Alliance founding convention to send out a direct mail piece asking for contributions. I got a good lesson in the glamour of campaigning when I spent a whole weekend signing and stuffing these mailers; but it was well worth the effort, because it brought in some much-needed money.

Overall, however, the organization failed to gel, and by mid-November it was apparent that we were falling seriously behind. We had no office space, no campaign pamphlet, little money, and no discernible fundraising plan. What we did have was a plan for a launch that would cost $60,000, even though we only had about $40,000 in the bank. Stephen and I realized in mid-November that the organization wasn't working and couldn't be saved. He therefore called all the paid people and told them he would have to terminate their employment, though John Williamson would stay a few more weeks as press secretary and First Past the Post would continue to do our web business. I admired the way Stephen did this; it would have been easier to tell me to fire everyone, but he didn't take the easy path. This willingness to handle the unpleasant side of things has continued to be one of his strengths in his subsequent political career. Even when he has to replace people, they appreciate how he delivers the bad news personally, and they often remain supportive and willing to work in other capacities in the future.

After the mass firing, Stephen thought seriously about calling off the whole campaign. Having spent three precious months with little to show for it, he was afraid that we might never be able to make up the lost ground. But our group of Calgary friends discussed it among ourselves and decided we could continue the campaign on a volunteer basis. When I went out to Stephen's house to bring him the news, I found him still uncertain, while his wife Laureen, who is as strong-willed as he is, was pushing him to make up his mind. The next day Stephen was still on the fence until Laureen finally got to him, saying, "If you don't think you can do it, you should quit now." At that, he smashed his fist on the desk and decided to go for it.

Still guided by the original strategy memo, we made a new plan for a stripped-down campaign, largely based on volunteers – Stephen's friends in Calgary, plus supportive MPs and staffers in Ottawa. The cost was to be about $250,000, more or less what we thought Keith Martin had spent when he had run his solo campaign for the leadership of the Canadian Alliance in 2000. Events would soon show that we were far too pessimistic, but it was crucial at that stage to have a plan that could be carried out without going into debt. Unlike the 2006 Liberal leadership candidates, who borrowed large sums to finance their leadership campaigns, Stephen was adamant that he would not go into debt.

Not only did we have to reorganize the campaign, we were faced with the untimely death of Peter Shuley, the BC Draft Harper coordinator, who died suddenly of a heart attack on 14 November. He had been instrumental in mobilizing a base of support in British Columbia, using the "Team BC" distribution list that he had developed. The loss affected Stephen deeply at a personal level. Politically, too, our BC organization was never the same after we lost Peter. Long after Stephen won the Alliance leadership, and even after the merger with the Progressive Conservatives, we continued to have problems getting all the factions in BC to pull together.

STARTING OVER

Once Stephen gave his approval to carry on, the Calgary volunteers went into high gear. Using a draft from Michele Austin, an assistant to MP James Rajotte, George Koch and I wrote the text of a campaign pamphlet, which George quickly got designed and produced through his wife's company, Merlin Creative. It used our new slogan, "Getting It Right," which had been contributed by Chris Matthews. It was, of course, a double entendre, emphasizing Stephen's conservative stance ("standing on the right") as well as his competence ("doing things right"). The paragraph on "Why Stephen Harper Is Running" illustrates the impression we were trying to create – stability, strength, determination, professionalism, and dedication to conservative principles:

> Stephen believes the Reform-Conservative Alliance is a party worth fighting for. He has a vision for a strong and successful party. He has the ability to transform that vision into reality. As a well-known conservative thinker, writer, and public speaker, he will powerfully communicate the party's policies to the public. Stephen will provide solid, professional leadership that will bring good government to the Canadian Alliance – and to Canada.

While George and I were working on the pamphlet, First Past
the Post got the campaign website ready, while John Weissenberger and Mark Kihn located office space and equipped it with
rented furniture. Keeping our minimal budget in mind, we leased
about 1,500 square feet in an unpretentious strip mall on Calgary's near north side. We would have needed twice that much
space if everything had been done there, but we made good use
of other locations. I had to be at the university anyway to teach,
so I kept in touch by using telephone and email. Similarly, correspondence was handled by a volunteer offsite, and we later
rented separate premises for a phone bank.

Given our financial position, we abandoned any idea of a
splashy launch. We simply concentrated on getting together the
$25,000 entry fee and getting our skeletal volunteer field organi-
zation to collect the three hundred signatures of party members
from thirty ridings required for entering the race. Stephen travelled to Ottawa on 2 December to tell the national press gallery
that he was running. Then, on 6 December, he walked into the
Canadian Alliance national office in downtown Calgary and
submitted the signature sheets, the $25,000 deposit, and various
other papers needed to become a candidate. He was the first to
enter the race officially.

Formal entry into the campaign brought two things that we
desperately needed for fundraising. One was the ability to offer
donors tax credits for their contributions to the campaign. Technically, they would make their donation to the party, and the
party would issue a tax receipt and pass 80 percent of the
amount on to the campaign, keeping the other 20 percent to help
defray the costs of conducting the leadership contest. We had
raised over $100,000 during the Draft Harper phase, but we
were running out of the well-to-do, committed supporters who
would donate without receiving any tax advantage. Now we
could appeal to the much larger universe of people who would
give as long as they got some benefit at tax time. The second
thing we received was the electronic database of party members,
both current and lapsed, going back to the founding of the Reform Party – about 300,000 names with "tombstone" information, i.e., mailing address and phone number. Our subsequent

campaign consisted mainly of mining this database for support
and money.

PLAYING BY THE RULES

There is no such thing as campaign strategy in the abstract; any viable strategy has to take into account the rules under which the
race is conducted. In the fall of 2001, the Canadian Alliance laid
down a set of rules for the leadership race that, though we had had
no say about them, were reasonably favourable to our campaign:

- Like the 2000 contest, this was to be a one-member, one-vote
  race, without any attempt to create balance by region, province, or riding. This was favourable to Stephen in that the largest part of the current Alliance membership was located in the
  West and had its roots in the Reform Party. It did not matter
  that Stephen's base was concentrated in one part of the country; a vote was a vote was a vote. Also, once we found we
  could raise money, we knew we could make universal member
  voting work for us, because we would have the financial ability to contact members through direct mail and telephone.
  None of the other candidates was able to afford to do this on
  the scale that we could.
- The decision rule was to be 50 percent + 1, i.e., an absolute
  majority of votes cast. If no one crossed over this threshold on
  the first ballot, there was to be a second ballot, limited to the
  top two finishers on the first ballot. This was at least mildly
  favourable to Stephen; being widely known, he was a plausible
  second choice for members who might have other first choices.
- The election was to be conducted by mail-in ballot. In one
  sense, this rule was probably neutral in its impact upon the
  candidates. The dynamics of universal member voting are
  pretty much the same whether ballots are cast in person at
  polling stations; registered via fax, telephone, email, or website; or sent in by mail. But since large numbers of voters are
  involved, the mail-in ballot favours a campaign, like ours, that
  was well enough organized and funded to mount an effective
  "Get Out the Vote" effort.

- Membership sales could continue up to three weeks before the first ballot was to be counted (20 March). Members would receive their ballots around 8 March 2002, which meant that some voters would have joined the party only about a week before they saw the ballot and could vote. This rule was mildly favourable to the Day campaign to the extent that their sales machinery was better than ours. It would have helped our cause if there had been a longer minimum waiting time between joining the party and voting, because that would have given us more time to bring our persuasion machinery into play and perhaps bring the supporters of other candidates over into our camp.

- The campaigns could sell new memberships, or people could join the party directly in a variety of ways – by mail, on the website, or dropping into the national office. However, third parties could not sell memberships on behalf of a campaign. This was different from 2000 and was a hindrance to the Day campaign; for they had effectively used third parties, such as Campaign Life, to sell memberships in the last race.

- There were to be no new membership sales between the first and second ballots. In the event, this didn't matter, because we won on the first ballot. If there had been a second ballot, however, the prohibition on new sales probably would have been helpful to us. Our machinery of direct mail and call centres was well designed to persuade existing members, whereas Stockwell Day's network of affiliations made it easier for his team to sell memberships in bulk.

- So-called "directed" donations could be made to the Canadian Alliance for the benefit of one of the leadership campaigns. The party would keep 20 percent of a directed donation, pass on the remaining 80 percent to the campaign, and issue the donor a receipt for a tax credit. Campaigns could keep 100 percent of donations made out to the campaign, but then the donor would not get a tax credit. Both rules worked well for us. Directed donations were the backbone of our populist fundraising, because most small donors require a tax credit in order to give. Beyond that, however, Stephen had a personal following of supporters who were willing to give directly to the campaign and forego a tax receipt.

• There was no upper limit on the size of donations, and corporate donations were allowable. In practice, this didn't matter because none of the candidates had the right connections at this time to raise large amounts of corporate money.

Overall, the rules were conducive to the kind of campaign we were prepared to run, so we had no cause to challenge them. It wasn't until the next race that I was to encounter the squabbling over rules that has been the hallmark of Tory leadership races since time immemorial.

ORGANIZING THE "CATTLE DRIVE"

The rules of the selection process strongly conditioned our organization. Because we did not have to win this race riding by riding, we did not need to create a complete field organization across the country. John Weissenberger recruited regional organizers but did not set up a full riding-by-riding network. We would have been particularly hard-pressed to create such an organization in Quebec, for we had almost no supporters there beyond a few libertarians associated with the Montreal Economic Institute and some English-rights activists whom Harper had befriended when he was president of the NCC.

Also, since there was no national convention of delegates, we did not need to create a cadre of influential supporters to work the convention floor, trying to solidify our own support while seeking second-ballot support from delegates committed to other candidates. A one-member, one-vote leadership race inevitably becomes a "cattle drive," in which the goal is to round up as many supporters as possible, make sure they have up-to-date memberships, and get them to mail in their ballots. With a good database of past and present members, you can do this largely through direct mail and telephone contact.

Our organization was exceedingly lean. We had no need of national and provincial chairmen and committees and similar advisory bodies because we did not need a full-scale field organization. Our financial position also played a role; because we were so worried about money at the beginning, we minimized the number of paid staff positions. In that respect, we may have gone too far. We definitely should have had a director of membership sales in addition to Devin Iversen as director of voter contact. Our failure to have such a director led to an inadequate membership sales plan and a lot of last-minute scrambling.

Overall, however, our organization was sound, as shown by the fact that we won on the first ballot and finished with money in the bank. Comparing this success with the failure of our first attempt to set up an organization for Stephen, I drew several conclusions:

- The campaign organization should be small and tight; you don't need a lot of external advisers.
- Decisions are best made by those who have to implement them, not by unaccountable advisers.
- Teamwork is important; things work best when the key people know and trust each other.
- Commitment, not cupidity, should be the main motivation. Use volunteers as much as possible. If remuneration is necessary, offer as little as possible, but pay a generous bonus to those who persist to a successful conclusion.

We adhered to this model in all subsequent Harper campaigns, thereby avoiding the organizational problems that plague many campaigns: overpaid consultants giving advice but not taking administrative responsibility; factional warfare between cliques; lack of clear lines of authority; everybody interfering in the business of everyone else. Of course, as our campaigns grew larger and more complex, we had to relax our approach somewhat. To make bigger campaigns work, you have to pay more people, and pay them better. You also need more external advisers, partly because you need to make more people feel involved, and partly because you need the advice. But we always aimed at a lean, nimble organizational structure and clear lines of authority, employing a cohesive and dedicated group of workers.

Also worth noting is the division of labour that developed very early in this campaign. I spent most of my time working on the business side of the campaign – budget, fundraising, direct mail, phone banks, membership sales, data-processing. The communications director served as press secretary travelling with Stephen;

there were no communications staff in the campaign office. Ken Boessenkool also gave his policy advice directly to Stephen and drafted speeches for him. I sometimes copyedited Stephen's speeches but never touched the content. Stephen also controlled the tour in as much as John Weissenberger, who served as national field organizer, tour director, and deputy manager, reported to directly to Stephen on tour issues. From the beginning, then, I was the business manager of the campaign but had little to do with policy, strategy, communications, and the leader's tour.

MINING FOR MONEY

Money was our greatest need in the early stages of the campaign, so Mark Kihn rushed out a direct mail piece as soon as we got the database. We mailed it on 12 December so that people who responded promptly could get a tax receipt for 2001 – and then get another tax receipt for 2002 if they gave again in the coming year. We limited this first letter to the approximately seventy thousand current members (reduced to about fifty thousand mailers by including all family members in the same envelope) because we had to bootstrap our way up and couldn't afford to pay for any more printing or postage at this stage. Several of us made small short-term loans to the campaign to finance this first mailer, but in the end Mark repaid the loans immediately because he was able to get thirty-day terms for payment from the mail house and the printing company.

We were hopeful that this would be a productive list because the Reform Party and Alliance had placed great emphasis on renewing memberships and securing small donations. People who were still with the party at this point would be highly committed to the cause and used to the idea of reaching into their own pockets to support their beliefs. Our appeal followed the time-honoured advice for raising money by direct mail – make people angry and afraid, and set up an opponent for them to give against:[29]

Imagine the Canadian Alliance didn't exist.
  Imagine no political party spoke for Canadians like you who cherish conservative principles and values. Imagine the only

alternative to Jean Chrétien's arrogant, spend-happy Liberals were Joe Clark's arrogant, spend-happy Red Tories.

Not a pretty picture, is it? ...

But here's the good news. You've finally got somebody fighting on your side!

Results started to come back after Christmas. There was one reply on Thursday, ten on Friday, and then I fretted all weekend, wondering how it would go. On Monday afternoon, after he had picked up the mail, Mark Kihn called me and said, "You'd better sit down for this. There are two hundred replies containing about $20,000." From that day on, we never had to worry about money. The adding machine tape for 31 December was twelve feet long because of hundreds of small donations totalling $50,000. Overall, this one letter brought in almost $400,000 from party members responding to the first sign of hope they had seen in many months.

We followed up as soon as we could with a second wave of direct mail to former members of the Reform Party who no longer had a current membership in the Alliance. Ultimately Mark sent about 90,000 of these letters, going back to people whose Reform membership dated from 1995 or later. We did not mail people whose membership had lapsed prior to 1995 because we thought that too many of them would be deceased, have a new address, or simply not be interested any longer. Our approach to these lapsed members was to portray Stephen as the embodiment of the Reform tradition. Knowing that the party had had the energy of a social movement, not just a political party, we took a chance on a highly personalized appeal:

You know Stephen. Maybe you remember him from the days when he was one of the Reform Party's most effective and energetic MPs. You may even recall he was a founder of the Reform Party and was its first chief policy officer. You may recognize him as a principal author of Reform's original "Blue Book."

You might remember all that because you were once a strong supporter of the Reform Party. Then something happened. You became disillusioned.

The party lost your trust. Perhaps, like many others, you came to believe the party had lost its direction, that it had turned its back on the principles and values you cherish.

But I hope the spirit which led you to originally join the Reform Party is still alive inside you. The spirit that gives you the strength and courage to fight for what's right.

That same spirit also burns inside Stephen Harper. It's the spirit of a true conservative – a true reformer.

This letter was also a big success, bringing in about $200,000 and four thousand membership renewals.

Our third wave of mail went out after membership sales had closed. Early in March, all campaigns received an update to the database containing information on approximately fifty thousand new members who had joined during the leadership race. Mark sent a letter to all of them, even to those whose memberships had been sold by Stockwell Day, Grant Hill, or Diane Ablonczy, or who had joined the party on their own initiative. We asked for their vote on the first ballot; or, if they were supporting someone else, to consider Stephen on the second ballot if it came to that. It was not primarily a fundraising letter, but Mark put in a "soft ask," and the letter brought in revenue more than covering its costs. It also served as a "Get Out the Vote" reminder to our supporters.

In addition to these three main waves of direct mail, we tried to treat our donors well. Rather than wait till the campaign was over, we sent out interim thank-you letters containing a sixteen-page press digest, entitled *Harper's Review*, which Mark Kihn, a journalist by training and trade, put together. With a donor coupon in this mailing, we got a substantial number of second donations. Then, after Stephen had won, Mark sent all donors a thank-you letter and a new edition of *Harper's Review*, which led to donations coming in for many months after the campaign was over. Overall, the campaign raised about $1.1 million from about 9,800 donors, for an average donation of $116. At least three quarters of that came from direct mail. Smaller but still useful amounts of money came from the website or from those who attended rallies. At each event, we would set up a table at the door and place on every chair an information package containing a donor reply envelope.

Mark ran a true populist fundraising campaign. Our largest donation was $20,000. We had only five donations of $10,000 or more and five between $5,000 and $10,000. There were ninety-eight contributions of $1,000 or more. There was only a handful of corporate donations, of which the largest was $5,000 from CanWest Global. The few corporate donations that we did get were from individually or family-owned corporations, where it was largely a matter of convenience whether the owner would write a personal or a corporate cheque. We got nothing at all from banks, airlines, mining companies, oil industry majors, forest products companies, the insurance industry, or any of the other traditional patrons of Canadian political parties.

The truth is that we really didn't try very hard with those sources. When we did make some inquiries, we were often told that it was corporate policy to give only to election campaigns and not to leadership races. We knew that wasn't true, because Paul Martin's leadership campaign was racking up unprecedented totals in corporate donations, but it didn't really matter. We could see that we could raise all the money we needed from small individual donations.

At the outset, when we were still worried about our financial position, we decided not to mail the approximately 100,000 lapsed members in the database who had joined after the foundation of the Canadian Alliance. We were afraid that they would not be supportive enough to be profitable for us and that contacting them might actually antagonize them. But we may have been too cautious here. Obviously, we couldn't persuade these people by stressing the Reform connection, but a properly couched appeal might have drawn thousands of them to rejoin the Alliance, vote for Stephen, and give money. Experience in subsequent campaigns has shown that it pays to be aggressive in prospecting lists of people who have any history of supporting conservative causes. Although we couldn't have afforded to send 100,000 of these letters at the outset, we could have sent, say, 10,000 as an experiment and then followed through if the results had been positive.

We did have one bit of unwanted excitement in our direct-mail fundraising. On 26 January 2002, someone from the National Alliance of Canada sent the Harper campaign a $100 money order made out to the Canadian Alliance Fund. Not recognizing the identity of the donor organization, Meredith McDonald – then a graduate student working in the Harper leadership campaign, now a speechwriter for the prime minister – databased the cheque and sent it on to the Canadian Alliance for processing. The National Alliance of Canada is just a few people with a post office box, but they are connected to the much larger and very sinister National Alliance of the United States. This is a racist, neo-Nazi organization founded by William L. Pierce, author of *The Turner Diaries*, the book that helped to inspire Timothy McVeigh's Oklahoma City bombing.

In mid-February, Diane Ablonczy, with whom I had worked closely in early Reform years, called to tell me about this racist donation to our campaign; she had heard about it from a reporter who had called her for a comment. I immediately ordered the money refunded with a letter saying, "Neither the Harper Campaign nor the Canadian Alliance accepts donations from organizations advocating racialist ideology." Once the National Alliance got that rebuff, they sent a copy of the money order to the *Sun* newspaper chain; and Anne Dawson, head of their Ottawa bureau, called me about it as part of the research for her story. Instead of just sticking to the main message that we had returned the money as soon as we found out about the contribution, I added the gratuitous observation that anyone could have set this up, the Liberals or even one of the other campaigns. I had no proof and shouldn't have said it, so I had to call the other campaigns and apologize for making accusations.

The story didn't go anywhere at the time, but the Liberals tried to resurrect it just before the 2004 election. Mike Robinson, one of the main Liberal spinners, said to Don Newman, "There were questionable donations that ended up in the media where white supremacist groups had given money, and – this is true, go read the newspapers – the National Alliance made a donation to Mr. Harper's campaign."[30] Again, the story fizzled, because Robinson was forced to admit that we had returned the money. He tried to insinuate there were other such donations, but there was no proof because there weren't any others. The lesson? There's nothing so dirty that your opponents won't try to use it

against you, so you have to watch every step and clean everything off your shoes, even if you stepped in it inadvertently.

LOCKING DOWN THE VOTE

Under strong advice from Scott Reid, we knew that we wanted
to win this campaign one member at a time, identifying and databasing Stephen's supporters and encouraging them to vote
when the time came. But how could we afford to do all the tele-
phoning that was required? To pay a telemarketing firm to call
the seventy-five thousand current members at, say $2 per voter
ID call plus $1 for a GOTV call to identified Harper supporters,
would have taken us close to $200,000, and that was just for
the original list of current members. Even more cost would
have been involved to make voter ID calls to new members
who joined during the campaign, and to make persuasion
callbacks to the undecided. That kind of expense seemed out of
the question for us in autumn 2001, so we had to canvass
cheaper alternatives.

One approach that we talked about was to use an autodialer.
For $10,000, we could have sent a recorded message to all cur-
rent members, asking them to press 1 if they supported Stephen,
2 if they were undecided, etc. This would have been better than
nothing, but voter ID through autodialing has important limitations. You don't know who's answering the phone: it might be
the husband or the wife, the babysitter or the mother-in-law, or a
polite burglar. And penetration is low. Most people will hang up
on an autodialed message before they get around to making the
response, or they will get confused by the instructions and press
the wrong button.

A second approach is the old-fashioned volunteer phone bank.
Install as many phone lines as you can afford, round up as many
volunteers as you can find, and give them printed lists of numbers to call. Preston Manning's leadership campaign had used
this approach in 2000. It's a lot better than nothing, but the
slowness of manual dialing limits productivity. We doubted that,
in the two months available, we'd be able to get through the
membership list with this method.

The best tool is a predictive dialer, that is, a computer programmed to dial numbers directly from the database. Callers
wearing headsets and sitting at computer terminals can key in
the ID responses and also sell memberships and take donations
over the telephone. However, the equipment is expensive and it
takes considerable training to make callers effective in using it.
In practice, if you want full-scale predictive dialer technology,
you have to go to a telemarketing company.

Devin Iversen, the assistant to Rob Anders, Stephen's successor as MP for Calgary West, came up with a solution. He and
some friends bought a stripped-down predictive-dialer system
and rented it to the Harper leadership campaign. These rigs
came in pods of five headsets attached to a central computer.
Each headset was matched not with a full computer keyboard as
in a commercial predictive-dialer arrangement but with a small
keypad like that of a telephone. The buttons on the pad could be
used to code and record up to twelve different answers to one,
but only one, question. So, after reading an introductory script,
volunteers would ask, "Who are you supporting in this leadership race?" Harper could be coded as 1, Day as 2, Hill as 3,
Ablonczy as 4, "undecided" as 5, etc.

Early in January 2002, we rented additional space in Calgary,
not far from the campaign office, and set up two pods of Devin's
dialers. Because of Stephen's reputation in Calgary, we were able
to get enough volunteers to keep these ten stations busy every
weekday and evening, plus Saturday during the day. We later expanded by setting up another ten places in Ottawa, under Scott
Reid's supervision, which we manned with a combination of volunteers and paid teenagers (we also paid some shifts of teenage
callers in Calgary toward the end of the campaign).

Using this system, we were able to call the entire list of current
members, plus updates as we received them. We made an ID for
everyone we could reach who would answer our question. Using
our most knowledgeable volunteers, we also made persuasion
calls back to those who said they were undecided. Finally, we
placed GOTV calls in March to the more than thirty thousand
identified supporters, reminding them to send in their mail ballots. If they had not gotten a ballot, we told them how to contact
the national office and get one.

Telephone calls were our main, but not our only, source of voter ID. We merged our lists of donors and of new membership sales with the telephone database, and we also made some identifications through email and fax blast-outs. But volunteer telephone calling was the workhorse of the voter identification effort.

SELLING MEMBERSHIPS

Our original campaign plan placed priority on persuading current members through direct mail and telephone calls, but we also made some provision for renewing or selling memberships to people who wanted to vote for Stephen:

- one could buy a membership on the Harper for Leader website;
- we distributed "info-packs" including membership application forms at every public meeting where Stephen appeared, and we set up a sales table outside the meeting room to sign up new supporters;
- Mark Kihn sent out a renewal letter, which was also a fundraiser, to about ninety thousand lapsed members, i.e., to those who had joined the Reform Party before 2000, but not to those who had joined the Canadian Alliance in 2000;
- John Weissenberger's field organization planned to generate membership sales by coordinating the work of riding-level activists.

However, we had neither a director of membership sales nor a separate staff for selling and processing memberships. Initially, we were satisfied with the results, as these methods brought in several thousand renewals and new sales. I remember an episode in mind-January 2002, when Stephen asked me whether I really thought he had a chance to win. I was feeling good because our direct-mail machine was flooding the office with money and our telephone operation was now in high gear. "You can't lose," I answered complacently.

This complacency was rudely shattered in late January when I attended a meeting of the Alliance caucus in Victoria, BC. I went out to discuss the campaign with Stephen's caucus supporters – by now more than two dozen. After I gave my view of how well things were going, I got a jolt from some of the caucus veterans. Art Hanger and Bob Mills, in particular, described how Stockwell Day's campaign was selling large batches of memberships, focusing on retirement homes, churches, and social conservative action groups. I went away thinking our campaign had under-emphasized membership sales and that we had better do something about it. Because he was in closer touch with the field organization, John wasn't as worried as I was, but he agreed that we should intensify our efforts.

At this point, we only had about five weeks to take corrective action, because sales closed at the end of February. As soon as I got back to Calgary, I convened the team to start brainstorming ideas for upgrading our sales effort. The best solution we found was to start pressuring our caucus supporters to crank up the workers in their ridings to sell memberships for Stephen. John Weissenberger spent hours, indeed days, on the phone, pleading with MPs to get busy. Cooperation was not universal, but supporters such as Art Hanger, Bob Mills, and Dave Chatters delivered on a large scale. Since a vote was a vote, it didn't matter that these sales were concentrated in a relatively small number of ridings.

Beyond that, because our fundraising was going so well, we could afford to throw money at a variety of approaches to boosting sales:

- The most conventional method was to hire a telemarketing company to make about twenty-five thousand calls to lapsed Reform members in ridings where we did not have an active, supportive MP.
- To contact the approximately 100,000 lapsed members that we had hitherto ignored because they had joined after the Alliance was formed, we hired a company with a high-capacity autodialer. Within an hour one Saturday morning in February, these people all got a message inviting them to rejoin and support Stephen in the leadership race. All they had to do was to press 1, and someone would call them back. Those who got the message on their voice mail got a number that they could call to purchase a membership. All in all, we got about 1,700 responses from this initiative and were able to convert about six hundred of them into sales.

- The most cost-effective initiative we took was to send an auto-dial message to all the identified Harper supporters, by this time close to thirty thousand. The message, in Stephen's own voice, told them that this was a close race against Stockwell Day and urged them to sell memberships to their family and friends. The phones in the campaign office rang off the hook for days as our supporters, spooked by the prospect of Stock being re-elected as leader, phoned in memberships for their wives and husbands, sons and daughters, mothers and fathers, and neighbours and workmates.
- Mark Kihn ran some ads in *Alberta Report* and the *National Post* with a response coupon for membership and donations.

The combined effect of all these measure unleashed a flood of sales in February, which in turn produced a new problem. Under the rules of the leadership race, each campaign had to process its own sales and submit them in batches of one thousand, using an electronic template provided by the party administration. In January, when our sales volume was smaller, I had hired some part-time students to do the data-processing; but they could not cope with the higher February volume, which had to be processed by the end of the month. I tried to solve the problem by turning to a databasing company to process the surplus, but that wasn't as easy as I thought. The sales forms were not always clearly legible, and bits of information were often missing. For this and other reasons, the company's keystroking contained a lot of errors, and we had to pay for double entry as a means of checking accuracy. Amid all the haste, we also got into problems of overlap and duplication between what was being processed in the campaign office and what was contracted out.

Another problem cropped up in February, too. When we had telephoned members for voter ID purposes, we had recorded their expressed preferences but had not thought of trying to renew their memberships, since we regarded them as members in good standing. But we had forgotten a detail of the Alliance system, which did not have a universal renewal date for all members. Rather, membership extended twelve months from date of payment. That meant that some (we estimated as many as four thousand) of the people we had identified as Harper supporters were due to have their memberships expire during the course of the campaign and might not get on the voters list, for which you had to have a valid membership as of 28 February 2002. It took a lot of last-minute scrambling to make sure these supporters were eligible to vote.

All this wrestling with sales, renewals, and data-processing gave me one of the worst bouts of insomnia I can remember. I would lie in bed at 3 AM, saying melodramatically to myself, "Am I going down in history as the campaign manager who lost his race because he couldn't get his sales processed?" But Maria Duhaime came to the rescue. As Art Hanger's constituency assistant, Maria had lived through Art's nomination race in 2000, when he sold fifteen thousand memberships in Calgary Northeast to beat back four Sikh challengers. Maria, who was already working in our little war room helping to arrange Stephen's travel and events, took over management of the data-processing, and told me to go home and get some sleep. She pulled it all together somehow, and at the end of February her big red wall thermometer showed sixteen thousand sales processed and submitted to the national office. We may not have sold as many as Day (their campaign claimed twenty-nine thousand), but we had sold enough to protect our lead. Even if we had not accelerated our sales efforts, we might still have won; but we would not have won on the first ballot, so all the confusion and insomnia was worthwhile in the end.

COMMUNICATIONS

Stephen rightly insisted that we focus our efforts on reaching the party members who could actually vote to elect the leader. He took the hard-headed economist's view that our resources – money, volunteers, and his time – were limited and therefore had to be rationed according to a criterion of utility. Proposals for all other activities, such as media appearances and interviews, photo ops, and meetings with community groups, would be strictly assessed according to whether they reached actual and potential members of the Canadian Alliance. This approach had several practical consequences for planning our campaign.

First, we spent relatively little effort soliciting public endorsements, except from current members of the Alliance caucus. We believed that support from sitting MPS was valuable because they had local organizations that could help us reach party members, but that other endorsements, e.g., from constituency presidents, or former MPS and party officials, would make little difference. Stephen's initial efforts, followed up by a round of my own phone calls, had yielded about a dozen caucus supporters. We then asked Charlie Penson, James Rajotte, and James Moore to continue working behind the scenes, and their quiet efforts eventually brought us endorsements and on-the-ground assistance from about half the caucus. We did far better in this respect than the other candidates; Stockwell Day had a dozen declared supporters, Grant Hill half a dozen, and Diane Ablonczy none except herself (her natural supporters had gone over to the DRC).

Second, we organized Stephen's tour around the imperative of meeting party members, while we did almost nothing to set up photo ops or elicit invitations to address community groups. Smaller events – lunches, dinners, receptions – were usually fundraisers. Beyond that, we tried to organize as many large evening or weekend rallies as possible. We always distributed envelopes and set up an information desk at such meetings, so they also helped our fundraising and membership sales.

Third, we put little emphasis on media for its own sake. We had no communications staff except for the three different press secretaries who accompanied Stephen at various times on his tour. The first was John Williamson, who was given notice in November as part of the purge of the Toronto staff, but who stayed on till the end of 2001. John later became national spokesman for the Canadian Taxpayers Federation and maintains a cordial but professionally distant relationship with the Conservative Party. The second was John Collison, a broadcaster who had built up a reputation in Winnipeg as a "shock jock." Collison wasn't the right choice to work for Harper, who wants self-effacing media people around him. He lasted only a few weeks, went back to talk radio, and later linked up with Ezra Levant's *Western Standard* radio operations. The third and last press secretary was Carolyn Stewart-Olsen, a former nurse who had worked in Reform communications in Ottawa but had not survived the internecine warfare. She was the perfect person to work for Harper – intensely committed, loyal, and self-effacing. She is now the prime minister's press secretary.

The campaign staged few photo ops and formal press conferences, although of course Stephen did interviews with reporters and columnists covering the campaign and appeared on talk shows that might reach party members. But overall, we put very little effort into "spinning" reporters and columnists. The main initiative we took beyond doing interviews while Stephen travelled was to have him give five major speeches that could be condensed for op ed publication in the National Post, Globe and Mail, and other metropolitan dailies. Once they appeared, we used the printed columns as enclosures in our mailings to potential voters and donors. Drafted mainly by Ken Boessenkool, these speeches and columns were fairly dense, policy-oriented productions, designed to present Stephen to the public as a serious thinker. We were trying to heighten the contrast with our opponents, none of whom, whatever their other merits, had a reputation as a policy wonk.

The plan was to keep the Canadian Alliance alive by running against Joe Clark and the Red Tories who wanted to absorb the disintegrating Alliance. That contrasted Stephen to Grant Hill and Diane Ablonczy, who were both running on an explicit pro-merger platform.[31] It also contrasted Stephen against Stockwell Day, whose leadership was associated with the factionalism and in-fighting that threatened the future of the Alliance. Merely by enunciating his position, Stephen could differentiate himself from his three opponents without having to mention, much less attack, them. As a practical matter, Stephen also wanted to avoid attacking his opponents because he hoped to win and knew he would need their cooperation afterward to reunify the party. In line with this strategy, Stephen had me replace his second press secretary, John Collison, after John made condescending comments to the National Post about Stockwell Day: "I would suggest that Stock Day is not the strongest policy wonk out there, that he is not the deepest policy thinker."[32] John's comments appeared in the morning paper, I accepted his resignation at midday after checking to see that Carolyn Stewart-Olsen was available, and I hired her later in the afternoon.

We did, however, go openly negative once against the Day campaign, in early February, when we were worried about their apparent lead in membership sales. I was in my car, driving back from a meeting with the company I had hired to keypunch our membership sales data, when I got a phone call from Elizabeth Thompson, a reporter for *The Montreal Gazette*. She told me that Campaign Life, the national anti-abortion organization, was trying to sell memberships on behalf of Day. President Jim Hughes had written to Campaign Life members, offering to accept their money, process their data, and submit their memberships to the national office of the Canadian Alliance. Such third-party sales had been legal in the 2000 race but were specifically forbidden under the 2002 rules. Our campaign was having so much trouble selling memberships and processing the data that the thought of the Day campaign relying on surrogates made me indignant. I went back to the campaign office, visited Campaign Life's website to check the facts, and then wrote a note of protest to Terry Horkoff, the party's chief electoral officer. It was an open-and-shut case, so the party very quickly told Campaign Life to stop claiming that it could sell memberships.[33]

Also, I made a rare intervention in the media, telling the *Globe and Mail* that Day was trying to win the Alliance leadership by stringing together a coalition of single-interest religious groups, including pro-life Roman Catholics, evangelical Protestants, and Dutch Reform members.[34] Stephen and Ken Boessenkool thought I had gone too far in being so specific, because many members of these same religious groups were on our side.

However, it kept alive concern among our supporters that Day might win the race, which was fine with us. We didn't want our supporters to think it was in the bag. Equally important, we wanted Hill and Ablonczy supporters to think that Day had a serious chance of winning and that the only way to prevent a Day victory was to vote for Harper. In order to ensure that all these groups would vote, we wanted them to be alarmed over the possibility that the Alliance might continue its disintegration. Campaign Life's *faux pas* was a perfect opportunity to heighten that fear.

Not just through this episode, but through everything that Harper said and didn't say in the final weeks, we were successful in creating the impression of a tight race. Newspaper headlines just before the 20 March decision day were full of phrases such as "too close to call," nail biter," and "down to the wire."[35] Some columnists were speculating that Day had apparently rallied to pull off a victory.[36] We were happy to let the media wallow in their own disinformation because we wanted our supporters to be motivated to vote.

In fact, we were sure that we were well ahead. Voter ID is not the same as scientific polling, but it gives a sense of how things are going, and our nightly calling showed us far ahead of Day, with Hill and Ablonczy not even on the map. It also showed Harper as the leading second choice, reassuring news in case we failed to win on the first ballot. In February, Grant Hill behind the scenes offered to shut down his campaign and throw his support to us if Harper would make some promises about vigorous pursuit of cooperation with the Tories. Hill's campaign manager, Tom Jarmyn, called me repeatedly around 15 February to try to make a deal, but we refused to promise anything. We didn't want to be beholden to anyone, and we thought that Hill would support Stephen on a second ballot if necessary.

To check our perceptions, I commissioned an inexpensive autodial poll of Ontario and Western members in late February after sales had closed. We didn't poll Quebec and Atlantic members because their numbers were few in comparison to Ontario and the West. The poll confirmed that we were far ahead among those who had been members when the race started, and also ahead, but not as much, among new members. It showed that we were well-positioned to win on the first ballot, with Harper at 49.9 percent and Day trailing at 23 percent. Ablonczy and Hill were far back with 6 and 4 percent respectively. When we looked only at original Reformers, even more, 55 percent, supported Stephen, whereas only 17 percent said they would support Day. The results suggested that Stephen's Reform base would offset any gains through new membership made by the Day campaign.[37]

Projection of the actual result depended on what assumptions one made about the likelihood that old Reform and new Alliance

Table 2.2

Canadian Alliance Leadership Results, 20 March 2002

Candidate	Votes Received	Percentage of Total Vote
Stephen Harper	48,561	55.0
Stockwell Day	33,074	37.5
Diane Ablonczy	3,370	3.8
Grant Hill	3,223	3.7
Total	88,228	

members would actually vote. My best guess at the time was that we very close to a first-ballot victory but not close enough to guarantee it. However, even if we didn't achieve victory on the first ballot, we would win a run-off against Day, because Stephen was the overwhelming second choice of Hill and Ablonczy supporters. In the event, Harper got 55 percent on the first ballot, suggesting low turnout among Day's new membership sales.

RESULTS

The Harper campaign got very favourable first-ballot results in this race, as shown in table 2.2. To establish the legitimacy of Stephen's leadership, it was important to win on the first ballot and by a wide enough margin to cut off any future attempts at internal opposition. In fact, Harper's first-ballot margin over Day, 55.0 percent to 37.5 percent, was perfect for that purpose – big enough to be convincing, but not so large that Day was humiliated. After demonstrating that he still had substantial support within the party, Day offered Stephen his unconditional support, thus setting the stage for reunification of the Canadian Alliance.

Also important was that Harper won the race while building a reasonably good image in the media. Not all observers were wildly enthusiastic, but most were willing to give him a chance. The *Vancouver Sun* noted Stephen's focus on policy, not politicking[38]; in Edmonton, headlines touted a "triumph of substance over style";[39] Lorne Gunter opined that Stephen did not win but rather that Day lost the race;[40] *The Montreal Gazette* cautiously called the victory "at least a start";[41] in Halifax, the opinion was that the Alliance under its new leader now faced a mammoth task of rebuilding;[42] and in the *National Post* Andrew Coyne called Harper "Manning with a mean streak."[43] Chantal Hébert's opinion in the *Toronto Star* was more or less typical of reaction at the time:

> The fact is that, in getting Harper as leader, the Ontario wing of the Alliance is as close to having one of its own in charge as it has ever been. By comparison with Preston Manning and even Day Harper is a fully bilingual national leader. He is comfortable with urban audiences. More importantly, and in particular, in sharp contrast with Day, he comes to the scene without any social conservative baggage. Indeed, by choosing him so decisively, the Alliance membership has signalled its willingness to ditch the party's social conservative credo, a move that many in Ontario have long described as a must if the Alliance is ever to expand in the province.[44]

The race in general, and our campaign in particular, helped to rebuild and revivify the Canadian Alliance. From December 2001 to March 2002, membership rebounded to 125,000; and enthusiasm went up as well as numbers. Turnout, i.e., the proportion of members casting ballots, was 71 percent in this race, compared to 60 percent in the first round of the 2000 leadership race, and 42 percent, 50 percent, and 66 percent in the Reform Party referendums of 1991, 1999, and 2000.[45] I'm convinced that the nature of our campaign helps to explain this high degree of participation. We sent at least one direct-mail piece to every member, and many got more than one, including thank-you letters for donations and postcard announcements of events. Similarly, we called as many people as we could reach at least once for voter ID purposes, made a second call to the undecided for persuasion purposes, and sent out various autodial announcements and messages to others. While a few members complained about the intensity of the contact, most seemed pleased to hear from a cause that meant a great deal to them.

This rekindled enthusiasm helped to restore the party's finances. During the crisis period, the national office had built up an internal debt of about $2 million by borrowing from the party's riding associations. That whole sum was paid back, with interest, in less than two years after Stephen became leader, due to increased levels of giving. The first direct mail piece after 20 March, which George Koch and I wrote, brought in over $400,000.

Another accomplishment of our campaign was not only to avoid debt but actually to make a small profit, based on campaign revenue of about $1.1 million. Stephen used some of this money to help pay his opponents' campaign debts, but most of it he simply kept in the bank for future contingencies. It turned out to be extremely useful in launching the next leadership campaign after the merger with the PCs, which came up on short notice. Given that Stephen had no wealth of his own and few wealthy friends or corporate connections, it was vital to stay out of debt and put some money aside for the future – otherwise his freedom of political maneuver would have been severely hampered.

There was much to be proud of in our campaign. Apart from a couple of mistakes (bad organizational plan at the beginning, inadequate plan for membership processing), we ran a well-conceived, economical campaign that achieved our major objectives. But there was also much to be modest about. Grant Hill and Diane Ablonczy never got any traction, and Stockwell Day was fatally wounded before the race ever began. He had been a formidable opponent in 2000 when he beat Preston Manning, but by 2002 events had driven his reputation down so that he could no longer raise money and attract staff. Many who had worked for him in 2000 worked for us in 2002. But the effort we mounted in 2002 might not have beaten the Day of 2000.

There were also shortcomings in the results that we did achieve. The rules encouraged us to run a database campaign without the necessity of building a riding-by-riding field organization. John Weissenberger's cadre of regional organizers proved very useful in the future, but at this stage we did not have control of all riding associations. Some socially conservative constituency presidents and councils remained skeptical of Harper, while other Tory-leaning ridings were still pursuing immediate cooperation with the PCs, even though Joe Clark remained leader. Stephen did not even have control of his own riding association, Calgary Southwest, which had been taken over by Ezra Levant. Ezra eventually gave up his nomination as the Alliance candidate in Calgary Southwest in order to let Stephen get a seat in the House of Commons, but the board remained filled with Ezra's handpicked supporters.

We didn't "fail" to get control of riding associations; rather, we never tried. But we did try and fail to get control of the party's National Council. This body was to be elected by membership mail ballot in conjunction with the leadership race. Candidates would run at-large for the thirty-two positions (three per province, one per territory). This was a major departure from past practice, in which the Council was elected by the delegates to the National Assembly. The new method turned the Council race into a name-recognition contest. How, for example, were the forty thousand members in Alberta eligible to cast ballots supposed to choose among eight candidates for three positions – eight candidates that they had probably never heard of before and probably not met during the race?

Under these rules, the winning strategy was clearly to use direct mail and telephone contact to bring the race to the voters, but that demands money and organization. We were prepared to pay for voter contact for Council candidates that we thought would be supportive of Stephen; and during the race I spent a lot of time on the phone with Scott Reid, James Rajotte, and James Moore, sharing rumours about who planned to run in various provinces and where their loyalties would lie. In the end, we paid for some direct mail in Ontario, but only in that province. The candidates that we wanted to support in Alberta – the only other province where there was a hotly contested race – felt that our backing might be counterproductive and asked us not to give any help. Unfortunately, they were wrong in their analysis, as shown by what a group of other candidates did. They sent a direct mail piece to every Alliance member in Alberta containing information about themselves, and all three were successful, because they were the only ones widely known, or at least recognizable, among all voters.

In the event, the Council that was elected turned out to be quite deeply divided, and not easy for Harper to work with. He spent a great deal of time and effort in the winter of 2002–03 to get the officers changed so that Council would not blockade him. All this was hardly visible to the public and perhaps not very important in the grand scheme of things, but it helped convince Harper that the Alliance could not go much farther on its own and needed to find a *modus vivendi* with the Tories.

3

Intermission, 2002–2003

After he won the Alliance leadership, Stephen asked me to go to Ottawa to become chief of staff of the Office of the Leader of the Opposition (OLO). I was intrigued by the offer, but it wasn't practical to accept it for the long term. My wife didn't want to move to Ottawa for an indefinite number of years, nor did I want really to break with my academic career. Marianne and I finally agreed that we would go to Ottawa for a year to help Stephen get set up there.

There did, however, have to be some delay. I was unable to do much for Stephen in the months of April through June 2002 because I was an expert witness for the Crown in the case of *Buffalo v. Canada*, and it was now time for me to testify in the Federal Court of Canada sitting in Calgary. I had begun to testify in January, but after two days the presiding judge, Max Teitelbaum, announced that he had been diagnosed with an illness and would have to adjourn. That was unfortunate for Justice Teitelbaum, but it was a blessing for me because it allowed me to get back to the campaign. John Weissenberger would have managed in my absence, but it would have been a burden on him because his day job was less flexible than mine.

I was on the witness stand for a total of about two weeks at different points that spring; and that, combined with the time necessary for preparation, took me away from politics. In particular, I could not play any role in Stephen's campaign in the Calgary Southwest by-election scheduled for 13 May 2002.

CALGARY SOUTHWEST

The by-election campaign was less entertaining than the events leading up to it, which were a small part of the much larger story of Stockwell Day's disintegrating leadership and Preston Manning's attempt to steer the remains of the Canadian Alliance into some kind of partnership with the PCs. Manning never left the Canadian Alliance, but in the summer of 2001 he gave some public encouragement to the thirteen breakaway Alliance MPs – almost all known to be strong Manning supporters – who had formed the Democratic Representative Caucus (DRC) in loose alliance with Joe Clark's Tories. Manning also let it be known that he would resign from Parliament early in 2002, and that Calgary Southwest would be a good venue for a joint Alliance-PC candidacy in the by-election that would be held to replace him.

Some Alliance members liked this idea, but others were uneasy about cooperating to this extent with Joe Clark when his public position was still basically that cooperation had to mean absorption into the Progressive Conservatives. In Calgary, Ezra Levant decided to block cooperation with the Tories in Calgary Southwest. With Sean McKinsley as his campaign manager, he went all out to take control of the riding association and get the nomination for himself. Raising tens of thousands of dollars, he rented five thousand square feet of vacant office space in a local shopping centre, where McKinsley installed his autodialer and a phone bank. They sold hundreds of new memberships as they got ready to take over the riding association at the next annual meeting in November 2001.

Initially, Stephen was quietly supportive of what Ezra was doing. If Calgary Southwest – Preston Manning's riding – made a deal with the Tories, it would have been a serious blow for the Canadian Alliance, for whose leadership Stephen was now running. I was also supportive of Ezra's efforts, for personal as well as political reasons. Ezra and Sean were both former students and now friends of mine.

On 21 November 2001, Ezra took control of Calgary Southwest. At a raucous meeting attended by 650 local members, his followers elected an entire slate of thirty new directors for the constituency association, including a couple of Ezra's family members. So far, so good – just effective street-level politics. But then he made remarks about "taking out the trash."[1] Many of the old board and their supporters had been working for Manning and Reform since the party was founded in 1987, and they did not take kindly to being taunted. Some left and joined the Progressive Conservatives, others stayed in the Alliance, awaiting a chance to regain control.

The new board set 19 December 2001 as the date for the meeting to nominate a successor for Preston Manning, even though Manning had not yet retired and was expected to continue serving at least until the end of January 2002. Rushing the nomination meeting this way made it difficult for anyone to mobilize to oppose Ezra. In normal times, the party's central administration might not have allowed such tactics, but these were not normal times. The meeting was held as scheduled, and Ezra was nominated by acclamation.

The Progressive Conservatives held a nomination meeting on 9 February 2002, at which Calgary lawyer Jim Prentice won a narrow victory over former Progressive Conservative MP Lee Richardson. The Liberals did not yet have a candidate but were rumoured to be planning to nominate a high-profile person who would be promised a cabinet position. What used to be a rock-solid Reform/Alliance riding was shaping up as an unpredictable three-way battleground in which almost anything might happen. Ezra said that to win such a competitive race he had to raise his profile by waging an expensive pre-writ campaign. Soon he was putting up billboards and running radio and TV ads slagging Joe Clark as "Kyoto Joe."

As it became clear that Stephen would win the Alliance leadership, we grew increasingly concerned about what Ezra was doing. Polls suggested that Ezra's takeover of Calgary Southwest, far from securing the riding as an Alliance bastion, had put it up for grabs to the PCs and Liberals. Moreover, once Stephen won, he would want to get into Parliament as soon as possible, and there was no vacant seat except Calgary Southwest. If he could not succeed Preston Manning in that seat, he would either have to lead the Alliance caucus without holding a seat or ask a sitting member to resign – neither being attractive options.

Only two days after he had won the nomination, Ezra had gotten in touch with me through Sean to propose some options. His three options, in order of preference were: (1) a sitting member of caucus could resign to open a seat for Stephen, as Scott Brison had done when Joe Clark became leader of the Progressive Conservatives; (2) he could resign his nomination in Calgary Southwest for the by-election but come back to that riding for the next general election, at which time Stephen could find another seat; or (3) he could resign permanently in favour of Stephen, and he and Sean could go to work for Harper's team.[2]

Stephen, however, refused to enter into any negotiations of that type, so I wrote back to Sean:

> Ezra has previously said in public that he will withdraw in favour of Stephen if conditions make that expedient. Now he seems to want to attach conditions to that offer. But Stephen has never asked Ezra to withdraw and does not wish to engage in bargaining over this question. Stephen's view is that MPs and candidates are free to make up their own mind on matters of this type. Should Ezra decide not to withdraw his candidacy, Stephen is confident that members of caucus, with the good of the party in mind, will help the new leader find a seat.[3]

On the evening of 20 March, after Stephen won, I told a TV reporter that the right thing was for Ezra to withdraw in favour of Stephen so he could get into Parliament as soon as possible. That was admittedly stirring the pot, but it was ready to boil over anyway. On 26 March, Stephen had a telephone conversation with Ezra. Behind the scenes, I had also been talking to Sean, telling him that it was not in their interest to stand in the way. Nonetheless, Ezra held a nationally televised news conference on 27 March to say that he would not step down. He tried to cast it as a matter of internal party democracy: "The decision is not mine nor even the leader's, but rather the decision of the grassroots."[4] Jean Chrétien, knowing or guessing what Ezra would do, had already called the by-election for 13 May, thereby ratcheting up the tension. There wasn't a lot of time left to sort this out.

Stephen looked weak for a few hours, but the reaction to Ezra's press conference was swift and savage. Alliance MPs, party members, voters, pundits – everyone condemned Ezra. With his phone ringing off the hook, a shaken Ezra announced the next day that he would surrender his nomination.[5]

After Ezra stepped aside, things moved quickly. Following the usual practice when a new leader first seeks a seat in Parliament, the Liberals announced on 29 March that they would not put up a candidate in Calgary Southwest, and Jim Prentice renounced the PC nomination on 30 March. Among major parties, only the NDP, which has never followed the convention of giving new leaders a pass, opposed Stephen. They nominated the Reverend Bill Phipps, pastor of Scarboro United Church in Calgary and former moderator of the United Church of Canada. Phipps was widely known for his left-wing politics but was not the sort of candidate to make a socialist breakthrough in Calgary Southwest. In addition to Phipps, there would also be Christian Heritage leader Ron Gray as well as an independent and a Green candidate.

Even though there was no real opposition, Stephen wanted to put on a respectable campaign. I couldn't help out because of my responsibilities in the *Buffalo* litigation, and Ken Boessenkool also had other obligations; but the rest of the leadership team moved over to work on the by-election campaign, with Glen Herring as manager. In the long term, the most important decision was to use Devin Iversen's predictive dialer technology to start identifying Canadian Alliance support in the riding. Manning had never needed to do this, and Ezra's team had only identified about a thousand supporters.[6] Stephen would need to know who his supporters were because he would have to deal with two potentially hostile blocs of Alliance members in the riding who would be liable to blame him for everything they didn't like – Ezra's followers, who controlled the board of directors, and the displaced Manning supporters, who were determined to get back in control and conduct inquiries into Ezra's campaign. Stephen badly needed to bring new people into the membership to blunt this conflict, and the first step was to find out who were his supporters in the general population. That was also the first step in the grassroots fundraising effort needed to restore the riding association to self-sufficiency. Devin and his volunteers made a good start, and the effort has continued since then. With the help of Mark Kihn's direct-mail campaigns,

Calgary Southwest has regained its financial health and has become able to assist less wealthy ridings across the country.

In spite of an energetic ground campaign with signs, door-to-door canvassing, and phone banks, the results were only minimally satisfactory. Stephen drew 71.7 percent of the vote, but that wasn't very impressive, considering that he faced no Liberal and PC opponents and that Preston Manning had won 64.8 percent of the vote in 2000 with all parties running. With no real contest, turnout was abysmally low, only 23 percent. Thus Stephen got into Parliament without further incident after Ezra stepped aside, but without any great show of enthusiasm on the part of the voters.

Nor was it a good night nationally for the Canadian Alliance. Seven by-elections were held simultaneously on 13 May. Although Calgary Southwest was the only one that we really expected to win, we had hoped for a decent showing in St. Boniface and Windsor West, but our candidates in those ridings garnered only 21.9 percent and 16.4 percent respectively. But if it was not a great night for Harper and the Alliance, it was a terrible night for Jean Chrétien and the Liberals, who lost two ridings – Windsor West in Ontario to the NDP and Bonavista-Trinity-Conception in Newfoundland to the Progressive Conservatives. The media coverage that night was more about the Liberal setbacks than the mediocre showing of the Alliance, but it was a sober warning that there was a long road ahead for the Alliance if it was going to become a governing party.

CHIEF OF STAFF

At Stephen's request, I made a trip to Ottawa in late March to review the staff and structure of the OLO. After that visit, I recommended that Stephen try to minimize disruption by leaving the current chief of staff, Jim MacEachern, in place. I would join the OLO in July 2002 as director of operations; one of my main responsibilities would be to start planning for the next federal election campaign. I would also be available for promotion to chief of staff if Stephen couldn't establish the necessary rapport with Jim. In fact, I only served as director of operations for a few weeks until early August, when Stephen decided that I should replace MacEachern.

Along the way toward becoming Stephen's employee, as opposed to the unpaid volunteer that I had been during the leadership race, I had to give up my role as a media pundit. I had spoken to the media very little during the leadership race; but once it was over I started to express some of my own views again in public. In April I published a paper for the Fraser Institute – "The Uneasy Case for Uniting the Right" – which I had been writing in summer 2001, before the leadership race erupted. Here is the concluding sentence:

> Conservatives and libertarians who see politics as a means of effecting change in public policy are more likely to achieve their goals by supporting parties with a consistent free-market outlook than by submerging themselves in "big tent" parties that may sometimes win elections but have no clear agenda for changing public policy.[7]

The paper became a minor stumbling block in organizing a Calgary Leader's Dinner as an Alliance fundraiser in 2002. Stephen worried about it, fearing that poor attendance might get his leadership off to a bad start, but he finally told me he would do it if I felt it would succeed. I thought we were on the way, but at the first planning meeting Calgary oilmen Jim Gray and Steve Snyder jumped on me over the Fraser Institute essay. They weren't interested in selling tickets for Harper's Leader's Dinner unless they were sure he was working toward eventual cooperation with the Progressive Conservatives. I managed to reassure them, but it was a good lesson in the dangers of expressing your views independently when you are working closely with the leader of the party.

Never a quick learner, I went on in June to publish a column in the *National Post* endorsing the general direction of Indian Affairs Minister Robert Nault's new bill, the *First Nations Governance Act*.[8] Stephen called me from Ottawa to say that our Indian Affairs critic wanted the Canadian Alliance to oppose Nault's bill. It finally sunk in that, if I was going to work closely with Stephen, I couldn't take public positions that might cause him political difficulties; so I agreed to stop publishing on current political issues and in general to stop talking to the media.

It is particularly dangerous for the chief of staff to talk to the media, for in that capacity you have too much access to confidential information. You know about the leader's moods, his ups and downs, his human weaknesses, his confidential conversations with other people, the advice he hears but rejects, the ideas he toys with but later abandons. All this may become important when the time comes to write history, but it has to be kept confidential when the political process is ongoing. Better for the chief of staff not to be put in a position where he might accidentally say something he shouldn't.

When I came to Ottawa, much of the leadership campaign team had already preceded me. As soon as he won the Alliance leadership, Stephen immediately appointed Ray Novak as his executive assistant and Carolyn Stewart-Olsen as his press secretary. After the by-election, he hired Maria Duhaime to run his Calgary-Southwest office. Devin Iversen was given a job in OLO Operations; Yaroslav Baran, who had done volunteer work for the campaign in Ottawa, became deputy director of communications. In the fall, Ken Boessenkool came to Ottawa to be Stephen's senior policy adviser. In early 2003, Mark Kihn moved from the National Citizens Coalition to become a fundraiser for the Canadian Alliance, while Meredith McDonald, who had assisted Mark during the campaign, got a job in OLO Research. The only senior figure from the leadership campaign who did not make the transition was John Weissenberger. Stephen and I wanted John to become director of OLO Operations; but in the end he decided he could not make the move, because of career and family considerations.

We also quickly built up the team by making several internal promotions, giving increased responsibility to people who had deep roots in the party going back to Reform days and were well known to others in the campaign team. Phil Murphy became deputy chief of staff, Debbie Campbell moved from correspondence to the crucial position of Stephen's logistics manager, and Steve Brooks moved from Grant Hill's office to become director of OLO Operations after John Weissenberger decided he could not take the job. Jim Armour, who used to be Reform's director of communications, was rehired from the private sector to be the OLO director of communications. In view of what lay ahead –

three more campaigns in the next three years – it was fortunate that we were able to augment the original leadership campaign team in a way that maintained its cohesion.

MEDIA MISHAPS

Stephen's first few months as leader were marked by a series of media misadventures that seriously affected his public image. When he was the MP for Calgary West, Harper had been known as media-friendly, ready to speak at length with reporters. Then, after he went to work for the NCC, he was much in demand as a pundit and TV panellist. But the situation of a party leader is fundamentally different from that of a pundit or an ordinary MP. As leader, you are the constant target of the communications departments of all the other parties. They dissect every word you say and do their best to get the media to report it in the most unflattering way possible. Like all new leaders, Stephen had to learn through experience how to operate in this adversarial environment.

The first episode was on 7 May 2002, when *Globe and Mail* columnist Jeffrey Simpson claimed Harper had told him that he "despised" his NDP opponent in the Calgary Southwest by-election, the Reverend Bill Phipps, former moderator of the United Church of Canada.[9] I wasn't present at the interview, so I don't know what Harper actually said to Simpson; but it is an axiom of democratic political ethics that you should differ with the ideas of your opponent without expressing dislike for the person. It is also basic political common sense, because you never know when today's opponent may become tomorrow's ally.

Moreover, Stephen became irritated with the *Globe* over a by-election campaign story attributing to him something that his campaign manager, Glen Herring, had said. Not content with sending in a letter of correction, he thought of filing a grievance with the Ontario Press Council; but we didn't proceed after learning how much the legal costs would be.

His most damaging faux pas came on 28 May, when he spoke of a "culture of defeat" in Atlantic Canada in an interview with Richard Roik of the *New Brunswick Telegraph Journal*:

"I think in Atlantic Canada, because of what happened in the decades following Confederation ... there is a culture of defeat that we have to overcome," Harper said.

"It's the idea that we just have to go along, we can't change it, things won't change," he added. "I think that's a sad part, a sad reality the traditional parties have bred in parts of Atlantic Canada."

"Traditional regional development programs are not very successful," he argued.

"They grossly distort the market and they not only fail to develop a lot of profitable enterprises, but over a long period of time, they have detrimental effects on potential opportunities."

Harper said Atlantic Canada also needs to see its gap in wealth with the rest of the country begin to narrow before the culture of defeat will recede, and he believes a federal government with a "can-do attitude" can also change opinions.

"These things feed on each other," he said.

"Atlantic Canada's culture of defeat will be hard to overcome as long as Atlantic Canada is actually physically trailing the rest of the country," he said.

"When that starts to change, the culture will start to change too."[10]

The next day, a motion condemning Harper passed unanimously in the Nova Scotia legislature.[11] The "culture of defeat" episode remained an impediment to his attempts to build support in the Atlantic region at least until the beginning of the 2005–06 election, when he finally offered an apology on radio.[12] Every time he travelled there, journalists put it into the story. It became like Pierre Trudeau's "Why should I sell your wheat?" comment, which never ceased to plague him in Western Canada.

Not long after this, Harper got into trouble over the Calgary Stampede, of all things. During the leadership race, the Canadian Alliance had neglected to schedule a barbecue or any other event for the 2002 Stampede. That was not Stephen's fault, but he compounded the damage by choosing to keep a low profile during the ten days of festivities in his home city. He tried to act like a private citizen, attending some events accompanied by family members yet not taking a public role, but it just didn't work. Both Paul

Martin and Joe Clark came to Calgary and flipped pancakes at Stampede breakfasts, allowing the media to paint Harper as a shirker.[13] That he was already scheduled to take a two-week family vacation in Mexico right after the Stampede encouraged further commentary on his alleged disappearing act. He said he needed some rest after months of campaigning, giving rise to comments about his stamina and commitment.[14] This was all trivial stuff, but it added up to weeks of less than favourable media coverage, on top of the "culture of defeat" fiasco. It wasn't a good start for a new leader.

Another problem arose on Friday, 13 September, when Stephen appeared on Fox News to discuss the anniversary of the 9/11 attack on the World Trade Centre and the Pentagon. When asked about a recent Ipsos-Reid poll that found that 84 percent of Canadians believed that the United States was at least partially responsible for being attacked, Stephen responded with a throwaway line, "Liberal pollsters will get Liberal results." Almost immediately, my fax machine spit out a demand for an apology from the lawyer for Ipsos-Reid, backed by a threat of defamation proceedings. Ipsos-Reid was obviously serious because their lawyer was Paul Schabas, one of the Canadian legal profession's stars. Harper hadn't mentioned Ipsos-Reid by name, and it wasn't even clear that he had alleged a connection to the Liberal Party, because the word "liberal" could just as well have been interpreted in the lower-case sense, referring to a certain ideology or worldview. But we got a quick introduction to how restrictive Canadian libel law is. Deputy Chief of Staff Phil Murphy and I talked to a retired judge and half a dozen lawyers, and we got essentially the same response from everyone: the comments were defamatory because, in context, they implied that Ipsos-Reid would massage its polling results to achieve political (Liberal) or ideological (liberal) objectives. Such an allegation was potentially damaging to Ipsos-Reid's commercial reputation as a scientific polling company. We could drag an action out for years, and we might hold the award to a minimum, but in the end we would almost certainly lose.

Remembering how Stockwell Day had weakened his leadership of the Alliance by his reluctance to settle the libel suit brought against him by Lorne Goddard, I didn't want to see

Stephen get caught in a similar trap. I brought in legal counsel to explain the issue to Stephen, and he signed a letter of apology that was released to the public on Monday, 23 September:

> Ten days ago, on the American television network Fox News, I made a comment involving liberal pollsters and liberal poll results. The statement is incorrect. We retract and withdraw same, and apologize to Ipsos-Reid for our error. We are pleased to make this clarification and apology, and regret any inconvenience and embarrassment that may have been caused.[15]

The apology led to one day of minor news stories, after which the issue dropped from sight completely and never reappeared. It was a successful exercise in damage control, and Stephen learned from the experience, so that he has never again, as far as I know, been seriously threatened with libel proceedings.

Stephen also had to learn one more lesson about controlling his mordant sense of humour. During Question Period on 23 October, when he was lambasting the Liberals for corruption, he said that Liberal ministers who had recently been fired or demoted for ethical problems had their photos plastered in newspapers "and, for all I know, in most of the police stations in the country." When Svend Robinson rose to say Harper was being unparliamentary in suggesting politicians are criminals, Stephen replied with a grin: "Mr. Speaker, I am sure the picture of the honourable member of the NDP is posted in much more wonderful places than just police stations."[16] Whatever exactly Stephen meant with his jibe, Robinson took it as an insult to his sexual orientation and told the media he would complain to the Speaker the next day.

Immediately after Question Period, Stephen invited staff into his office to discuss the situation. He said he hadn't meant his remark to refer to Robinson's sexual orientation, that he had been thinking of all the crusades, from environmentalism to euthanasia, in which the BC MP had boosted his profile. We all said essentially the same thing, that he could never win a fight on this issue, and that he had better apologize right away. He immediately picked up the phone and apologized to Svend, then repeated his apology in the Commons the next day. There was a bit of unfavourable media commentary to the effect that his apology wasn't sincere enough, but Robinson accepted it, and the issue quickly died. Again, the experience increased Stephen's caution about making off-the-cuff comments and quips in public.

All in all, Stephen faced a steep learning curve during his first six months, but the experience was beneficial. He became more cautious about what he said in public and learned how to avoid gaffes and lawsuits.

MEDICARE

Before Stephen left for his vacation in Mexico, I gave him some reading to take along. It was a new book by President Bill Clinton's former political adviser, Dick Morris, entitled *Power Plays: Win or Lose – How History's Great Political Leaders Play the Game.*

One of the famous concepts in this book is "triangulation," which Morris used to describe appropriating part of your opponent's program. Two chapter-length examples in his book were "George W. Bush Moves the GOP toward Compassionate Conservatism" and "Bill Clinton Leads His Party to the Center."[17] Another example would be Tony Blair's acceptance of Margaret Thatcher's economic reforms. "Triangulation" is a genuine act of statesmanship. The leader has to recognize that democratic politics requires acceptance of deeply rooted popular views, even when they were originally associated with opposing parties.

Health care had been an enormous political problem for Reform and the Canadian Alliance. It was not a major part of Preston Manning's original issue set, but the party could hardly avoid taking a position on such an important topic. For the market-oriented Reform Party, introduction of market-based elements into national health-care policy seemed obvious. But the Liberals attacked all of Reform's proposals as amounting to "two-tier" or "American-style" health care, leading to the famous episode in the 2000 Leaders' Debate when Stockwell Day held up his hand-lettered sign, "No Two-Tier Health Care."

Stephen's "triangulation" on health care amounted to avoiding this trap by matching or even outbidding whatever the Liberals proposed. Harper would go on to support the National Health Accord negotiated between Ottawa and the provinces in

2003, to excoriate Paul Martin at every opportunity for having cut health-care transfers to the provinces, and to stress that the public system provided the only health care available to him and his family (in contrast to Paul Martin, who patronized the private Medisys clinic in Montreal). This led to some tension between Harper and the libertarian wing of Canadian conservatism, which he addressed head-on on 29 April 2005, when he said to a Fraser Institute meeting in Calgary, "The ability to pay cannot control access to necessary medical services for ordinary Canadians, and it will not in a national Conservative government."[18] Publicly asserting this difference from a major group of supporters was a "Sister Souljah moment" (in 1992 Bill Clinton criticized hip-hop artist Sister Souljah for her remarks about white people).[19]

When he had been president of the National Citizens Coalition, Stephen had endorsed expansion of private medical-care alternatives,[20] but he had never believed that the federal government should take the lead in a sweeping privatization of health care. He takes seriously the constitutional division of powers, according to which health care is a provincial responsibility. Just as he disapproved of the federal government using the spending power to bludgeon the provinces into conformity with a certain model of public health care, so he would disapprove of the federal government forcing provinces to privatize health care. As far back as I can remember, his view has been that the federal government should live up to its financial commitments but should otherwise let the provinces exercise their constitutional jurisdiction.

LEADERSHIP STYLE

When I became chief of staff, I encountered an arrangement that had been developing since April and was already well established. Basically, Stephen acted as his own chief of staff for communications, policy, and tour. For communications, he presided over a daily morning issues meeting in which the principal attendees were Director of Communications Jim Armour, Deputy Director Yaroslav Baran, Press Secretary to the Leader Carolyn Stewart-Olsen, Press Secretary for French Media Dimitri Soudas, and Senior Policy Adviser Ken Boessenkool. For travel and scheduling, he met with Logistics Manager Debbie Campbell. I did not usually attend these meetings because there really was nothing for me to add. Stephen wanted to get advice in these areas directly, not through the chief of staff.

Stephen's hands-on approach to policy, communications, and tour was only a special case of his approach to being Opposition Leader. He also dealt directly with several other key areas, such as caucus management and relations with the national executive of the party. I don't know if he ever read Richard Neustadt's classic book *Presidential Power*, but his approach was a bit like that of Franklin Roosevelt in the White House:

> Not only did he keep his organizations overlapping and divide authority among them, but he also tended to put men of clashing temperaments, outlooks, ideas, in charge of them. Competitive personalities meshed with competing jurisdictions was Roosevelt's formula for putting pressure on himself, for making his subordinates push up to him the choices they could not take for themselves.[21]

Rather than funnelling everything through a chief of staff or principal secretary, Stephen's penchant for dealing directly with a wide range of advisers allowed him to transcend gatekeepers, leaving him truly in charge of all matters that he regarded as important.

Stephen's approach to being leader of the Opposition was a form of "flat" or "hub-and-spoke" leadership, in which numerous subordinates get a chance to give their advice directly rather than funnelling everything upward through a few senior officials acting as gatekeepers and filters. The system can work very well, but it does require the spokes to stay in close communication, to make a rim around the hub, so to speak. As soon as Phil Murphy and I realized what the challenge was, we worked hard at meeting it. Our two offices were side by side, and we spent a lot of time briefing each other on our areas of responsibility. I asked him to look after personnel and space allocation, leader's tour, and House of Commons issues, while I spent much of my time dealing with the Canadian Alliance offices in Ottawa and

Calgary and particularly liaison with fundraising. Fortunately, I had excellent personal relations with the members of Stephen's immediate staff, and I often met with them informally to discuss whatever problems they were having.

Although hub-and-spoke management creates some difficulties, it is better than many alternatives. For one instructive example, read Paul Well's description of how Paul Martin was controlled by his long-term staff members, who called themselves "the Board." They refused to let other staffers deal directly with Martin even when that was his explicit wish. In Wells's view, some of the worst mistakes of the Martin government resulted from the Board's incestuous groupthink.[22] Harper's arrangement prevented would-be gatekeepers from gaining this kind of control over his decision-making.

The main area where things broke down was in relations with the National Council. Some councillors were enthusiastic about the new leader, but others were lukewarm at best. A complicating factor was that Council President George Richardson's son, Adam Richardson, had been a candidate for the Alliance in 2000 in the New Brunswick riding of Tobique-Mactaquac, had come close to winning, and was now the OLO's regional representative in Atlantic Canada.

When we decided to replace Adam, George and a some other councillors from the Atlantic provinces reacted strongly. They claimed that the leader wanted to downgrade their region, even though there was a plan to hire a new Atlantic regional liaison person. The Council became virtually paralyzed as meeting after meeting was taken up with discussion of the Adam Richardson affair, factions polarized, and personal relationships broke down. Finally, after months of this acrimony, a large enough group on the Council coalesced to vote George Richardson out of office and replace him with one of the Manitoba members, Don Plett, who went on to become chairman of the Interim Council of the Conservative Party after the merger and then was elected president of the National Council at the 2005 Montreal convention.

Apart from this nasty, time-consuming war within the National Council, Harper's first year as leader was managerially successful. The caucus was small (only sixty-six elected in 2000,

with a couple of defections afterward) and included only one
senator, Gerry St Germain. All factions had been so badly
bruised by the infighting of the previous year that no one wanted
to go public with dissent. The Liberals had a stable majority;
and, while the Alliance was the Official Opposition, no one considered it a serious contender to topple the government in this
Parliament or form a government in the next. Thus the degree of
media scrutiny was lower.

Stephen's desire to manage his personal activities directly gave
me wide latitude to run the rest of the show in the OLO, and indeed there was a lot to be done. The factionalism and changes in
leadership since 2000, with the inevitable firings and resigna-
tions, had been hard on the organization. There were several vacancies, including key areas such as the youth program; salary
schedules had become distorted through wave after wave of
emergency hires; and normal personnel practices in recruitment
and staff assessment had been relaxed in favour of quick fixes.
Now that we had settled the issue of leadership, it was time to
stabilize the OLO by filling vacancies, readjusting salaries, setting
up personnel evaluation procedures, and compiling an administrative manual. Phil Murphy took responsibility for a lot of this
work. Fully bilingual, with an MBA from the University of Ottawa and nine years experience on the Hill, he was a good complement to me – a unilingual academic from the West with no
prior experience in Ottawa.

I also spent a great deal of time on relations with the party.
The Reform and Canadian Alliance head office had always been
in Calgary, but one of Stephen's first steps as leader was to authorize the establishment of a party operations office in Ottawa,
managed by Barry Yates, the newly recruited director of political
operations. Barry and I spent a lot of time working out the relationship between his office and the OLO, particularly with regard
to the party's field organization. Like all parties, the Canadian
Alliance had field organizers who performed a range of tasks
that benefited both the party and the OLO. At the time, administrative arrangements for these organizers were chaotic. Barry
and I made a deal, which we called the "Concordat" (we never
settled who was the pope and who was Mussolini), to set up
proper supervisory mechanisms.

Liaison with fundraising was another area that occupied a lot of my energy because much of it involved the leader attending events, calling major donors, and approving the use of his name in written appeals. We were trying to revive the Canadian Alliance Leader's Dinners, which, after raising huge amounts of money in 2000, had fallen into desuetude during the time of troubles. We were more or less successful in this, but it took a lot of my effort because Stephen is very demanding about the execution of events and would not let party officials plan major fundraisers unless I was observing to make sure his expectations were met. With stable leadership and patient attention to detail in our Leader's Dinners, direct mail, and phonathons, the party was able to pay off all the Alliance debts when it merged with the Progressive Conservatives in 2003.

My most important mandate was to start organizing the Canadian Alliance campaign for the next federal election, which at that time was expected to be about eighteen to twenty-four months away. The actual work is done by party staff and volunteers, as well as external consultants and contractors; but there has to be a sturdy connection to the leader to make sure the preparations match what he wants. This was the most daunting challenge of my entire professional career. I had just successfully organized and managed a leadership campaign; but that enterprise, in which we spent about a million dollars, was an order of magnitude smaller than a federal election campaign, in which we would have a spending limit of about $17 million. I had no experience in preparing for a national election campaign, and none of the senior people who had run the Reform and Canadian Alliance campaigns were available. Preston Manning's main organizers – Rick Anderson, Cliff Fryers, Morten Paulsen, Ian and Ellen Todd – would have been controversial now because of their association with the DRC. Bryan Thomas, who had done Reform and Alliance advertising, had given up his London agency and gone into a media production business in Calgary with Cliff Fryers. Stockwell Day had used at various times a number of people from Alberta provincial politics, including Rod Love, Hal Danchilla, and Terence Kowalchuk. Trying to bring them back would have caused as much internal trouble as attempting to rehabilitate Preston's organizers. So, with no

senior and experienced organizers on hand, how were we supposed to plan a campaign?

The answer lay in bringing together the campaign knowledge
that was dispersed among senior members of the OLO and party
staff. All had worked in previous campaigns, if not at the top, at
least close enough to the top that they could observe what was
going on. With that in mind, I started to convene regular meetings of a body I called the Chief's Management Advisory Committee (CMAC). I gave it such an odd name because I remembered
something Preston Manning had once said: "Always give your
campaign planning committee a prosaic name so you won't be
bothered by people trying to get on it." At the beginning, the
main participants were:

- Election Readiness Coordinator for the Canadian Alliance
  Caucus Randy White
- Deputy Chief of Staff Phil Murphy
- Senior Policy Adviser to the Leader Ken Boessenkool
- Director of Communications Jim Armour
- Deputy Director of Communications Yaroslav Baran
- Director of Research Mike Donison
- Manager of Opposition Research Dave Penner
- Press Secretary Carolyn Stewart-Olsen
- Manager of Leader's Logistics Debbie Campbell
- Executive Assistant to the Leader Ray Novak
- Barry Yates, director of political operations, Conservative
  Party
- Dimitri Pantazopoulos, the party's pollster (occasionally at-
  tended)

We were later joined by:

- Director of Operations Steve Brooks
- Political Adviser to the Leader Tom Jarmyn
- Deputy Chief of Staff Ian Brodie
- Doug Finley, director of political operations, Conservative
  Party, after he replaced Barry Yates

We gradually worked through all aspects of the national campaign, recounting experiences, pooling our knowledge, and

agreeing upon future directions. Because I knew less than anyone else about campaigning, I mostly presided over the discussions without imposing my own views, announcing a decision when consensus seemed to be reached. Participants would take responsibility for certain areas, draw up proposals, then bring them back to the group for discussion. Once one of these subplans was approved, the person in charge would report regularly to CMAC about progress in their area. During this period, we took three initiatives that put a stamp on the campaign eventually waged by the Conservative Party in the spring of 2004.

First, the party undertook development of a new Constituency Information Management System (CIMS). The Reform Party and the Alliance had had a chronic problem of losing all voter identification data acquired during campaigns. A telephone call centre, located in Alberta, had made hundreds of thousands of calls in the 2000 campaign, but because of a dispute with the contractor hired to organize and run it, no data were ever turned over to the party. Some constituency associations had data from local phone banks and door-knocking, but the data were not available to the national office. The Alliance national office had an excellent database of current and past members, but no voter identification data. We were starting from zero as far as direct voter contact was concerned.

CIMS was a modified version of the Trackright system developed by the Ontario Progressive Conservatives. Theirs was a voter ID management system; we wanted to go further by incorporating financial data into CIMS. The most important feature of CIMS was that it was available to users at both the national and riding levels. For example, if the national party sold a new membership and entered the tombstone data in CIMS, that same information would become available to the local riding association, which could then approach the new member to volunteer in the local campaign or put up a lawn sign. Similarly, if the local campaign found a new supporter by door-knocking and entered the data in CIMS, the information could be used in national fundraising programs. The national party would own and maintain the central computer plus the database software, thus ensuring that all data would be saved from one election to the next.

Devin Iversen became the main apostle of CIMS. My own role was simply to give it internal political support so that it received

approval from the leader and the Canadian Alliance National
Council, who would have to authorize payment for the develop-
mental work. After approval, implementation was turned over
to a three-man committee: Devin Iversen, representing the OLO;
Cyril McFate, from the party's administrative staff reporting to
the National Council; and Tom Jarmyn, representing the Council itself. With this committee, we hoped to have all the ultimate
users of the system involved in its development.

In building CIMS, we made all of what I now know to be the
classic mistakes of information-technology projects. We turned it
over to a committee without hiring a professional IT manager.
Because the techies were the only ones who really understood
what was going on, they acquired too much influence and
loaded the system down with "feature creep." It was often behind schedule and over budget. Linking it to existing accounting
and membership software was a nightmare. By the time the 2004
election was over, the party had acquired enough computer
hardware to manage a moon launch. Stephen once referred to it,
in a moment of exasperation, as "the Conservative Party's own
gun registry." Yet, if we had taken the slower, more conventional
route, we probably would never have got the system built because of all the delays caused by the merger, leadership race, and
two elections. And CIMS ultimately proved its worth in the elections of 2004 and 2006, helping us to win many close races in
British Columbia, Saskatchewan, Manitoba, and Ontario.

The second initiative was the discovery of the Responsive
Marketing Group (RMG), a Toronto-based telemarketing company with a long history of doing work for the Ontario Progressive Conservatives as well as other parties of the right in Canada.
Or, to be more precise, RMG discovered us. In early spring 2003,
RMG President Michael Davis contacted me. He must have been
taken aback when I asked him who he was and what was he selling. But he persisted and came up to Ottawa for a presentation.
RMG was so successful with an initial prospecting experiment
that the party very quickly gave all our voter-contact work to
that company.

Our relationship with RMG linked nicely with our development of CIMS. RMG was already familiar with a CIMS-style system because of the work they had done with the Ontario PCs,

and CIMS provided a receptacle for the hundreds of thousands of records generated by RMG's large-scale calling programs.

The third step we took was to find an advertiser. As mentioned, Bryan Thomas was now out of the business and might have been internally controversial in any case. We therefore deputized Director of Communications Jim Armour to look for a replacement. Jim beat the bushes in Toronto and Ottawa without much luck. Many firms have no interest in doing political work, and those with interest and experience were already aligned with the Liberals or Progressive Conservatives. Finally Mark Kihn found Watermark Advertising Design, a medium-sized firm in Calgary. It was a perfect fit for the Canadian Alliance. Their best-known client was Mark's Work Wearhouse, a retailer appealing to many of the same demographic and geographic groups that supported our party – Western, male, stable working class, and middle class. The owner, Steve Bottoms, had been a supporter since Reform days and was enthusiastic about working for Stephen Harper.

The campaign plan we were constructing at that time wasn't really a plan to win the election but to increase our number of seats from sixty-six to eighty or ninety, to make a decent breakthrough in Ontario, to bury the Tories, and to establish ourselves for the future as the only conceivable alternative government. For that sort of plan, you produce a few ads that express your point of view, and you run them as much as you can afford, wherever they will do the most good, hoping to win over the additional voters you need to win targeted seats. Meanwhile the Liberals are cruising, beating back any opponent that threatens to break out of the pack, while appealing to the electorate as the only party with a realistic chance of forming a government.

However, the merger, of which we had no inkling in early 2003, changed everything. As the Conservative Party, we would be duelling with the Liberals, going all out to win, even if only a minority government. In that situation, political advertising becomes a dynamic game of volley and response. The other side trains its guns directly on you, and you have to be able to respond quickly with new ads to deflect attacks and open up new fronts against your opponents. But our team had never been through that kind of experience and did not have a plan for it.

FOREIGN POLICY

Reflecting on his first year in office as prime minister, Harper said:

> Well, I've said one of the big surprises I have had on the job has been the degree to which international affairs occupies my time, my workload and my actual responsibilities, the amount of travel. I try and minimize my travel. I still travel a lot, and I think it's just reflective of the fact that we are in a global world and a global economy and for many, many problems, there really are not national boundaries any longer.[23]

His previous experience had mainly been in domestic politics, but his record as Opposition Leader shows that he was never afraid to take positions on international issues. The war in Iraq is probably the best example.

On 17 March 2003, Jean Chrétien announced in the House of Commons that Canada would play no role in the US-led Iraq invasion. He emphasized that Canadian participation would have come only if the Security Council had approved the action and that this approval had not occurred. "If military action proceeds without a new resolution of the Security Council, Canada will not participate."[24]

Stephen responded on 20 March with an eloquent speech in the House of Commons, which, though it did not call for sending Canadian troops to Iraq, supported the US initiative:

> We in the Canadian Alliance support the American position today on this issue because we share its concerns and its worries about the future of the world if Iraq is left unattended ...
>
> We will not be neutral. We will be with our allies and our friends, not militarily but in spirit we will be with them in America and in Britain for a short and successful conflict and for the liberation of the people of Iraq.
>
> We will not be with our government, for this government, in taking the position it has taken, has betrayed Canada's history and its values. Reading only the polls and indulging in juvenile and insecure anti-Americanism, the government has, for the

first time in our history, left us outside our British and American allies in their time of need. However, it has done worse. It has left us standing for nothing, no realistic alternative, no point of principle and no vision of the future. It has left us standing with no one ...[25]

We printed the speech in pamphlet form and mailed out thousands of copies. As far as I could judge, there was strong support from the grassroots of the party.

Stephen also drew from his speech to expound his position in interviews and op eds. In a 22 March column in the *Ottawa Citizen*, he argued that the so-called "coalition of the willing" had the legal authority to act:

> Security Council Resolution 678, adopted in November 1990, authorized the use of all necessary means, not only to implement Resolution 660, which demanded Iraq withdraw from Kuwait, but also to implement all subsequent relevant resolutions and to restore international peace and security in the area. Resolution 687, which provided the ceasefire terms for Iraq – not an armistice – in April 1991 affirmed Resolution 678. Security Council Resolution 1441 itself confirmed that Iraq has been and remains in material breach of its disarmament obligations, a point on which there is unanimous approval.[26]

Columnists said he was out on a political limb with respect to the divisive issue. Chantal Hébert saw him "standing precariously on a narrow pro-war ledge of public opinion,"[27] and Don Martin suggested that "in a Parliament filled with cooing Canadian doves, [Harper] circles alone as the hawk."[28] CTV and the *Globe* commissioned a poll around this time that suggested two out of three Canadians supported Chrétien's handing of the issue.[29] An Ipsos-Reid poll released 27 April 2003 found Liberal support at 50 percent, with the Alliance far behind at 14 percent, virtually tied with the Progressive Conservatives at 13 percent.[30]

Not everyone was supportive of the PM's position, however. Very harsh criticism came from US Ambassador Paul Cellucci, who said Americans were "disappointed" and "upset" that Canada was not standing by its ally to the south, adding, "There is no

security threat to Canada that the United States would not be
ready, willing and able to help with."[31] The C.D. Howe Institute
called Chrétien's decision "gratuitous" and said Canada-US relations had plummeted to their lowest level since the 1960s.[32] An interview with Brian Mulroney revealed that he held much the same
sentiment. "I think this is juvenile delinquency elevated to parliamentary proportions," he said, and called the policy of neutrality
"a classic example of followership, not leadership."[33] Don Cherry
devoted an entire episode of Coach's Corner to promote his position that Canada ought to be backing the US in its efforts.[34]

Almost as soon as Stephen became prime minister, he began to
take an active role in foreign policy. In his first few months of office in 2006, he claimed virtual ownership of the Canadian mission in Afghanistan by travelling there to spend time with the
troops, then pushing through a House of Commons resolution
to extend the Afghan mission for two more years. He tilted deci-
sively toward Israel when it retaliated against Hezbollah in Leb-
anon. Even at the cost of jeopardizing a meeting with the prime
minister of China, he criticized the Chinese human rights records.
When he received the Woodrow Wilson award on 5 October
2006, his speech sounded almost Wilsonian:

> ... we will only merit this honour if we lead the country – and
> if we lead it in understanding that all nations of the world will
> share a common future for better or for worse.
>   We will lead Canada toward that better world.
>   We will build the relationships and the capabilities which
> will allow us to preserve our sovereignty, to protect our inter-
> ests, and to project our values – just as Woodrow Wilson
> wished for all of our nations.[35]

PERTH-MIDDLESEX AND
THE ROAD TO MERGER

The Perth-Middlesex by-election, held 12 May 2003, illustrated
the weakness of the Canadian Alliance in Ontario and propelled
Stephen toward seeking closer cooperation with the Progressive
Conservatives. The road to merger began in Perth-Middlesex.

Perth-Middlesex is a largely rural riding in Southwestern Ontario. Its largest city is Stratford, home of the famous summer
drama festival. Outside the arts community in Stratford and
some unionized auto workers, the riding tends to be conservative. It sent a Progressive Conservative MP to Parliament every
year from 1953 to 1993, when PC/Reform vote-splitting allowed
the Liberal John Richardson to be elected. But it had never been
a particularly strong riding for Reform or the Canadian Alliance;
we had finished third there three times in a row, getting only
23 percent of the vote in 2000.

Richardson was already sick in 2000 and probably would not
have run in that year except for Jean Chrétien's sudden rush to
hold a fall election. Though easily re-elected, the sixty-nine-year-
old Richardson was not well enough to carry out his duties and
finally announced his resignation on 11 October 2002.[36] The
district remained without representation in Ottawa for over six
months until on 6 April, four days before the legal deadline, the
prime minister announced that a by-election was to be held.

The Canadian Alliance riding association in Perth-Middlesex
had about $30,000 in the bank when Richardson made his an-
nouncement but otherwise was not in good shape. Volunteer
numbers were low, and the association was controlled by gatekeepers who appeared more interested in keeping people out
than bringing them in (the president and his wife later defected
to the Liberals). Trying to turn things around, the party quickly
arranged for the nomination of Marian Meinen, a Reform-
Alliance activist who lived just outside the riding in a northern
suburb of London. The owner of a construction company and
the mother of six sons, she had never been a candidate before.
Barry Yates, the party's director of political operations, also sent
down someone from Ottawa to be a resident adviser, in effect an
unofficial campaign manager. At this stage, I had little connection with Perth-Middlesex because it was considered a party
matter, not OLO business.

The PCs nominated Gary Schellenberger, the owner of a paint-
ing/decorating business and a former councillor in local government. He had run in 1997 and 2000, placing second behind
Richardson each time. A first Liberal nomination meeting on

12 December 2002[37] selected Dr Rick Horst as the Grit candidate from a field of six contenders.[38] However, the result was
nullified when questions arose as to the integrity of the voting
process,[39] and after it emerged that Horst was a member of the
provincial NDP.[40] Brian Innes, a local crop farmer and brother-
in-law of Liberal MP Tony Ianno, won the second vote, held on
1 February 2003.[41]

Sam Dinicol, the NDP candidate, was a twenty-three-year-old
student living in Toronto. He had run in the district in the 2000
federal election, coming fourth with 6.7 percent of the vote.[42]
Ron Gray, the Christian Heritage leader who had run in the Calgary Southwest by-election, announced he intended to file his
nomination papers at the Stratford returning office on 21 April,
almost at the last minute.[43] His candidacy was a nuisance for us,
as it promised to bleed off some Alliance voters.

Although an Alliance campaign office was opened, there
seemed to be little progress in attracting volunteers and building
a viable campaign. Stephen grew more and more concerned because he wanted the Perth-Middlesex by-election to demonstrate
what the Alliance could achieve in Ontario; at least superficially,
it seemed that there was an opportunity for us. The Liberals
were internally divided, the Tories had re-nominated a two-time
loser, and the New Democratic candidate was a student from
outside the riding. But we were hardly in a position to coast to
victory on the problems of the other parties; we would have to
mount a strong campaign to have any chance of winning.

Around the beginning of December, Stephen asked me to call
Doug Finley, who had interviewed earlier in the year for the job
of director of political operations, which eventually went to
Barry Yates. Doug, a Scottish immigrant then living in New
Brunswick, had been working on campaigns ever since 1966,
when he had helped the first candidate of the Scottish National
Party ever to be elected to Parliament. In the intervening years,
he had evolved from his youthful Marxism and nationalism to
manage dozens of federal, provincial, and municipal campaigns
in four Canadian provinces for the Liberals, Progressive Conservatives, and Canadian Alliance. Early in 2003, we sent Doug
down to Perth-Middlesex to take over the campaign, which at

that point was in sad shape. Much of the money had been spent, but little else had been accomplished. There were few volunteers, little organization, and no discernible plan. Using both his volunteers and a small telemarketing company, Scott Reid had been attempting to do voter ID for Marian, but the data were seriously corrupted and not very useful.

Doug took over on the ground, writing a plan, creating an organization, and finding volunteers, while I tried to coordinate the external volunteer resources that could be made available to help in Perth-Middlesex. Working from Calgary, Chris Matthews sent out direct mail to raise money for the campaign and put up a website. Mark Kihn got some simple radio ads produced and took care of the local media buy on behalf of the party. To give Doug some much-needed help, various party staffers volunteered for a week or two to help in the local campaign office. Later in the campaign, van loads of volunteers went down to help with door knocking and GOTV. Devin Iverson used his stripped-down predictive dialer to set up a voter ID and GOTV effort in Ottawa, using local volunteers. One side benefit was that Devin and Doug were able to try out micro-targeting and voter contact methods that later became staples of our ground campaigning in national elections

Stephen visited Perth-Middlesex five times,[44] and other caucus members also went there frequently. Stephen even approved holding a Canadian Alliance caucus meeting in Stratford while he brought his family along to celebrate his daughter Rachel's birthday; but an ice storm turned the logistics into a nightmare, and then Chuck Cadman sat on Rachel's birthday cake and Jenni Byrne shouted at him while the TV cameras rolled. Even apart from that farce, the utility of having so many MPs visit the riding was questionable. Valuable volunteer time is consumed in meeting and entertaining visiting dignitaries – time that might be better spent knocking on doors or manning phone banks. Also, sending so many caucus members to Perth-Middlesex raised the stakes psychologically. MPs began to think that this must really be an important battle if they were being sent there to help. It was risky to raise the stakes this way when we could not be sure of controlling the outcome.

Without Doug Finley's efforts, we might well have finished fourth, behind not only the PCs and Liberals, but also the New Democrats. Doug, however, managed to find some volunteers, both from within and outside the riding, and to set a respectable ground campaign in motion. But just as we were starting to build some momentum, our chances of finishing better than third were frustrated when, on 1 May, the local press printed a letter about the Kyoto Accord that Marian had published in the *Calgary Sun* on 5 September 2002. The prime minister, she wrote, "just wants to do what's politically expedient, as usual, and as usual the unthinking masses in Ontario are in agreement." She also went on to say, "But what do I know, I'm so out of the loop that I actually joined the Canadian Alliance and became president of our riding association. I think I live in the wrong part of Canada."[45] She might have survived re-publication of the letter if she had been a well-known long-term resident of Perth-Middlesex; but, for someone from outside the riding who was just getting acquainted, the effect was devastating. When Marian had first been nominated, we had done opposition research on her and had given her local campaign a file including this letter. But with the changeover in management, the information never reached Doug Finley, so he had no strategy for blunting the letter's bad effects.

As if that was not bad enough, there was another flub around the same time at a well-attended all-candidates debate. One of our advance men, wearing a walkie-talkie headset, was accused by a Tory of coaching Marian over the airwaves. Instead of just denying the patently false allegation, he replied sarcastically, "Yeah, I'm bouncing radio waves off Marian's husband's eye patch" (he had recently had cancer surgery). The coaching allegation got amazing currency and travelled around the riding for days, in spite of John Reynolds's attempt to kill it with bluster in the House of Commons:

The PCs simply could not understand why our candidate, Marian Meinen, could give thoughtful and intelligent answers to difficult questions. Marian Meinen, or any other woman for that matter, does not need coaching to out-think any PC candidate or even any PC Member of Parliament.[46]

The campaign turned ugly in other ways, too. Six days before the vote, three hundred of Marian's campaign signs were vandalized with spray-painted swastikas and the words "stop fascism."[47] That same day, in an email to the Meinen campaign, Frank Doyle, the editor of the *St Mary's Independent*, threatened to encourage voters not to vote for the Alliance. Upset that the party had not bought any advertising in his paper, Doyle fired off an angry missive:

> Jenni [Byrne], Thanks for all your phone calls recently seeking free publicity for your candidate. It seems we made a mistake in giving your candidate coverage in the Independent, (front page photos etc) because as a result you did not consider us for any advertising. As we are the most read paper in St. Mary's and area, (with the highest circ) and our readers tell us we have a huge influence when we write (each and every week – check with either of your two supporters over here) we thought that you might support small business (which we are) rather than the big chain newspapers. Now that we know where your party stands on small business, we will surely re-pay your patronage in this week's Friday edition, when we plan to devote as much space (including the editorial) as possible to encourage voters not to vote for your party. Not only do we intend to do it this week but we will never give your party any coverage – ever. Thanks again for everything. Frank.[48]

After offering him the option of retracting his threats of bad press, we forwarded the email to the media, which ran the story immediately.[49] As well, we lodged a formal complaint with the Ontario Press Council, on the grounds that these actions were a breach of journalistic ethics. But it was just desperate posturing on our part – Marian was done like dinner.

When the votes were counted on 12 May, the results were dismal for the Canadian Alliance (see table 3.1). The PCs had won, and both they and the NDP had grown at the expense of the Liberals, while we had gone backward in terms of popular vote. Any way you parsed it, the news was bad for the Alliance. We had failed to come up with a candidate from within the riding, which does not matter much in urban races (Stephen Harper

Table 3.1
Perth-Middlesex Election and By-Election Results

	2003 By-Election (%)	2000 General Election (%)
Liberals	30.5	40.4
PCs	33.8	30.5
Canadian Alliance	17.5	23.3
NDP	15.2	6.7
Christian Heritage	2.9	

does not live in Calgary Southwest, and Paul Martin does not live in LaSalle-Emard), but is important in rural races. Both the local riding association and the national party structure had performed sluggishly until we found Doug Finley to galvanize them. We lost badly even though we arranged for all sorts of outside volunteer help. In the end, voters who were looking to punish the Liberals preferred the known PC candidate, Gary Schellenberger, and his reassuring slogan, "Change You Can Trust," to the unknown Alliance candidate with the perhaps unsettling slogan, "You *Do* Have a Choice." Worst of all, it gave the Progressive Conservatives a big boost as they headed toward their leadership selection, scheduled for the end of May 2003.

Yogi Berra said, "It ain't over till it's over." In politics, it's never really over. There's always another day and another chance, if not for you, then for the next candidate, the next leader, the next party. Stephen's response to this defeat was to decide to make a serious play for cooperation with the PCs. Joe Clark had resigned as leader of that party, and a leadership race was underway, to be won by Peter MacKay on 31 May. Even though MacKay signed a deal with David Orchard not to consider cooperation with the Alliance, Stephen thought that MacKay might be open to persuasion. Thus the defeat in Perth-Middlesex became the prelude to reuniting the conservative family in Canada.

4

The Conservative Leadership Race, 2003–2004

The outcome of the Perth-Middlesex by-election convinced Harper that it was essential to pursue cooperation with the Progressive Conservatives now that Joe Clark was about to retire. He was not deterred by the outcome of their leadership race, which Peter MacKay won by promising David Orchard in writing that he would make no agreement with the Canadian Alliance. In fact, the deal with MacKay encouraged Stephen to take the initiative, for it had to have made the more right-wing PCs unhappy. And if MacKay would make a deal with Orchard, maybe he would make another deal with Harper. I had almost nothing to do with what followed, because I was now back in Calgary and Stephen relied on Tom Jarmyn, who was with him in Ottawa, as his main assistant in the unity negotiations.

Stephen, after contacting Peter in the first week of June, announced at the Canadian Alliance Leader's Dinner in Calgary on 12 June that he was interested in cooperation with the PCs:

What has become clear is that we must focus on achieving the minimum necessary to build from there. What is that? A single slate of candidates. We will continue to talk with PCs about the framework necessary for a single slate, and I urge all of you, members of both our parties, to promote the conditions for that to come to fruition.[1]

At the Toronto Leader's Dinner on 16 June, he asserted that, in spite of Peter MacKay's deal with David Orchard, rank-and-file Progressive Conservatives wanted cooperation with the Alliance:

> They do not want David Orchard's vision of the PC party – a PC party that exists to fight the Canadian Alliance. They do not want, or need, an "opposition to the opposition." They want our parties to prepare, not to do battle with each other, but to do battle with the Liberal party ... David Orchard cannot be allowed to have a veto on Canadians' choices in the next federal election.[2]

Peter Mackay responded in a speech to the Confederation Club that he "was open and interested" in having discussions on unity.[3] When he bumped into Stephen in the lobby of the House of Commons, he said, "You and I have to talk."[4] He and Stephen met in Belinda Stronach's office on 26 June. The Magna heiress had been taking her own steps since early June to push the unification of the two parties. Did she at that point expect that she would run for the leadership of a united Conservative Party? Probably not.

Stephen and Peter reportedly agreed on the need to move quickly to reach a Labour Day deadline,[5] and they each appointed teams of three emissaries to discuss matters further: former MP Ray Speaker, Senator (and former PC Party President) Gerry St Germain, and MP Scott Reid for the Alliance; former MP and Deputy Prime Minister Don Mazankowski, former Ontario Premier Bill Davis, and PC House Leader Loyola Hearn for the Tories. Very early on, Harper accepted Mazankowski's proposal that the negotiations should strive for merger rather than mere cooperation or even an electoral coalition.[6] Stephen was impatient to push ahead, but the Tories moved very slowly. MacKay remained in regular contact with Orchard, and repeatedly referred to the rule in the PCs' constitution requiring them to run a candidate in every riding.[7] The Tory delegates did not come to a meeting until 21 August and cancelled several subsequent meetings in August and September. Progress was so halting that Harper started "an extended game of orchestrated media leaks," designed to steer the Tories back to the table.[8] On

8 October Stephen chased Peter MacKay to Toronto, confronted him in the airport, and got him to meet later that night at Belinda Stronach's house.[9]

Harper made concession after concession. "The founding principles of the new Conservative Party of Canada," according to Bob Plamondon, "were lifted virtually verbatim from the PC party constitution – the same words, in the same order."[10] There were a few additions, but they did not include any trademark Reform policies, such as Senate reform and direct democracy. But two sticking points remained, one bigger and one smaller. The smaller one concerned the fate of nominated candidates. Harper had proposed that "the selection of CA and PC candidates shall be grandfathered to the Conservative Party, and further CA and PC nominations meetings shall immediately cease."[11] The Tories were opposed to this because a much larger number of Alliance candidates had already been nominated. They feared that grandfathering in this way would shut PC candidates out of the most winnable ridings.

The bigger issue was the formula for choosing the leader of the new party. Harper's original proposal was the one-member, one-vote, mail-in procedure used in the 2002 Canadian Alliance leadership race.[12] The PCs were willing to accept a membership vote rather than the delegated convention format in which Peter Mackay had triumphed; but they would not accept one-member, one-vote, under which the 110,000 Alliance members would have swamped their forty thousand members. (The numerical disparity was even greater than these numbers suggest, because a sizable minority of the PC membership consisted of David Orchard's followers, who would not stay around in case of a merger.) Thus the PC emissaries put forward the system used to elect Joe Clark in 1998: a membership vote weighted equally by riding. Each constituency would receive one hundred points, which would be divided among the leadership candidates in proportion to the percentage of votes received in the riding. Victory would require an absolute majority of points, with some form of second ballot or second count being required in case no candidate got an absolute majority (50 percent + 1) of points on the first count.

Equality of members versus equality of ridings – it was a classic clash of principles in which each side advocated a principle advancing its own interests. The equal-member model treats all members equally, which is the norm in a democracy. However, it also encourages the party to remain bottled up in areas of current geographic strength rather than expanding into areas of weakness. Leadership candidates can win by appealing to the membership in areas where the party is already strong, as we did in the 2002 Alliance race.

In contrast, the equal-riding model reminds parties that, in order to win a national election, they have to have support in many parts of the country. A leadership candidate has a strong incentive to develop support everywhere, because every riding has one hundred points to be won. But the obvious problem with the equal-riding model is that, at least in its pure form, it takes no account of the size of the local membership. A riding with ten members has just as much influence in the process as a riding with one thousand members, which encourages manipulation and outright corruption in the "rotten boroughs." Where memberships are very small, candidates are tempted to use tactics such as buying memberships, busing in "instant members" with no long-term interest in the party, striking real members off the list, and moving the voting site to a location that favours one side (like the living room of a riding organizer).

With something to be said for and against both principles, it was logical to seek a compromise. One could, for example, allocate a maximum of one hundred points to each riding but stipulate that the full one hundred points would go only to ridings with one hundred or more voting members. Thus, a riding with, say, ten voters turning out would have only ten points to be divided among the candidates. Mathematically, each member's vote would be worth one point in ridings with one hundred or fewer members. Small-membership ridings would still be treated more favourably, but not so much more favourably as in the Tory equal-riding model, according to which the votes in a ten-voter riding would each be worth ten points.

Harper was open to such a compromise, and his emissaries proposed several different formulas, but the PCs were adamant. It was their way or no way, not only for leadership selection but also for selecting delegates to the party's founding convention, at which a constitution and policy book would be adopted. When I had lunch with Stephen in Calgary on 11 October 2003, he sounded frustrated and quite pessimistic about the prospect of transcending this deadlock to reach any unity agreement.

Of course, more than principle was at stake. Even after merger, there would be a large number of rotten boroughs, including most of Quebec and the Greater Toronto Area, much of Atlantic Canada, the three northern territories, and some scattered ridings in Western cities such as Winnipeg and Vancouver. Neither party was strong in these areas, but the Tories tended to be stronger than the Alliance. The most plausible winning strategy for a candidate from the PC side would be to sweep Quebec, the GTA, and Atlantic Canada while picking up enough points elsewhere to squeak over 50 percent. Without the rotten boroughs, no Tory candidate would have a chance. For his part, Harper was pursuing merger with the intention of becoming leader of the new party; he assumed that Peter MacKay would also be in the contest. He did not want the leadership-selection formula to confer an advantage upon MacKay or any other potential Tory opponents.

Stephen pondered his options over the Thanksgiving weekend, then called Peter Mackay on 14 October to tell him he would accept the Tory demands, including a new round of candidate nomination meetings as well as the equality-of-ridings leadership selection formula.[13] Three years afterward, Hugh Segal lauded Stephen's decision as "an act of supreme statesmanship."[14] More prosaically, Harper just kept saying yes until the other side ran out of reasons to say no. When the merger was announced to the public on 16 October, the Agreement in Principle contained the following provisions entrenching the Tory equality-of-ridings leadership selection formula:

The leadership will be conducted on a One-Member, One-Vote Point System:
- It is very similar to one-member, one-vote, but allows for each riding to be weighted equally, thus giving each riding access and importance in the process.
- Each riding is worth 100 points (i.e., 100%). Leadership candidates are assigned a point total based on their percentage of the vote in each riding. For example, if Candidate A

received 50% of the vote, he or she gets 50 points. If Candidate B received 20% of the vote, he or she gets 20 points.

- To win, a candidate must obtain a majority of points from across the country.
- Preferential ballot (single transferable vote) will be used. [My note: "preferential ballot" is the correct label for what was done; "single transferable vote" is incorrect.][15]

"Harper's wager" was a gamble that he could accept any Tory formula and still win the leadership race. It was risky, but not recklessly so; the weeks of negotiations had shown him much about the weakness of the PCs. As his subsequent victory showed, it was the right decision for him at the time, though it left the new party with the continuing problem of rotten boroughs, a dilemma that remains for the future to resolve.

Bob Plamondon claims that Stephen would have been willing to accept Joe Clark as temporary leader of the merged party while the leadership race was conducted,[16] but Clark immediately denounced it as a proposal to terminate the Progressive Conservative Party, "and I think that would be a loss to Canada."[17] Four other members of the twelve-member PC caucus, including former leadership candidate Scott Brison, also refused to go along with the merger. In the Senate, Norman Atkins, Lowell Murray, and Elaine McCoy decided to retain their designation as Progressive Conservatives, sitting as representatives of a party that no longer exists. Prominent PCs outside the caucus, such as anti-free-trade crusader David Orchard and Mulroney-era Minister Sinclair Stevens, also denounced the merger. They and their supporters in the PC Party migrated in different directions. Some, like Brison, joined the Liberals. Others, like Clark, declared that they were now independent but supported particular Liberals in the 2004 election (Clark worked for Anne McLellan in Edmonton and Scott Brison in Nova Scotia). Still others went to the Greens (former Green leader Jim Harris used to be a Tory) or to the newly founded Progressive Canadian Party, where they became a nuisance when Chief Electoral Officer Jean-Pierre Kingsley allowed them to adopt the PC abbreviation. And then there was MP Keith Martin, who also denounced the merger and went over to the Liberals – the only significant defection from the Reform/Alliance side.

The defectors generally claimed to be from the more "progressive" or left-wing side of the PC Party, which had won a great deal in the unity negotiations, including the all-important selection rules for choosing the leader and delegates to national conventions. To be sure, they had lost the word "progressive" in the party's name, but the same word reappeared in a commitment to "progressive social policy" in the founding principles of the new party.[18] Why did they not stay in the merged party and continue to fight for their particular version of conservatism, as did those who elected to form the Conservative Council headed by BC Tory activist Rick Peterson?[19] Perhaps some, like David Orchard, whom Joe Clark once called a "tourist" in the Progressive Conservatives,[20] had views that were simply too far removed from the median member of the new party; but most did not seem that distant from the moderate conservatism to which Harper committed himself in the aftermath of the merger.

"This is not my party," Joe Clark said, as he announced his departure on 8 December. "This is something entirely new."[21] But the only thing that was new was that Joe Clark and the Red Tories were no longer in control. Clark's subsequent statements on this subject continued to make little sense. On 25 April 2004 he told CTV, in words that did us serious damage in the 2004 election, that he preferred Paul Martin to Stephen Harper:

> I would prefer to go with the devil we know ... I'm that concerned with the imprint of Stephen Harper, not only what he stood far in the past, but the way he has led this party ... I don't believe that the Harper party can get away with the masquerade that it is the Progressive Conservative party that was broad enough to attract support from a wide cross-section of Canadians.[22]

Harper has led the party in a moderate direction, often matching the Liberals on key points of policy; but Clark could only see extremism, in contrast to Brian Mulroney, who noted that Harper was building a "moderate, successful Conservative party."[23]

FIELD OF DREAMS

Having returned to Calgary in June 2003, I was leading our efforts to organize a Canadian Alliance campaign for the next federal election, expected for spring 2004 after Paul Martin would have become Liberal leader. But as soon as the merger was announced I shifted gears from planning for a federal election to organizing Stephen's campaign for the leadership of the new party.

The rules of this leadership race gave it a different character than the Alliance leadership race of 2002. Adoption of the Tory principle of equality of ridings meant that we would have to work to find support everywhere, not just where we were already strong. I expressed it in a formulation that Stephen often repeated: "In the first race, we could win by building on strength. In this race, we have to address our weaknesses." Specifically, that meant building a comprehensive field organization so we could sell memberships and locate Harper supporters in every riding in the country. Ten votes in one of the rotten boroughs in Quebec might be as important as a thousand votes in one of our bedrock Alberta ridings.

"Harper's wager" definitely involved some risk. With rotten boroughs constituting more than a third of the 308 ridings, there was a serious chance that Harper could have been beaten by a strong Tory candidate, particularly a Francophone and/or native son from Quebec. On paper, the premier of New Brunswick, Bernard Lord, was the perfect candidate to beat Harper. Born in Quebec but raised in New Brunswick, fluently bilingual, blessed with one of those ethnically androgynous names that can be interpreted as either French or English, a lifelong Tory who had restored his party to power in New Brunswick with a crushing majority in 1999, Lord looked like a dream candidate for the Tories who wanted to block Harper. He would also have had John Laschinger, the most experienced campaign manager in Canada, at his side.[24] Tories talked Lord up in the first few weeks after announcement of the merger, but he had his own problems. He wasn't well known at the federal level. His majority had unexpectedly been reduced to one seat in the New Brunswick election of June 2003, and he suddenly seemed like less of a winner. If he left his vulnerable provincial government in the lurch to go questing for the federal Holy Grail, he might appear to be bailing out of a difficult situation. Only thirty-eight years old at the time, he chose to wait.

The Tories also took a run at promoting Mike Harris, but that never really got off the ground. Unable to speak French, tired from his years as premier of Ontario and preoccupied with family matters (separation and reconciliation with his wife, then divorce and remarriage), he was visibly not very interested; he announced on 2 November 2003, that he would not run.[25]

Another Tory "white hope," much less plausible than either Lord or Harris, was Larry Smith, publisher of *The Montreal Gazette*. Smith, a bilingual lawyer from Montreal, had played fullback with the Montreal Alouettes in the 1970s. He was Commissioner of the CFL in the 1990s, in the period when the league made its unsuccessful expansion bid into the United States, and then president of the Alouettes, beginning in 1997, when the team staged its successful comeback into the CFL. Although he seemed to have some of the attributes necessary to do well in the race, Smith had never run for political office at any level and had no political organization of his own. His candidacy was never a serious proposition, even though some Tory organizers promoted it for a while.

Other potential candidates also considered running – Peter MacKay, Jim Prentice, Chuck Strahl – but when they tested the waters they found that the support they needed, particularly financial support, simply wasn't there. MacKay and Prentice were still recovering from the 2003 PC leadership race, and MacKay was doubly discredited because of his pact with David Orchard. At one stage, Prentice announced that he would run, but he withdrew on 11 January 2004, after a failed phone-bank experiment made it obvious that he would not be able to attract volunteers and donors to pay for a campaign.[26] When I had called Jim in the fall and not so subtly suggested it would be a waste of his time to run, I hadn't gotten anywhere, but financial realities turned the trick.

The underlying problem for would-be candidates from the PC side was that they lacked the ability to conduct grassroots fundraising, while their potential corporate supporters were tapped out from having donated to the recent PC leadership race as well

as to Paul Martin's leadership campaign. Moreover, Belinda
Stronach was starting to vacuum up corporate money. When I
heard rumours in fall 2003 that she might run, I did not take
them seriously at first because Belinda herself denied them,[27] and
in any case she seemed like a non-starter. Like Larry Smith, she
had never run for political office; and unlike Smith she was not
even bilingual. If Smith could not run, how could Stronach? But
I started to believe the rumours in December when I requested
Senator Gerry St Germain, one of our main fundraisers, to ask
Belinda for a contribution. In view of the large amounts she had
given MacKay in the recent Tory race,[28] and because of her inti-
mate involvement in the unity process, I was expecting at least
$50,000 and hoping for $100,000. When Gerry reported back
that she would not give a dime, I knew she was serious about her
own candidacy.

She announced her decision to run on 20 January 2004, promising "to bake a bigger economic pie."[29] Lacking political experience, unable to speak French, wooden in manner despite her
striking good looks and fashionable wardrobe, she was far from
the dream candidate the Tories had been seeking. Yet her financial resources meant that we had to take her campaign seriously,
particularly because she used her money to assemble a "dream
team" of experienced campaigners. Mike Harris put her together
with John Laschinger, who had just finished managing Peter
MacKay's successful run for the PC leadership. Laschinger pulled
together an all-star team of conservative campaigners, to which
Harris contributed former top aides and associates, such as Deb
Hutton, Guy Giorno, and Janet Ecker. Geoff Norquay and Andrew Skaling also worked on communications. The database
manager was Doug Earle, not a well-known name to the public
but a highly skilled practitioner of voter ID and GOTV through
direct mail, website, and phone banks. Jaime Watt acted as a
campaign adviser because his communications firm – Navigator
– had been handling the Magna account for years.[30]

Laschinger also used Stronach's money to hire experienced
political operatives across the country: Rod Love, former chief
of staff and campaign manager for Ralph Klein; Morten
Paulsen, former director of operations of the Reform Party; Ian
Todd, former executive assistant to Preston Manning; and Rick

Anderson, Manning's strategist.[31] In Quebec he hired virtually all the Tory organizers, most of whom had worked for MacKay in the PC leadership contest.[32] Through our national co-chair, Michael Fortier, we approached some of these people, arranged a meeting with Harper, and offered them our standard rate; but they almost all went with Belinda, reportedly at more than three times what we could afford to pay.

Belinda herself didn't frighten us, but the combination of her money and the reputation of her campaign team gave us cause for concern. We were worried about Quebec because we knew our weakness there. The rotten-borough strategy was self-evident, and Laschinger's years of experience with the PCs, reinforced by Belinda's unlimited wealth, gave him the knowledge and connections to implement it. We were quite concerned in the beginning, especially when Belinda's organizers turned out an audience of 1,300 for her at a breakfast event in Calgary.[33] When I saw that, I resolved to run as strong a campaign as possible while taking nothing for granted. In the end, however, Belinda was simply not a sufficiently experienced, polished, and persuasive candidate to pull it off, no matter how strong her team was.

A confounding factor was the candidacy of Tony Clement. Tony, a former Minister of Health for the Ontario PCs and one of the founders of the Canadian Alliance, was an experienced and credible candidate, though not ideal for this race. Harper cut him off from the more conservatively minded members of the new party; and, though he could speak French, he was not well known in Quebec. He was also burdened with having lost his last two races (leadership of the Ontario PCs, re-election to the Ontario legislature). Moreover, Belinda's candidacy absorbed much of the financial and organizational support that he might otherwise have expected to garner in Toronto. Many who were led by personal ties to work for Tony, such as Toronto lobbyist John Capobianco and lawyer Bob Dechert, would otherwise have probably supported Stephen, and our team maintained friendly relations with them behind the scenes during the campaign. Privately, they were caustic about Belinda for undercutting Tony, whom they saw as more deserving of the opportunity to be the Eastern candidate against Harper.

A straight fight between Harper and Stronach might have polarized and even split the new party. Having Tony, whose roots
were in the Ontario PCs but who had been one of the founders
of the Alliance, in the race helped blunt the cleavage between the
federal PCs supporting Stronach and the old Reformers gathered
around Harper. From personal contacts as well as polling, we
knew that a majority of Clement supporters would have Harper
as their second choice; so even if he bled support away from us
on the first count, his candidacy did not jeopardize our ultimate
chances of winning.

In the end, the most important fact about this race was who
did not get involved – not Bernard Lord, not Mike Harris, not
any other candidate who would have been able to sweep the rotten boroughs; and certainly no one of Reform background who
would have been able to challenge Harper on ideologically conservative turf. Was this just good luck? Perhaps, but it also reflected Harper's strength. Anyone researching the possibility of
running against Harper would quickly have seen that he had the
support of 90 percent of the Alliance caucus, he would be able to
raise all the money he needed from the grassroots of the party,
and he already had in place a campaign team that, if not highly
experienced, was enthusiastic and cohesive. *Si vis pacem, para
bellum*, runs the old Latin adage: "If you want peace, prepare
for war." Our organizational strength was an exercise in deter-
rence that helped bring us a war we could win.

BUILDING THE TEAM

The core of the campaign team would be much the same as in
Stephen's previous leadership race. I would be the manager, Carolyn Stewart-Olsen the press secretary, Ray Novak Stephen's executive assistant and body man on tour, Mark Kihn the chief
fundraiser, Devin Iversen the database coordinator, and Eric
Hughes the financial agent. Ken Boessenkool stayed in the OLO
to advise Interim Leader Grant Hill, but he did quite a bit of volunteer speechwriting for Stephen. This campaign would be based
in Ottawa, which meant that John Weissenberger, who was still
living in Calgary, could not play the same kind of role as he had

in 2002. He did, however, help out as volunteer chairman of the field organization in southern Alberta.

But even if the core members were the same, the team would have to be enlarged for this campaign. For one thing, we needed an honorific level of organization to meet the expectations of those from the Progressive Conservative side. Thus Stephen appointed John Reynolds, the Canadian Alliance House Leader, and Michael Fortier, a Montreal investment broker who had run for the leadership of the PCs in 1998, as national co-chairs, and provincial co-chairs were added as time went on.

We also needed a bigger media operation. Whereas in the earlier campaign Carolyn had handled all media relations, we now hired Yaroslav Baran to issue press releases from the campaign office. Yaroslav also held daily telephone briefings with a so-called "regional spin team," a network of communications people around the country, hired on part-time contracts to improve our coverage in both local and national media. It was a useful innovation that we would repeat in the 2004 national election campaign.

In the Alliance leadership race, tour organization had been rudimentary – just Stephen on the road with Ray Novak and Carolyn Stewart-Olsen, while John Weissenberger and some volunteers were back in the office making travel bookings, renting venues, and keeping in touch with local contacts. Stephen's tour organization had naturally expanded once he got to Parliament as Leader of the Official Opposition; so now, in addition to Ray and Carolyn, we had a tour director (Debbie Campbell), a scheduling assistant (Christina Chu), event organizer (Vida Brodie), and an advance man (Denis Gagnon) who, as a retired Mountie, also performed some security functions. All these people moved from the OLO to the leadership race when the time came.

This campaign would also feature formal televised debates, and for debate preparation we were fortunate to get Michael Coates, the president of Hill and Knowlton Canada. Mike was one of those who tried to recruit Harper for the PC leadership in 1998.[34] He thought Harper was the best candidate in this race, so he stepped forward to volunteer his services. He not only became a trusted all-around adviser, he put together a rehearsal team who approached these events like the televised leaders' debates in a national election. These debates weren't nearly that stressful, but the preparation experience was invaluable for the more taxing national leaders' debates soon to follow.

Because of a much bigger membership list, we could no longer rely entirely on Devin Iversen's stripped-down predictive dialer rigs. Fortunately, Michael Davis came up with an innovative proposal to do voter ID and telephone fundraising at the same time. We used Devin's volunteer phone bank for the task of calling the much smaller Tory side of the list and for persuasion of the undecided – areas where the more personal touch of volunteer callers was helpful.

Finally, the equal-riding system of choosing the leader demanded that we construct a nationwide field organization to fight for points in every constituency. We started by borrowing virtually the entire field organization of the Canadian Alliance. Doug Finley by that time had become director of operations of the Alliance, and his two chief lieutenants at the national office were Jenni Byrne and Stacey Sherwood. When the leadership race began, those three, plus almost all the Alliance field organizers, took leave from the party and went to work for the Harper leadership campaign. Doug then enlarged this skeleton crew by hiring temporary full- or part-time organizers to ensure relatively even coverage across Canada. The result was a field organization extending into almost every riding, which became the basis of future Conservative Party ground campaigns.

Quebec, where the Alliance had maintained only one field organizer (Michel Rivard in Quebec City) was a special challenge. After Belinda's campaign hired all the Tory professional organizers, we put together a motley crew of paid organizers and volunteers, consisting of former Tories, Reformers, provincial Liberals, ADQistes, social conservatives, and evangelical Protestants. They were a ragtag group, not used to working with each other, but they delivered 33 percent of Quebec's points to Harper, thus eviscerating Belinda's rotten-borough strategy and opening the pathway that eventually led to winning ten seats in Quebec in the 2006 election. Those who provided leadership were Michael Fortier, who as the Francophone national co-chair had a special interest in Quebec; Richard Décarie, who had been at different times associated with the provincial Liberals as well as the PQ when Daniel Johnson was leader; and Judith Seidman, a former Brison-for-leader supporter, who added a lot of energy to the Montreal office.

With overtime assistance from Alliance staffers Cyril McFate and David Schellenberg, we set up a modest campaign office on the sixth floor of the Varette Building at 130 Albert Street, the same building where the Canadian Alliance maintained its Operations office and where the national office of the Conservative Party of Canada is now located. I had an office there during the leadership campaign, but I divided my time between Ottawa and Calgary because fundraising (Mark Kihn) and budget administration (Eric Hughes) were being done out of Calgary.

PAYING THE BILLS

At the start of the first Harper leadership campaign, we had had almost no working capital and no clear idea of how we would raise money or how much we might garner in contributions. This time we were starting with the surplus left from the previous leadership campaign. According to federal law, this money was Stephen's personal property. Apart from using some of it to help his opponents pay their campaign debts, he chose not to spend any, leaving it in an account managed by Eric Hughes. It was, therefore, available as start-up money once the merger was announced. We also had our invaluable list of about 9,600 people who had contributed to the first campaign. Since only eighteen months had passed since that campaign, the contact information on our donor list was still fresh.

Stephen's time as leader of the Canadian Alliance, particularly the experience of organizing Leader's Dinners, had significantly expanded our fundraising potential among high-end and corporate donors, through contacts such as Michael Fortier and Laurent Benarrous in Montreal; Thom Bennett, Manny Montenegrino, and Mike Coates in Ottawa; Linda Frum and Susan McArthur in Toronto; Gwyn Morgan in Calgary; and John Reynolds and Gerry St Germain in Vancouver. With fundraisers of this calibre, we knew we could do much better at the high end than we had the first time around, even though our mainstay would still be grassroots contributions.

The surplus from the first campaign would soon be exhausted by start-up expenses such as leasing and equipping the campaign office, putting up a website, printing pamphlets, getting a campaign song written, and ordering T-shirts, buttons, noisemakers, and all the other items of tour kit that we would need. Thus I started immediately to raise more money, beginning at a dinner in late October, when I was in Ottawa for a campaign planning session. I challenged Gerry St Germain, who was sitting across the table from me, to pledge $5,000 if I would do the same. We quickly shook hands on it. Then, at the end of the evening, he playfully punched me on the shoulder and said, "You let me off easy, Flanagan. I would have given $10,000 if you'd asked." But $10,000 from two people in one evening was a good start.

I then approached all the senior staffers in the OLO and the Canadian Alliance, asking for $1,000 apiece. The pitch was easy: "Stephen has to win this, or we're all going to be looking for new jobs." Just about everyone chipped in. I also made personal appeals to some outside contractors and other keen supporters who were able to afford generous contributions without worrying about a tax credit. Jim Abbott, the MP for Kootenay-Columbia, raised a substantial amount by asking all the members of the Alliance caucus for contributions. In addition, Mark Kihn quickly used our donor database, sending personalized letters to all who had donated $1,000 or more in the last campaign. These were proven loyalists, so we didn't mind asking them for money even though we were not yet able to offer a tax credit for donations.

These early measures ensured that we had ample funds to get started. Beyond that, I originally assumed that we would have to wait for the formal start of the campaign to crank up the populist fundraising machine, because effective grassroots fundraising at the grassroots level requires the ability to offer tax credits. We thought, however, of a way to get started earlier – ask the Canadian Alliance National Council to authorize tax credits for directed donations to any Alliance member who planned to campaign for the leadership of the merged Conservative Party. As in the earlier leadership race, it allowed us to offer tax credits in two tax years to those willing to donate twice.

Once that motion was passed in November, our fundraising started in earnest. Mark sent out a letter, not just to prior Harper donors, but to the entire current membership of the Alliance – over 100,000 names. Later, when the merger made it possible for us to get the PC membership list, he mailed those people, too. As in the first campaign, direct mail set up a revenue stream that sustained the entire campaign, supplemented by contributions made on the website, envelopes distributed at rallies, and aggressive telephone fundraising. Mark also was our contact point with RMG, and the money they raised on the telephone came very close to paying for the entire voter ID and GOTV effort.

The other feature that distinguished our fundraising from that of the first Harper campaign was the much greater success of our high-end and corporate effort. Our major donors included such well-known companies as Power Corporation, Bell Canada, Rogers, Onex, Grant Forest Products, CanWest Media, and En-Cana. Most of these large companies were supporting the process rather than committing themselves solely to Harper, so they also gave to one or both of the other campaigns. Overall, we raised about $2.7 million from about 16,000 donors, for an average donation of $142.[35] About half the total came from 1,829 donations of $200 or larger. The other half came from about fourteen thousand donations smaller than $200. Like the first campaign, it was basically a grassroots effort, though with a stronger high-end and corporate component.

Actually, I would find it impossible to say exactly how much we raised. The Leadership Election Organizing Committee (LEOC) decided retroactively that the campaign did not officially begin until after the merger was approved (12 December 2003 was the date chosen), so we did not have to report money received before that date. Things also got very confused at the other end. When Mark Kihn sent out a thank-you letter to all sixteen thousand donors, he include a "soft ask" for donations to cover any "clean up" costs. That brought in almost $500,000 in a revenue stream that continued for months after Harper won the leadership on 20 March 2004, and the donor list swelled to eighteen thousand.[36] By the time this was happening, I had gone on to manage the 2004 national election campaign and start preparations for the election to follow that. I never fully understood these final problems, and it didn't seem worth investing the effort to get a complete grip on them because Mark Kihn and Eric Hughes assured me that it was all going to work out. And it did work out. In the end, we paid all our bills and still had a comfortable surplus.

On the expenditure side, the main story of the campaign was the increase in costs imposed by the party. In autumn 2003, before I knew what the rules would be, I estimated our expenditures at approximately $1.7 million. However, LEOC imposed much higher levies than I expected and also required us to participate in an expensive final event in Toronto, which added about $200,000 to our campaign costs. In the end, we spent about $2.5 million, including levies to the party. There were times in January and February, after I learned about the additional costs imposed by the party, that I wondered whether our fundraising would be able to keep up. This was in marked contrast to the Alliance race, in which we had severe financial worries at the beginning, but smooth sailing once our direct-mail program got under way. In this campaign, we started off without much concern because we had the surplus from the first campaign and we were able to raise money quickly, but we developed concerns in the middle of the race because of unexpected rules imposed by LEOC. In both cases, however, Mark Kihn's grassroots fundraising sustained us, and we were able to win while gathering a significant surplus. With twenty separate mailings, he pushed our supporters hard, but they responded generously.

POSITIONING

Our 2002 campaign had had an ideological emphasis. Our slogan, "Getting It Right," suggested an ideological position as well as managerial competence, and Stephen's main message was the need to preserve the Canadian Alliance as a genuinely conservative party, not to let it come under the control of Joe Clark and the Red Tories. Things were different this time. When Peter MacKay decided not to run, the way was open for Stephen to present himself as a unifier of factions, the father of the merger. Along this line, he chose as a campaign slogan the phrase "One Conservative Voice." The French version – "Une seule voix conservatrice" –

had a useful double entendre in that "voix" can mean "vote" as well as "voice." The subtext was that the unification of the two parties would create an opportunity to beat the Liberals.

Our campaign pamphlet reflected this new direction. On the front page, along with a picture of Harper looking casual and friendly in a blazer and crewneck sweater, we printed the reasons "Why Stephen Harper should be Your *First* Choice." All were personal rather than ideological in character:

- Stephen Harper is a family man who understands the country.
- Stephen Harper is educated, experienced, capable, and professional.
- Stephen Harper is a proven unifier and coalition builder.
- Stephen Harper is an established national leader.

Political philosophy was relegated to the inside of the pamphlet under the heading "What I Believe." Traditional Harper conservatism was refined to present a more moderate image: higher levels of public funding of health care, use of the federal gas tax for municipal infrastructure, and a "made-in-Canada approach to reducing pollution and improving the environment." This last point amounted to opposition to the Kyoto Accord couched in a more positive way.

Early polling conducted by Dimitri Pantazopoulos showed that Stephen had a substantial lead among the membership, so he expected to win. Wanting a unified party behind him to contest the impending federal election, he planned to avoid attacks on the other candidates and spend his rhetorical energies during the campaign criticizing Paul Martin and the Liberals. We could differentiate him from Belinda Stronach and Tony Clement simply by stressing his attributes and achievements – his political experience, bilingualism, and record as a winner.

FIGHTING ABOUT RULES

Since all my political experience had been in the Reform Party and the Canadian Alliance, I was only dimly aware of the grand Tory tradition of waging leadership races in the form of fights over the rules. But I was forced to become a quick learner as rules fights became the major disruptive factor in an otherwise smooth campaign.

The LEOC provided for in the merger Agreement in Principle was perfectly designed to promote such fights. It was to consist of an equal number of members appointed by the leaders of the Canadian Alliance and the Progressive Conservatives, with no neutral chairman to break ties.[37] At the time the merger was negotiated, Stephen definitely knew he would run and Peter MacKay was contemplating it. The two leaders saw this provision as being in the interest of both, by making it harder for an outside candidate to take over. However, it set up a stalemate when Stephen appointed four Alliance loyalists and Peter appointed four Tories, almost guaranteeing a confrontational atmosphere of deadlock.

After the Alliance Executive Council's decision to offer tax credits to donors even before the race was officially under way gave him a fundraising advantage, Stephen announced that he thought the campaign should be run under the rules of Bill C-24, which would come into effect on 1 January 2004. This would mean limits of $1,000 on corporate donations and $5,000 on individual donations. We could easily live with those limits because of our large grassroots fundraising potential, whereas any challenger from the Tory side (particularly Belinda Stronach) would need to rely on corporate and high-end donations. Political campaigning induces self-righteousness, so we thought we were on the side of the angels; but it must have looked to the Tories as if we were just advocating rules that favoured our side.

Another factor, which I did not appreciate until afterward, was that the Conservative Fund, led by Irving Gerstein, former Chair of the PC Canada Fund, wanted to make as much money as possible for the party through levies on the leadership race. From their point of view, it would be silly to prohibit corporate donations and set low limits on individual contributions because that would limit the three campaigns' total fundraising potential. The Fund wanted the campaigns to raise as much money as possible so that its cut would be maximized – not an unreasonable position for those responsible for balancing the party's books.

The LEOC was not scheduled to meet until January, so it seemed that the new rules might triumph by default. However, Bill C-24 contained a provision (s. 67) allowing a leadership campaign to be run under the old rules – no limits on any kind of contribution except for a prohibition of offshore donations – if the campaign began before 1 January 2004. People from the Tory side took advantage of this loophole. They persuaded the interim leader of the merged party, Senator John Lynch-Staunton, to write to Jean-Pierre Kingsley, chief electoral officer of Canada, informing him that the race had already begun. We did not learn about this until Kingsley's affirmative reply was reported in the press on 27 December.[38] It looked to us as if our potential Tory opponents were conniving with the interim leadership to fix the rules to their advantage. It led us to encourage our four LEOC appointees to dig in and not make any compromises when that body started to function.

Once the LEOC began to meet in January, it produced a draft set of rules for the race that gave our campaign team many concerns. We opposed the party's heavy levies on money raised by campaigns; we wanted some limits on the size of donations; we feared that the proposal for fax voting in the advance poll and in remote constituencies would be open to ballot-tampering; we thought that a four-hour window for voting was much too restrictive, especially in British Columbia, where it would mean voting 7–11 AM on Saturday morning; and we didn't like the idea of an expensive final event in Toronto. The tenor of the draft reinforced our suspicion that the LEOC was being influenced by advisers hostile to Harper. We tried to seek changes through the LEOC's consultation process, but before we got very far another rules issue arose that did not involve the LEOC *per se*: membership.

An old tradition in both Liberal and Progressive Conservative leadership and nomination races is "vote farming," i.e., bulk-buying of memberships using outside money. This is an essential tactic in procuring instant members to stack nomination or delegate-selection meetings. To get people with no real interest in the party to cast a vote, you have to buy memberships for them. We were opposed to the practice, not only for moralistic reasons but also out of hard-headed political calculation. We knew that Belinda's only chance was to use her money to swamp the rotten boroughs with new members, and we didn't want to make that easier by entrenching vote farming in the rules.

Late in January, party officials sent us draft membership rules that would have allowed contributions of up to $5,000 for the purpose of purchasing memberships for others. I opposed that vehemently in a conference call; and, when I sensed that I was not making much headway, I told Yaroslav Baran to leak the story to the press.[39] The publicity was instrumental in getting the offending clause deleted, although it further inflamed the rapidly worsening relationship between our campaign and party officials.

In the name of consistency we then had to accept a provision that prevented family members from purchasing memberships for one another. In operational terms, that meant that each membership application would have to be personally signed by the applicant; or, if a membership was sold over the phone, there would have to be a separate credit card number for each person. This seemed inconvenient and unnecessary; after all, the evil that we were concerned with was the farming of hundreds or thousands of memberships at a time, not a husband renewing his wife's membership when he renewed his own. But we learned to live with the new rules.

In the meantime, LEOC battles were raging, of which the first concerned fundraising. We were very unhappy with many provisions of the funding rules that the LEOC distributed for comment, especially the following:

- no upper limit on the size of contributions;
- no restriction on corporate donations;
- $50,000 non-refundable entry fee and $50,000 refundable compliance deposit;
- 10 percent levy to the party on all donations;
- an additional 10 percent "processing fee," with a minimum of $10, on all "directed donations," which had to be run through the party in order to generate a tax credit for the donor;
- 10 percent levy to the party on all expenditures (minus a few exempt categories).

We were least bothered by the $50,000 entry and compliance fees because we had enough money to cover them; these were, however, a major challenge for the Clement campaign, which was just getting under way and had money problems. Still, we saw these fees as part of an effort to turn the leadership campaign into a cash cow for the party. In that context, we were most outraged by the "processing fee" on directed donations, which we saw as a punitive, almost confiscatory, tax on grassroots fundraising.

Our fundraising strategy was to generate thousands of small contributions through direct mail and telephone calling. Such contributions would average about $100 in size, but more than half of them would be smaller than that. Consider a $25 directed donation: under the draft rules, we would have to pay 10 percent = $2.50 as a general levy plus a processing fee of $10, leaving us $12.50 to spend. When we actually spent that amount, we would have to pay another 10 percent = $1.25 as a levy to the party on expenditure. Total taxes to the party on a contribution of $25 would thus be $13.75, leaving us a net benefit of $11.25, or 45 percent of the whole. Compare that to a hypothetical contribution of $1 million from Belinda to her own campaign. She would have to pay a levy of 10 percent = $100,000 on the donation, plus 10 percent = $90,000 when the balance of $900,000 was spent, leaving a net benefit of $810,000 = 81 percent of the original contribution. We argued that this was unfair to our campaign and unwise for a party that needed to encourage grassroots fundraising for the future, when C-24 would prohibit big contributions. If we had been certain that we were going to win, we needn't have objected, because the money would be in the party's coffers for Harper to use once he became leader; but we weren't taking anything for granted. At the time, we saw Belinda, with her money and experienced campaign team, as a serious threat, so we were fighting hard over every nuance of the rules.

Coordinating somewhat with Tony Clement's people, who had related concerns, I made vigorous submissions to the LEOC. In the end, we got a couple of worthwhile changes. The minimum $10 charge on directed donations was deleted, which mitigated the impact on grassroots fundraising. Also, the LEOC increased the contribution levy from 10 percent to 20 percent on amounts over $25,000, which restored rough parity in the treatment of high-end and low-end donations. With these changes, we no longer thought the rules were grossly biased against us, though we still considered it a revenue grab by the party. On that issue, however, where you stood really depended on where you sat. When I was managing the leadership campaign, I resented the party levies; but later, when I came to manage the Conservative election campaign of 2004, I appreciated the party's healthy financial condition, which was due in part to taking in as much money as possible from the leadership campaigns.

With the funding issues resolved partially to our satisfaction, attention now shifted to the question of how voting for the new leader would be carried out. This debate went on for weeks and caused tensions in the campaign that made the funding arguments seem like mild disagreements. To understand the debate, we must go back to leadership-selection rules contained in the merger Agreement in Principle:

The leadership will be decided on March 19–21, 2004.
- To be eligible to vote, a person must be a member in good standing of the Conservative Party of Canada by February 29, 2004.
- The leadership election organizing committee will be responsible for the conduct of the leadership race and determining the method of voting, with a preference to voting in person at polling stations.[40]

The Progressive Conservatives had used "voting in person at polling stations" in the leadership race that elected Joe Clark in 1998. The Canadian Alliance had employed a mail ballot in 2002 but had used voting in person at polling stations in 2000, when Stockwell Day beat Preston Manning and Tom Long. Stephen preferred "voting in person" because he thought it was less susceptible to fraud than mail ballots, telephone voting, or internet voting. If I had been asked, I would have spoken in favour of voting by mail, which I had observed to work smoothly in 2002, but I had no part in these negotiations.

The tight timeline imposed by the Agreement in Principle – membership cutoff 29 February, voting 19–21 March – made any use of a mail ballot difficult. In 2002, the Alliance had managed to use a mail-in ballot within a similar time period, but that was with a smaller voters' list contained in a better organized database. In 2004, the simultaneous merger of two parties and introduction of a new computer system (CIMS) would have made it hard to mail out over 200,000 ballots and get them returned and counted in twenty days.

However, the "preference to voting in person at polling stations" expressed in the Agreement in Principle left two problems unresolved. One was the conduct of the advance poll. As in general elections, the imposition of a specified day for voting requires other arrangements to accommodate those who cannot vote on the particular day chosen. The commitment to hold the vote during a weekend, Friday-Sunday, 19–21 March, raised the prospect that some members might be excluded no matter which day was chosen – Muslims on Friday, Orthodox Jews and certain Protestant sects on Saturday, other devout Christians on Sunday. It therefore seemed essential to have an advance poll, but how to conduct it?

The second problem concerned so-called "remote ridings." In addition to the three very large Territorial ridings, most provinces have one or more large constituencies in which it is impractical for all members to vote in person at one polling place. This problem is solved in general elections by having multiple polling places, but the LEOC and party staff maintained that, given the state of the membership database, it would be impossible to produce mutually exclusive voters' lists for multiple locations within ridings. There were, it was said, simply too many problems in address and postal code data. I still think these problems could have been solved; but party officials, committed to the view that they couldn't be solved, refused to tackle them, so that in practice they became insoluble as time ran out. A complicating factor was that several of the most determined and competent party staff, including Doug Finley, Jenni Byrne, and Devin Iversen, were on leave to work in the Harper Campaign and were thus unavailable to the party to deal with these technical issues. The solution put forward by party staff for both the advance poll and remote ridings was fax voting, which deeply alarmed our campaign team.

After the bruising battles over membership and fundraising rules, we were becoming more suspicious of the intentions of Belinda's team. From our point of view, it seemed that Belinda's organization had gotten control of the LEOC members appointed by MacKay and was using them to force through rules favourable to their campaign. I know now that this view was unfair to the LEOC members, but that's the way it appeared in the heat of the campaign. We hypothesized scenarios in which Belinda's organization would collect fax ballots for the advance poll and remote ridings (which were often rotten boroughs), fill them out, and send them in, swamping the votes of legitimate Conservative Party members. These scenarios were far-fetched, but they were real to us at the time.

The result was a stalemate on the LEOC that lasted until mid-February. By that time, things were getting desperate. Membership sales were to end in two weeks, and the party still had no rules for conducting the advance poll and the voting in remote ridings. The four members appointed by MacKay were advocating fax voting, while the four members appointed by Harper were holding out against it. I was getting stressed out by the endless phone calls from members of the Harper team telling me how dangerous fax voting was, and my own calls to members of the LEOC urging them to stand fast against it.

The breaking point came on Valentine's Day, Saturday, 14 February. Several members of the LEOC had gone away for the holiday weekend, and a subcommittee had been deputized to reach a solution on fax voting. Multiple phone calls during the day convinced me that one of the Harper appointees on the LEOC was about to cross over and support fax voting. I couldn't really blame him. A decision had to be made, and the refusal of party officials to develop plans for other alternatives meant that it would be fax voting or nothing. I therefore bowed to the inevitable and gave it my blessing, with two qualifications. One was that, to reduce the chances of voting fraud, anyone voting by fax would have to fax copies of two photo ID documents, along with the actual ballot and a signed cover form. The other condition, less precisely formulated, was my impression that only a relatively small number of ridings would be declared "remote."

That evening Marianne and I went to a Valentine's Day dinner and dance. As the wine flowed, I gradually unwound and made a decision that I should have made weeks ago: I would stop dealing with the LEOC myself. The other campaigns, more used to Tory practices, had appointed lawyers for liaison with the LEOC, a sensible idea because lawyers are trained to carry out negotiations over rules. I therefore asked Mike Donison, director of research in the OLO and a lawyer with substantial knowledge of electoral law, to be my volunteer representative to the LEOC. Mike dove into the task with gusto, keeping me informed while flooding the LEOC with paper and burning up the phone lines with "our" members. That released me to concentrate on urgent operational tasks, such as fundraising and voter ID, which I would have had to slight if I had continued to spend most of my time on the LEOC.

The Valentine's Day decision was by no mean the end of the story of fax voting. I had thought that the LEOC might declare a dozen or so ridings to be remote, but it soon became apparent that the number would be much larger. After some days of uncertainty, and in spite of our continuing vehement protests, the LEOC finally announced that sixty-three out of 308 ridings (20.5 percent) would be considered remote. Doug Finley and Devin Iverson worked up a plan for partitioning the database so that multiple polling places could be designated in all but the largest ridings, but their effort went for naught; the party was determined to go ahead with fax voting. The large number of ridings designated as remote, combined with the advance poll, meant that perhaps 25 percent of the votes in the leadership race might be cast by fax ballot. Stephen, as well as the rest of our campaign, was outraged; it was hardly what he had in mind when he agreed with Peter MacKay upon "a preference to voting in person at polling stations."

This battle over fax voting lasted for weeks, right up to the end of February, and was by far the most acrimonious LEOC issue, but there other areas of controversy. One issue concerned the final event. The LEOC wanted to hold a large, convention-style event on the final weekend of the race, 19–21 March, to serve as a media-intensive launch for the new leader of the new party. I was initially skeptical of the idea because it seemed to be a very large expenditure of money for little permanent gain; but my opposition was mollified when, at an early meeting, the LEOC agreed (at least, I thought they agreed) to hold the event in Ottawa. That would make it smaller in scale and also less expensive for us, since most of our campaign team was located in Ottawa. The nation's capital is also the home of the national press corps, so that seemed to make it a logical venue for this sort of event.

A few days later, however, the LEOC announced that the event would be in Toronto – and not only in Toronto, but in the Metro Convention Centre, perhaps the most expensive venue in Canada. At that, I resumed my opposition and even wrote a letter threatening to boycott any such event. I let it drop, however, because Stephen, though initially also opposed, became more open to the idea as he became more confident of winning. In retrospect, I was mistaken on this issue; I was thinking in financial terms that were appropriate for the Canadian Alliance but too parsimonious for the new Conservative Party. It did turn out to be an effective launch for the new leader facing an imminent election.

A related issue was more significant, however. The LEOC worked backward from media deadlines associated with the final event – specifically the need to have it wrapped up by 5 PM Eastern Time on Saturday, 20 March – to decree that the window for voting could only be four hours long on one day; and in British Columbia that meant voting from 7 to 11 AM Pacific Time on a Saturday morning, so that votes could be tabulated for an afternoon announcement before the cameras in Toronto. I thought, and still think, that this decision was too cavalier toward the membership, particularly in the West. A four-hour time slot hardly offered them an adequate opportunity to vote. In Macleod in Southern Alberta, for example, it could take up to two hours to drive to the single polling place. I didn't see this as unfair to our campaign in particular; rather, it was unfair to the membership in general, and it certainly contributed to the low turnout in this race. But our protests availed nothing.

Appropriately enough, my relationship with the LEOC ended with one final, farcical fight over rules. Early in March, I commissioned our pollster, Dimitri Pantazopoulos, to carry out a sample survey of the membership according to a methodology he had designed to predict the final point totals. The basic idea was to draw a sample of 1,232 (four respondents from each riding) and then use provincial breakdowns to predict the division of points in the ridings in each province. The results of this poll were quite favourable to us and proved to be extremely close to the actual result on 20 March. Dimitri then suggested that COMPAS, headed by Conrad Winn, would be interested in doing a similar poll for publication by the *National Post* shortly before the convention. Stephen agreed that that would be a good way to build our momentum going into the final weekend, so I gave Dimitri's fieldhouse permission to draw a sample from the membership database and pass it on to COMPAS. Winn's results, published on 13 March, were almost exactly the same as Dimitri's and were indeed a powerful morale booster at the end.[41]

As required of all campaign managers, I had signed an undertaking to use the membership database solely for contesting the leadership race and not to give copies of the data to outside parties for other purposes. I saw no conflict in what I had done; getting Winn to carry out his public poll was a deliberate campaign tactic to build our profile and demoralize our opposition. But John Laschinger, staring at defeat and looking for anything he could use, complained to the LEOC that I had broken the rules by letting a commercial pollster use a sample drawn from our copy of the membership database. I was, he said, going outside the campaign framework by helping COMPAS and the *National Post* do business. This was surely theatre of the absurd. Twelve years ago, Laschinger had written: "The campaign manager's job is to win elections not public esteem. They all bend the rules when they consider it expedient to do so."[42] And again: "When all else fails, the final recourse is simply to make it up, to invent a poll. There isn't a campaign manager alive who hasn't done a little creative leaking, fibbing, or inventing in his time."[43] Given those views, it was a bit rich for him to be making a fuss about what I had done.

The LEOC, after spending much time on this, decided there hadn't been any infraction. They did, however, ask our campaign to list a deemed expense of $10,000 to represent the cost of the poll that Winn had conducted, since we had allowed him to draw the sample and had regarded the poll as part of our campaign tactics. Because of the new expense on our books, we then had to pay an additional 10 percent levy of $1,000 to the party, which was well worth the price to bring this episode to a close.

THE CAMPAIGN

We started the tour in Ottawa on 12 January 2004, with the splashy sort of launch that we had not been able to afford in 2002 – rented premises, big screen, noisemakers, lights, a special song, and people bused in from Quebec. It cost about $60,000, which I resisted at first, fighting a series of losing battles with Jim Armour and Vida Brodie over noisemakers and other expenditures that I thought were frivolous. But it was worth the money because it convinced observers that we were ready to operate at a national level.[44] Subsequent events could not all be so lavish, but they were carefully organized and well attended. In the first campaign, we had learned how to turn out a crowd with post cards and autodial messages, and now we pushed even harder to make sure that the room was always full.

Stephen was introduced by Ontario MPP John Baird and former PC leadership candidate Michael Fortier, to emphasize the point that he was not just a Western Reformer.[45] His speech drew striking contrasts between himself and Paul Martin – contrasts that would also work against Belinda Stronach when she entered the race, though he did not mention her at this time:

> I warn you that I am no Paul Martin. I have not been packaged by an empire of pollsters and media managers. I have not been groomed by the experts and the influential. I was not born into a family with a seat at the cabinet table. I grew up playing on the streets of Toronto, not playing in the corridors of power. When I left home for Alberta, I had to get a job. I wasn't on loan to the corporate elite. I'll never be able to give my kids a billion-dollar company, but Laureen and I are saving for their education. And I have actually cooked them Kraft dinner – I like to add wieners. When my family goes on vacation, it isn't on a corporate executive jet. I pay for the ticket and we stand in line to get a seat with everyone else.[46]

Belinda's campaign, which invested very heavily in media, may have got more coverage than ours did, but we didn't regard media as the prime battleground. We just had to do well enough there to avoid getting in trouble while we won the campaign through voter ID and GOTV. Media coverage in a leadership race is diffused across millions of people who are not even members of the party, whereas voter ID and GOTV focus on those who are going to vote.

We started by asking Michael Davis at RMG to call the entire list of active members (over 100,000) who had come from the Alliance side. When that was done, RMG started calling the new names that we got from sales updates, mostly after the sales cutoff on 29 February. In the meantime, Devin Iversen set up a volunteer phone bank to phone former Progressive Conservatives. We went that route because we thought they would need more persuasion and information about Harper, which volunteers can do better than paid callers.

In February, we also asked RMG to do some sales work by calling through the list of lapsed members. They sold a couple of thousand memberships this way, but there were problems of time because fewer than half the people who said they would rejoin would pay by credit card over the telephone. That meant RMG had to send out a printed reply form, which led to delay and sometimes failure to follow through. We probably should have started the renewal sales program much earlier; though if we had we might have run into financial problems, as it was not self-funding.

Overall our membership sales efforts were not impressive; we only processed about ten thousand memberships through our campaign, including website sales, RMG telephone sales, and sales made by the ground force in our field organization. At one point, I personally got on the phone and sold five memberships to friends in Quebec to show our field organization in that province what could be done. I was so worried about Quebec that I even told Dimitri Soudas to sell memberships to his soccer buddies in Montreal.

We should have done better in sales, but it turned out not to matter much, for two reasons. First, the current membership was already large – about 150,000 at the start of the race. The

Interim Council had decided to extend through the leadership race the membership of everyone who was a member of either founding party at the end of 2003, so much of the sales work was in effect done for us. Also, while we were campaigning for Harper, candidate nominations were taking place in most ridings outside Quebec, and local aspirants were selling memberships to boost their own chances. Many races featured candidates who made a point of stressing their support for Harper, so their membership sales were almost as good for us as if we had made them ourselves. These names were put on the party list as they were processed, so we could reach them through voter ID.

The overlap of the leadership race with local candidate nominations has given rise to the fairy tale that the Harper campaign team tried to defeat Belinda in her race to win nomination in Newmarket-Aurora. "The guy behind the grassy knoll, trying to take out his main rival, had to be Stephen Harper," writes Don Martin. "Harper operatives were seen working at Brown headquarters. Endorsements from the former leader appeared on Brown's campaign literature. Her staff wore Harper T-shirts."[47] Stephen had indeed given a testimonial for Belinda's opponent, Lois Brown, as he had for a number of other candidates coming from the Canadian Alliance side. Because of the simultaneous timing of the contests, many of the local people working for Lois Brown were also Harper supporters. Our campaign team, however, sent no operatives into Newmarket-Aurora; even if we had wanted to, we had none to spare. Belinda may believe that Harper and his team made a special effort to block her nomination in Newmarket-Aurora, but that's simply not true. In fact, it's arguable that we were responsible for getting her elected to Parliament three months later because, by organizing the voter ID and GOTV program that built up her lead in the advance polls, we secured her narrow margin of victory.[48]

By the end of the campaign, after pooling the results of RMG's voter ID, Devin Iversen's persuasion calls, and our miscellaneous sales, we had assembled a list of about eighty-five thousand identified Harper supporters, which meant over 100,000 people, taking into account other voters in multimember households. We then tried to drive these people to the polls through a massive GOTV campaign involving riding-level committees as well as postcards and live calls from RMG to every identified supporter.

Two auxiliary efforts were also important to GOTV. One simply involved dispensing information. Due to problems in the database and the party's use of fax voting in remote ridings and the advance poll, there was confusion on the ground about when, where, and how to vote. The party set up an information hotline with less than adequate capacity to handle all the requests for information, so we also set up our own phone bank to respond to queries.

The other initiative was more novel. After it became clear that we would have to live with fax voting, Doug Finley thought of buying sixty-four portable fax-printer-scanner machines to use in remote ridings. At an expense of about $20,000 plus shipping costs, it was an excellent investment. We sent the machines to our local organizers, with instructions on how to use them to facilitate voting in these far-flung districts. Sometimes they were set up in central locations in stores or office premises, while in other cases our workers took them from house to house. The portable machine was versatile enough to scan and photocopy identification documents and then fax them, together with the ballot, to the official number. The machines were a welcome aid, and so was the presence of the workers, who could help voters fight their way through the unfamiliar rules.

Another way in which this campaign differed from the previous one was in the use of endorsements. We had cared little for endorsements in the Alliance campaign, except to get the support of caucus members who could help in tangible ways with their riding teams. Then, we had had the support of about half the caucus; this time we had the support of about 90 percent of former Alliance caucus members. But that still wasn't enough because they were all in the West, except for the two Ontario members, Scott Reid and Cheryl Gallant. We had to show regional strength through endorsements in Ontario, Quebec, and the Atlantic provinces; and of course we also had to show support from the PC side.

Of the seven members of the Conservative caucus who were former PCs, the only one to come out in Stephen's favour was Greg Thompson, the member for New Brunswick Southwest. We therefore spent considerable time and effort courting former Progressive Conservative MPs (e.g., Gerry Weiner in Montreal), current and former PC members of provincial legislatures (e.g., John Baird in Ottawa), and those who at one time or another had held senior positions in the federal PCs, such as Rick Morgan, Peter MacKay's chief of staff; Denis Jolette, PC national director; and Brian Mitchell, treasurer of the party.[49] We did not put up huge numbers, but we got enough former PCs, especially in Ontario, Quebec, and Atlantic Canada, to endorse Stephen to dispel the illusion that his support came only from the Alliance side. Our debate coordinator, Michael Coates, and our national co-chair Michael Fortier, who had been high-level players in the PCs for more than twenty years, were particularly helpful in this regard.

The quest for PC endorsements revealed how the PC political culture differed from the Reform/Alliance milieu to which I was accustomed. The PC Party, though it had built a mass membership and donor base starting in the 1970s, was in many ways still a network of local notables. Brian Mulroney had become legendary for playing to this culture with his use of the telephone. He would regularly call not just MPs and senators but also junior staffers and local organizers. I met no end of former Tories who told me about their calls from Mulroney; I even met one who still had a recording of his call from the prime minister. That sort of telephone contact had never been the norm in Reform or the Alliance. I used to joke with the Tories that the only time as a Reformer you ever got a call from the leader was to tell you that you were fired.

Throughout the campaign, I was bombarded with requests that I get Stephen to call so-and-so. I sometimes said to those making the requests, "You want Stephen to call one Tory, but I've got a phone bank calling thousands of them." In line with our general grassroots orientation, our strategy was to contact large numbers of former PCs directly through our organization rather than have the leader spend a lot of time on the phone with a small number of people.

ANALYSIS OF RESULTS

The Conservative Party announced the results from the first count of the ballots on 20 March 2004, which by chance happened to be the second anniversary of the announcement day in the Canadian Alliance leadership race (see table 4.1). Because Harper won over 50 percent of the points, the first count was also the final count, and he was declared the winner.

Table 4.1
Conservative Party Leadership Results, 20 March 2004

	Total Points	Percentage of Points
Harper	17,296	56.2
Stronach	10,613	34.5
Clement	2,887	9.4

Superficially, the result seemed satisfactory, and in many ways quite like that of the 2002 Canadian Alliance race. Harper had won a majority on the first count and had bested his closest opponent by more than 20 percentage points, so his victory was decisive and beyond challenge. Yet the closest challenger (Stockwell Day in 2002, Belinda Stronach in this race) had gotten over 30 percent, enough to take some pride in the result. It was particularly important that Belinda had not been humiliated, because she was the candidate of many members from the former Progressive Conservative side. This result seemed to say they could hold up their heads because, at 34.5 percent, they represented a large element of the new party that could not be ignored.

The provincial breakdown was also satisfactory from the point of view of moving forward with Harper as leader (see table 4.2). He not only had won the huge majorities in the West that everyone expected; he had also won a clear majority in Ontario and pluralities in New Brunswick and the three Territories. Even where he had not led, he had generally gotten a respectable share – over 30 percent in Newfoundland, Nova Scotia, and Quebec. Only in tiny Prince Edward Island could his support be called weak.

So far, so good; but deeper analysis is disconcerting. For one thing, only 97,397 valid votes were cast. Based on a voters' list of about 208,000 names, that represented a turnout of just 47 percent – far below the turnout of almost 71 percent achieved in the 2002 Canadian Alliance race. What caused this falloff in participation? One possible explanation is that many of the new members had been recruited in local nomination contests and may not have been interested in the leadership race. Beyond that, however, a combination of factors made the ballot exercise unfriendly to voters:

Table 4.2

Conservative Party Leadership, 2004

	Harper's Percentage of Points
NFLD	32.9
PEI	21.5
NS	37.3
NB	45.9
QUE	33.4
ON	57.0
MB	73.4
SK	82.5
AB	84.9
BC	79.9
TERR	47.4

- The ballot window of four hours was inconvenient, particularly in the far west, where it meant starting at 7:00 AM on a Saturday.
- The decision to have no more than one polling place in each riding made it hard for many members in rural ridings to vote. We will never know how many members, facing a round trip of two or three hours to vote, said, "It's just not worth it."
- Fax voting was also inconvenient for many people. If you live on a farm or out in the wilderness in one of these remote ridings, it may be a very long drive to find a store with the right hardware (both photocopying and faxing were required to submit a valid ballot). The cash cost might be several dollars, depending on local charges. Submission of two photo IDs may sound like a simple requirement, but some older people no longer have driver's licenses, passports, or any photo ID at all.
- There were many computer errors in the lists for all three polls (advance, remote fax, and in-person). No systematic evidence is available, but we received endless anecdotal accounts of members' names being left off the list altogether or appearing in the wrong constituency, indeed sometimes in the wrong province. There were a lot of problems in the database, including bad

Table 4.3
Impact of the Voting System upon the Candidates, Conservative Party
Leadership, 2004

	Total Votes	% of Votes	% of Points	Efficiency
Harper	67,143	68.9	56.2	0.81
Stronach	25,345	26.0	34.5	1.33
Clement	7,968	8.2	9.4	1.15

legacy data from the predecessor parties, sloppy or incomplete data entry for new members due to pressure of time, and software bugs in CIMS. Stephen called me a few days before the vote and said with evident concern, "Everyone I know has been left off the list" (referring to people who wanted to use the advance poll or remote voting). We were concerned about fairness, but from what I heard later, supporters of the other candidates had just as many problems. Indeed Belinda's campaign had requested on 11 March 2004 that the leadership selection event be postponed because of data problems.[50] The database problems did not favour or harm any one candidate, but they certainly contributed to low turnout overall.

Further analysis of the data also highlights the problem caused by rotten boroughs in the equal-ridings model of voting. Consider table 4.3. Harper received almost 69 percent of the votes cast (first preferences) but only 56 percent of the points. The system worked against him in that he converted votes into points with only 81 percent efficiency. Stronach, on the other hand, got 26 percent of the votes but 34.5 percent of the points. The equal-riding system multiplied the impact of her vote with 133 percent efficiency. Clement fell in between the two extremes, but the system also worked positively for him with an efficiency of 115 percent. Comparing the impact at the extremes, we could say that the system was 133 percent / 81 percent = 164 percent as favourable to Stronach as to Harper.

In this race, it could be argued, the favouritism was beneficial to the party and even to Harper. He still won handily, while the equal-riding point system, by softening the impact of his huge

Table 4.4

Votes, Points, and Power Indices in the 2004 Leadership Race

	Total Votes Cast	Total Points	Power Index*
NFLD	683	700	1.02
PEI	1,120	400	0.36
NS	2,910	1,100	0.38
NB	2,916	1,000	0.34
QUE	3,195	7,500	2.35
ON	38,156	10,600	0.28
MB	4,906	1,400	0.29
SK	4,489	1,400	0.31
AB	24,046	2,800	0.12
BC	14,833	3,600	0.24
TERR	143	300	2.10

*Power Index = Total Points/Total Votes Cast.

lead in votes, made the Progressive Conservative portion of the new party feel more at home. That was a worthwhile result if judged in light of the Agreement in Principle, whose spirit was a cooperative merger of equal parties, not a takeover by the numerically larger party. However, the data also suggest the viability of a rotten-borough strategy in future leadership contests. Assuming that the distribution of members stays more or less as it is now, candidates will get far more bang for their buck in Quebec, Newfoundland, and the Territories than in the rest of the country, as shown by the provincial breakdown in table 4.4.

The power index, defined as the number of points allocated to a province divided by the number of votes cast in that province, measures the power of voters in that province. At one extreme, each voter in Quebec awarded 2.35 points to their preferred candidate; while, at the other extreme, a voter in Alberta awarded only 0.12, or about 1/8 of a point. That means that a vote cast in Quebec was worth 19.6 as much as a vote cast in Alberta (2.35/0.12). To take a less extreme example, a vote in Newfoundland was worth three to four times as much as a vote in

Ontario, the rest of Atlantic Canada, or the West, and 8.5 times as much as vote in Alberta. In my view, these disparities are too great and could be dangerous to the party in the long run. How long will members in Alberta support a system that gives them only 1/20 the per capita influence of members in Quebec? If it is going to succeed, the Conservative Party has to expand its support in Quebec; but it also cannot succeed without retaining its membership and financial base in Alberta.

These disparities, while perceptible at the national level and glaring at the provincial level, became downright ludicrous at the local level. One practical definition of a rotten borough would be that fewer than one hundred votes were cast in the leadership race. There are, of course, pockets of weakness everywhere, so there were five ridings in the West and five in Ontario that were rotten boroughs by this definition. But in Ontario and the West, such weakness was an infrequent exception, whereas it was the norm in Quebec (72/75), Newfoundland (4/7), and the Territories (3/3). There were even three ridings where fewer than ten votes were cast: Labrador (eight), Argenteuil (eight), and Rivière du Nord (nine). Contrast that to the eleven ridings in Alberta, one in BC, and three in Ontario where more than one thousand votes were cast. In these extreme comparisons, a vote in a rotten borough is worth more than a hundred times as much as a vote in a riding where the membership is large and enthusiastic.

To explore the effect of a possible rule change, I have reworked the preceding table, changing the number of points per province according to a modification of the equal-riding rule that has often been proposed: each riding gets one hundred points unless fewer than one hundred votes are cast, in which case it gets as many points as votes (see table 4.5). Under this revised formula, a province can never have more points than votes cast, so its power index can never be greater than one. The major changes wrought by the revision are to reduce Newfoundland from 1.02 to 0.71, and Quebec from 2.35 to 0.98. No jurisdiction is now more than 8.5 times more favoured than Alberta, compared to 19.5 under the pure equal-riding model. The system still exhibits a bias toward provinces where the party is weak, but the disparities are not quite so dramatic. This is a compromise that could work if it is ever adopted.

Table 4.5

Votes, Revised Points, and Power Indices in the 2004 Leadership Race

	Total Votes Cast	Total Points	Power Index*
NFLD	683	488	0.71
PEI	1,120	400	0.36
NS	2,910	1,100	0.38
NB	2,916	985	0.34
QUE	3,195	3,139	0.98
ON	38,156	10,447	0.27
MB	4,906	1,297	0.26
SK	4,489	1,392	0.31
AB	24,046	2,800	0.12
BC	14,833	3,551	0.24
TERR	143	143	1.00

*Power Index = Total Points/Total Votes Cast.

The issue of rotten boroughs, by the way, should also be of interest to the Liberal Party. The party did not publish riding-level vote totals in its 2006 leadership race, but it was reported in the press that only about 6,500 Liberals voted in Quebec, and that fewer than one hundred members voted in eight ridings.[51] The most extreme case was Abitibi-Baie-James-Nunavik-Eeyou, where only two Liberals voted (both for Bob Rae, meaning he would get fourteen delegates on the first ballot, if indeed that remote riding could find fourteen people to attend the convention). Any Canadian party that uses any version of the equal-riding model to select its leader has to face the rotten-borough problem.

5
Getting Ready, 2004

DURING THE LEADERSHIP RACE

The leader's importance to a Canadian political party sets real limits on how much campaign preparation can be carried out without knowing who the leader will be. No matter who the leader is, the party will need to set up a war room, lease a jet and buses for the tour, and nominate candidates; but the most politically sensitive matters are specific to the leader. If Belinda Stronach had won the leadership race, her election platform, campaign slogan, and advertising would have been quite different from Stephen's. She would also have wanted to bring in John Laschinger and other senior members of her leadership campaign team to run the election campaign for her.

Many from the OLO and the party left to work on Harper's leadership campaign, but some stayed to continue working on generic election preparations useful to any future leader. This meant building on Alliance plans, because the PCs had not yet begun formal election planning, though they did have useful connections, such as their past association with Greyhound Canada. I continued to loosely coordinate these efforts during the fall, but once the leadership race formally got under way in January 2004 I could no longer do that because Harper's campaign manager could not be directing the efforts of OLO and party staff. However, I did call most of the team together for one meeting at Phil Murphy's apartment in late February or early March to review the state of election preparations and ensure that progress was taking place on essential files.

Communications and policy were in the hands of a troika of OLO employees (Political Adviser to the Leader Tom Jarmyn, Senior Policy Adviser Ken Boessenkool, and Director of Communications Jim Armour), assisted by Dimitri Panatazopoulos of Praxicus, who had been the Canadian Alliance pollster. They continued to work with the Calgary-based Watermark communications firm, which had been selected months ago, before the merger was even thought of. One area where they could move ahead was graphic design, which is not dependent on the leader. Watermark produced a new logo, colour scheme, and overall look for the Conservative Party that are still in use – a blue "C" around a small red maple leaf, all set against a white background. It was an attractive design with a sense of movement; everyone seems to like it. Having the design in place made it possible to forge ahead more quickly on advertising, signs, pamphlets, and other communications items when the time came.

Ken Boessenkool, meanwhile, did some preliminary work on a possible election platform. In December 2003, Ken had helped a committee of caucus chaired by Peter MacKay to prepare a consolidation of Alliance and PC policies highlighting the common ground between the two predecessor parties; this document, often known as the MacKay Report, served as an interim policy manual for the new party. There was also a research program over the winter, both quantitative and qualitative, to serve as a basis for both advertising and policy development.

While we were off doing the leadership campaign, someone decided to use radio to run some inexpensive pre-writ attack ads against the Liberals. Watermark produced several clever ads, including one in which a Jamaican voice talked about Paul Martin and Canada Steamship Line's offshore investments. As soon as that ad played, the Liberals accused it of racism, and Conservative caucus members either ran for cover or joined in the denunciation. Inevitably, Stephen's opponents in the leadership race tried to blame him for the ad. The whole episode reinforced the wisdom of not doing creative until there was a leader in place to set a direction and take responsibility for what was produced.

Space for the impending general election campaign was not a big problem. The Canadian Alliance had already increased its space on the seventeenth floor of the Varette Building in downtown Ottawa in anticipation of an election, the Harper leadership campaign leased a suite on the sixth floor of the same tower, and the Progressive Conservatives had their headquarters in a nearby building. With rewiring and reconfiguration, the merged party would have adequate space to run an election campaign, though being split up on different floors was not ideal. Also, the Canadian Alliance was already well underway with CIMS when the merger took place. The merger and leadership race tested it far harder and faster than anyone had expected, but it was good preparation for the election, no matter who the leader would turn out to be.

The new leader would have to haul the media around the country during a national election in the five-week madness known as the Leader's Tour. Phil Murphy, now chief of staff for Interim Leader Grant Hill, took overall responsibility for tour preparations, though of course he had to work closely with party officials, since the party would negotiate the contracts and pay the bills. The first necessity was to lease a jet for the tour, and for that we went to Air Canada. We had been having desultory discussions with that company when we were still the Canadian Alliance, but things went better after the merger. In the end, we negotiated a satisfactory contract with Air Canada and were delighted with the service they gave us during the campaign. For buses, we ended up dealing with Greyhound Canada, who had been providing buses for Conservative federal and provincial campaigns for the past twenty-five years. Our efforts turned out to be successful inasmuch as we had buses ready to go when the writ was dropped, which was the most important thing. However, we made two mistakes.

First, based on planning that we had done for a Canadian Alliance campaign, we requested the lease of six buses, three for Ontario and points east, and three for the West. Within each set of three, one was to be the leader's bus, configured for Harper and his staff, while the other two would be media buses. Even if that was the right choice for an Alliance campaign, it was not optimal for a Conservative campaign. Targeted ridings for the new Conservative Party were located heavily in Ontario, so the leader had to spend a lot of time there. For symbolic reasons, he also had to be seen in Quebec, where we had no targeted ridings, and in Atlantic Canada, where we had only a few. We also had targeted ridings in the West, but they were mainly in widely separated urban areas – Winnipeg, Regina, Saskatoon, Edmonton, Vancouver, and Victoria. Thus, when the Leader's Tour was in the West, it had to hop by air from city to city, which made it difficult to use our leased buses. We often had to rent day buses from Greyhound to do events in particular cities because we couldn't get our leased buses there in time across the vast distances.

We also overinvested in technology for the buses. With a combination of leased and purchased equipment, we tried to set up a satellite communications system that would allow reporters to file their stories from the buses. It was a beautiful dream, but it didn't work out too well. Sometimes our equipment didn't work as promised; sometimes reporters brought incompatible equipment with them or simply lacked computer savvy. We ended up renting day rooms in hotels and paying for temporary phone lines to be installed so that reporters could file their stories in the traditional way. Given the pace and pressure of a Leader's Tour, there is simply no time for experimenting with new technology.

In this campaign, we had no comprehensive plan for a secondary or surrogate tour, that is, travel and public appearances by party notables other than the leader. This was more of a limitation than an outright mistake; I decided not to proceed in this direction because there was no item for it in the budget I had inherited and our team was already stretched to the limit planning the absolute essentials of the impending campaign. We would include a secondary tour in the plan for the 2005–06 campaign, when we had more time to get ready.

In the summer of 2003, I had pulled together a small committee to prepare a budget for a Canadian Alliance campaign. We had devised an overall campaign budget of about $12 million, much less than our legal spending limit of $17.5 million, but as much as we thought the party could afford. It wasn't a plan for a true national campaign, because we knew that our effort would be largely token in Quebec and parts of Atlantic Canada. We set aside about $800,000 for voter contact, calculating that the national campaign would spend about $20,000 apiece in forty targeted ridings, using phone banks and direct mail for voter ID, persuasion, and GOTV. We wanted to concentrate our resources on the relatively small number of ridings where our incumbents were threatened or where we had a reasonable chance of picking up new seats. However, $800,000 was definitely on the low side for what we hoped to achieve, and we would probably have added to that sum as our planning progressed.

During the leadership campaign, officials not involved in that race worked with RMG and with Andrew Langhorne, who had been the voter contact coordinator for the provincial PCs in Ontario, to develop a more expansive program for the merged party. Based on some encouraging polling results, the number of ridings to be included rose to fifty or more, and the total expenditure soared. Irving Gerstein, president of the Conservative Fund, had given the green light for the Conservative Party to spend its full legal limit of $17.5 million in the national campaign; and much of the increase went into voter contact. Certainly an increase in that area was warranted, but there were other needs to be met, too. The advertising for a Conservative campaign should have been different in character and more expensive than for an Alliance campaign, yet no increase had been made there. Also, a Conservative campaign would have to spend more in Quebec than an Alliance campaign would have, but nothing had been provided for Quebec. Finally, the draft budget had no contingency allocation; everything had been fully allocated. That was completely impractical. You can't go into a $17.5 million campaign with every dollar already committed.

GATHERING UP THE THREADS

Stephen won the leadership of the Conservative Party on Saturday, 20 March 2004. Paul Martin had said that he wanted an election soon after becoming prime minister, and at that point there was much speculation that he might ask for the writ to be dropped as early as Sunday, 4 April. So we feared we had only two more weeks to complete our preparations for a national election. The need for haste helps to explain why the Harper leadership campaign team moved on without much expansion to plan the campaign for the general election. Clearly there was talent on the Clement and Stronach teams, but it takes time to integrate new people, and we feared we had no time. Also, after all the rules fights, considerable animosity, which would require time to settle, lingered toward Belinda's team.

But even if major enlargement of the team wasn't on the agenda, we did have to make some quick organizational changes. On Sunday, 21 March, Stephen and I and a number of staffers returned from Toronto to Ottawa on the train. On the way, I asked Vida Brodie if her husband Ian, deputy chief of staff in the OLO, was ready for the bigger challenge of running the party. When she said yes, I recommended to Stephen that he appoint Ian Brodie national director of the Conservative Party. It wasn't job recruitment at its most scientific, but we had no time to waste.

Stephen also decided to promote Ken Boessenkool, his senior policy adviser, to the more encompassing role of political adviser, which integrated policy with communications and general political strategy. Effectively, Ken became co-manager of the impending campaign, responsible for working directly with the leader on policy, strategy, and communications. Although Ken responded with three months of almost superhuman effort, we were objectively short-staffed in policy and communications, and that hurt us in the late stages of the campaign. However, that must be put in the context of having to carry out the merger, the leadership race, and the national election campaign within six months.

On Tuesday, 23 March, I had to start wrestling with another major issue, one I simply had not foreseen. Michael Fortier, who was national co-chair of the Harper leadership campaign and was scheduled to play the same role in the upcoming Conservative election campaign, drove over from Montreal to see me. His simple question staggered me: "How much money are you going to give to Quebec?" I hadn't thought of giving anything. Quebec had always been peripheral to Alliance campaign planning, and in general the Reform/Alliance tradition was that constituencies and candidates paid for their own local campaigns, perhaps with a bit of help from the national campaign or transfers from well-heeled Alberta and BC riding associations. But I quickly learned that we had inherited another Tory tradition – subsidies to the Quebec campaign.

There is less of a tradition of grassroots fundraising in Quebec than in other provinces, and that weakness was compounded by the tiny size of our party's membership in the province. In the past, major corporations headquartered in Montreal, such as Power Corporation, Air Canada, Bell Canada, and Canadian Pacific, had picked up some of the slack, but Bill C-24 now limited corporate donations to $1,000. I wasn't happy about it, but it quickly became apparent that there would be no campaign in Quebec unless the national party helped to pay for it.

That put me in a quandary. The budget I had inherited included no contingency fund, no allocation for a Quebec ground campaign, and no line item for a Quebec media buy other than English-language overlap from the national network buy. I told Michael I would do what I could but that I couldn't possibly find as much as he would like from a budget that was already fully committed.

I went back over the budget and made cuts to almost everything except advertising, which was already underfunded. The impact was heavy on the voter-contact program, but that was the only place I could find large amounts of money. I then promised a sum to Michael for the Quebec ground campaign plus a further amount for a Quebec media buy. Some money was left over to be set aside as a much-needed contingency fund. Michael was glad to get anything but kept trying for more, so after a week or two I took myself out of it, telling him he would have to deal with Operations Director Doug Finley over the subsidies for the Quebec ground campaign. That way Doug could tell him, "Flanagan won't give us any more money."

In the end, we gave modest subsidies to many local campaigns, depending on how promising they seemed. Candidates had to sign a note to repay the subsidy if they got a rebate from Elections Canada, but only twenty-two of seventy-five got the 10 percent or more of the popular vote necessary for receiving a rebate. Beyond that, the national campaign set up an office in Montreal with some rudimentary administration, and we paid for signage on public streets (lawn signs on private residences are not common in Quebec). Spending even more money on the ground war in Quebec would not likely have gotten better results in 2004, because most local campaigns lacked the volunteer base required to make good use of more money. I concluded that, if more money was to be spent in Quebec in the future, it should be on advertising. Without the volunteer base necessary to conduct politics through personal contact, advertising seemed like the best bet to change voters' minds.

While dealing with these pressing issues of budget and senior campaign personnel, another urgent concern was to get a campaign slogan approved. It is essential to have the slogan, as a short statement of the campaign's central theme, before producing the platform, ads, lawn signs, pamphlets, and other communications materials. Based on the research program they had conducted over the winter, Ken, Jim, Dimitri, and Watermark were recommending "Demand Better." Release of the Auditor General's report on Adscam in February 2004 had brought questions about Liberal integrity to the fore, but there was still no public proof of outright corruption, even though we had our suspicions. The research suggested that people weren't ready for charges of corruption; they saw Adscam more as a matter of waste, and seemed particularly upset when they thought about what could have been done with the money wasted on advertising agencies. "Demand Better" appealed to these sentiments. Without making direct charges of corruption, it suggested that the Liberals had mismanaged the government and that the Conservatives could do better.

Stephen, who is always cautious about approving wording, especially slogans, asked me to get some reactions from members of the caucus. Racing to get so many things done at once, I made a classic hub-and-spoke mistake, convening a discussion group of Conservative MPs without including any of the people, such as Ken Boessenkool and Jim Armour, who had worked on the slogan up to this point and could have explained the thinking and research behind it. The group quickly went off track as someone (I can't remember who) came up with a new slogan, "Ready to Govern." The MPs in the room liked it, but it was completely off the strategy that Ken and Jim and Watermark had been developing, which was to keep public attention focused on the Liberals' misgovernment. "Ready to Govern" would have thrown the spotlight directly on the Conservatives, and those of us responsible for designing the campaign were dubious that the public was ready to think in these terms.

The genie was out of the bottle, and we had to stuff it back in again – quickly. Fortunately, Dimitri Pantazopoulos was scheduled to conduct some focus groups, so we asked him to include a dial test of various possible slogans, including "Demand Better" as well as "Ready to Govern." It wasn't a big risk, because variations on both themes had already been tested during the winter research program. As expected, "Demand Better" did indeed score the highest, and Stephen finally accepted it when we showed him the numbers. He then asked Ken, Jim, and Dimitri to reconvene the caucus focus group, show them the results, and get them on side prior to a presentation to a full meeting of caucus.

With the slogan in place, work on advertising could go ahead. I was involved, though more to make sure that things got done on time and on budget than to be part of the creative thinking. We produced four ads before the writ was dropped – two negative and two positive. Since we didn't like the execution of one of the negative ads and never used it, we actually had only three ads going into the campaign.

Our best ad was undoubtedly the negative ad entitled "Carousel." With calliope music in the background, it showed janitorial staff heedlessly throwing bags of money into a dumpster. Produced by White Iron, a Calgary company led by Bryan Thomas, who had done advertising for Reform and the Canadian Alliance, it was eye-catching and ear-catching, as well as funny, and it captured what the public knew about Adscam at the time – that there had been a lot of waste and mismanagement. We played it in heavy rotation during the campaign, and it attracted a lot of favourable comment from advertising executives and other informed observers. Our nightly polling also showed that it was getting through to voters.

The negative ad that we decided not to use showed a woman at her kitchen table bemoaning all the things that could have been done with the money that the Liberals had wasted. It was conceptually sound and in line with the research, but the execution didn't seem quite right. The actress went over the top in her grief, looking more as if she were mourning the death of family members than criticizing bad public policy. The problems couldn't be fixed with any footage we had in the can, so we never used it.

The two positive ads both focused on the leader. The first one, in two slightly different versions, showed Stephen in his office with his jacket off, looking honest, hard-working, and business-like. It was meant to counter Liberal attempts to demonize him as a reckless ideologue. The second Harper ad showed Stephen in various shots with supporters and family members, combined with mood-altering music and an uplifting script about dedication to making Canada better. "Commitment," as we called it, played well with Stephen's supporters, but it may have seemed corny to voters not already predisposed to support him.

In retrospect, there was a serious weakness in this suite of ads. Neither "Carousel" nor the two versions of "Harper in the Office" nor "Commitment" had any positive policy content. "Carousel" memorably expressed the idea that the Liberals couldn't be trusted, but by itself it might have led voters to turn to the NDP or the BQ – anyone but the Liberals. The Harper-focused ads communicated the idea that Harper could be trusted to govern because of his personal qualities, but they did not give any idea of what policies a Conservative Government would enact. It was a gap we never filled in our TV advertising, though we did have some policy-oriented radio ads. This shortage of policy content in our advertising later facilitated the Liberals' attack on Harper's "hidden agenda." If your own ads aren't forthcoming about your policy agenda, you make it easier for your opponents to say you must be hiding something.

Another grave weakness in our advertising program was a lack of planning for the rest of the campaign. The few ads that we did produce were probably sufficient for the first couple of weeks. But we had neither a plan nor the budget to be responsive during the campaign. What we did was more on the model of commercial advertising – come up with one or two well-conceived, well-produced ads, and run them over and over. Exposure through repetition is the mantra of commercial advertising, but this only applies up to a point to political advertising. The crucial difference is that in a commercial campaign you don't have opponents attacking you and jamming your message, whereas that is the essence of a political campaign in which you are actually contending with another party to form the government. In previous Reform and Canadian Alliance campaigns, the party had never really been in a position to win, so its advertising was closer to the commercial model – produce a few ads to encapsulate your message and play them as much as you can afford. We didn't appreciate that it would be different this time, that we would need to be responsive to Liberal attacks, that we would have to play a game of serve and volley with our main opponents.

Stephen asked repeatedly that we should envision Liberal attacks and be ready to counter them. But, spooked by what had happened with the radio ads during the leadership campaign and fearing that negative ads would reinforce the Liberals' line that Stephen was "scary," we rejected hard-hitting negative scripts, believing that an emotional spot like "Commitment" was the best response to attacks. In any case, our advertising program, designed to win perhaps ninety to ninety-nine seats, wasn't well set up to produce tougher counterattack material. Our production budget was far too small in the first place, and we spent most of it producing the three ads that we had ready to go when the writ was dropped.

Watermark was a wonderful company to work with. Their people were fast, efficient, and always came in at or under budget. Their designs were outstanding, and the ads they created were cleverly conceived, faithful to the research, and well produced. If this had been the Canadian Alliance campaign that we had planned for, it would have been an exemplary success story. But, when it turned into a Conservative campaign that gave us a realistic shot at actually beating the Liberals, the campaign team did not have the right experience to take advantage of the opportunity and come up with a new plan.

A third weakness in our advertising was in our approach to French content. Going back to the Canadian Alliance roots of our campaign team, there were no Québécois or Francophones within our advertising group. On Watermark's recommendation, we retained a small, bilingual Montreal firm – Mediavation – for the French side, but their circumscribed role was to translate English ads and signs into French and arrange for distribution in

Quebec, not to do original creative work in the Quebec environment. Thus, Mediavation took our English slogan, "Demand Better" and came up with a French equivalent – "C'est assez" – meaning approximately "We've had enough" or "We're fed up." The trouble with this approach was that it failed to take account of the unique political situation in Quebec. In the other provinces, if a voter wanted to "demand better" than the Liberal government, voting Conservative was the logical choice because the Conservative Party had a realistic chance of winning seats and forming an alternative government. But in Quebec the Conservative Party was still a fringe party, struggling to get above 10 percent of the vote and win even one seat. Convincing Francophone voters that they had "had enough" might logically lead them to vote for the Bloc Québécois, because that was the obvious way to beat the Liberals in Quebec. A national campaign needs a slogan for Quebec that is conceived within the unique political configuration of that province.

Similar problems dogged our Quebec advertising. Because there was no dialogue between actors in "Carousel" and "Commitment," it was technically easy to do a French voiceover for those ads; and we shot "Harper in the Office" in separate English and French versions, with Stephen saying his lines in both languages. So our French-language ads looked and sounded all right, but they were not created in the Quebec context. They treated the Liberals as the main opponent, whereas we should have given people reasons not to support the Bloc Québécois.

While we wrestled with the slogan and with advertising, we also had to be working on many other fronts. There was so much to be done so quickly that I had no time for micromanagement. I delegated extensively, trying only to coordinate loosely and to ensure that everyone stayed within budget. Phil Murphy, deputy campaign manager and Stephen's chief of staff, dealt with Air Canada and Greyhound. Debbie Campbell, Ray Novak, and Vida Brodie coordinated with Ken's scripting team to prepare a travel plan and to identify staff for the tour. Logistics and events people in the war room, communications and logistics people to travel with the tour, plus advance teams to crisscross the country ahead of the tour, ensuring that events were properly set up, amounted to more than fifty people altogether.

Phil also worked closely with Jim Armour and Yaroslav Baran to identify a dozen or more communications staff who would work in the war room. Communications Director Jim Armour would travel with the tour, so Yaroslav was nominated to manage war-room communications.

In staffing tour and communications, we tried to bring in as many former Progressive Conservatives as possible to reinforce the Harper campaign team. Some of these were at lower levels, such as manning communications desks and advance teams, but others were quite senior. Of particular note were Boomer Throop, who functioned as associate tour director in Ottawa; Geoff Norquay and William Stairs, who along with Yaroslav made up the senior communications people in the war room; Maureen Murphy-Makin, who supervised the production of briefing notes for the tour; and Leslie Tomlin, who became the senior advance person. At the same time we were also bringing in new people from the Alliance side, such as Mark Cameron and Patrick Muttart, who worked with Ken to plan the campaign.

Ian Brodie, as the new national director of the Conservative Party, took over the physical preparation of the war room, which involved hurried movement of walls, furniture, and wiring. The CIMS computer system was a special challenge, because there had not been much time for training users in the field, and the system had acquired a bad reputation during the leadership race. Ian hired about a dozen young people to man the help desk while Doug Finley worked to refine and simplify CIMS operational requirements to the point where campaigners at the constituency level could make effective use of it. It was time-consuming and expensive but ultimately successful.

Conservative Fund Chairman Irving Gerstein took charge of fundraising, so that I scarcely had to think about it. I worried about keeping within budget but not about raising the money. Indeed, one could argue that the campaign was paid for wholly by the provisions of Bill C-24. At the beginning of the year, we received our entire annual subsidy of over $7 million, calculated as $1.75 times the number of votes received by the Canadian Alliance and Progressive Conservatives in the 2000 election. For this election, we could also count on receiving from Elections Canada a rebate of 60 percent (50 percent in future elections) of the amount expended by the national campaign. If we spent the legal limit of $17.5 million, the rebate would be over $10 million. Hence the sum of the annual subsidy plus the rebate was enough to pay for the whole national campaign, so the only real problem was managing cash flow. To that end, Irving arranged a line of credit from a bank consortium, and we were off to the races. It was a totally different situation from the two leadership races I had managed, where raising money always had to be my primary concern.

Another thing we needed for the campaign was a new website. We asked Watermark to take responsibility so that the look of the website would be consistent with other campaign materials. Watermark, like most communications agencies, doesn't do this work in-house; they subcontracted the job to a website developer, who dealt more or less directly with our webmaster, Steve Brooks. Steve suggested to the developer that he have a look at John Kerry's presidential campaign website, which had several features that he wanted to emulate. But the developer, it seems, went much farther than mere imitation. He lifted parts of the actual code from the Kerry website, then incorporated those lines of code into the website he was developing for us. Reportedly, it was done in such a way that someone logging on to our website would also have registered a hit on the Kerry website.

Completely unaware of this, I told Steve to put the new website up for testing a couple of weeks before the writ drop. Within a couple of days, a technically savvy Liberal sympathizer had discovered the plagiarism and the cross-connection with the Kerry website. He told Liberal über-partisan Warren Kinsella about it in an email, assuming that Kinsella would inform the Liberal Party, who would publicize it and leave us looking woefully incompetent. Kinsella, however, detests Paul Martin and his team for the way they deposed Jean Chrétien. Even though he doesn't support the Conservative Party, Kinsella also likes Stephen Harper as a person. Here's a typical statement from Kinsella's blog. The words are from 12 October 2005, but the sentiments were the same in spring 2004:

I don't like Stephen Harper BECAUSE I dislike Paul Martin. They're not connected. I disliked Paul Martin long before Stephen Harper appeared on the scene, believe me.

I like Harper, as does every member of my family, because he phoned my Mom after my Dad died. Even when I – the clichéd Liberal Attack Dog – had been bashing his party for years. That phone call surprised me, a lot, and it forced me to re-evaluate some views I had. I concluded that Harper was smart, decent and not ... scary.

I dislike Martin, as does every member of my family and all of my friends, because of what he did to former colleagues of mine, and to the Liberal Party and – now – to the country.

Rather than informing the Liberal organization, Kinsella for-warded the email to Phil Murphy. Thus forewarned, we pulled the website off the internet before the embarrassing story could become public. Fortunately, Steve Brooks had another developer working on a website to use after the election was over, so he rushed development of that site and managed to get it up in time for the election. Dodging that bullet buoyed our spirits, making us feel we had some luck on our side.

Doug Finley, who returned from the Harper leadership cam-paign to his position as the party's director of political opera-tions, was once again in charge of candidate nominations. Most of our stronger ridings had held nomination meetings during the leadership race, and almost all those candidates were satisfac-tory, except for a couple who had slipped through the screening process and now had to be weeded out. But there were still many vacancies to be filled in our weaker areas, especially Quebec, ru-ral Newfoundland, and the northern Territories. Doug managed to field a full slate of 308 candidates – no mean feat, considering that Reform and the Canadian Alliance had never managed to do that, and the Progressive Conservatives had also missed the mark in 2000.[1] In some ways, it might not matter much if a party has no candidate in a riding it has no chance of winning; but the absence of candidates furnishes attack points if you are actually close to a national victory. Also, C-24 has changed the financial calculus. To get a candidate to run in a weak riding, the national campaign often has to promise some degree of financial support; but that subsidy will now normally be regained through the new federal subsidy to the national party of $1.75 per vote per year. Suppose, for the sake of argument, that you have to promise a candidate $10,000 in special support to run in a weak riding where the local association has practically no fundraising capacity. Suppose, further, that the candidate receives a very modest four thousand votes. At $1.75 per vote, that translates into an increased subsidy of $7,000 per year to the national party. The initial expense of recruiting the candidate is more than recovered after two years, and there is a clear profit every year after that until the next election is called.

Mike Coates wanted us to hold a weekend campaign kickoff event for all candidates in Ottawa. It was a good idea, but we just didn't have the capacity to set it up in the time available. Doug Finley organized some local training sessions, supplemented by conference calls and Internet hookups; but such measures couldn't fully replace the excitement and impact of a well-organized candidate college. It is possible that we would have had fewer problems with candidate "bozo eruptions" if we could have gotten them all together for a weekend training session – although our worst problems arose with incumbents, not with rookie candidates.

Another thing Doug had to do was to rebuild the party's field organization. Part of that was relatively simple – just moving the Harper leadership field staff over to the party's employment. As always, however, Quebec required special attention. The extreme weakness of constituency associations meant that Doug had to hire extra staff and set up a provincial campaign office to handle functions such as financial administration and printing that ridings handle for themselves in the rest of the country. Quebec consumed a disproportionate share of Doug's time jockeying with local people, some of whom seemed more interested in controlling the Quebec organization rather than expanding its support among voters.

Quebec was the most severe case, but we also had difficulties in other parts of the country fitting the national campaign together with local aspirations. Part of the problem was a difference in traditions between the Reform/Alliance and Progressive Conservative sides of the party. Reform/Alliance campaigns had been quite centralized, with little machinery mediating between the national campaign and constituency campaigns. The PC tradition, on the other hand, was to appoint provincial and regional campaign committees, chairmen, even managers, with some role in candidate recruitment, fundraising, advertising, event organization, and media relations. People from the PC side often complained that they felt shut out from the national campaign, and they were not assuaged by the standard Reform response that they should involve themselves in a constituency campaign. They wanted to play a bigger role at a provincial or regional level.

Advised by John Reynolds, Michael Fortier, and Doug Finley in the selection of names, Stephen tried to reach a compromise by appointing two or three campaign co-chairs in each province. They were knit together into a national campaign advisory committee co-chaired by Reynolds and Fortier, but they did not have provincial campaign committees of their own (at least not in a formal sense recognized by the national campaign; some may have convened informal advisory groups). The national campaign also hired a "regional spin team," composed of media-relations people located in various parts of the country; and some of these, notably Colin Metcalfe in Vancouver, also played larger roles as local coordinators. But there was no template for such activity; everything depended on local personalities and circumstances.

A modern Canadian campaign has to be highly centralized, due to legislated rules on fundraising and spending caps as well as the requirements of the information age. But there is a role for local committees in recruiting candidates, organizing multi-riding events, getting local campaigns to help each other, and dealing with local media. Inventing the right organizational structures for all of this is still a work in progress within the Conservative Party. We were far from having it all together in the spring of 2004.

While all this was going on, Doug and I were also setting our direct voter contact (DVC) program in motion. I kept closely involved in this because it was a major item in the budget. The goal of the program was to win the close races that the Canadian Alliance had lost in the 2000 election. We, therefore, made a preliminary definition of marginal or "Blue" ridings as those in which our margin of victory/defeat in 2000 was close enough to be affected by an effort at voter mobilization. That was the basic idea, although it wasn't quite that simple because we had to allow for the change in riding boundaries for the coming election and the effects of the merger. We also designated some ridings as Blue because the incumbent was retiring.

Most candidates were delighted to get the extra help, although inevitably there were a few who stayed out, thinking they didn't need it or could arrange the equivalent services in their own way under their own control. As part of the standard package, we asked each candidate in a Blue riding to make a contribution, while the national campaign would chip in much more for telephone calling and direct mail in a cooperating riding. While the national campaign would arrange and manage all the mail and calling, the local campaign would be expected to access the voter identification data through CIMS to make its ground campaign more effective.

The first step of DVC was voter identification over the telephone, to build up lists of Conservative supporters to be driven to the polls in the closing GOTV effort, to locate undecided voters that we could attempt to persuade through direct mail and further calling, and to identify hardcore partisans of other parties whom we could ignore from then on. The national party in 2004 had no data of this type except for lists of current and past members, although some ridings had local databases built up in previous campaigns.

While we started calling in ridings that were definitely in the program, Doug Finley and his staff worked furiously to bring in other Blue ridings that had not yet made a commitment. Both predecessor parties had strong traditions of constituency autonomy, so we couldn't just order ridings to climb aboard. We had to show all candidates the advantages of the program and demonstrate that they would receive far more in value than they were being asked to contribute.

Meanwhile Stephen and Ken Boessenkool were continuing to work on the campaign platform. It was supposed to be a closely controlled process because Stephen didn't want the platform released too early. Everyone remembered how, in 2000, Stockwell Day had made the flat tax his signature policy before the election was called, only to have the Liberals counter with their own proposal for a tax cut. Boessenkool, now assisted by Mark Cameron and sometimes by other OLO staffers, was the main draftsman, subject to final approval by the leader.

I wasn't involved at all until the middle of May, when it was time for Watermark to start editing and formatting the document for printing. Quite a bit of work was required, as the platform was a forty-four-page, text-heavy document without pictures but with several complicated, multi-page fiscal tables. Because I was in Calgary at least part of the time, I took over supervision of the editing and formatting process, once the composition was more or less finished. While that was going on, we were all caught by surprise when the platform was leaked on 14 May. The timing of the leak coincided with Stephen's speech to the C.D. Howe Institute in Toronto about some of the fiscal aspects of the platform.

Ken was so devastated that he offered his resignation, but we never did find out the source of the leak. For a while, I was worried that I might have been the inadvertent source because I had left a printed copy in my Ottawa office, where someone from the cleaning staff might have been able to pick it up; but that turned out to be a copy of a different draft than the one that ended up in the press. Watermark hired a forensic specialist to conduct an internal audit, and they practically tore their computer system apart but could find nothing. Similarly, Phil Murphy had the IT people in the House of Commons audit staff email but found no record of the platform being sent where it wasn't supposed to go. We'll probably never know what happened unless someone decides to include it in their memoirs.

The headlines and coverage around the leak were favourable. Terence Corcoran, writing in the *Financial Post*, was extraordinarily positive, calling the platform "a little masterpiece of political strategy and a brilliant mirror of the soul of the New Conservatism."[2] To be sure, the leak tipped off the Liberals ahead of time where we were heading, but none of their policy announcements seemed designed to blunt the effectiveness of our platform. Indeed, their campaign rhetoric dealt hardly at all with our platform; they attacked Stephen for his "hidden agenda," not what he said but what he didn't say. The main damage that the leak caused was in making the platform less newsworthy later on in the campaign, leading to our decision to release the whole thing quite early.

Ken Boessenkool was also responsible for planning the Leader's Tour, so he left much of detailed writing of the platform with Mark Cameron while he turned his attention to the tour. Ideally, the five-week national campaign should be a unified narrative, a story with thirty-five chapters supporting a central theme. The leader's appearances, interviews, photo opportunities, and speeches should all be integrated into the unfolding story. Ken and Stephen's basic conception of the storyline was to use each day to discuss a different aspect of the platform, so that by the end of the campaign voters would have an overall idea of what the Conservatives stood for. Unfortunately, however, Ken and the other writers (Jim Armour, William Stairs, Mike Storeshaw) weren't able to draft the entire plan before the writ was dropped; the best they could do was to plan the first twenty-five days, the period up to the leaders' debates.

I wasn't worried about it at the time; it seemed logical to preserve some flexibility at the end, depending on where we stood coming out of the debates. But what we should have done was to prepare scenarios in advance for at least three possible endgames – trailing badly, dead heat, and in the lead. Without that advance planning for the endgame, Stephen was forced to improvise in the last ten days, with the unfortunate results described in the next chapter.

The platform, entitled *Demanding Better*, was drafted not as a catalogue of all the party's positions on every conceivable issue but as a program that the Conservative Party could enact if it formed a government after the election. It reflected Stephen's often-stated view that the new party was "moderate, modern, and mainstream." In that connection, the silences in the platform spoke volumes. There was nothing about bilingualism, multiculturalism, abortion, and capital punishment. Rather than a critique of immigration, the platform promised "speedier recognition of foreign credentials and prior work experience."[3] On gay marriage, the platform took a process position, holding "that Parliament, not unelected judges, should have the final say on contentious social issues like the definition of marriage" (the Supreme Court had not yet decided the Liberal Government's reference on gay marriage).[4]

The platform led off with a call for "better accountability," which included two major areas. One was a clean-up of the "waste, mismanagement, and corruption" revealed by the Auditor General's report on the Quebec sponsorship scheme. Specific proposals were to expand the jurisdiction of the Auditor General and to create an independent ethics commissioner, "appointed by Parliament, not by the Prime Minister." In a broader vein, there was also a set of political reform measures hearkening back to the old Reform *Blue Book*, such as fixed election dates and the election of Senators. Conspicuously absent, however, was any mention of direct democracy, which had caused so much trouble in the 2000 Canadian Alliance campaign.[5] Politically, all of this was tied to the critique of Liberal corruption that we would be making every day in the campaign. None of these points was earthshaking in itself, but taken together they allowed us to say that we were not just critics, that we had a positive program of "better accountability."

Our appeal to voters' pocketbooks came under the heading of a "better economy," marked by policies to "lower taxes, control spending, and create jobs." It is worth repeating the specifics along with some parenthetical comments:

- Reduce the federal tax rate on middle-income Canadians by more than 25 percent. (This was to be done by raising the thresholds on tax brackets and reducing some of the rates. It was perhaps unwise to have used the 25 percent figure because, without careful analysis, it seemed to suggest a 25 percent reduction in total tax burden, which was far more than we were promising. This may have fed the plausibility of later Liberal charges that we would create a "$50 Billion Black Hole.")
- Introduce a $2,000 per child deduction to reduce the tax burden on families with children. (This was a deliberate pitch for the vote of young parents, a group that, according to our research, was not supporting the Conservatives as much as we would have liked but might be won over. It's also probably relevant that Stephen has two small children and Ken four, so they're aware of the economic problems of young families.)

- Reduce premiums to eliminate the annual surplus in the Employment Insurance Act. (The Liberals subsequently moved in this direction.)
- Invest in infrastructure by transferring at least three cents of the gas tax to the provinces. (We had to do something like this to compete with Paul Martin's cities and infrastructure promises, but it was also part of our policy of remedying the "fiscal imbalance" between Ottawa and the provinces.)
- Introduce a new Registered Lifetime Savings Plan that will allow Canadians to withdraw their money tax-free. (This would have addressed the anomaly that RRSP savers sometimes face *higher* marginal tax rates after retirement.)
- Control government spending and pay down the national debt. (This was targeted at the Liberals' practice of underestimating the annual budget and then spending it when it materialized.)
- Cut wasteful corporate subsidies in order to reduce taxes for all businesses. (This was the politically riskiest part of our fiscal program, because subsidies to business, while unpopular in the abstract, are difficult to remove in specific cases. Government support for Bombardier, for example, is almost an article of civil religion in Quebec, as is support for the automobile industry in Ontario.)
- Invest in research and development, especially medical and scientific research. (Elimination of the capitals gains tax was buried in the further discussion of this point.)
- Support Canada's farmers, fishers, and forestry workers. (This was a portmanteau heading for a grab-bag of appeals to specific interests, such as elimination of the Wheat Board monopoly on Western wheat and barley, continued support of supply management in dairy and poultry, and financial help for the softwood lumber industry in its NAFTA battles with the United States.)[6]

There was also a section on health care, most of which was defensive in nature. Following Stephen's triangulation on this crucial issue, it promised more money for the public system, supported the 2003 Health Accord, and stayed away from privatization. On the positive side, it promised to "propose to the provinces a federal program for catastrophic drug coverage"[7] and to "commit one percent of federal health funding to the funding of physical activity," including amateur sport.[8]

There were dozens of promises under the headings of "better communities" and "better security," dealing with diverse matters of criminal justice, environmental policy, and advanced education. Some were predictable, such as repeal of the long-gun registry and zero tolerance for child pornography. Others were more surprising, such as the promise to spend "$4 billion over ten years to clean up contaminated sites such as the Sydney tar ponds."[9] The biggest-ticket items were for increasing our support of the Canadian Forces, including an immediate budget increase of $1.2 billion, growth of the Regular Force strength to at least eighty thousand, and equipment upgrades for tanks, heavy-lift aircraft, and maritime helicopters.

Three pages of financial tables used five-year federal Department of Finance figures to show that our program of tax cuts and targeted spending increases was affordable. The conclusion: "There is significant fiscal room in the coming years for a Conservative government to address Canadians' priorities, such as investing in health care and our military, and reducing taxes."[10] The main differences from the Liberals' budget figures were to lower their projected spending path in non-priority areas and to make a more realistic forecast of surpluses and to draw them into the overall fiscal plan, rather than treating them as windfalls to be dispensed for year-end political gains.

Almost everything in the platform, except perhaps draconian cuts to business subsidies, was politically feasible, and there were not too many concessions to special interest groups. The whole program had been costed and found to be affordable. There were few highly controversial positions that would have provoked acrimony without winning anyone's support. In spite of some inconsistencies, the platform as a whole would have moved public policy in a conservative direction – lower taxes, less onerous economic regulation, stricter enforcement of the criminal law, and a stronger military. Although it didn't contain everything that all Canadian conservatives wanted, it had at least some things that most conservatives desired to see, and very little

that was outside conservatism altogether. By showing that we
had rational, feasible ideas about what we would do as a government, the platform was a major factor in helping us to do as well
as we did in the election.

With the benefit of hindsight, however, I think that the communications strategy for the platform could have been better. We
used the platform to prove that we were trustworthy, but we
campaigned more by talking about the Liberals' misdeeds than
by expounding the virtues of our own program – "keeping the focus on the Liberals," as Ken called it. Thus we did not try to
make the platform reader-friendly. With forty-four large pages of
text, three pages of tables, and no pictures, it was hardly designed
for mass distribution. It was more like a throwback to the Reform Party's first *Blue Book*, which Stephen had written for the
1988 campaign. This time, we printed a minimal number of copies for distribution to the national media. We did no policy-based
ads for television. We did draw on the platform to produce about
a million dollars worth of radio advertising in targeted ridings,
but in retrospect I think that money was largely wasted. It's very
difficult to communicate policy messages in short radio ads because most of the time people aren't listening with full attention.

In the second half of the campaign, we produced a shortened
version of the platform that local campaigns could print and dis-
tribute using their own resources. Some ridings took advantage
of the opportunity, but they were probably well-organized campaigns with lots of volunteers, so I doubt that the short version
of the platform swung many (or any) ridings for us.

Overall, how well prepared were we for the campaign? In
some respects, we were almost miraculously well prepared, considering how little time was available. We had sufficient money,
a rationalized budget, and effective financial controls; adequate,
well-equipped space for the war room; a smoothly running
Leader's Tour with attractive buses and collateral materials; a
full set of candidates supported by paid field organizers and volunteer provincial chairs; television ads ready to be played; a
well-thought-out platform; a daily plan up to the debates; and
an extensive, carefully planned voter-contact program, backed
by a new computer system, to maximize our chances of winning
close races in targeted ridings. In some ways, we proved to be

better prepared than the Liberals, even though they had had all the time in the world to get ready. Our designs looked better, our Leader's Tour ran more smoothly and attracted bigger crowds, our messaging resonated with voters in the first part of the campaign, and our voter-contact program delivered the goods in close races. But I would be the first to emphasize how lucky we were that Paul Martin waited two full months after Stephen was chosen leader before he asked for an election. I hate to think of what it would have been like if we had had only two or even four weeks to get ready. Why did the Liberals wait so long? Were they themselves not ready, or did they fear public opinion would punish them if they did not give the new Conservative leader a decent opportunity to prepare his campaign?

We also had serious deficiencies, which hurt us badly toward the end of the campaign and probably cost us a victory that might have been attainable:

- We were never really in the game in Quebec. Though we had a full slate of candidates, many were token, and almost all were underfunded. Our slogan, platform, and advertising were conceived in English without the Quebec situation in mind, and then translated into French.
- Our initial advertising was all right, but we were not prepared to be responsive during the course of the campaign. The research and production budgets were inadequate for that purpose; but even if more money had been set aside we didn't really understand the dynamic requirements of advertising in a duel for victory.
- Because at the start we hadn't really expected to win, we had no endgame plan. Only the first twenty-five days were scripted, and we had not written down what we would do under the various scenarios that might prevail toward the end – ahead, behind, or very close. Without clear endgame plans to follow, we drifted, improvised, and generally failed to meet the daunting challenges of the final phase of the campaign.
- Lack of endgame planning was exacerbated by an inadequate command-and-control structure. As will be shown in detail in the next chapter's account of the campaign, our decision-making process was simply not up to the stresses of the final phase.

6

National Election, 2004

In line with the Liberal campaign slogan, "Choose Your Canada," Paul Martin opened the 2004 campaign by polarizing against Stephen Harper, whom he tried to associate with US values. After visiting the governor general, Martin spoke to reporters outside Rideau Hall: "You can have a country like Canada. You can have a country like the United States. That's a choice you can make. But you cannot have a health-care system like Canada's ... [and] social programs like Canada's with taxation levels like those of the United States."[1] It was similar to what Jean Chrétien had said on the opening day in 2000 against Stockwell Day: "This election offers two very different visions of Canada, two crystal clear alternatives."[2] Both Liberal campaigns were negative to the core. As Stephen Harper said, the Liberals were running a "campaign of fear."[3] Their main effort was devoted to making voters afraid of the new party of the right – the Canadian Alliance in 2000, the Conservatives in 2004. The strategy worked better in 2000, when it led to a majority government, than it did in 2004, when it led only to a minority government.

Due to our frantic efforts over the preceding two months, we were more or less ready when the writ was dropped on 23 May 2004. The tour jet was standing by, refitted buses were in Ottawa, staff had been hired, and those working in the war room had moved into their new quarters several days ahead of time. The first week of the tour plan, which was to hopscotch across the country from coast to coast stopping in major media markets along the way, went off smoothly. The message plan of that week was to attack the Liberals for their waste and mismanagement.

The only real hitch at the beginning occurred with our advertising. The ads had been produced, the media buy was mapped
out, and a line of credit was approved by the bank consortium.
However, we couldn't actually get the money from the banks until the writ was dropped, and the networks wouldn't run the ads
until they received the money. Paul Martin went to the governor
general on the Sunday of the Victoria Day long weekend, which
meant that the banks couldn't put the money in our account until Tuesday morning. It then had to be wired to Watermark,
which had to transfer it to the networks. As a result of this cumbersome arrangement, our advertising didn't really get going until day 5 of the campaign – Thursday. We put our ads on our
website on day 2 to create a little media coverage,[4] but we
weren't actually running them on air. We were anxious about it
at the time, but it didn't really do us any damage and may have
even helped by freeing up some extra money to be spent in the
last weekend, when the planned buy was probably too light. In
any case, we learned from experience and had a more flexible arrangement in place for 2006.

The second week of the tour mainly consisted of bus travel
through rural Ontario, hitting as many "Blue" ridings as possible – the ones that we hoped to win. Policy rollout started seriously now, as Stephen would release a chapter of the platform in
a message event, with a rally for partisans in the evening. He
then unveiled the entire platform in Toronto on Saturday,
5 June.[5] Saturday in Toronto was chosen because we wanted to
release the platform at a large mid-day rally, but the choice was
not optimal from a media point of view. The *Globe and Mail*
and the *National Post* do not publish on Sunday; and even for
newspapers that do have a Sunday edition, the weekend is not
the best time to get attention for political news. We didn't really
care because we thought the pre-writ leak of the platform had
undermined its news value in any case. The damage was minor,
but it did allow our opponents to claim that we were trying to
hide our policies.

The platform had been composed in English, so it had to be
translated into French before printing, and that caused a near-
disaster. Several French-language mavens got into the act and
kept submitting duelling versions of the wording, while Phil

Murphy and I were desperately trying to make sure the English and French matched each other. At the last minute, there were some changes to row labels in the French edition of the fiscal tables, which had an effect on column alignment that we didn't notice. Fortunately, Steve Brooks caught it about an hour before the print run was to start, so the master could be corrected. If Steve hadn't noticed the problem with the tables, we would have printed English and French platforms with different versions of "the numbers." I never told Harper this story; he had enough to worry about as it was.

Apart from these secondary issues, there was a bigger problem associated with our platform release, which we did not appreciate until much later. Because there had not been time to hold a policy convention after the merger, the Conservative Party had no official positions on many issues. It seemed logical, therefore, to get the platform out fairly quickly, to define ourselves in the public mind. Hence the decision to have Harper talk about large chunks of the platform each day and to release the whole platform at the end of the first two weeks. What we underestimated, because we had never run a national campaign before, was the difficulty the leader would face in dealing with the media after the platform had been released. He was carting the media around the country in the Leader's Tour, and they expected him to generate news each day. If he did not have new policy to announce, they would go after him with their own questions, thus transferring control of the agenda from us to them.

Overall, however, the first three weeks seemed quite successful. We started about six points back of the Liberals and fell even further behind in the first few days before our ads began to run, but then we started to climb and overtook them in our internal polling on day 14 and maintained a two or three point lead through most of week 3. What accounted for this striking, if temporary, success? The main factor was probably the leader's performance on tour in this period. He looked relaxed, explained our policies clearly, and allowed reporters to ask lots of questions, to which he gave calm, enlightening answers. Beyond that, the tour ran on time and reasonably smoothly, except for some problems with our overly ambitious technology on the buses, and reporters seemed to take those little glitches in stride.

Our advertising was not dazzling, but it matched our earned-media messaging, and it was effective in these early weeks, once it got going. "Carousel" drew attention to Liberal waste and mismanagement, and the ads showing Stephen in his office introduced a still-new party leader to a national audience.

Candidate gaffes were the only thing that went visibly wrong in the first three weeks. On 27 May (day 5), the *Moncton Times Transcript* published a long interview with Conservative official languages critic Scott Reid under the inflammatory headline, "Harper government would overhaul bilingualism, requirements for mandatory bilingual services would be eased under Tory government: candidate." Stephen was flying in the tour jet when this came out, but later that day he accepted Reid's resignation as critic, and Scott put out a statement that these were his personal views, not party policy or the leader's position.[6] Then on 1 June, the *Globe and Mail* published highlights of an interview of Jill Mahoney with our health critic, Rob Merrifield, in which he said he thought it was useful for women to receive counseling before having an abortion.[7] The subheading was inflammatory – "Urges mandatory third-party counseling" – even though Merrifield had been moderate in his comments; he didn't say that a Conservative Government would legislate such a requirement, and only a few days earlier Paul Martin had said, "I think you should always refer to counseling."[8] It was infuriating to be hammered in the media for saying nothing different than the prime minister had said. Nonetheless, Merrifield's intervention worked at cross-purposes with Stephen's position that he would not legislate on abortion, so Rob quickly had to follow Scott Reid's example: resign as critic, and stress that this was only a personal view.

Stephen immediately distanced himself from their comments. It seemed to work as far as public opinion was concerned; our polling numbers never wavered in spite of the publicity surrounding these candidate gaffes. At this early stage, it seemed that people were willing to give us the benefit of the doubt as long as the leader himself stayed on message.

McGill University's Observatory on Media and Public Policy used content analysis techniques to track daily coverage of the campaign in seven major metropolitan newspapers. According to their data, Harper and the Conservatives received far more favourable coverage than Martin and the Liberals in the first two weeks. We began at a net score of about 0, i.e., neutral, while the Liberals started at around -25. The Conservative Party's score held up for the first week but started to slide in the second as candidate gaffes accumulated. Harper, however, remained at his strong initial level for the first two weeks.[9]

We benefited from exceeding people's low expectations in these early weeks. Observers were surprised that our campaign seemed well organized and professionally smooth in contrast to Paul Martin's frantic style. The tour was running on time, crowds were large and enthusiastic, the leader was calm and rational, the ads were low-key but pointed, and Watermark's designs made everything look good, from the bus wrap to the banners and posters at rallies.

But moving ahead after two weeks of a national campaign is like leading after the first quarter of a football game. It's nice, but a long way from winning. Indeed, the game became more difficult for us as soon as pollsters reported that we had taken the lead. It started to dawn on voters that voting for the Conservatives would not just punish the Liberals, it might actually elect a Conservative Government. Media coverage for Harper became much more negative in week 3, dropping from close to 0 to the range of -10 to -15, while Martin's coverage, though still more negative than Stephen's, was becoming more favourable.[10] We were in for heightened scrutiny, which would put unbearable stress on the weaknesses in our preparation. Three of these weaknesses combined in a way that proved fatal over the last half of the campaign:

- We had no plan for being ahead in the race. Our writing team (which was too small and overworked) had thought that, once the platform was released, we could revisit parts of it in more detail, but that didn't work out well in practice. Thus the way was opened for the media to take control, to ask the leader about his plans for government, or to get him to comment on candidate gaffes. Without a workable day-by-day plan, Stephen had to start improvising.
- Our decision-making system was flawed. Our pipeline between the war room and the tour was too narrow, Stephen didn't get

enough information coming out of polling or the ground campaign, and those of us back in the war room didn't hear
enough about the leader's concerns.

- Our advertising was fine at the start but became less effective
  when we started to de-emphasize "Carousel" in favour of
  "Commitment." We had neither a plan nor a budget for producing new ads to counter the attacks that the Liberals would
  soon launch against us.

Even though we maintained our lead in the polls for most of
week 3, we started to lose control of the agenda. On 8 June, the
national media discovered (courtesy, I assume, of Liberal opposition research) a *Western Catholic Reporter* story on what Conservative MP Cheryl Gallant had said at a pro-life rally on
13 May 2004 – that there was "absolutely no difference" between abortion and the recent terrorist beheading of US reporter
Nicholas Berg. This wasn't a gaffe in the usual sense, because it
hadn't happened during the campaign and Gallant wasn't a
critic and hadn't claimed to be speaking for the party. Still, it put
the focus back on abortion, which wasn't supposed to be part of
our script. Stephen tried to distance himself as best he could, saying, "Abortion is going to go on one way or the other, and I
think it's part of life, rightly or wrongly. I wouldn't say I like
abortion, but I think abortion is a reality that is with us."[11] This
wasn't strong enough to make the controversy die, so Stephen
tried again on 9 June: "I have no intention of supporting abortion legislation, so there's no way that abortion rights are going
to be overridden by my government. I have no intention of introducing abortion legislation, and I think the chances of any being
passed in this Parliament are virtually non-existent."[12]

We didn't seem to be in trouble at the moment. Polls were
showing us in the lead, Senator Anne Cools had just defected
from the Liberals to our side, and outspoken Liberal MP Carolyn
Parrish called the Liberal campaign "a comedy of errors ... like
the Keystone Kops running around."[13] Yet Harper's reference to
"this Parliament" was troubling, as were other statements that
he would not prevent backbenchers from bringing private member's bills to restrict abortion. In an intellectual sense, both statements were true; a prime minister cannot prevent private

members from introducing bills, nor can he make binding commitments about what future Parliaments might do. But statements like these are better suited to the calm mood of a university seminar than the overheated atmosphere of a national campaign. Our opponents seized upon them to allege that Harper had a long-term agenda on abortion different from his short-term position in this campaign. Thus, as the week went on, he found himself dealing with more and more questions about abortion and other hot-button social issues, especially now that there was really nothing new to say about the platform.

The relationship with the tour media was becoming increasingly testy, so, in an attempt to bring them to heel, we started staging his media scrums in the midst of party events. Thursday, 10 June, in Brampton was particularly edgy. Stephen wanted to talk to the largely Sikh audience about immigrants' professional credentials, but reporters wanted to ask about the recent comment of Kitchener-Conestoga candidate Frank Luellau that gay relationships were unnatural.[14] Harper scrummed for what seemed forever, answering one question after another about gay rights, while partisans hissed and booed the media. The *Toronto Star*'s Tonda MacCharles got so upset she held up the tour bus while she sat outside to settle down. We had an hour of excitement in the war room when we got distorted phone reports that she had been threatened with a knife, perhaps a Sikh kirpan, but there proved to be nothing in the rumour.

Meanwhile, hoping to move our still-anemic numbers in Quebec, Stephen had started to talk in public about the possibility of a majority government. He first mentioned it in Aurora on the evening of 9 June, when he appeared at a local event with Belinda Stronach.[15] From then on, even if he did not mention it in his formal remarks, he was bound to be asked about it at every scrum, particularly in light of what happened on 10 June. That was the date of the famous Liberal conference call to which someone gave the *Globe and Mail*'s Jane Taber the call-in number and pass code. She was startled to hear campaign manager David Herle tell the meeting that the "Liberals were in a spiral" – downward, not upward. Naturally that became the headline in the *Globe and Mail* on 11 June, strengthening the impression that the Conservatives might really win the election.[16]

At the 10 June meeting, Herle announced that the Liberals were about to release attack ads against the Conservatives. They had, in fact, run some pre-writ attack ads in newspapers and on television, referring viewers to a "Stephen Harper Said" website for more details.[17] Ken Boessenkool worked all night to put up a rebuttal website, and we thought we had weathered those attacks without much damage. When the writ was dropped, the Liberals shifted to positive ads featuring Paul Martin in conversation with Canadians. Those ads were forgettable, and, as far as Dimitri could measure through his polling, had almost no impact. But their new attack ad was certainly memorable, both in iconography and in script:

> (Female narrator; deliberate diction; ominous music.) Stephen Harper would have sent our troops to Iraq (stock footage of tanks and soldiers crossing desert).
>
> He'd spend billions on tanks and aircraft carriers (stock footage of ship at sea), weaken our gun laws (close-up of gun pointed at camera), scrap the Kyoto Accord (stock footage of industrial pollution).
>
> He'd sacrifice Canadian-style healthcare for US-style tax cuts (close-up of oxygen mask descending onto camera, cut to doctors wheeling patient on gurney).
>
> He won't protect a woman's right to choose (desperate teenage girl rocking on floor).
>
> And he's prepared to work with the Bloc Québécois (pan over Gilles Duceppe).
>
> Stephen Harper says that when he's through with Canada (zoom out on flag), we won't recognize it.
>
> You know what? (Flag begins to burn and disintegrate.) He's right. (Fade to black.)[18]

Reportedly, the Liberals had not originally planned to be this negative but felt they had no choice in view of the lead the Conservatives were building. When they focus-tested this ad in Mississauga on 4 June, they were impressed with the results. "I have never, in all my marketing experience, witnessed as powerful an impact for a single ad in a focus group as I saw that night," Jack Bensimon, the head of Liberal advertising, said after the campaign.[19]

Harper's public response was that the ad was over the top and would backfire on the Liberals. Maybe so, but we had no effective plan for responding to such negative ads. While we kept playing "Carousel," we increased the rotation of "Commitment," which showed him and his family in a rather sentimental light. We wanted something new at this point to counter the Liberal onslaught, and "Commitment" was all we had. Ken Boessenkool and Jim Armour played with some negative scripts, but we never settled on a counterattack. We still feared that hard-hitting negative ads would reinforce the "scary" image that the Liberals were pinning on Harper.

As week 3 ended, the tour came back to Ottawa so the leader could begin debate preparation. The French debate was scheduled for Monday, 14 June, the English for Tuesday, 15 June. Harper wanted a thorough preparation for his first experience in a national election debate, so we had set aside three days, Friday through Sunday, for Mike Coates and his team to prep the leader. Ominously, our polling numbers plunged over the weekend, giving the Liberals back the six-point lead they had enjoyed at the outset. At the time, we weren't too worried; we attributed the decline to Harper's debate preparation, which caused him to "go dark" while the other party leaders continued to do public events. Though not everyone agrees with me, I now think it would have been smarter to attribute the decline to the combination of what had happened in week 3 – obsolescence of our daily plan, loss of control over the news agenda, focus on abortion and other social issues, and the release of powerful negative ads to which we had no response.

About this time there also took place the single craziest event of the campaign, at least from my point of view. Greyhound had given us a team of six bus drivers headed by Fred Watson, who had been driving in Conservative campaigns for twenty-five years. Fred was much more than a bus driver; he was also the team leader and chief contractor for the renovations to the bus. He's highly experienced and very good at what he does, but he would also be the first to admit that he can be outspoken. As of 10 June, I hadn't even met him because he had been dealing with Phil Murphy, with whom he didn't get along. Then on the night of 10 June, I got a late call that Fred was threatening to go directly to Harper over some grievance or other.

"That's it," I said to myself, so next morning I told Phil Murphy to call Greyhound and ask for new drivers. Thinking it was all settled, I went out to Stornoway for the opening meeting of debate preparation. There I met Ray and Carolyn, wearing long faces and telling me that it was unthinkable to run the tour without Fred. When I got the same message from Tour Director Debbie Campbell and Wagonmaster Dave Penner, I knew I had made a big mistake. Everyone closest to the tour was telling me they couldn't do it without Fred Watson.

Back at the war room, I talked to Associate Tour Director Boomer Throop, a former PC who had worked with Fred in other campaigns. He offered to drive me out to the Ottawa motel where Fred and the other drivers were holed up. So I went out there that afternoon and re-hired them, after having fired them in the morning. You can't persist in a mistaken decision when it means ignoring the unanimous advice of those who are closest to the issue. The drivers were kind enough to come back to work, and they did a first-class professional job during the rest of the tour.

Returning to the main narrative, Harper did well in the debates, and our numbers shot up afterward. Duceppe, of course, as the only native Francophone, could not help but win the French debate by a large margin. However, Stephen had done all right in the French debate. Paul Martin was superficially more fluent, but Stephen actually spoke more correct French, which seemed to make a good impression. For many Francophones in Quebec, it was probably the first time they ever heard Harper speak French, and they seem to have been pleasantly surprised that he could function in the language. Our support in Quebec, which had reached a low of 6 percent of 14 June, the day of the French debate, went up for six straight days afterward and eventually reached a high of 17 percent on 23 June.[20]

The English debate on 15 June was such a madhouse that the format was abandoned in the next election. The almost unlimited interruptions allowed by the rules rewarded rudeness and rendered the whole thing incoherent. Stephen, however, triumphed in public opinion by remaining calm, controlled, and polite. On the first day after the English debate, print media seemed to think Martin had done better, but voters did not see it

Table 6.1

Distribution of Seats Based on Advance Polls
and Special Ballots, Canadian General Election, 2004

Conservatives	125
Liberals	117
NDP	16
Bloc Québécois	49
Independent	1

that way.[21] In a large Ipsos-Reid post-debate poll (n = 2000), 37 percent of respondents said Harper won, compared to 24 percent for Martin, 18 percent for Layton, and 6 percent for Gilles Duceppe.[22] Conservative support surged dramatically in our internal polling after the debates, climbing daily from 30 percent on 15 June to 41 percent by 18 June. Meanwhile the Liberals slipped from 32 percent to 26 percent. We had opened up a fifteen-point lead by 18 June, though we should have paid more attention to a rise in undecided respondents from 15 percent to 22 percent over the same period of time. Public polling was also showing us in the lead, though not as much, because pollsters were reporting results of a three- or five-day roll. Dimitri had enlarged the size of our nightly sample after the debate, so we were able to put some confidence in his one-night results, which indicated our growth more dramatically.

Our new lead may have been more fragile than we realized, but it was real enough, as shown by the results of the advance polls. We won a narrow victory among the 9.2 percent of ballots cast in the advance polls on 18, 19, and 21 June, plus the 1.8 percent of special ballots cast by soldiers who were out of the country and other voters who were outside their home ridings on elections day. We received 34 percent of these votes, as compared to 37 percent for the Liberals, but our advance and special vote was efficient in terms of seats[23] (see table 6.1). Although our lead melted away in the last ten days, the advance polls helped to elect ten Conservative MPs who would have lost counting only election-day ballots but had rolled up a big enough margin in the advance polls to win their seats.

Table 6.2

Distribution of Seats, Canadian General Election, 2004

Party	Election final, including advance polling	Election Day ballots only
Liberals	135	139
Conservatives	99	89
NDP	19	23
Bloc Québécois	54	56
Independent	1	1

Table 6.2 compares the official election results in terms of seats with those that would have resulted from the election-day count only. The main explanation of the difference between advance-poll and election-day trends is undoubtedly that we finished weakly while the Liberals finished strongly; but our Get Out the Vote (GOTV) program must also be kept in mind. We were actively pushing our identified supporters in targeted ridings to vote early. That we won ninety-nine seats, instead of the eighty-nine that we would have won if only ballots cast on 28 June had been counted, was partly due to the way our popularity peaked just before the advance polls, and partly due to the effort we made to get supporters to vote early. One must, however, beware of drawing sweeping conclusions about the effect of advance polls.[24] We lack good evidence about the voting behaviour of those who take advantage of advance polls to cast their votes early. Efforts to encourage partisans to vote early may affect *when* the vote is cast but not necessarily *whether* and *for whom*. It is probably going too far to state categorically that we won ten extra seats because of our GOTV efforts in the advance polls. Nonetheless, it cannot have hurt our cause that we got those votes in the bank ahead of time.

Returning to the story of the campaign, debate-induced euphoria must be taken into account in understanding what happened next. We thought that Harper had won the debates, and we were surging everywhere, including Quebec. We were determined to leverage this advantage into victory, even a majority government, by winning some seats in Quebec. We had been reluctant to tour outside of Montreal and Quebec City because we were so weak on the ground, but we now planned a bus tour from Montreal to the Eastern Townships and north to Quebec City, covering rural ridings where we thought we might be able to make a breakthrough. Though there wasn't a lot of money available, I authorized some additional radio advertising in the same general area, the "triangle" between Quebec City, Montreal, and the Eastern Townships.

Stephen also sounded increasingly bullish in his public statements. The day after the English debate, he said, "There are no safe seats for the Liberals anywhere, any more. None in Atlantic Canada, none in the West, or in Quebec and in Ontario."[25] He also announced that he was appointing a transition team including Hugh Segal and Derek Burney, both former chiefs of staff to Brian Mulroney. It's understandable why he made that announcement. He was leading in the polls, and as Stephen Clarkson has written, "As a leader with a strong chance of defeating the current government, it would have been irresponsible for him not to prepare for office."[26] But, necessary as the announcement may have been, it heightened the scrutiny on Harper and the Conservatives as possible winners.

Normally, the leader of a major party with a chance to form a government would have appointed a transition team well before the election; getting ready to govern is a major task that takes months of work, with one of the biggest jobs being the compilation of a "talent book" of names for hiring in the PMO and ministers' offices as well as appointments to the Senate, the courts, and commissions and agencies. Because of the merger, the leadership race, and the hurried preparations for the election campaign, we hadn't done any of that. Thus the transition team appointed in the final two weeks of the campaign could only undertake the merest beginning of what needed to be done. At Stephen's request, I worked with Burney and Segal to prepare a road map of the first three weeks in office of a Conservative Government – dealing with congratulations from foreign leaders, appointing a cabinet, meeting the new caucus, preparing for any immediately pressing appointments or international obligations, and so on. In the time we had, we couldn't compile a talent book, so staffing a new Conservative Government would have been a scramble if we had won.

So, amid talk of surging polls, majority governments, and transition teams, Stephen set off for Montreal and then a bus tour of rural Quebec, hoping to boost our support in the province from around 15 percent, which we had attained after the debates, to 20 percent or more, the point at which we might win a few seats. It seemed to us like a rational strategy at the time, but former Liberal pollster Michael Marzolini sees it as a fatal miscalculation:

In the last week Harper spoke continually of forming a majority government [my note: not actually true, but the impression was out there], scaring voters who might have trusted him with a minority but certainly not with a majority. This disastrous strategy, which prompted an electoral run on the bank, was aimed at attracting Quebec voters ... [27]

Be that as it may, our attempt at a closing surge quickly ran into obstacles, of which the first was Ralph Klein. On 18 June, Paul Martin jumped on the news that Alberta Premier Ralph Klein would release a new health-care policy that might conflict with the Canada Health Act. "He's hoping he'll have a silent partner in Ottawa by the name of Stephen Harper," Martin said. "Someone who will not speak up for the Canada Health Act ... and someone who doesn't care. Well, unlike Stephen Harper, I do care ... And unlike Stephen Harper, I will look Ralph Klein in the eye and I will say no. Unlike Stephen Harper, I will defend medicare."[28] That controversy, dragging on over the weekend and into week 5, certainly did nothing to help our stagnant poll numbers. It was particularly frustrating for Stephen because he thought he had put that issue to bed, and here it was coming back, not as a campaign mistake as had happened in the 2000 election, when Jason Kenney opened the door to charges of advocating two-tier medicine,[29] but as a wholly unexpected incursion from outside.

There was no need for Klein to make those comments in the closing stages of a federal election. Was it just the general sloppiness that marked the final years of his time as Alberta premier, or was he being deliberately mischievous? Was he paying Harper back for the "Alberta Agenda" letter of 2001? It is perhaps relevant that he had no personal relationship with Harper. After becoming Conservative leader, Stephen put a lot of effort into cultivating the four Progressive Conservative premiers in Atlantic Canada, but he never had a meeting with Ralph Klein. (Yet cultivating a relationship with Ralph Klein is no guarantee that he won't say something damaging. Stephen did meet with him prior to the 2006 election and was rewarded with a public statement from Klein to the effect that "Harper can't win").

Then came the famous child-pornography fiasco. Tightening the laws against child pornography had been a cause for the Canadian Alliance ever since 1999, when the British Columbia Supreme Court had accepted John Robin Sharpe's plea that "artistic merit" could justify possession.[30] In the meantime there had been several votes in the House of Commons in which the Liberals had frustrated attempts to take the "artistic merit" defence out of the Criminal Code, though they did rename it "public good." *Demanding Better* stated, "We will pass legislation that will adopt a zero tolerance policy for child porn, eliminating the so-called 'public good' defence."[31]

On 17 June 2004, Michael Brière, accused of murdering Holly Jones, testified in a Toronto court room that child pornography had led him to kidnap, rape, and murder the little girl.[32] At the communications meeting in the war room the next morning, several people argued vigorously for taking advantage of this news report to highlight our policy on child pornography, which hadn't yet received much attention. I remember Maureen Murphy-Makin being very nervous about it; we should have listened to her.

Early in the afternoon a release went out with the unfortunate title "Paul Martin supports child pornography?" It was one of those mistakes that should have been caught but wasn't. There was a troika running communications in the war room – Yaroslav Baran, William Stairs, and Geoff Norquay. William did a lot of liaison with the spin team across the country, and Geoff was a frequent TV panellist, while Yaroslav was the main operations manager. All material that went out was supposed to be checked by at least two, and preferably all three, of them; but Yaroslav was the only one around when this release was ready, and he made the fateful mistake of approving and sending it out on his own authority. Here is how he later described what happened:

On the day of the child pornography reality check, the system broke down somewhat. It was a particularly busy day, and I was the one who signed off on the reality check. In fact, I was the one who commissioned it, based on the fact that Paul Martin and Jack Layton were being reported in the media as having respectively pledged their unequivocal support to end all manifestations of child pornography, and citing this as a "priority." These declarations, of course, begged the question, "oh really?" Their respective records were against them, as the content of the reality checks revealed. Furthermore, it had been decided in our morning meeting that we would generally go after Martin for his hypocrisy on the issue ...

When the reality check in question came, I made one deletion from the body (it originally had five bullets, rather than four), then let it go, as William and Geoff were not in the office at the time, for a sober second check. The headline, in the heat of battle, did not strike me as too personal. In fact, it did not strike me as being personal at all, but rather a reflection of policy history. Our party has always held that if you do not eliminate the loopholes that allow child pornography, then you are tolerant of it. That is how I read the title, but a second set of eyes would, no doubt, have read it in a sense that would have flagged it as being unduly personal.

It is completely my responsibility that this slipped through the cracks on the approval side. I should never have allowed our triple-review process to be compromised just because it was a busy day. As we all know in hindsight, it is better for nothing to go out than for a flawed piece of work to go out.[33]

The release went out in the early afternoon while our tour cavalcade was making its way across Quebec. Stephen, riding in the leader's bus, did not see it, but reporters in the media buses got it on their Blackberries, and the Liberals had time to egg them on with further Blackberry messages demanding an apology to Paul Martin. When the tour stopped for a local event and Stephen got out, he was literally trapped against the side of the bus by a crowd of reporters demanding answers about a news release he had never seen and didn't even know was coming. Would he apologize to Paul Martin for implying that he endorsed child pornography?

Before answering, Stephen convened a quick conference call with his communications advisers on the tour and in the war room. I wasn't on the call; but, according to Paul Wells, some wanted to kill the story with a quick apology,[34] while others wanted to be more aggressive. The group decided not to apologize but to withdraw the release and re-issue it under a new title, "How tough is Paul Martin on child pornography?" Harper then went on to defend the content of the release, saying that the Liberals "have had multiple opportunities to do something about it and they have systematically refused."[35] Martin demanded an apology in his usual exaggerated way: "This is personal. I am a father and I am a husband. And he has crossed the line and should apologize." Most of the media sided with him.

I wasn't part of the crisis management, but when I learned about it later, I wondered whether Stephen should have apologized. He could have said, "It was a mistake. The person who made it has been reassigned. I don't think Paul Martin personally supports child pornography, but the Liberal record ..." I joked with the communications people who had been in on the call, "You guys are all too young. If you'd been married as long as I have [forty years], you'd know you have to apologize right away." But being a smart-ass after the fact is easy. We would have taken a heavy hit on this no matter what Stephen said. Apologies don't work very well in the heat of campaigns because they make you look weak and draw attention to your mistake, as happened with Kim Campbell's famous apology in the 1993 election over Conservative ads that the Liberals managed to construe as a personal attack on Jean Chrétien's facial paralysis.

The hit was indeed heavy, but because of the nature of polling we lost a day in recognizing it. The episode took place in the late afternoon, so it did get some play in the evening national news; but polling started around 6 PM before most Canadians would have become aware of what had happened. Thus our Saturday-morning tracking results, which reflected opinion as of early Friday evening, were the most favourable of the entire campaign – 41 percent of decided voters for us, compared to 26 percent for the Liberals. We thought we might have dodged the bullet. But the Saturday morning newspaper headlines were brutal, especially in Ontario; and there was quite a different story in Saturday night's polling numbers, which we saw on Sunday morning. I got a sick feeling in my stomach when I saw that we had dropped 10 points in one night while the Liberals had gone up 12 and now led us by 7 points. Stephen's favourability index in newspaper coverage also turned down and continued to fall for several days thereafter.[36] The horse race between the Conservatives and Liberals returned to neck-and-neck, and never again would we have a continuing lead. Our chance at a majority government had disappeared overnight.

It was not yet ordained, however, that we could not squeak through with a minority government. That we would lose was decided in the final ten days by a combination of bad luck for us, cunning Liberal tactics, and our own inability to react to both. In the heady days when we seemed to be on the move, it had been decided to start the final week by visiting ridings in Ontario, such as Sault Ste Marie, that we had not been expected to win. That would demonstrate that we were on our way to a majority government. The tour would then skip across the West where we were fighting close races – Winnipeg, Regina, Victoria, Vancouver, and Edmonton – to finish with a victorious day-long cavalcade of all six buses from Edmonton to Calgary.

That plan may have made sense when it was formulated in week 4, but in light of the child-porn setback it was clearly wrong for week 5. Rather than cruising to a majority government, we were fighting desperately to squeak out a plurality. It was crystal clear not only from Dimitri's polling but from the intelligence pouring in to Doug Finley from his field organization. It would have been a good idea to restructure the final week to begin with a Western swing and then finish in Southern Ontario, where three dozen suburban and small-city ridings that we thought we could win were suddenly at risk, but our decision-making process bogged down and we were unable to make the necessary changes.

So we limped into the final week with the wrong tour plan and lots of stories about how Harper was refusing to talk to the media. Meanwhile, things continued to go wrong in other venues. Sunday, 20 June, brought stories about a letter from the OLO, dated 9 June 2004, dealing with the legislated requirement for Air Canada to offer services in both English and French everywhere in the country. The letter said that Air Canada should come under the same regulations as other airlines – the view of Air Canada's management, and the position that the Conservatives had espoused before the election. But in the heat of a campaign, it could be attacked as being against bilingualism. "I would never have thought," said Paul Martin, "that I would see a leader of a political party, like Stephen Harper, express ambiguity on official languages."[37] The letter should never have been sent, but OLO correspondence staff apparently thought it was all right to send this one because it expressed a previously enunciated policy. We took stronger steps in 2006 to ensure that correspondence staff didn't create issues during the campaign. Our Quebec polling numbers continued to rise for several days after disclosure of the letter, but it did cost us another day in trying to recover from the child-porn damage.

It was nerve-wracking to be in the war room as we staggered through the final week. Out tour plan was wrong, and Stephen, though he did continue to do interviews with broadcast media who were not on the tour, was barely talking to the tour media.[38] A local reporter described the situation when the tour hit Sarnia on 24 June:

> Circling like sharks with cameras and microphones ready, the journalists grumbled that they'd had just seven minutes this week to ask questions directly of the man who would be prime minister.
>
> Their spirits didn't improve much when Thursday's scrum was also cancelled without explanation.[39]

Every morning our overnight numbers were a little lower, and we were hoping we could just hang on for a slight minority edge when the votes were counted. But the Liberals' shrewd plan for the final weekend brought them a minority government – a tarnished prize, considering the high hopes with which Paul Martin had become prime minister six months ago – but still entailing control of the executive government.

The Liberals began their final push on the morning of Friday, 25 June, with Paul Martin holding a press conference to screen a Randy White interview by Vancouver filmmaker Alexis Fosse

Mackintosh. Before the election had been called, Mackintosh had been making a sympathetic documentary on gay marriage entitled *Let No One Put Asunder*. On 19 May 2004, four days before the writ was dropped, she had sought out Randy as an opponent of gay marriage, as she later explained in an interview:

> [Question:] You were the person who did the now infamous Randy White interview, where he talks about using the not-withstanding clause more frequently, and specifically against gay marriage. The release of the interview was a real turning point in the election campaign. How did you get the interview in the first place?
> [Answer:] Randy White was a wonderful interview. I was very direct from the start. I said I was doing a documentary on same-sex marriage and that I wanted someone from the "no" side who could articulate that position. He was very open to do that, he spoke very clearly and articulately, and he spoke the feelings of his constituency. He got 20,000 more votes than his nearest competitor. The people in the Abbottsford area really want him to represent them.[40]

Having gotten her interview, Mackintosh let it travel to the Liberal Party, even though *Let No One Put Asunder* had not yet been released. On 15 August 2004, Mackintosh's documentary would win an award at a CBC-sponsored gay film festival in Vancouver.[41]

White's interview was enormously damaging. Not only was he a senior member of caucus and former justice critic, he identified himself with the party as he spoke about gay marriage and the notwithstanding clause:

> Well, my position and the Conservative Party's position are identical ... If the Charter of Rights and Freedoms is going to be used as the crutch to carry forward all of the issues that social libertarians want, then there's got to be for us conservatives out there a way to put checks and balances in there. So the "notwithstanding" clause, which that was meant for when it was originally designed, should be used, I would think that not just the definition of marriage, but I think you'll see more

uses for the "notwithstanding" clause in the future. And I sincerely hope it is, because the Charter of Rights and Freedoms, I think, you'll even see that redefined as the Charter of Rights and Freedoms and Responsibilities, which is really needed for an amendment.[42]

Randy summed it up with this pithy line: "To heck with the courts!"[43]

The interview was perfect for the Liberals because it seemed to show that Harper really did have a hidden agenda: his carefully crafted positions on abortion, gay marriage, and perhaps other issues were just for show, and the real Harper would come out of the box if he won the election. It was powerful message to take into the final weekend when, traditionally, about 25 percent of voters make up their minds.

Earlier in the campaign, after the Scott Reid, Rob Merrifield, and Cheryl Gallant problems, Ken Boessenkool and I had split up the list of Conservative incumbents running for re-election and had called as many as we could reach, while Doug Finley's field organization talked to candidates who were running for the first time. We spoke about the importance of message discipline, about focusing on their ridings and staying away from the national media, particularly CTV, whose election bus was stalking our candidates. Both Ken and I talked to Randy at different times and found that he was the only caucus member who aggressively rejected the need for such advice. "Why are you calling me?" he asked. "I've been in Parliament for eleven years." But if Randy had confessed that he had given this bombshell interview that was sitting out there waiting to explode, we could have done something about it. As Yaroslav Baran likes to say, "You can spin anything if you have time." We could have gotten the story out well before the final weekend with a statement from Randy that he did not speak for the party, or that he had been set up. But there was little to be done now. Ken and I talked of expelling him from caucus, but Stephen was wiser than that. Such an exaggerated reaction would only have made a bad situation worse by pouring fuel on the flames of controversy.

The weekend just got worse as Stephen continued his swing through the West, when he should have been in Ontario. Speaking in Edmonton in his last televised appearance before his faux-triumphant motorcade to Calgary, he evoked memories of the Reform Party: "For more than a decade, the West and Alberta, in particular, have been demanding change. This is where it all started, and I've come here to tell you today, change is on the way in this country."[44] Such rhetoric may have helped us eke out a couple of tight victories in the West, but it did not reassure nervous voters in Toronto, Hamilton, London, Kitchener, and Waterloo, where dozens of seats were at stake.

Our multiple problems in earned media were the major story of the campaign, but advertising also played a role. As described earlier, the Liberals opened with positive ads featuring Paul Martin talking with people, then suddenly switched to an over-the-top negative ad. In the first three weeks, we asked questions every night in our tracking polls about whether respondents had seen Liberal ads, whether they remembered what the ads were about, and whether they would make them more or less likely to vote Liberal. As far as we could tell, the early Liberal ads, both positive and negative, were helping us more than they helped the Liberals. We wrongly concluded that Liberal ads wouldn't hurt us, and stopped asking about them in our polls because there were some other things we wanted to study. That proved to be a big mistake, because the Liberals moved on to less hysterical negative ads that became effective when our campaign mistakes seemed to validate them. One, entitled "The Stephen Harper We Know" and evoking the hidden agenda, fed on the news coverage of Ralph Klein, the Air Canada letter, and Randy White. Another series of ads, which ran in slightly different versions in different parts of the country, associated Harper with former Conservative leaders such as Brian Mulroney, Mike Harris, and Grant Devine. These played on fears that a Harper Government might return to the deficit-spending ways of Mulroney and Devine, just as George W. Bush had been chalking up large deficits in the United States. Doug Finley was getting reports from the field that these ads were working, but we didn't have hard numbers to prove it because of our decision to stop polling on Liberal ads.

The Liberals would have attacked our fiscal projections under any circumstance because Paul Martin's record as finance minister was one of their strengths, which they had to use. But the fiscal presentation in our platform made the attacks more plausible. In an attempt not to look like "slash and burn" conservatives who intended to take an axe to the roots of government, *Demanding* Better had accentuated the positive, emphasizing tax cuts and spending initiatives but giving no specific information about proposed spending cuts, even though it promised to "take a prudent approach to budgeting that keeps spending growth under control."[45] The platform's fiscal projections, however, showed federal program spending growing by only 13 percent (about 2.5 percent a year compounded) over the five-year term of a Conservative Government, from $142.5 billion in 2004–05 to $160.8 in 2009–10.[46] Some of the most expensive federal programs, such as old-age pensions, are driven by demography and cannot be made less costly without major legislative change. Thus, holding the growth in program spending to less than 2.5 percent a year meant there would have to be serious cuts somewhere to reach that target. In the absence of clarity about where those cuts would come, it was plausible for the Liberals to suggest either that the cuts wouldn't happen and the budget would spiral into deficit – the "$50 billion black hole" – or that the cuts would be draconian and gut essential services as Harper implemented his real "hidden agenda." The Liberals advanced both critiques simultaneously, not worrying about the contradiction. Then in the final weekend they brought out "Think Twice, Vote Once," playing it in heavy rotation in crucial media markets, such as southern Ontario. It capitalized on all the fears that our final ten days had awakened in potential swing voters.

Of course, even if we had continued polling on Liberal ads, our lack of production budget meant that we weren't set up to respond effectively. We produced only one new ad late in the campaign. Called "Cookie Jar," it showed a hand reaching into a big jar to steal cookies. At this stage of the campaign, when the Liberals were carpet-bombing us with all-out attacks, it was like bringing a knife not just to a gun fight but to an air raid. It was a brutal experience, but it was also an invaluable lesson that helped us win in 2006. Don't believe that negative ads will backfire. They may, if they are badly done; but the late-campaign Liberal ads were very good. And don't dismiss negative ads just because they seem to have no immediate effect on your polling numbers, for weeks of repetition can create doubts in voters' minds that affect their final decision. Against such an experienced and capable opponent as the Liberals, you cannot win without a complete arsenal of negative ads to offset the effect of their attacks.

Like everyone else, we were surprised by the results on election day, in which we finished a full seven points (37 percent to 30 percent) and 36 seats (135 to 99) behind the Liberals. We were mentally prepared to accept that we might lose, but not by that much. Dimitri had been showing us just two or three points behind the Liberals in the latter part of week 5. The commercial pollsters who were also calling it a dead heat have been criticized for halting their surveys too early, but Dimitri kept polling over the weekend and reported that our support actually improved on the Sunday before the vote. Perhaps Michael Marzolini was right that none of the pollsters in 2004 had an adequate correction for non-voters, who constitute a major problem for prediction when turnout plunges as low as 61 percent, as it did in 2004.[47]

All subsequent research has found that the Liberals did very well at the end of the campaign. André Turcotte, for example, reports that 40 percent of those who made up their minds in the final weekend voted Liberal, as compared to 33 percent of those who had made up their mind before the campaign started. The trend was the opposite for the Conservatives, who received the support of 32 percent of those who had decided before the campaign but only 26 percent of those who decided in the final weekend.[48] Since a quarter of voters claimed they did not make up their mind until the final weekend, this difference is enough to have had an appreciable impact upon the actual results.

Actually, what happened is more complex than just a choice between Liberal and Conservative. Our weakness in the final ten days, combined with the strength of the Liberal endgame, did persuade some Conservative-leaning swing voters to regard us as too risky and either vote Liberal or stay home; but it also persuaded some left-leaning swing voters in southern Ontario, who would have liked to vote NDP, to stay with the Liberals for fear that a vote for the NDP would actually help elect Conservative members of Parliament and thus lead to a Harper Government. In other words, Liberal scare tactics made strategic voting an important factor at the margin by convincing some potential NDP supporters that they had to vote Liberal to prevent the greater evil of a Conservative victory. This is an old Liberal tactic, commonly known in campaign war rooms as "scaring the shit out of the Dippers," but it worked once again. The NDP, who had been polling around 20 percent most of the campaign, ended up with only 15 percent of the vote and 19 seats.

Of course, the NDP leadership was aware of what the Liberals might do, and they had their traditional response, "Liberal, Tory; same old story." In this campaign, they hoped to neutralize Liberal scare tactics in advance with an advertising campaign painting Harper and Martin in the same colours:

> In one of the English-only ads, a map of Canada gives way to a split screen of Harper and Martin, followed by a big photo of Bush.
>
> As the images flash by, a female voice can be heard saying "Both Paul Martin and Stephen Harper want to bring Canada closer to George Bush, but Jack Layton thinks we can be good neighbours while still maintaining our values and independence."[49]

Bringing President Bush into these ads unintentionally helped the Liberals, because to most Canadians it was more plausible to see Harper, not Martin, as the leader closest to Bush.[50]

Strategic voting is a complicated phenomenon, and anyone who tries to promote it is likely to cause some unintended consequences. The Liberal tactics may have helped us win thirteen of fourteen seats in Saskatchewan (and perhaps a couple in British Columbia), where there were close races in which the two leading candidates were Conservative and NDP. Under those circumstances, voters switching from the NDP to the Liberals to defeat the Conservatives nationally would have helped elect the Conservative candidate locally. But there were far more seats in southern Ontario and metropolitan Vancouver where the close races were between a Liberal and a Conservative, so that "scaring the shit out of the Dippers" helped promote Liberal victories.

All in all, our more experienced opponents taught us a series of painful but useful lessons in the final days of the campaign.

The leader learned that there would have to be better management of his communications with the tour media; he would have
to retain control of the agenda and not let himself become the
target of persistent questioning in areas far off the campaign
plan. Other candidates saw how much damage could be done by
thoughtless remarks that played into opponents' hands. Campaign staff realized the importance of having a full-scale, dynamic, responsive advertising campaign. Learning these lessons
was unpleasant in 2004 but paid off in victory in 2006.

In assessing the 2004 campaign, we should not lose sight of all
the things we did right in a very short period of time. We showed
that we could master the basics of campaigning – a full slate of
308 candidates; a tour that kept to schedule; large, enthusiastic
rallies; good-looking campaign materials; and informative
nightly tracking polls. These may sound mundane, but the Reform, Alliance, and Progressive Conservative campaigns of
1993, 1997, and 2000 had sometimes lacked these basic elements. We also had a thoughtful platform based on serious research. We did not lose in 2004 because of positions we took or
didn't take; we lost because of positions that we were unable to
prevent our opponents from ascribing to us. We had to learn
how to go from flypaper to Teflon.

Another thing that we did very well was financial control. We
had a budget for a fully funded campaign, and we stuck to it re-
ligiously. Of course, there were shifts from category to category,
but we kept within our global limit. Even though there is a cap
on national campaign spending, it is easy and legal to exceed it
by transferring expenditures to local campaigns that are not able
to spend up to their own legal limits. That may be wise in some
circumstances, but it would have been a waste of money in
2004. Ideally, we should have had a bigger advertising budget,
but I'm not sure that our command-and-control structure would
have allowed us to make good use of the money. Under the circumstances, it was better that we stuck to the budget because we
ended 2004 in the black and ready to fight another election at
any time.

Another major accomplishment in 2004 was to improve our
local campaigning. As mentioned in the last chapter, the Canadian Alliance had not been good at winning close races. In the

2000 election, the Alliance won only four out of eighteen races (22 percent) in which the margin of victory was 5 percent or less, and nine of thirty-four (26 percent) in which the margin was 10 percent or less. In our preparations for the 2004 campaign, we had hoped to improve that performance by creating the CIMS database and instituting a nationally controlled direct voter contact (DVC) program, as well as by better training and technical support at the local level. The PCs had had a similar problem in 2000, winning only two of seven races (28 percent) where the margin was 5 percent or less, and four of eleven (36 percent) where the margin was 10 percent or less. Neither party had a modern DVC program to identify supporters and drive them to the polls.

In 2004, the haste in which we had to prepare for the campaign meant that Doug Finley, the director of operations for the Conservative Party, had little time for candidate training, although he did what he could with weekend seminars, conference calls, and internet hook-ups. The main weapons we had at our disposal were the new CIMS database and the nationally controlled DVC program, which we planned to deploy in targeted ("Blue") ridings. Before the merger, the Alliance had planned to target forty ridings, but we pushed it up to sixty after the merger to take advantage of new opportunities, and up again to sixty-seven during the campaign when we thought we were surging ahead.

The change between 2000 and 2004 was little short of phenomenal. In 2004 we won 64 percent of races (twenty-five out of thirty-nine) in which the margin of victory was 5 points or less. All the other parties were in negative territory: the Liberals won 46 percent of such races, the NDP 33 percent, and the Bloc 25 percent. To show how important close races were to the Conservatives in 2004, consider the following: of the ninety-nine seats that we won, fifteen were won by two percentage points or less. On the other hand, we only lost five seats where the margin was 2 percentage points or less. Winning 75 percent of these very close races saved Harper's leadership so that he could fight another day. As it was, there was quite a bit of grumbling about not living up to the expectations that arose during the course of the campaign. Suppose that the percentage of wins and losses in very close races had been reversed, so that the Conservatives, instead of winning fifteen of twenty close races, lost fifteen of twenty. That would have resulted in a Conservative caucus of eighty-nine rather than ninety-nine, and with that result there might have been more pressure on Stephen to resign.

As a result of the merger and all the new practices that we introduced in the 2004 campaign, the Conservative Party became a formidable opponent on the ground in close races. It is less clear how much of the improvement was due to the very costly DVC program. We are still working on ways to disentangle multiple causes and effects when we evaluate our campaign practices. Local victories are the joint result of large number of factors – including the identity of the national party leaders, advertising and media management in the national campaigns, the choice of local candidates, and changing demographics within the riding – all of which are outside the control of the candidate. Political science research indicates that the local campaign accounts at best for a few percentage points of difference. But in a close race where the winner gets the whole prize, every point is worth fighting for.

CANADA'S PUNIC WARS

Perhaps Stephen Harper's most important accomplishment in the 2004 campaign was to demonstrate that he and the new Conservative Party belonged on the national stage. For a considerable period of time, it looked as if we could win. Eventually, the Liberals regrouped while we made mistakes that cost us a victory, but it was a good showing for a new party and a new leader who had only had two months to get ready for their first national campaign. We were the first party of the right since 1993 that had been able to run a full slate of candidates and raise the money for a completely funded national campaign. Even though we lost, we showed that we were on the way up while the Liberals were on the way down.

The many skeptics who said that the merger between the Canadian Alliance and the Progressive Conservatives was not additive, that the new Conservative Party of Canada would not receive the sum of the 25.5 percent vote share that the Alliance had gotten in 2000 plus the 12.2 percent that went to the PCs, proved to be right in an arithmetic sense. The Conservatives received only 29.6 percent of the vote in 2004, so obviously a lot of votes went missing – about eight points of the total vote. Those defecting voters, however, did not accrue to the benefit of the Liberals, who also lost vote share – about four points – from 40.8 percent in 2000 to 36.7 percent in 2004. Many of the defectors must have stayed home or scattered to the NDP, Greens, Bloc Québécois, and smaller parties.

This scattering meant that the merger fulfilled expectations politically, if not arithmetically. Even while losing 8 percentage points of the so-called "right wing" vote, the Conservative Party was able to increase its seat total from seventy-three at dissolution (seventy-eight in the 2000 election) to ninety-nine. Even more important, that increase, coupled with gains made by the NDP and BQ, was enough to bring the Liberals down to a minority – and an unstable minority at that. It was unstable in the sense that no single party could keep the Liberal minority Government in power; after giving up the Speaker, the Liberals would need the support of the NDP plus independent Chuck Cadman to get a bare majority of 154 out of 307 votes (Cadman had been a Conservative but had run successfully as an independent in 2006 after losing the Conservative nomination battle in his riding). The result, to be sure, was a loss for the Conservatives – and a bitter loss, because for a time outright victory had seemed to be within reach – but it set up the short-lived Martin Government for defeat eighteen months later.

I like to compare the 2004 election campaign to the first of the three Punic Wars. In the First Punic War, Rome made the comparatively modest gain of taking Sicily from Carthage, which still remained the dominant power in the western Mediterranean. In the Second Punic War, Rome got control of the Iberian Peninsula and much of North Africa, reducing Carthage to secondary status. And in the Third Punic War, Rome defeated Carthage, razed it to the ground, and plowed salt into the fields so that nothing would ever grow there again, thus fulfilling the slogan of Cato the Elder that "Carthage must be destroyed!" (*Carthago delenda est*).

To continue the analogy, the 2004 election was our First Punic War, in which bringing the Liberals down to a minority government constituted modest progress. We fought our Second Punic War in 2005–06, got control of the government, and reduced the Liberals to opposition status, burdened with inadequate fund-raising and seeking a new leader. But what of the coming Third Punic War? Should our slogan be, *Liberales delendi sunt* ("the Liberals must be destroyed"), even if that were in our power? Objectively, it would probably be more in our interest to beat the Liberals down to about 20 percent of the vote, where they could duel for year with the NDP over Official Opposition status. Of course, none of this is really within our power to determine. Canadian voters will determine what happens.

In regional terms, our greatest achievement was to make a long-awaited breakthrough in Ontario, where we won 31.5 percent of the vote and twenty-four of 106 seats. Obviously, we had hoped to win even more, but twenty-four seats were enough to be considered significant. Equally important, they were the right seats for a conservative party to win as an Ontario beachhead. They were rural, small-town, and outer-suburban seats where the right-wing vote had traditionally been strong both federally and provincially. Some of these areas had voted Conservative for a hundred years until they encountered the split between Reform and the PCs. That this was a redoubt, not just a beachhead, would be shown in 2006, when we held every one of these twenty-four seats except for Belinda Stronach's, which we had lost when she defected to the Liberals.

The merger was also highly successful on the prairies. We went from twenty-four of twenty-six seats in Alberta to twenty-six of twenty-eight; in Saskatchewan we added three new seats, going from ten to thirteen of fourteen; and in Manitoba we held the five seats we had inherited while adding two seats in Winnipeg. This was an important regional breakthrough, for neither party of the right had held any Winnipeg seats since the crack-up of the Mulroney coalition. Vote-splitting had been hurting us there, just as it had in Ontario.

In the four provinces of Atlantic Canada, we did proportionately about as well as in Ontario – 30 percent of the vote and seven of thirty-two seats. The difference was that here we were not adding new seats but merely retaining the same number of seats that we held at dissolution. Also, our vote share in the region fell, not just below the total of the Alliance and PC vote but below the PC vote itself in 2000. It was obvious that voters in Atlantic Canada were still reticent about the new brand; and realization of that fact would lead Stephen to apologize early in the next campaign for his infamous "culture of defeat" remark.

Quebec, where we won no seats and only 8.8 percent of the vote, was a very weak performance. Our expectations were never high, but for a few days in week 4 when we were at 15 percent or even higher in the polls, we hoped we might be able to win a seat or two. The magnitude of our loss in Quebec led to Harper's dogged efforts, described in the next chapter, to improve in the province and ultimately to the breakthrough of 2006, when we elected ten candidates.

British Columbia was a strong performance in objective terms – twenty-two of thirty-six seats and 36.2 percent of the popular vote – but it was a disappointment in terms of expectations because in 2000 the Alliance had won 49.4 percent of the vote and twenty-seven of thirty-four seats. We didn't go into the campaign planning to lose five seats in BC, but that's what happened. Our slippage in BC, which got even worse in 2006 in terms of seats (though not in terms of popular vote) is a challenge for the Conservative Party, though unfortunately there is no agreement on the explanation of what is wrong.

One theory often heard from former Reformers and Alliance members is that the new Conservative brand doesn't sell well in BC because it is not populist enough. It is too establishment-oriented and does not appeal to those voters (numerous in BC) who were open to both the NDP and Reform/Alliance. There may be some truth in this, but it also needs to be remembered that 2000 was an exceptional election. The NDP that year was reeling from disclosures of corruption in the provincial government, which severely tarnished the federal brand even though they had nothing to do with federal politics. The NDP took only two seats and 11.3 percent of the vote in the federal election of 2000, less than half of their long-term historical average. In 2004, they bounced back to win five seats and 26.6 percent of the popular vote. Indeed, they bounced back even further in

2006, with 28.5 percent of the vote and ten seats. Perhaps the Alliance was just lucky in the timing of the 2000 election in BC, and the Conservatives should not expect to do as well ever again unless the NDP takes another dive. In any case, whether the problem is the merged Conservative brand or the self-generated ups and downs of the NDP, our party clearly has problems on that front.

Another explanation for our weakness in BC in 2004 is the growing popularity of the Liberals, who went from 27.7 percent of the vote and five seats in 2000, to 28.6 percent of the vote and eight seats in 2004. The Liberals had the advantage of their great strength among Chinese and South Asian voters, who continue to move into British Columbia, especially Vancouver, in large numbers; but they also pursued aggressive political strategies in BC, recruiting star candidates (David Emerson) and crossovers from other parties (Ujjal Dosanjh and Keith Martin), and identifying themselves with popular BC issues (the 2010 Winter Olympics, the Pacific Gateway). Harper fought back by mimicking Liberal stands on these issues and, after the 2006 election, recruiting David Emerson into his cabinet, with the hope of decapitating the Liberal organization in BC.

It is probably unrealistic for the Conservative Party to expect to dominate BC in the way it dominates Alberta. Vancouver is a much larger city than Calgary or Edmonton, there is a much larger immigrant population, and organized labour is far more powerful and politically aggressive than in Alberta. All these conditions tend to work against Conservative support. The Conservatives should continue to be the largest party in BC, but we will have to look elsewhere for most of the gains required to form a majority government.

7

Getting Ready Again, 2004–2005

2004

The results of the vote on 28 June 2004 were something of a shock. We had thought we might lose; but we expected at least to finish close to the Liberals, not to trail by seven percentage points of popular vote and thirty-six seats. Bringing the Liberals down to a minority government was important in terms of setting up our ultimate victory in 2006, but at the time it seemed like a minimal success.

Stephen was less than buoyant the next day, as recounted in the *Calgary Herald*:

> In comments on his campaign jet the morning after the Liberals eked out a minority win, Harper didn't rule out resigning the leadership of the party he helped build six months ago.
>
> "I'm going to take a little bit of time with my family, obviously I'm already talking to people across the country," he said when asked by reporters if he planned to soldier on as Conservative leader.
>
> "My sense is our people are pretty happy with where we've come in a short period of time."[1]

Many thought he was seriously considering resigning as leader, but I think he made these remarks to test sentiment in the party. If there was to be any attempt to overthrow him, he wanted to flush it out early. Reaction both within and outside the party was almost universal that he should stay on and lead the Conservatives into another election, so speculation about his resignation quickly died away.

Meanwhile, I agonized over the mistakes we had made. After a couple of weeks of obsessively replaying the campaign in my mind, I decided I wanted out. I was afraid I could not do better the next time, and I was nostalgic for the tranquility of university life. I also thought maybe Stephen would welcome the chance to find a more professional campaign manager. I called him and told him I wanted to quit; but when he urged me to stay on, the tone in his voice told me that he really did want me to continue. I agreed, therefore, albeit under slightly different conditions. Since we didn't expect a new election for at least a year, we decided that I could go back to teaching half-time at the university, while devoting the other half of my time to organizing the next campaign. Ken also told Stephen that he had taken him as far as he could, and that he should recruit Patrick Muttart as his political adviser. Ken then resigned from the OLO and went to work for Hill and Knowlton in Calgary.

The immediate task was to assess what had worked well in the last campaign and to figure out how to fix what had gone wrong. Contrary to the legend that grew up in the media toward the end of the 2006 campaign, there was no highly organized, well-structured review process that zeroed in on the problems and quickly came up with solutions. The senior people in the campaign wrote assessments that we passed around by email, but we refrained from holding a group retreat because we didn't want to touch off a round of damaging media stories. Everyone agreed that our fundraising, financial administration, field organization, and direct voter contact programs were basically sound and needed only marginal adjustments. We also readily agreed on what needed more fundamental change:

· We had to build an "indigenous" Quebec campaign, including "made in Quebec" advertising and communications.
· Our advertising had to become more regionally diverse and responsive to attacks from other parties.
· The leader's tour would have to be reorganized to do a better job of communicating the platform. The 2004 tour had

succeeded much better in logistics than in communications. We would have to have a daily plan that reached to the end of the campaign.

- Our war room communications would have to become more responsive to attacks and more capable of destabilizing our competitors.
- We had to have a better command-and-control structure, with better exchange of information between the leader's tour and the war room.

It was easier to agree upon what needed fixing than actually to fix it. None of us knew exactly what to do about these big challenges, but we started to grope toward improvements.

Stephen himself took personal control of the Quebec file. His first move was to give more prominence to Josée Verner, who had gotten 31 percent of the vote in the Quebec City riding of Louis-St Laurent, finishing second to the BQ candidate. Harper appointed Verner a member of the caucus and the shadow cabinet, as critic for the Minister of the Economic Development Agency of Canada for the Regions of Quebec and for La Francophonie. He also put Josée on the OLO payroll, with the full-time job of building the Conservative brand in Quebec. Several Francophone staff from Quebec were hired to work for the party in the field and for the OLO in Ottawa, in an attempt to create a French organizational, communications, and research presence within the overwhelmingly English Conservative establishment.

Stephen's other big initiative was to insist that the Conservative policy convention be held in Montreal in March 2005. This would challenge the party to find enough Quebec delegates to put up a respectable showing. It also represented a substantial personal risk for him, because he would have to face a leadership review at this convention. Holding it in Montreal would make it easier for the Red Tory members of Toronto, Quebec, and Atlantic Canada to attend, and harder for Harper's bedrock supporters from the West to get there.

None of these efforts bore any fruit for a frustratingly long time. Membership and support levels in Quebec remained flat until the middle of the 2005–06 election campaign. Although she worked hard, Josée had trouble pulling together the Conservative factions

in the province. Our support there was badly splintered among
Red Tory, ADQ, provincial Liberal, and religious social conservative groups, all of whom seemed to spend more time fighting each
other and sniping at the leader than building the party. Nevertheless, Stephen never gave up on his dream of making a breakthrough in Quebec. He repeatedly visited the province in the fall
of 2004 and kept searching for candidates and organizers, even
when many (including me) grumbled that he should be spending
more time in Ontario.

Even though I initially had no idea how I would do it, I told
Stephen that I would deal with advertising. Fortunately, Mike
Coates came to the rescue by introducing me to his friend Perry
Miele. Perry had worked as a staffer on the Hill and then gone
into the advertising business in the late years of the Mulroney
period. He built up the Gingko agency for commercial business
while he did political advertising under the Hogtown brand. He
accumulated priceless experience in political advertising by
working on a number of federal and Ontario PC campaigns.
More recently, he had sold Gingko to an international company
and moving on to investment banking. Though no longer in the
advertising business, he had connections he could mobilize to
build a virtual agency for the Conservative Party, like the Liberals' Red Leaf virtual agency spearheaded by Jack Bensimon of
Bensimon Byrne.

I first met Perry in August 2004, when Mike Coates brought
him along on one of his business trips to Calgary. We went out
for a steak dinner at Hy's, and the next day I took them fishing
on my favourite stretch of the Oldman River, where it comes out
of the mountains at the Livingston Gap. Perry is a serious fisher-
man who has published articles in fishing magazines, so I wanted
him to have a good experience, but nothing went right. To start,
Mike closed the car door on Perry's thousand-dollar Sage fly rod
and broke all four sections of it (fortunately the manufacturer
honoured the lifetime no-fault guarantee and rebuilt it). Then,
after we walked to the river, we found that a thunderstorm had
turned it chocolate brown instead of its usual brilliant blue-
green. Perry taped his rod together and actually found a few fish
in the turgid water; but every time he would hook a trout, his
broken rod would collapse and he would have to pull in the line

hand over hand. It wasn't exactly what we had expected, but we laughed a lot and got to know each other. More seriously, Perry and I talked at length about how to construct a virtual agency using a Toronto media buyer and creative teams from Toronto, Montreal, Calgary and perhaps elsewhere.

At this early stage of assessment, we weren't yet able to analyze all our problems with the media, but we did come up with some useful insights:

- We needed to plan the tour right to the end so that the leader wouldn't be forced to improvise.
- We should plan in advance for multiple possible endgames.
- We needed more communications staff on the tour to help deal with the media.
- The leader needed a senior adviser with him on the tour to provide better communication with the war room. This would also be a key part of creating a better decision-making process.
- We should hold fewer rallies and more message events, and schedule these message events earlier in the day in order to get a jump on the news cycle.
- The war room had to do a better job with "destabilizers" directed at the other parties. Our performance in that department had been weak in 2004. We were constantly reacting to their attacks rather than putting them off balance with our own.

Ken recommended that we start immediately to develop a "moving script," so as to be ready whenever an election might come. Maybe I should have pushed harder on this file, but I assumed Stephen would make it happen when he was ready. In the meantime I concentrated on establishing the infrastructure for the next Leader's Tour. Given our good relationship with Air Canada, it was an easy decision to go back to them. We were more conflicted about Greyhound, so we spent several months researching other possibilities. We found, however, that the few other charter companies in Canada with truly national reach were not interested in having their buses torn apart and rebuilt to fit our specifications. In the end, we realized Greyhound was our best bet, and in a December meeting with senior management we worked out the kinks in our relationship.

We did not, however, simply want to repeat what we had done in 2004. We realized that six buses – three for the east and three for the west – were too many, that we couldn't really use a full fleet of three Western buses because of the great distances in Western Canada. We decided, therefore, to lease four buses – a leader's bus and two media buses for Eastern Canada, and a somewhat simplified leader's bus for Western Canada. We would rent day buses for the media to complement the leader's bus when the tour was in the West. That was our plan at the time, though in the end we rented only the three buses for the East, and did everything in the West with day buses. Leasing fewer buses saved several hundred thousand dollars in rental and conversion charges and helped us afford the eight-week 2005–06 campaign.

Another thing we did in fall 2004 was draw up writ-period and pre-writ campaign budgets to guide our planning. One of our strong points in 2004 had been strict financial control, and we wanted to continue in that vein. For many line items, the new campaign budget closely resembled its 2004 counterpart, but we were determined to spend more on advertising. We therefore cut voter contact considerably, and many other things less drastically, in order to set aside more funds for advertising, including creative, production, and the media buy.

In early fall 2004, we also started to build on the success of our DVC program. Michael Davis and Andrew Langhorne came up with a broad set of suggestions for reconfirming and enlarging our pool of identified supporters. Working on those suggestions for the last two years, we have now built up a "voter vault" of millions of Conservative supporters. We contact them frequently by direct mail, email, and telephone to find out about their policy concerns and the depth of their support. This continual cultivation of the grassroots is an important part of the success of the Conservative Party.

EARLY 2005

Late in 2004, Stephen decided to try to use same-sex marriage, which would be on the Parliamentary agenda for the first half of 2005, to pry part of the ethnic vote away from the Liberals. He instructed me to get Perry Miele, who had now more or less assembled his virtual agency in Toronto, to develop some simple print ads on marriage, translate them into appropriate foreign languages, and run them in ethnic weeklies in early 2005. Ethnic voters – especially Chinese, Indo-Canadians, and Italians – were the main target, but we also decided to place English and French versions of the ads in Roman Catholic newspapers, as well as in rural weeklies in Ontario and Atlantic Canada where we had lost to the Liberals in 2004 by close margins.

One can debate whether same-sex marriage was the right issue, but Stephen's basic thinking was sound. Just as the Conservative Party will never become a majority party without some support in Quebec, it also needs to cut into the traditional Liberal bastions of Roman Catholic and immigrant voters, who have sustained that party over generations.[2] In terms of the "three sisters" theory that Stephen and I had developed to guide the rebuilding of a conservative coalition, ethnic voters have now become a "fourth sister" that must be drawn into the Conservative voting coalition if it is to achieve long-term success. The Republicans have pursued similar strategies in the United States. They haven't yet made great progress with African-Americans, but they do get a majority of the ever-growing Asian vote. Ronald Reagan appealed successfully to Roman Catholics, and George W. Bush worked on the Hispanic vote. There is no law of nature that says Roman Catholics and people of colour have to vote for a left-of-centre party; indeed, the basic values of these voters are often more conservative than liberal.

The ad campaign offered a chance of attracting large numbers of new supporters, but there was also a risk of losing some existing support among Red Tories by stressing opposition to legalizing same-sex marriage. "I would not have run the ads," Belinda Stronach said after they came out in print; and Peter MacKay, with whom she was now a romantic item, groused in public that he had not been consulted. Stephen's response was typical: "I've never considered caucus a focus group for advertising."[3]

In the end, we spent about $300,000 to produce, translate, and run print ads in dozens of ethnic, Catholic, and rural weeklies over several weeks in early 2005. As advertising goes, this was a minuscule campaign, but it attracted a lot of attention in major media outlets. In the next election, we won most of the rural

ridings in which we ran these ads, and our vote share among Roman Catholics also went up, but it is hard to trace cause and effect. We also attracted some ethnic candidates and workers to the
Conservative cause, but the election results were disappointing.
None of our numerous new visible minority candidates across the
country got elected, and we didn't win the ridings in Montreal,
Toronto, and Vancouver where the ethnic vote is decisive.

We started to speed up our campaign preparations in early
2005. With a new budget in the offing, there was an increased
probability that the opposition parties might precipitate an election. I told a meeting of caucus in January that the campaign
team's goal was to be ready to go whenever they might decide to
bring down the government. Brave words, but the reality was
not so simple! Not enough progress was made on scripting because the people now on the team in Ottawa were not the ones
who had done the scripting in 2004.

We therefore did what we could in early 2005 to get ready for
an election. We told Watermark to start designing print materials
such as lawn signs, posters, and pamphlets; and we commissioned the usual research effort to underpin an advertising campaign – a national baseline poll and focus groups in key markets
across the country. But I breathed a little easier after Stephen's
controversial decision to support the Liberal budget and take
credit for its proposed corporate tax cuts and increased military
spending. "There's nothing in this budget that would justify an
election at this time," Harper said. "In fact, I'm a lot happier
than I thought I would be. The major priorities in this budget are
Conservative ones."[4] On 9 March 2005, the Conservatives ab-
stained when the budget was voted upon.[5] That made a spring
election seem unlikely, meaning we could all concentrate on the
Montreal convention.

THE CONVENTION

Stephen's decision to hold the convention in Montreal had faced
us with a double challenge: getting a respectable number of delegates from Quebec, where the party was weak; and encouraging
his loyal supporters from the West to attend, so there would not
be any embarrassments in the leadership review. Using surplus

money left over from Stephen's campaign for the Conservative leadership, we hired Rob Griffith, who had managed Stephen's local campaign in Calgary Southwest, to track the delegate selection process. He and John Weissenberger called all the ridings in the West and parts of Ontario, making sure that slates of Harper-friendly delegates were being put forward. We also paid for autodial messages to encourage members identified as Harper supporters to turn out at these selection meetings. We quickly discovered that Stephen was overwhelmingly popular in the West, though there were isolated pockets of two types of opposition: traditional Tories, who would probably be unhappy with any leader from the Reform side, and Reform populists, who thought Stephen's leadership was too dictatorial. It was slightly alarming that, in Calgary and Vancouver, these two opposition factions were beginning to find each other and make common cause; and indeed that turned into a more serious problem on the floor of the convention in Montreal.

The main task at the convention was to achieve the political objectives required to carry us into the next election. A committee consisting of Nicky Eaton, Gary Lunn, Patrick Muttart, and Ken Boessenkool had worked for weeks planning the event. Ken also worked with Stephen to draft the necessary policy resolutions and plan the voting agenda to make sure they would have a good chance to pass. Securing results was the job of Doug Finley, who set up an operations centre at the convention (we didn't know until publication of Don Martin's book that Belinda Stronach also had her own operations centre, run by John Laschinger).[6]

Four important battles were being waged simultaneously at the convention:

- Stephen Harper had to score well in the leadership review. We wanted Harper to get at least 80 percent because we thought that would deter any future sniping and subversion from opponents and malcontents.
- A number of policy issues that would be important for the coming election were up for debate at Montreal. Although Stephen had not wagered his prestige by engaging in open advocacy, he hoped the delegates would adopt positions he regarded as politically essential, including:

- A completely free vote in the House of Commons on legislat-
  ing same-sex marriage (the position he had taken from the
  beginning);
- A promise that a Conservative Government would not introduce or support any legislation on abortion (to prevent being
  trapped by an issue that had hurt us in the 2004 election);
- Endorsement of official bilingualism and recognition of the
  "fiscal imbalance" in the federal system (essential to his
  Quebec strategy);
- Support for supply management (required for a party such
  as ours that is so dependent on rural votes in Ontario and
  Quebec);
- Dropping the Reform heritage of direct democracy (referendum, initiative, recall), which had proved so problematic in
  the 2000 election campaign.

- A constitution for the Conservative Party had to be approved
  at Montreal. The draft put power primarily in the hands of the
  leader and secondarily in the hands of the chairman of the
  Conservative Fund, who was appointed by the leader. Against
  this was a movement, supported both by old Reformers who
  wanted to make the party more populist and Red Tories who
  wanted to weaken Harper, to subordinate the Conservative
  Fund to the National Council, thus eroding the leader's control
  over fundraising and financial management.
- Another constitutional issue involved the formula for electing
  future leaders. Equal representation by riding had been the formula used in the merger "Agreement in Principle," but changes
  could now be made through constitutional amendment. Scott
  Reid was planning to bring an amendment to modify the equality formula slightly, by providing that an EDA would not get its
  full number of points for leadership selection unless it had at
  least one hundred members.

In the all-important leadership ballot, Harper received 84 percent support, high enough to squelch any claims that the party's
members were unhappy with his leadership. Harper's own performance did more than anything else to ensure a strong endorsement. Friday evening, he gave perhaps his best speech to date
(composed with help from David Frum), stressing the harmonious

diversity of the party: "This is the party of Jason Kenney and Jim Prentice; of Belinda Stronach and Stockwell Day; of Peter Mackay and John Reynolds; of Preston Manning and Brian Mulroney."[7] For two years, Ray Novak and Carolyn Stewart-Olsen had been trying to get Harper to use a teleprompter. He had experimented with it once at a minor occasion, but this was the first time he had used it for a major speech. It improved his delivery considerably, and he has used it consistently for major occasions ever since. Ray and Carolyn blanched when I joked afterward that it had worked so well that Stephen should start using it to address Ben and Rachel at home. "Don't joke about it," they said; "it took too much effort to get him to try it." Harper is adventurous politically, but he is a true conservative by temperament in anything that affects him personally.

On the policy front, all the necessary resolutions passed without any real arm-twisting; delegates had drawn the lessons of past campaigns and were in a mood to vote for electoral success, not doctrinal purity. The only close call involved fiscal imbalance, which was initially defeated in an early-morning workshop session when some Quebec delegates failed to show up. The problem was resolved by re-introducing it in another workshop as an economic policy.

The constitution was a tougher challenge. Early workshop votes made it clear that there was substantial support for party "democracy," i.e., putting financial and organizational management under the control of the elected National Council rather than the appointed Conservative Fund. In an attempt to persuade delegates that the party was already under sound management and that constitutional amendments were not needed, Conservative Fund Chairman Irving Gerstein addressed a lunch-time plenary session and released an unprecedented amount of information about our finances and fundraising programs. But his presentation, which had worked extraordinarily well with caucus just a few weeks ago, couldn't reach such a large audience. Three thousand delegates eating boxed lunches had trouble focusing on spreadsheets and fiscal projections.

Seeing that they still faced substantial opposition over the constitution, Doug Finley and Ian Brodie worked out a late-night compromise with the insurgent forces. The leader could still

appoint the members of the Fund as well as the executive director of the party, but the appointment would have to be approved
by the Council.[8] Both the leader and the Fund would have to report quarterly to the Council, and the Council would have the
right to be consulted about the budget, though its approval
would not be required.[9] A compromise that everyone could live
with, it reversed the tendency of both the Reform Party and the
Progressive Conservatives in the 1990s to put fundraising and financial administration under the control of the elected council.[10]

When Scott Reid's motion for an adjustment to the equality-of-
ridings formula passed at an early-morning workshop on Friday,
18 March, Peter MacKay rushed out and spoke to the media in
apocalyptic terms about how this change threatened the future of
the party because it attacked a fundamental principle of the
merger. Stories immediately started flashing around the country
about the peril to party unity. Influential party members such as
John Reynolds, assuming that MacKay as deputy leader was
speaking for the leader, quickly supported him. Delegates in general, fearing that unity was threatened, swung over to Peter's side,
and Reid's resolution died an early death. In spite of that, Peter's
immoderate language led to threatening headlines after the first
day of the convention, such as these beauties:

"Tories face new divide: MacKay fuming over a bid to quash
unity provision"[11]
"Angry MacKay warns merger in jeopardy"[12]

Harper was furious that MacKay's unexpected action was
stepping all over his own message, but at this point there was no
good response.[13] The MacKay affair, however, proved to be a
mere hiccup. Rebound headlines in the following days were uni-
formly positive as the party's unity behind Harper became obvious to even the most cynical reporters. "Harper wins over party
skeptics," was the theme of Peter O'Neill's wrap-up story in the
Vancouver Sun.[14] Maybe Peter MacKay even did us a favour by
creating a little drama of threat and recovery – first we were tot-
tering on the brink of dissolution, then we were uniting around
the leader in a cloud of good feeling. I would have preferred
Scott Reid's motion to pass, perhaps in amended form, but its

defeat did not create any problems in the present. Harper's leadership was secure because of the 84 percent vote of endorsement, and there would be no new leadership race to worry about.

At the end of the day, we were quite satisfied with the convention. We had attracted 3,600 people to Montreal and broken even financially on the event, presented a united front around the leader, and passed both the constitution and the policy book that we needed to move forward. In a post-convention poll, Praxicus showed that our convention had had a more positive effect on voters than the Liberal convention that had been held a few weeks earlier. While not complacent, we were daring to relax a little. The convention about which we had fretted for months was successfully concluded, and there seemed little chance of an early election because Stephen had announced his support of Ralph Goodale's budget. I was beginning to think my wife and I would get to use the airline tickets for a June trip to Europe that we had booked in a moment of optimism.

THE ELECTION THAT WASN'T

The feeling of relaxation, however, did not last long. In early April, astounding revelations seeped out of the Gomery Commission hearings as Jean Brault began to testify. On 29 March, Justice Gomery had temporarily imposed a media ban on reporting the testimony of three witnesses,[15] but the Conservative Party was allowed to have an observer there who was keeping us informed. Also, an American blogger – "Captain Ed" of Minneapolis/St Paul – was posting the highlights of testimony after getting them from someone attending Gomery's daily sessions.[16] As lurid revelations about money in paper bags and kickbacks to the Liberal Party poured out, Liberal support started to sink in the polls and ours started to rise. Don Martin called it "Canada's Watergate,"[17] and an Ekos poll published on 11 April gave us a seven-point lead over the Liberals in Ontario.[18] A spring election suddenly seemed possible again. In a conference call in early April, we decided to put our campaign preparations into high gear.

Certain things were relatively easy to do on short notice, and our fundraising had been so successful that Irving Gerstein could

give us the green light to spend whatever was necessary. Ian Brodie's assistant, Jaime Beauregard, who was already looking for
war-room space, found that our current landlord had an appropriate vacant suite just around the corner from party headquarters. Deputy Campaign Manager Doug Finley was in Ottawa all
the time and so could proceed immediately to get this space wired
and equipped while he also worked on a staffing plan. We already had a detailed plan for voter ID to be done later in the year
as part of the preparation for an anticipated 2006 election, so we
told RMG to get it done in April and May; that changed the cash
flow somewhat but didn't fundamentally alter the 2005 budget.

We were a bit further behind on developing our advertising,
but the basic research had been done over the winter. Polling and
focus groups had shown that we faced two major hurdles if we
were to push ahead of the Liberals. First, our policy profile was
weak; we did not really "own" any major issue areas except for
criminal justice. It was not surprising that voters perceived the
Liberals to be stronger than the Conservatives in social-policy
areas such as health care and the environment; but it was dis-
couraging that voters also preferred the Liberals for cutting
taxes, managing the economy, defending the national interest,
and improving Canada's relations with the United States. The
second finding was that voters saw Paul Martin as a better
leader than Stephen Harper. Harper's rating had gone up for a
while during the 2004 campaign but had fallen at the end and
had stayed down ever since.

After seeing the research, Perry Miele proposed a simultaneous
attack on these problems in a program of positive advertising.
His virtual agency would create ads associating Harper with our
signature policies in fields such as tax cuts and child care. And
because Harper at the time was individually not strong in the
public eye, the ads would promote a "team" concept, showing
him discussing policy with some of our younger, more photogenic caucus members, such as Rona Ambrose, Josée Verner, Diane
Finley, Rahim Jaffer, and Peter MacKay.

Stephen accepted the team concept, but he was most concerned about policy content in the ads. After a long talk with
him on this subject in April, I sent Perry the following message:

WE MUST DEFINE OURSELVES IN OUR OWN ADS FROM THE
OUTSET BEFORE THE LIBERALS DEFINE US. He [Stephen]
came back to that point repeatedly. I think you intend to do
that in the brand ads. They must have policy content – special
prosecutor, tax cuts, child care, etc.

To emphasize the point, I attached a long quotation from Australian Prime Minister John Howard, the gist of which was that
an opposition party could not hope to win simply by criticizing
the government. "People," said Mr Howard, "are looking for a
sharper definition of what the alternative government stands
for."[19] But it was difficult to carry this out at the time because
we didn't have the platform yet.

Brand ads would be one side of the equation; the other would
be hard-hitting fact-based ads of the type that we had lacked in
2004. Perry's people had come into possession of an unflattering
picture of Paul Martin, around which they proposed to build a
series of ads on themes such as "You can't afford Paul Martin."
After Stephen approved the general concepts, Perry and his team
plunged into a full-scale creative and production process. In the
end, they created and produced a suite of eight brand ads, plus
story boards for several fact-based ads to appear later in the
campaign. It was a real foot race, but we would have been ready
to go if we had defeated the Liberals on the 19 May vote.

Patrick Muttart, incidentally, was a great help in getting ready.
Already in Toronto as an employee of Jaime Watt's Navigator
agency, he volunteered to work with Perry, who was no longer in
the advertising business and thus did not have an agency at his
disposal. Patrick's presence helped considerably in driving the
creative and production activity forward.

Perry's team also came up with the English campaign slogan,
"Stand Up for Canada." Around the world, Conservative parties
rarely win elections unless they become identified as the party of
patriotism; certainly that has been true of the Republicans in the
United States and the Conservatives in Great Britain. But we
would have to work to reclaim the ground of Canadian patriotism
that the Liberals had managed to appropriate for themselves.
"Stand Up for Canada" would be a first step in that direction.

Obviously, we would need a different slogan in Quebec. Republik, the agency that Perry had recruited to work with us in Montreal, offered several proposals that we discussed at a May meeting in Ottawa. Richard Décarie, then deputy chief of staff in the OLO, came up with the final wording: "Changeons pour vrai," which might be translated as "Let's really change things." This slogan was directed against the impotence of the Bloc Québécois, which, while claiming to defend Quebec's interests, could never be part of a government and thus could never bring about the changes that might appeal to Quebec voters. The choice of slogan reflected the strategic situation in Quebec, in which many of our winnable seats in and around Quebec City were held by the Bloc, not by the Liberals. The slogan also fit perfectly with the advertising that Republik wanted to develop, stressing the powerlessness of the Bloc to effect real change. My favourite among their creative concepts, which played on the French verb "débloquer," meaning "unblock" or "liberate," showed a bicycle rider pumping hard but going nowhere because the front of his bike was attached to a stationary block of cement, not a rolling wheel. Compared to where we had been in 2004, we were miles ahead in conceptualizing our Quebec campaign. We were not just translating concepts and scripts conceived by Anglophones for English Canada, we had advertising and a slogan rooted in Quebec's political dynamics.

All aspects of campaign preparation were now in hand except for platform, message, daily scripting, and tour planning. Although some work had been done to update the 2004 platform, it could not have been finalized before our policy manual was voted upon at the Montreal convention. It was now crucial to get the platform finished as soon as possible because scripting and the tour schedule depended on the contents of the platform.

I received what I was told was the final platform on Friday, 6 May. From a literary point of view, it needed a lot of editing. I worked throughout that Mother's Day weekend (survival of my marriage is the real miracle!), rewriting it twice, getting it under eighty pages, making it consistent in format and easier to understand. Then I forwarded it to Watermark to be formatted for publication, only to learn that the "final" version I had received was not really final. For the next several days, changes continued to drift in as people in Ottawa had further thoughts.

In the midst of trying to keep up with these changes while proofreading Watermark's work, I made a potentially catastrophic mistake. Wanting to send a newly rewritten version back to Ottawa, I clicked the "Send" icon and off went our top-secret platform draft to the wrong person. I did not realize anything was wrong until a day passed without a response. When I called, I learned that my new re-draft had never been received and people were wondering where it was.

The incorrect address I had used belonged to someone who had a name quite similar to my intended recipient but who had left the employment of Parliament several weeks previously and thus had not accessed his account even though it was still open. Once we understood what had happened, Phil Murphy got the parliamentary IT staff to go into the account and delete the file containing the platform. There was no record that the platform had been forwarded to anyone else, and no report of a leak ever appeared in the media, so we escaped without damage.

This never-used 2005 platform was more like a longer version of its 2004 predecessor than like the one that eventually helped us win the 2006 election. Although it was full of detail, it lacked the imaginative policies that came to define our later campaign. Not that the content was bad; indeed, it was full of moderate, feasible proposals to make government work better. But it needed to be reworked to appeal more to ordinary voters.

An equally serious problem was difficulty in preparing a day-by-day plan for communicating the contents of the platform. Nothing of this type had been done while the platform was under preparation, and staff had trouble coming to grips with the challenge even after the platform was completed. When I look back at that spring, I see that we were caught up in trying to force an election, to the detriment of actually preparing for it. Ken Boessenkool, who had led the scripting process in the last campaign, was now back in Calgary and no one in Ottawa seemed to be able to push the scripting forward. Ken was in Ottawa frequently that spring but could not galvanize people into action. At one point, I asked Doug Finley to call staff together, but still no results were forthcoming. Ken then came out to Ottawa about two weeks before we hoped to defeat the government and got some work going, but it was dangerously little and late. If we had actually defeated the government on 19 May, we would have been going into a campaign with only the first week already planned and an unclear macro-messaging strategy. The writing team would have had to work like madmen to draft all the speeches and news releases required for the rest of the campaign. It could have been disastrous, given what we had learned in the last campaign about the dangers of improvisation.

FORTUNATE FAILURE

After putting the campaign team on high alert in early April, Stephen chose to proceed in stages rather than try to get an immediate vote of non-confidence. He declined to support the Bloc Québécois, which wanted to press for a non-confidence vote at its next Opposition Day, scheduled for 14 April. This was partly a strategic decision: he didn't want to go into a national election triggered by supporting a BQ motion. But it was also practical: we didn't have a completed platform, a campaign script, or television ads in the can, and it would take several weeks to finish developing these indispensable campaign tools.

In the meanwhile, the Liberals pulled out all the stops in order to stay in power. They withdrew the budget implementation bill from the order paper, so they could not be defeated on that front. They also postponed all Opposition Days until the end of the session, thus forestalling any vote of non-confidence introduced by an opposition party.[20] On the political front, they ratcheted up their attacks on Harper, depicting him as angry, power-hungry, and in bed with the Bloc Québécois. They also started cutting deals with provinces, cities, and special interest groups, offering funding that, they said, would not be forthcoming if their government was defeated. That tactic succeeded brilliantly in stirring up an angry swarm of premiers, big-city mayors, and special-interest apologists, shouting that an early election would threaten their vital interests.

Carried away by the Gomery revelations, we had made a classic mistake of political gamesmanship; we hadn't given our opponents enough respect. We had failed to think through the options they possessed and the tactics they could employ. We were trying to implement a plan conceived without full attention to what our cunning, experienced, and desperate opponents might do to save their skins.

Another surprise came on 21 April, when Paul Martin requested national media time to address the nation. He apologized – sort of – for Adscam, saying he and the Liberal Party in general should have been more vigilant; but such a frail apology carried little weight with the public. More importantly, he promised to call an election within thirty days of receiving Justice Gomery's final report, then expected for 15 December 2006.[21] That would have implied an election in early 2006, about eight months away – time enough for the Liberals to absorb Gomery's findings and reposition themselves as the party of the new broom – no more far-fetched than many other Liberal transformations over the years.

Stephen thought Martin "looked weak" when he made his speech, and polling suggested that was correct in the short term. We had been one or two points ahead of the Liberals ever since 8 April. After Martin's speech on 21 April, our lead started to grow even larger, so Stephen felt confident about the next step in the plan. Parliament was to recess on 22 April and reconvene on 2 May. He therefore instructed caucus members to go back to their ridings and consult their voters on whether they should force an election. But this was risky because polling had been showing all along that voters were not keen on an early election. When asked whether they wanted an election right now or would rather wait for the Gomery report, far more picked the latter option. The Liberals would have had the same information from their own polling, which had led, no doubt, to Martin's televised promise of 21 April.

On 26 April, Paul Martin and Jack Layton made a deal to keep the Liberals in power. Layton, noting Martin's weakness in his televised speech, saw the opportunity to advance his party's policy objectives by throwing Martin a lifeline. The price Martin had to pay was to rewrite his budget – cancel $3.6 billion in tax cuts for business and add $4.6 billion in expenditures for various areas favoured by the NDP.[22] Now the Liberals and NDP could unite around talking points that this Parliament was working for the people of Canada, and it would be wrong to cut short its life. That left only the Conservatives and the Bloc wanting a speedy election. Liberal spinners could have a field day with Harper's alleged lust for power and Duceppe's desire to break up the country.[23] The whole strategic situation had shifted to our detriment, but Stephen denounced the budget accord as fiscally irresponsible, saying that it closed the case for an election.[24] Only a few days ago he had told caucus members to ask voters whether they wanted an election, but now he was saying that an election was essential, even as the Liberals finally had a semi-plausible reason to postpone it.

There was a special Conservative caucus meeting on the evening of Monday, 2 May, when Parliament reconvened. Stephen got the support he wanted from caucus for defeating the government, but Belinda Stronach publicly opposed the strategy of an early election before she walked into the meeting.[25] She could have spoken her mind inside without repercussions, but making her opposition public was a different matter altogether. The next day, Stephen called her in for a meeting with the Conservative House Leader and Whip as witnesses. He reportedly told her to stop undermining his leadership and that he would see to it that she never became leader herself.[26]

Belinda took her revenge on 17 May when she defected to the Liberals. I was at the OLO that Tuesday morning, meeting with Jason Kenney and Geoff Norquay before another meeting scheduled with the leader at 10 AM, when Ray Novak came in to say that Belinda was going to make an announcement that morning. Ray had received a call from Peter MacKay's office; Belinda had just told Peter that her decision to defect was final. According to published accounts, she and Peter had been up most of the night discussing it, and for a time he thought he had dissuaded her, but in the end she decided to make the break.[27]

You have to admire the ice water in Belinda's veins. She had attended our candidate training college and campaign kick-off over the weekend, chatted with dozens of people, and never let on a thing. Conservative House Leader Jay Hill told me later that he had spoken with her a long time that weekend and she seemed very well adjusted to the party. She was well adjusted to the party – just not to our party. Incidentally, it is untrue that I embarrassed Belinda at the candidate college by using a picture of her in a warning against bad media optics.[28] I did speak to nominated candidates at the event, but I didn't talk about media and I didn't say anything about Belinda. These and other stories in Don Martin's credulous biography of Belinda seem to be an attempt to create a legend that she was driven out of the Conservatives by an unkind leader and his henchmen.

Our media response to Belinda's defection was not as good as it should have been. We had information on Belinda's overspending in the Conservative leadership campaign, and in fact some of the information had been leaked two months previously;[29] but no one thought to Blackberry it to the reporters at her press conference until it was too late. The story did get out, but just barely, and it never had any impact because it was so poorly handled.[30] I remember thinking at the time, "this has got to change."

After Belinda's defection, our chances of winning the non-confidence vote scheduled for 19 May came down to the four independents. We knew Caroline Parish would vote with the Liberals, because on 19 May, after a bout of abdominal pain had led to a doctor's visit, she said, "Come hell or high water, there's no frigging way I'm going to let one ovary bring the government down."[31] We expected David Kilgour and Pat O'Brien to vote with us; these latter two had left the Liberal caucus over same-sex marriage and no longer had any desire to support Paul Martin. Independent Chuck Cadman was the swing voter. If he voted with the Conservatives in favour of the motion, it would carry by one vote and we would have an election. If he voted with the Liberals, there would be a tie, which the Speaker would break in favour of the Liberals, and they would continue in government.

Doug Finley wanted to make one last attempt to persuade Cadman to rejoin the Conservative caucus, but Chuck was very sick with skin cancer – he would be dead in two months[32] – and wasn't answering his phone. I dropped into Doug Finley's office about 1 PM on 19 May, just a few hours before the scheduled vote on our non-confidence motion, and found he couldn't get through to Chuck. I called John Reynolds, who called Gary Lunn, who was able to get us fifteen minutes with Cadman at 3 PM. Chuck was gracious when he received us in his Parliamentary office, but he was visibly tired, and I could see that he wasn't up to negotiating a return to caucus. The last thing he wanted right now was an election. I knew then that we would lose the vote, which we did a couple hours later.

That Doug and I made this last desperate try with Cadman shows how we were all caught up in the attempt to force an election. We were fully aware of how far behind our campaign scripting was; in fact, we were in the middle of working with Ken and others to kick-start the scripting process. Nonetheless, we did everything we could toward defeating the Liberals in the House of Commons. It's an excellent example of how the passions of politics lead to decisions that later make you scratch your head.

As if failing to defeat the Liberals wasn't enough for Stephen, he was also burdened the same week with the Gurmant Grewal affair.[33] In their drive to stay in power, the Liberals tried to entice several of our caucus members, including Belinda Stronach, Inky Mark, Lee Richardson, and Gurmant and Nina Grewal, to join the Liberals or at least sit as independents. Apart from Belinda, they were particularly interested in Gurmant, because he and his wife Nina had two votes, which would stabilize their margin of victory. Gurmant entered into discussions with fellow Sikh Ujjal Dosanjh, and then with Paul Martin's chief of staff, Tim Murphy. At a certain point, he started to "wear a wire" and record their conversations. He produced four cassettes plus a "highlights" reel, which he turned over to the OLO communications department. The tapes were not easy going because much of the conversation was in Punjabi. OLO communications staff, in trying to produce a digital version for posting on the internet, got the "highlights" tape mixed in with the four originals. The result was a posted version with breaks in it that were diagnosed by some experts as evidence of tampering.[34] Stephen finally called in Doug Finley, who sent the communications staff home and brought in a whole new team of people to work day and night through the weekend and sort out the mess. But it was too late to undo the damage because Stephen, having been given inaccurate information, had gone out on a limb to support the accuracy of the "Grewal tapes."[35]

On top of all that, there was also the Labrador by-election scheduled for 24 May 2006. Doug Finley had recruited the former mayor of Labrador City as our candidate, and we were going all out to win this historically Liberal seat because it would destabilize the tenuous Liberal control of the House of Commons. The party chartered a jet for Harper so that he could spend the weekend in Labrador campaigning for our candidate. But it turned into another disappointment as the Liberal candidate, the president of the Labrador Metis Association, held onto the seat.

Failing to defeat the Liberals on 19 May was depressing at the time, but it turned out to be a blessing in disguise. When the NDP decided to support the Liberals, the strategic configuration shifted against us. We would have been sailing against the current, propelled by an overly detailed platform without dramatic selling points and steered by a scripting team scrambling to get a few days ahead. It would have been hard to win under those circumstances.

Belinda Stronach's defection was also a serious blow. Though it helped in the long run by removing a permanent source of disaffection from the party, it dropped our standing in the polls by several points. Belinda delivered a cutting attack on Harper when she announced her defection: "I've been uncomfortable for some time with the direction the leader of the Conservative Party has been taking ... . I do not believe the party leader is truly sensitive to the needs of each part of the country and how big and complicated Canada really is."[36] It didn't help when Stephen commented, "I've never noticed complexity to be Belinda's strong point."[37]

Three days before her defection, Ipsos-Reid had reported that we were leading the Liberals 31 percent to 27 percent.[38] Our internal polling was not quite as favourable, but still showed us neck-and-neck with the Liberals. Then, in one night, we went from being tied with the Liberals in our tracking poll to three points behind.

In the long run Belinda's departure was beneficial, but in the short run the Conservatives and especially Stephen Harper suffered a heavy blow in Ontario public opinion. Many Ontarians seemed to see Harper as responsible for driving Belinda out of the party. That, together with the fallout from the Grewal affair and the Liberal attacks on Harper as angry and power-hungry, would keep us down in the polls for several months. An 8 June

Decima Research poll showed the Liberals 14 points ahead of the Conservatives: 37 percent to 23 percent.[39]

On the positive side, this failure forced Stephen to confront weaknesses in his organization. It cost him weeks and even months of gloom, but he emerged stronger, tougher, and more resilient, surrounded by a bigger, more capable, more unified campaign team. Future historians will see his response to adversity as his political coming of age. Those close to him that summer say the turning came about 5 PM on 16 June 2005, when Peter MacKay came into his office carrying a football. Stephen loosened his tie and said, "Let's go." Then the two of them went out on the Parliamentary lawn and played catch for about twenty minutes, creating odd photo ops of Harper wearing a business suit while throwing a football. When I saw the picture at my breakfast table in Calgary, I smiled because I knew this (for Stephen) unusually spontaneous act meant he was ready to stop second-guessing himself over his recent reverses and get back on the campaign trail.

COPING WITH ADVERSITY

After the debacle on 19 May, I had to make some personal decisions. When we failed to force an election, we entered a pre-writ campaign of uncertain duration, probably six to ten months. There needed to be a campaign manager in Ottawa all the time to look after the details of enhanced travel, policy development, and communications required by an extended pre-writ campaign. I could not manage it properly from Calgary, even with a lot of commuting, because a major part of what needed to be done involved staff in Ottawa. Our failure to be entirely ready for a spring campaign in 2005 illustrated the dilemma. If I had been in Ottawa all the time, I could have driven the scripting forward, but I couldn't be in Ottawa all the time because I was teaching half-time at the University of Calgary. I decided, therefore, to resign as campaign manager and recommend that Stephen replace me with Doug Finley, for whom my respect had been steadily growing. Doug was a much more experienced campaigner than I was, and I felt he could do a better job than I could, particularly because he was a full-time employee located in Ottawa. It would not be an abrupt transition, for as deputy campaign manager he was already dealing with a large share of campaign business.

I also decided it was time to challenge Stephen with some observations about his leadership style and how it interacted with his organization. A number of things that had not gone well the past spring – including platform development, scripting, and the fiasco of the Grewal tapes – reflected deeper organizational issues. So I wrote a long memo for Stephen to analyze what I saw as the main problems. I suggested that he had pushed his hands-on style of political management, laudable in itself, beyond the point of diminishing returns. He was so deeply involved in managing policy, strategy, and communications that his own ability to make decisions was becoming overloaded. The memo was quite hard-hitting in spots, but Stephen took it in stride. He thought about it for a few weeks and then invited me to dinner to discuss it further. Afterward he initiated the changes that took "Harper's Team" from a contender to a winner.

To reorganize his office and link it more effectively to the campaign machinery, Stephen appointed Doug Finley as deputy chief of staff while also continuing as campaign manager. Not long afterward, he appointed as his new chief of staff Ian Brodie, who had been deputy chief of staff in the OLO until he became national director of the Conservative Party in April 2004. This allowed Doug Finley, who lives for campaigning and had no desire to be an OLO administrator, to return to the party and spend all his time getting ready for the campaign that Paul Martin had already announced for next winter.

Another important change in personnel over the summer was the acquisition of Patrick Muttart. Patrick, now in his mid-thirties, had a longstanding relationship with Stephen because he had begun his political career as a Hill staffer for the Reform Party. After a few years of that, he became the marketing director for a hotel chain, then took a job with Navigator, Jaime Watt's communications firm in Toronto, where he had gotten wide exposure to political disciplines such as polling, advertising, and media management. Patrick had worked in our war room in the 2004 campaign, helping Ken Boessenkool with daily scripting, and he had also helped Perry Miele prepare our advertising in spring 2005.

Ken Boessenkool called me in June to say that Patrick would be interested in moving to Ottawa and working in the OLO. He had been held in Toronto by personal factors that were no longer relevant, so now he could make the move. Ken and I both called Phil Murphy and Doug Finley to recommend that Patrick be hired, and they made it happen in August.

We had never had someone like Patrick on the campaign team – a high-level strategist with an ability to think in visual terms and dramatize policy. Ken Boessenkool, as a trained economist, tended to think in dry analytical terms. Patrick, in contrast, has an eye for colour schemes, photo ops, sound bites, advertising, and all the other things that bring political communications to life. We already had the ingredients of successful communications – opposition research, policy advice, graphic design, advertising, polling – but we needed someone like Patrick, with the flair to make them work together and support each other.

Another new member of the team who went on to make an important contribution was Lawrence Cannon, a former cabinet minister in Robert Bourassa's Liberal Government. Harper's speechwriter, Paul Terrien, had met Cannon in Outouais local politics and had interested him in running for the Conservatives. In August 2005, Stephen made Cannon deputy chief of staff in the OLO and deputy director of the Conservative Party, becoming in effect the Quebec lieutenant. Whereas previously many of our Quebec people had had an ADQ flavour, Cannon brought along his deep provincial Liberal connections, including ties to Jean Charest, whom he had encouraged to run for the Liberal leadership. He also imposed a new level of discipline on the factionalized Quebec organization, helped by the fact that around this time Stephen made his peace with the Tory old guard in Quebec, finally accepting their proposal for an organizationally separate Quebec wing of the Conservative Party.[40]

While staff reorganization was taking place behind the scenes, the biggest public news was Stephen's summer tour. He was determined to travel all summer, to do the barbecue circuit across the country, as a way of showing that he was not giving up despite his spring setbacks. In fact, he took no holidays that summer; Laureen, Ben, and Rachel accompanied him much of the time on the tour. It was the right thing to do, to show the flag in spite of being wounded; but it did not gather much favourable publicity. Our communications people said things that led the media to interpret it as an image makeover – finally Stephen Harper was going to learn how to do retail politics.[41] Thus the national coverage – when there was any national coverage – was all about whether Stephen had really changed, and reporters could always find some one, like John Crosbie in the following quotation, to say he hadn't:

> Among our friends, the women think he's scary. Christ Almighty, Paul Martin is ten times as scary. But they believe Harper's cold. And he is cold. He doesn't have human warmth. He's not able to even work a room. He doesn't want to meet people. The thing that saved the Pope [John Paul II], who had some pretty reactionary policies, was that he genuinely wanted to meet people. Unfortunately, Harper needs that, but he hasn't got that at the moment. [42]

At times, the press seemed deliberately malicious, as in the headline on a Brian Laghi story in the *Globe and Mail*, "Majority Want Harper Replaced, Poll Shows."[43] According to a Strategic Counsel poll reported in the story, 59 percent of Canadians wanted Harper replaced as leader of the Conservative Party. But the same poll showed that 52 percent of Canadians, also a majority, thought Paul Martin should be replaced as leader of the Liberal Party. Harper may have been marginally worse off than Martin in public opinion, but to single him out in the headline without mentioning Martin was grossly unfair.

There was also a lot of pressure at the time for Harper to release the platform for the coming election campaign. Much of that pressure came from the Mike Harris Tories, who remembered how they had won in 1995 by releasing the Common Sense Revolution a year before the election. But Stephen has always believed in holding back the platform until after the writ is dropped, so opponents cannot steal the best parts or adjust their own policies to counteract it. If the platform is kept secret till the writ drops, the leader can make new daily announcements during the campaign, whereas it is harder to speak daily about something already in the public domain.

The other public thing Harper did in the late summer of 2005 was to run the brand ads that Perry Miele had produced in the spring. These showed Stephen in a campaign office, holding policy discussions with telegenic members of caucus, such as Peter Mackay, Josée Verner, Rona Ambrose, and Diane Finley. The point was to highlight key areas of policy while showing that Harper had a team around him. The party ran these TV ads in late August and September, mostly in targeted Ontario ridings. The ads may have produced a slight temporary upward movement in our polling support, but we knew that three weeks couldn't produce a lasting effect. However, they demonstrated our financial muscle and showed our loyalists that we were still in the game.

Some observers liked the ads, others found them contrived; but the punditi rarely know the research behind the ads, the strategy they're based on, and the nature of the media targeting. The ads certainly caught the attention of the Liberals, if for no other reason than that it is unusual for a party to spend so much money on advertising when no election writ is in the offing. Here are some snippets from emails between two senior Liberal advertisers, Jack Bensimon and Jack Fleischmann:

Bensimon, 23 August: The conservatives just announced a new TV campaign to air in Ontario. The slogan is Project Canada: Stand Up for Canada.

Fleischmann, 23 August: Saw the daycare ad this morning on NewsNet ... Harper has chosen to become a regular guy with middle of the road policies and great big smile ...

This campaign points to a strategic shift – away from the "all sleaze, all the time," messages of the last election toward a media campaign that attempts to contrast their "less intrusive government/greater choice" vs. Liberal waste and mismanagement. They're moving as fast as they can toward the centre with arguments that sound reasonable and feel right. They clearly recognize they can't afford to be painted into the same extremist corner and they're moving hard to set the agenda for the next campaign. These messages are more finely crafted than anything they've done up to now. The content is much stronger, the writing crisp. The tone is moderate, hopeful, upbeat. Someone over there is finally paying attention to the research, it seems ...

I'd say we should take a look at producing material that scratches the paint on their bright new Buick ... A few weeks at, say, 150 points a week ought to do it. Radio, too.

Bensimon, 24 August: I agree with Jack F. on the strategic shift. He makes good points about the Conservative strategists finally understanding their own problem. I'm just not as impressed with the execution. Although it is better than they've done before.

As for a response ... unless money is no longer in short supply, I wouldn't spend a nickel until the writ is dropped ...[44]

In addition to showing that Liberal security had been breached, the exchange illustrates their financial limitations. Even though they were the government, they did not feel able to respond to our ads with some of their own.

Meanwhile, Patrick Muttart was rethinking some aspects of our platform to enhance its appeal to ordinary people. Patrick was particularly impressed by the success of Australia's John Howard in winning four elections in a row. Howard has appealed to what he dubbed the "battlers," families struggling to raise their children on a modest income – working hard, paying their taxes, playing by the rules, to paraphrase rhetoric that we would use in the coming election. The Australian influence, already present in Patrick's mind, grew even stronger after Brian Loughnane, the national director of the Australian Liberal Party, came to our Montreal convention and made a presentation to some senior staff. Patrick and I went out to dinner with him, leading to further information-sharing and subsequent meetings between Stephen Harper and John Howard.

In effect, Patrick set out to recast our appeal in terms familiar to John Howard's battlers. To make it understandable to our advertising team, he created fictional people to epitomize our core and swing voters, as well as those who would probably never support us.[45] "Steve and Heather" typified one part of our core support: in their forties, married with three children, Protestant, with Steve owning his own business. Another core voter was "Eunice," a widow in her seventies, also Protestant, living on a modest pension but owning her own home. "Dougie" – single, in his late twenties, working at Canadian Tire – represented one type of swing voter. He agreed with us on issues such as crime and welfare abuse, but he was more interested in hunting and fishing than politics and often didn't bother to vote. He was potentially supportive but hard to reach. "Rick and Brenda," a common-law couple with working-class jobs, represented another set of swing voters, as did the better-off "Mike and Teresa," who probably would be Conservative core supporters except for their Catholic background. And to exemplify people who would never vote for us there was Zoë (affectionately named after the president's daughter in "West Wing"), twenty-five, single, with a degree in sociology, practicing yoga and eating organic food in her central-city apartment; and "Marcus and Fiona," a high-income couple with no kids, professional jobs, feeling part of the establishment and loving it.

Patrick concluded that the brand ads produced in the spring might be right for Zoë, or for Marcus and Fiona, but we were unlikely to change their minds no matter what we did. Those ads weren't quite right for the swing voters we needed to reach – people like Rick and Brenda, or Mike and Teresa. A bit edgy, filming our most photogenic MPs with a moving camera, lots of action bordering on hurly-burly, the ads appealed to the artistic sensibility of the creative types who work in advertising agencies – not surprising, because senior advertisers tend to be like Marcus and Fiona, while junior ones often resemble Zoë. So Patrick spent a lot of time with our ad team that fall, describing the kind of people we had to reach. He summed it up by telling them, "You buy your coffee at Starbucks, but these people get their coffee at Tim Hortons."

Patrick and Perry's work with the advertisers led to a new generation of English brand ads that we played in heavy rotation in the first part of the 2005–06 campaign. Capturing the mood of a low-budget suppertime newscast, they showed Stephen being interviewed by a media host, with a very ordinary-looking person asking a simple policy-related question and Stephen giving a low-key answer. Rather than edgy or artistic, the ads were artfully middle-brow – designed to reach the sort of people most likely to change their vote from Liberal or NDP to Conservative.

Although many observers said they were hokey, they were well-conceived for the job they had to do – to communicate the essence of our policy to middle-aged or older, family-oriented, middle-income people without high levels of formal education. These were our swing voters, the people who would bring us victory if we could just bring them on side.

Ian Brodie also went back over the platform in autumn, reshaping it to fit this more populist understanding of conservatism. One big change was in taxation.[46] Like the 2004 platform, *Demanding Better*, the spring 2005 platform draft advocated a set of changes to personal income tax exemptions and marginal rates in various brackets. It was technical and not easy to describe concisely – also prone to be stolen by the Liberals, who did in fact announce cuts in personal income taxes just before being defeated on 28 November 2005. In contrast, the version of *Stand Up for Canada* produced in fall 2005 called for an immediate one percent cut in the GST, from 7 percent to 6 percent, to be followed by another one percent cut before the end of a new Conservative Government's mandate.[47] It was catchy, highly visible, easy to communicate, and unlikely to be stolen by the Liberals, given the radical flip-flop on the GST that they had made after being elected in 1993.

Demanding Better had proposed a technocratic set of proposals for better funding of health care. They were reassuring enough to serve as a shield against attacks, but they weren't clear or catchy enough to attract many votes. The spring 2005 draft featured an unfortunately named "Ten Year Plan" to reduce wait times, but the fall 2005 version of *Stand Up for Canada* was much stronger, with a "Patient Wait Times Guarantee."[48] Again, it was something noticeable and memorable, not just wonkish ruminations about restructuring the system. Unless they have no faith at all in the source, voters will take a guarantee over a ten-year plan any day.

Then there was a whole package of family policies. The centrepiece was the $1,200/year "Choice in Child Care Allowance."[49] Its predecessor in *Demanding Better* had been a $2,000 per child deduction in the personal income tax. The Choice in Child Care Allowance, like the GST cut and the Patient Wait Times Guarantee, was deliberately reconstructed to become more visible and easier to understand. It also, by the way, became more universal; a tax deduction helps only those who earn enough to pay income tax, whereas an allowance goes to all parents, even those who pay no income tax.

Each of these three items – tax cuts, reduction in health-care wait times, and a preference for families over institutional child care – was an extension and reworking of the 2004 platform and indeed of positions that Harper had taken ever since becoming leader of the Canadian Alliance in 2002. But *Stand Up for Canada* also contained some new proposals for grants and reductions in personal and corporate income tax, all meant to be highly visible and easily understandable:

- $1,000 Apprentice Incentive Grant[50]
- Apprenticeship Job Creation Tax Credit[51]
- Tools Tax Deduction[52]
- increase from $1,000 to $2,000 in the pension income tax amount eligible for a federal tax credit[53]
- exemption of the first $10,000 of student scholarship income from taxation[54]
- $500 textbook tax credit[55]
- $500 tax credit to parents for registration fees and memberships for physical fitness activities for their children[56]
- federal tax credit for use of public transit.[57]

Taken together, these proposals communicated a powerful political message – that we cared about working people and their families, that we wanted to help parents, children, students, apprentices, tradesmen, commuters, and retired people. As populist economic conservatism, it worked like a charm in the election. It's far easier to stage a message event and photo op around children's physical fitness or textbooks or work boots than it is around a decrease in the marginal rate of the third bracket in the personal income tax.

One important innovation in the spring 2005 platform did survive into the final version of *Stand Up for Canada* – a more relaxed attitude toward federal subsidies to business. In 2004, *Demanding Better* had been highly critical of subsidies and had linked their deletion to reductions in business taxes:

Government should help all businesses to create jobs by keeping taxes low and creating a strong economic climate, not help a select few with special favours.

A Conservative government will seek to reduce or eliminate corporate subsidies of up to $4 billion per year. Savings generated will be used to reduce taxes for all businesses.[58]

Across-the-board opposition to business subsidies disappeared from the spring draft and did not reappear in the final version of *Stand Up for Canada*.

All in all, the team made a great deal of progress in the summer and autumn of 2005, which confirmed that I had made the right decision by stepping aside so we could have a campaign manager in Ottawa all the time. As manager, Doug kept everything we had built up in preparing for a spring election – a carefully planned budget, the new advertising team, CIMS and the voter contact program, the arrangements with Greyhound and Air Canada, and the personnel for the tour and war room. But while maintaining existing assets, he and the rest of the reconfigured team in Ottawa – Ian Brodie, Patrick Muttart, and Lawrence Cannon – also managed to make the OLO more functional, bring discipline to the Quebec organization, create a clearer strategic focus around populist economic conservatism, and rework our advertising and platform to suit that focus. We were now far better equipped to fight an election than we would have been in the spring of 2005.

8

Winning the Race, 2005–2006

Following the spring 2005 misadventure, Stephen said that he would not again try to force an election without the NDP on side.[1] We were mentally preparing for an election in early 2006. The prospect was not encouraging, for the Liberals would have had a chance to receive Justice Gomery's final report, accept his findings, and go to the voters on a reform platform, including a new budget.

Meanwhile the New Democrats, alarmed by the Supreme Court's *Chaoulli* decision legalizing private health-care insurance in Quebec, were trying to get Paul Martin to take steps to "protect" public health care. But Martin resisted their demands; and when the first Gomery report came out on 1 November, NDP strategists decided it was time to end their partnership with the Liberals.[2] I got a call on 6 November 2005 from one of their senior people, whom I knew slightly. "It must never be known," he said melodramatically, "that I have called the most right-wing political scientist in Canada." Actually, as I learned later, others in the NDP were making similar calls to senior Conservatives. It was a full-fledged charm offensive to bring about cooperation with our party.

The caller went on to explain the problem facing the NDP. Many of the top people wanted an early election, but some of their supporters thought their alliance with the Liberals was "progressive" and worth maintaining. They couldn't afford to appear too eager to vote non-confidence, not least because an immediate vote would result in a campaign spanning the Christmas holidays, so they wished to propose a House of Commons resolution calling on the Liberals to hold an election in January. They didn't want a straight non-confidence vote until they had given the Liberals this opportunity to accept a "reasonable compromise."

Stephen, who felt he had been abandoned by Layton in the spring, was skeptical at first,[3] but he finally agreed to meet with Layton and Gilles Duceppe on Sunday, 13 November. At that meeting, the three opposition leaders agreed to follow the NDP two-step. Layton made his motion on 21 November for the Liberals to commit to calling an election in January 2006, which the Liberals rejected as unprecedented and non-binding. On 24 November, Harper then introduced his own simple motion: "That this House has lost confidence in the government." All three opposition parties supported it in a vote on 28 November, and the election writs were issued on 29 November. This was the only time in Canadian history that a federal government has fallen on a non-confidence motion unattached to a specific issue.

NDP tactics in 2005 worked quite well for their cause. First they extracted $4.6 billion in spending concessions in exchange for propping up the Liberals in the spring, so they could tell their followers they were making Parliament work for them. Then they left the alliance with the Liberals at just the right time. Layton had learned from the Liberal surge late in the 2004 election that they were the real obstacle to his party winning more seats. "We have to somehow figure out," he had said shortly after that election, "how to counter the campaign of fear that the Liberals have so successfully used time and time again."[4]

There is some room for the NDP to grow at the expense of the Conservatives in BC and Saskatchewan, but their potential play is bigger against the Liberals. There were forty-five ridings in 2004 in which the Liberal and NDP candidates were the top two finishers; twenty-four of these had a margin of ten percentage points or less, and the Liberals won fifteen of these twenty-four. Moreover, there is good reason to think that NDP losses to Conservatives were abetted by the Liberal endgame tactics, for six of these losses were extremely close, i.e., by less than two percentage points, and could easily have been caused by potential NDP supporters voting Liberal to "stop Harper." Certainly that was the conclusion of the veteran New Democrat MP Lorne Nystrom, who lost narrowly in the Saskatchewan riding of Regina-Qu'Appelle: "The big shift happened when people tried to decide whether to go NDP or Liberal ... . It's nothing complicated. If the vote divides, you lose. That's what happened tonight."[5]

When Layton decided to pull the plug on Martin, it was the first step in a larger strategy, which they executed fairly consistently throughout the campaign, to prevent the Liberals from swamping the NDP by evoking fear of the Conservatives. It helped the NDP increase its popular vote from 15.7 percent to 17.5 percent and its seat total from nineteen to twenty-nine. No matter how well designed our campaign had been, it would have been hard for us to win if the NDP had not held up its end.

PREPARATION

Entering the new election, we had retained and improved those things that had worked well in 2004, including grassroots fund-raising, using all the tools of direct mail, telephone solicitation, and email; strict financial controls to guarantee staying within budget; travel contracts with Air Canada and Greyhound, with the rough spots ironed out in the latter relationship; a nightly tracking poll conducted by Praxicus; and an aggressive, nationally controlled program of direct voter contact, now enlarged to cover sixty-seven targeted ridings. Doug Finley had set up a special unit at the national office to offer these targeted ridings assistance with campaign literature and other aspects of local campaigning. He also introduced a secondary tour as a fully integrated part of the campaign, designed to send high-profile speakers such as Deputy Leader Peter MacKay and former House Leader John Reynolds to targeted ridings.

Once again, Doug had recruited a full slate of 308 candidates, but with more strength than in 2004. For 2005–06, we had former provincial legislators and cabinet ministers, such as Jim Flaherty, John Baird, and Tony Clement in Ontario, Lawrence Cannon in Quebec, and Fabian Manning in Newfoundland, as well as some former federal MPs, such as Garth Turner in Ontario and Jean-Pierre Blackburn in Quebec – all of whom succeeded in winning new seats for us. A related factor was that many candidates who had run strong but unsuccessful races in 2004, e.g., Laurie Hawn in Edmonton and Josée Verner in Quebec City, were running again and were now much better known to voters. Candidates of this type were quite successful in winning new seats in 2006.

We had also gone a long way toward fixing those things that we had diagnosed as not working well in 2004. For advertising, we had Perry Miele's larger, more experienced team and a much bigger budget, with a suite of brand ads ready to go, preparations for fact-based ads well advanced, and ideas for responding to the Liberal attacks that were certain to come. We also had an advertiser – Robert Beaudoin at a Montreal agency, Republik – who could give us an indigenous campaign in Quebec, rooted in the political culture and dynamics of that province. We were confident that we would not let ourselves be outgunned in the paid-media air war, as had happened in 2004.

For managing relations with the media, we had introduced many changes that we hoped would give us greater control over our message. On the Leader's Tour, we had chief of staff Ian Brodie as a senior adviser close to the leader; Marjory LeBreton as a spinner to talk to "the boys on the bus"; and extra communications staff to give them information and take care of their needs. We also had a plan for early-morning policy announcements to get our story out early each day, show voters exactly what we stood for, and protect the leader from being forced to improvise. The tour itself would run through the full eight weeks, though on a much reduced basis between Christmas and New Year's. We considered the idea of a Christmas "truce," but we didn't trust Martin to keep it, fearing he would do tsunami memorials or other "non-political" events to gain favourable coverage in the off period. We also made some important changes in war-room communications. Ken Boessenkool now had a bigger team for scripting and speechwriting, which was essential if we were going to control our message, and they had outlined a full eight-week script, with multiple endgames.

We also enlarged the communications staff, and we added Jason Kenney with a mandate to put the Liberals on the defensive. To prevent another child-porn fiasco, I was appointed "Editor

General," responsible for approving all releases before they went out. This did not mean relying on my own judgment so much as making sure there was ongoing consultation with all the other senior communications strategists in the war room – Yaroslav Baran, Jason Kenney, and Keith Beardsley. Almost everything that went out was unanimously approved by the four of us, or at least by three if someone was unavailable. A couple of minor mistakes were made along the way, but the system worked well enough to prevent public embarrassments.

Another improvement over 2004 was better communication between the tour and the war room. Ken and the scripting team had daily calls with the leader to update and revise the script. Beyond that, Doug Finley arranged for at least two and usually three conference calls every day, in which as many as ten or twelve people from both tour and war room participated. The calls were cumbersome at times, but involving so many people ensured that important issues got raised. Stephen could tell us if he wasn't happy with war-room communications, and we could tell him if we thought he was off message. A few shouting matches were a small price to pay for better results.

A final innovation was something we had not even considered in 2004 – links with the blogosphere. Blogging had grown exponentially in the meantime, and there was now a group who called themselves the "Blogging Tories." Not being a blogger myself, I wasn't even aware of them until Adam Daifallah gave me the news at the May 2005 meeting of Civitas. I called Stephen Taylor, whose "Conservative Party of Canada Pundit" vies for prominence with Steve Janke's "Angry in the Great White North," to get things started. Doug Finley subsequently appointed people to monitor the blogosphere and to get out stories that were not quite ready for the mainstream media.

SHAKY START

In spite of all of these preparations, our campaign got off to a ragged start. Stephen was blindsided in his first press conference by Allan Woods of CanWest, who asked him, "Do you love this country?" Taken by surprise, Harper didn't have a good answer ready.

"Well, I've said Canada is a great country," was all he could muster at that moment. He did better in the afternoon, when he said that Liberals believe that "people who don't vote Liberal, don't love their country. This is what we've got to expect. It is mean and it saddens me. I believe Liberals do love this country, but they love power too much."[6] But it still allowed Martin to pontificate about how much he loved Canada, even if Harper couldn't say it.

Stephen's first announcement was a promise to hold a vote in the House of Commons on whether or not to introduce legislation to repeal same-sex marriage.[7] Many observers said he was shooting himself in the foot, but it was an intelligent tactic to dispose of the issue early, rather than late in the campaign when large numbers of voters make up their minds. On the second day, Stephen couldn't tell the media the names of the candidates who were on the platform with him in Quebec City.[8] Also, Peter MacKay publicly opposed the need for a special federal director of prosecutions, even though it was a major feature of the accountability plank that Harper presented that day.[9] I then arranged for Peter to get his own daily briefing, and he was a trooper from that point on. He travelled tirelessly on secondary tour, and he stayed solidly on message for the rest of the campaign.

Behind the scenes, a number of other things went wrong in the early days. Funny now but not so funny at the time, when the Leader's Tour group went out to the airport on the first day, they found that Air Canada had put the wrong campaign slogan on the jet – the 2004 slogan, "Demand Better," rather than the 2005 slogan, "Stand Up for Canada." Fortunately, that could be fixed quite quickly, and the media never learned about it. In the war room, we had trouble getting releases out in the first few days. I thought things had been approved when I signed off, but Yaroslav Baran, following instructions he thought he had received, was also seeking approval from a couple of other people, making our system impossibly slow. No sooner did we get all that straightened out than our email system crashed, and our backup provider could not handle the long distribution lists that we employed to send out releases to the media. For several days, our staff had to waste time chopping long lists into multiple batches of fifty in order to send out media releases.

With all these early glitches, Stephen understandably started demanding that we put out something – anything – to put pressure on the Liberals. At a mid-morning conference call on 30 November, we discussed celebrity Liberal blogger and Paul Martin speechwriter Scott Feschuk's slighting reference to "socially awkward *Omni* subscribers." We all thought Feschuk was referring to Omni Television in Toronto, which broadcasts foreign-language programs for ethnic audiences. Although we couldn't figure out why the Liberals were allowing Feschuk to trash their ethnic core vote on their party website, we thought maybe we could use it. So Jason Kenney arranged a quick news conference to denounce the Liberals for their insensitivity to new Canadians. Then we learned that "*Omni*" referred not to the Toronto television station but to a defunct US science-fiction magazine unknown to us prosaic Conservatives. Jason had to endure looking silly for a few hours, though I doubt many in the Canadian media understood "Couch Boy" Feschuk's nerdish reference to *Omni* better than we did.

We had leaks in the first week. CTV knew about the GST cut before the announcement, and CBC's Julie Van Dusen got wind of our health-care policy the evening before it was announced on Friday, 2 December.[10] Doug Finley said he would look for the source. I'm not sure what he found, but we had no further policy leaks after that, though tour destinations sometimes got out.[11] Leaks of this type may seem like a small thing, but our communications strategy was premised on having something new each morning, so we had to maintain security until the actual announcement. Divulging the destination prematurely might allow reporters to guess what the announcement was about.

We also dodged what could have been a major embarrassment with our advertising. While intending to send out our brand ads to media outlets, our Toronto ad people mistakenly sent a DVD containing all ads, including fact-based and response ads. Fortunately, they discovered their mistake quickly and called back the courier shipments, so only the *Toronto Sun* actually received the DVD, and Yaroslav Baran was able to get that back without anyone ever opening it.[12]

In retrospect, our shaky start was not very harmful because we diagnosed our errors quickly and found the right corrections, while no one got overly upset. Our core team was much the same as in 2004, so we had been through worse than these silly glitches and could keep things in perspective. It was a good omen for the rest of the campaign.

GETTING UNTRACKED

Stephen started each day early with a new policy announcement, dominating the news for the day and showing the wisdom of saving policy announcements for the campaign. The accompanying media release and backgrounder were written in easy-to-digest bullet form, with online sources included for quick verification by reporters. The first week, it was the Accountability Act, including a special prosecutor for political corruption; reducing the GST from 7 percent to 6 percent immediately, and ultimately to 5 percent; the Patient Wait Times Guarantee; and a major increase in military spending, recruitment, and procurement. The second week included the Child Care Allowance, tax cuts for small businesses and seniors' pensions, and increased spending on cancer research. The early announcement strategy worked perfectly, giving Stephen a message at his daily press conference, reducing mischievous questions from the media, and handing reporters a major story to file early in the day. Waddell and Dornan summarize the effect:

> It was a mechanism to seize control of the news agenda, to dominate the day-to-day coverage, and it was therefore a media management technique. Compelled by their own responsibilities to document each announcement as it came, the media as a result had few openings or opportunities to raise issues that were not on the Conservatives' playlist.[13]

A lot of work was required behind the scenes to put on these seemingly smooth performances. The scripting team would have the speech and associated news release and backgrounder ready, but Stephen would always go over the material the afternoon or evening before the event, sometimes calling for major changes. Ken Boessenkool and his team would often be rewriting till midnight. Our heroic translator, who sacrificed her health on the altar of our election campaign, would make all the final changes in the French text overnight. Then I would come in at 6 or 7 AM to proofread everything, making sure the release and backgrounder matched the speech and (working with Philippe Gervais) checking that all documents said the same thing in both French and English. Sometimes there was another round of last-minute changes as we scrambled to send the material out to the Leader's Tour for a 9 AM or even 8 AM event. We had to hustle to do it in time, but after a couple of early stumbles we got pretty good at it, even though the tour people were often biting their nails. Ray Novak suggested that we should put on an overnight crew of writers, editors, and translators, but we didn't have to go that far – fortunately so, because it would have stretched our personnel too thin.

The Liberals made few policy announcements in the early days of the campaign because, as in 2004 and 2005, they had rushed out a huge number of governmental spending promises just before the anticipated writ drop. Expecting us to be all negative in the early weeks, they apparently hadn't given serious thought to the communications challenge of how to sustain an eight-week campaign when all your announcements have been made in a "jumbo policy fire sale"[14] before the campaign even begins. When observers drew unflattering comparisons between our emphasis on policy and the Liberals' silence, they reacted by improvising. On 6 December, Paul Martin unveiled a new child-care "policy" that consisted of extending existing promises from five to ten years – a commitment that no government can realistically make unless it expects to abolish the constitutional requirement of holding elections every five years. On 8 December, Martin went to Toronto to propose a total ban on handguns as a crime-prevention measure – even though handguns have been outlawed for decades in Canada for almost everyone except target shooters and law-enforcement personnel, and most gun crime is committed with handguns that are already illegal. With our improved communications between the war room and the tour, we were able to find the right rejoinder to these and other Liberal announcements. We didn't debate the details, we just dismissed them as "phony" – making promises that couldn't be kept, banning handguns that were already illegal.[15] It fit into our narrative that we were the party of new ideas while the Liberals were the party of corruption, desperately clinging to the perquisites of power.

Once the leader's morning message was out to the media, the strategy group in the war room devoted much of its effort to destabilizing the Liberals. Jason Kenney's goal was to arrange a news conference or event each day, while Yaroslav Baran and his staff kept up a steady stream of reality checks and other releases against the Liberals, plus talking points for our own people. Yaroslav made a particular effort to get material via Blackberry to reporters travelling with the other campaigns, so they would have probing questions to ask the leaders. Keith Beardsley's research team kept us primed with material drawn from media databases as well as our own extensive quotation database. Our war room had tried to do most of these things in 2004, but we were more effective now because we had more people to work with, better research support, and more experience to draw on. Three examples illustrate our improved capacity.

On 7 December, Paul Martin flew to Montreal to address the United Nations summit on climate change. In front of delegates from 175 countries, he boasted about Canada's commitment to curbing greenhouse emissions. Then at his press conference he played the anti-US card: "To all those countries that are still reticent – including the United States – I want to say this: we have a global conscience, and now it's time to listen to that conscience. It's time to join with the international community and get down to work."[16] Liberal strategists thought the Montreal meeting was a dream venue, but we had a nasty little surprise for them, in the form of a reality check that Yaroslav Blackberried to reporters on the Liberal tour just in time for them to ask questions at Martin's newser (see figure 8.1).

When reporters asked Martin about this at his press conference, he was taken by surprise and had no good answer. It got into the television footage and played over and over that day, stepping on the story that the Liberals were trying to create. We had had similar information in 2004 but had never succeeded in getting it into the news cycle, so Dave Penner, our wagonmaster on the Leader's Tour, had forwarded it to me for reuse in this campaign. That it

Figure 8.1

REALITY CHECK

Paul Martin: The High Flying Polluter
Flies in to environmental conference on loud, gas guzzling jet

FOR IMMEDIATE RELEASE
December 7, 2005

OTTAWA – Liberal Leader Paul Martin flew in to Montreal today to boast about his clean air record. Um, but he flew in quite the gas guzzler! Paul Martin is jetting around in a Boeing 727 – one of the world's noisiest and most environmentally unfriendly aircraft. Conversely, the Conservative campaign plane is an Airbus 320 – widely respected for its low greenhouse gas emissions and noise control.

- According to the European Commission, "The noise level of an Airbus 320, is around 20 dB less than that of a Boeing 727 40 years ago. And when it comes to aviation fuel consumption – and thus the volume of greenhouse gas emissions – the reduction is around 70%." http://europa.eu.int/comm/research/rtdinfo/en/28/aero3.html

- Statistics released by the Air Transport Association of Canada in 2002 reveal that the Boeing 727 burns 1,289 gallons of fuel per hour, compared with the Airbus 320 which burns just over half that amount, at 767 gallons per hour. (*Globe and Mail,* June 11, 2004)

- Even Boeing admits that its old 727s are archaic noise polluters: "Airplanes that utilize older, less-effective noise technology are being retired. Very few still are flying in countries where the overwhelming majority of the world's fleet is located. The noise levels of airplane operations will continue to decline dramatically as airplanes such as the Boeing 727 and 737-200 are removed from service." http://www.boeing.com/commercial/news/feature/quiet.html

Paul Martin once called on all governments to put a "shoulder to the wheel" to meet promises to cut greenhouse gases (*Toronto Star,* January 20, 2005). Clearly there's a gap between Mr. Martin's rhetoric and his actions.

---

worked so well this time was due to the Liberals' presumption in
having Martin step forward on climate change while his government's real-world performance left so much to be desired (Canada
was actually losing ground in meeting greenhouse-gas emissions
targets and had a poorer record than the United States, whom
Martin was taunting). Their noisy, dirty, inefficient campaign jet
became an ideal metaphor for their Kyoto policy; and it also
didn't hurt that their jet was leased from a Liberal donor, which
we didn't put in this release but made sure reporters knew about.
Perfect timing was also critical for getting into the story; reporters
need material when they need it, and if it doesn't reach them at the
right time, they won't use it, no matter how good it is.

The second example was triggered by Liberal communications
director Scott Reid's performance on 10 December. Speaking
about our child-care allowance on a Saturday-morning TV panel,
he uttered his immortal line, "Don't give people 25 bucks a week
to blow on beer and popcorn." This was part of the Liberals'
talking points, not just an idle slip of the tongue, for Liberal
strategist John Duffy said something very similar on TV later that
weekend.[17] They were trying out a new attack line, but it boo-
meranged on them.

Jason Kenney immediately saw the potential and got our child-
care critic Rona Ambrose to fly from Edmonton to Ottawa for a
Monday-morning news conference. Jason arranged for local parents and toddlers to be there, with hundreds of dollars worth of
beer and popcorn for props. TV loved it, and it helped keep the
story alive for days. In 2004, our campaign spokesmen would
have huffed and puffed, but we wouldn't have had the capacity
to put together an event on short notice and carry it off effectively. Compelling visuals make all the difference in fighting for
time in the news.

A third example of our new capacity was the way in which
Scott Reid's hospitality expenses reached the blogosphere. Our
researchers happened to have the information due to an earlier
"Access to Information" request. In normal times, no one would
have cared. Reid had submitted only thirty-two claims between
1 January and 15 June 2005, none of them large.[18] A New Year's
dinner meeting at D'Arcy McGee's costing $22.71 was fairly
typical. As communications director for the prime minister, it's

hardly surprising that he would sometimes talk business over beer in an Ottawa pub. But campaigns are not normal times, and his "beer and popcorn" remark, followed by Rona's press conference, had made his doings newsworthy, so the information placed on the blogosphere soon started appearing in the newspapers. To be sure, this was a very minor skirmish, but big wars are won by winning lots of little battles.

These three examples are ones that worked well; many others fizzled. But in the aggregate our destabilization capacity provided a dimension to our campaign that was largely missing in 2004. Even when they didn't hurt the Liberals badly, they helped keep them on the defensive and reduced their ability to attack our leader as he took the high road of policy.

WAGGING THE DOG

When the Liberals get in tough, they always play identity politics. In the middle of December, they put on an audacious identity-politics counterattack that showed they could still teach us a lot about campaigning. It boosted their poll numbers in the pre-Christmas period and might have carried them to victory, if they hadn't made so many subsequent mistakes.

It started on 7 December, when Paul Martin spoke to the climate-change summit in Montreal and took a swipe at the United States. On 9 December, he made an unscheduled trip back to Montreal to appear with Bill Clinton while the former US President tore strips off George W. Bush's climate policy. Meanwhile US Ambassador to Canada David Wilkins entered the fray: "It appears that often times, some officials, in order to build Canada up, attempt to tear the United States down. I'm sure the election plays a role in that or is to some extent a cause of that."[19] The same day, Ambassador Frank McKenna sought a meeting with the State Department in Washington, and afterward Canadian Government sources put it out that American officials had rebuked McKenna for Martin's criticism of their country's environmental record.[20]

That really irritated the Americans, because McKenna had sought the meeting, whereas Canadian Government spokesmen were making it seem that he had been called in for a reprimand.

Thus Ambassador Wilkins jumped in even more energetically on 13 December, when he said to a Canadian Club luncheon in Toronto, "It may be smart election-year politics to thump your chest and constantly criticize your friend and your No. 1 trading partner. But it is a slippery slope, and all of us should hope that it doesn't have a long-term impact on our relationship."[21]

That set the stage for a vintage Paul Martin performance in a lumberyard in Richmond, BC. In the midst of an otherwise lacklustre press conference, he suddenly drew himself up, looked straight into the camera, and delivered his lines: "I am not going to be dictated to as to the subjects that I should raise. I will make sure that Canada speaks with an independent voice now, tomorrow and always, and you should demand nothing less from your Prime Minister."[22] It looked corny watching the event, but it provided a powerful clip to be played throughout the day's news cycle. In the war room, we were wishing we could get Stephen to do the same thing more often. We pushed him repeatedly to deliver set-piece lines to generate clips for repeated play, and he got better at it as the campaign wore on.

The Liberals had done it – they had wagged the dog! They had precipitated a diplomatic row with the United States in the middle of an election campaign in order to mobilize the forces of Canadian nationalism and anti-Americanism. They were on a roll, and they carried their momentum into the first round of leaders' debates, scheduled for 15–16 December in Vancouver. We had talked about a destabilizer to disrupt Martin's debate preparations but hadn't come up with anything. The Liberals, in contrast, had dredged up a 1997 speech that Stephen had given to the Council for National Policy, a US conservative discussion group holding a meeting in Montreal. Stephen at the time was vice-president of the National Citizens Coalition. Speaking, he thought, off the record, he referred to Canada as a "Northern European welfare state in the worst sense of the term" and told the mostly US audience that "your country, and particularly your conservative movement, is a light and an inspiration to people in this country and across the world."

When I became chief of staff in 2003, one of the first things I did was to organize a "Harper research" program to collect everything he had ever written or said in public. I personally went to

Toronto to comb through the records of the National Citizens Co-alition. But this speech was not in their files, nor had it ever been published. Unknown to us, however, it was sitting on a website associated with the Council on National Policy, under the misspelled name "Steven Harper." Belinda's campaign had it in 2004, but it never became a factor in the leadership race.[23] Our researchers failed to discover it; but Liberal opposition research, which is always very thorough, found it and saved it for just the right time. The Liberals tipped off the CBC and Canadian Press to the existence of the speech on the afternoon of 14 December, just as Stephen was in the midst of debate preparations in a Vancouver hotel. Not only did it distract him and disrupt the debate team's work, it fit perfectly into the portrait that the Liberals were painting of Martin as Canada's defender against the United States and Harper as an obsequious suck-up to the Americans.

After conferring with Marjorie LeBreton on the tour, we decided to go with the line that the speech had been delivered tongue-in-cheek and quotes taken out of context didn't really represent Stephen's views.[24] Playing down its importance seemed to be the right tack to take; it reinforced the impression that we were talking about policy while the Liberals were bent on dragging up old stuff. Various pundits proclaimed that the speech was old, Harper had evolved, and so on. The Liberals had played perfect ball but didn't get all that much bounce.

Not much happened in the French debate, but the Liberals had another trick up their sleeve for the English debate, opening a new front in the war of identity politics. Martin blindsided Gilles Duceppe, delivering set-piece lines as he had in the Richmond lumber yard:

Mr. Duceppe, let me say to you that the Supreme Court, the Constitution of Canada and international law all make it very, very clear that you cannot have a unilateral declaration of independence. Let me say, also, that I am a Quebecker and you are not going to take my country away from me with some trick, with some ambiguous question ... This is my country. And my children were born and raised in Quebec ... A sovereignty [sic] a question of international recognition. You're not going to get international recognition if what you do is violate the Constitution of Canada, if you violate international law ...

And certainly, and as prime minister of this country, I will defend the unity of our land.[25]

Stirring stuff! It would even have been courageous if Martin had said it in French the night before. But by speaking in English, Martin wasn't really confronting Duceppe; he was only trying to make English voters think he was their protector against the separatist threat, just as he was their defender against the Americans. Again, it looked corny watching the whole debate, but it was effective theatre when it was packaged as a separate clip. Naturally it ran over and over in the following days, while Harper's thoughtful but lengthier answers to questions were harder to excerpt. To reinforce the point, Dave Ellis, the CTV pool producer travelling with the tour, asked Stephen immediately after the debate, "Do you think you lacked passion?" It was a prompt for a story posted later that evening on the CTV website, and it became the tag line for the debates – that Martin had passion, whereas Harper did not.[26]

On the strength of his scripted passion, Martin "won" the debate. Decima reported 31 percent for Martin, 20 percent for Harper, and 17 percent for Layton. Ipsos-Reid had it closer, 34 percent to 30 percent, but still with the advantage to Martin over Harper.[27] Although observers were generally saying that we were running a good campaign, the Liberals had moved public opinion in their own direction. Yet their gains proved to be temporary because their positions, though tapping into powerful wells of emotion, were fundamentally phony. There wasn't really any quarrel with the United States; it was all a figment of Liberal spin. And Martin wasn't really confronting Quebec separatism; he had shown his lack of courage by tackling Duceppe in English rather than French (can you imagine Pierre Trudeau going after René Lévesque that way?). Martin's ploy in the English debate, though it worked for a few days in the opinion polls, actually set the stage for Harper's breakthrough in Quebec.

TURNING POINTS

We were a little discouraged after the first three weeks. We felt we were executing our campaign as planned, and there was a lot of favourable commentary about it in the media. Our internal

polling showed that voters were aware of our policies and view-
ing them supportively, but there wasn't any change in top-line
numbers. We were still running about six points behind the Liberals – basically no improvement since the writ had been
dropped. However, we were tied with the Liberals among voters
who said they were following the election closely, and we were
starting to "take ownership" of issue areas such as tax cuts, going beyond our original strength in criminal justice. On the basis
of similar data, Michael Marzolini publicly predicted on 17 December that we would overtake the Liberals in the New Year,
and he proved to be correct.[28]

The first turning point was Stephen's speech to the Chamber
of Commerce in Quebec City on 19 December. The only new
policy item in the speech was a commitment to allow Quebec to
be represented at UNESCO, a promise that Paul Martin had made
earlier but reneged on.[29] Stephen also spoke of "open federalism" and promised to address the "fiscal imbalance." Importantly, he also promised to curb the federal spending power,
which has been used to drag the provinces into signing on to federally initiated social programs. He had said those things before
without striking a chord, but this time observers were impressed
and Quebec media commentary was friendly. Perhaps the pack-
aging helped; the speech was presented as a "Quebec Platform,"
and Stephen spoke with feeling about the province and its role in
Canada, with a touch of modesty about himself:

> The foundation of Quebec City is also the birth of the state
> that became Canada. We must never forget that Canada was
> founded in Quebec City and founded by Francophones. That
> is why I say that Quebec is the heart of Canada, and the
> French language an undeniable part of the identity of all Cana-
> dians, although I admit that some of us cannot speak it as well
> as we should.[30]

Once Stephen's speech had established his credibility in Quebec,
we followed up with a lot of policy-oriented radio ads. There
may not be as many conservatively oriented voters in Quebec as
elsewhere in Canada, but there certainly are some, and we
wanted them to know about our positions.

Whatever exactly happened with Stephen's speech, it paved the way, through its favourable reception in the French media, to a massive shift in voting intentions.[31] Voters started to come our way, defecting from both the BQ and the Liberals. It was the culmination of all that Stephen had invested in Quebec over the last three years – the French lessons in his office, the frequent trips to speak to small crowds, hiring more Francophone staff for the OLO and the party, the decision to hold the policy convention in Montreal, the recruitment of lead candidates such as Josée Verner and Lawrence Cannon, and the building of an indigenous Quebec campaign, with advertising rooted in the political culture of the province.

One should not, however, put too much emphasis on the speech itself. Polling data show clearly that there was no shift toward the Conservatives and away from the BQ and Liberals in Quebec until after the start of the New Year.[32] The speech seems to have given Harper and the Conservatives credibility in the eyes of Quebec voters, and then our ads and subsequent events in the campaign brought some of them over to our side. In any event, the speech helped us push back the Liberals' identity politics assault against us on the Quebec front; suddenly, we could plausibly argue that we were more in touch with Quebec voters than the Liberals were. In the first leaders' debate, Martin had dared Gilles Duceppe to debate him "on every street corner, in every city, and in every town and village in Quebec."[33] When Duceppe said he would accept the challenge, Martin backed off; and Stephen then offered to debate Gilles Duceppe head to head, forcing Duceppe to decline.[34] Stephen even went on the offensive, accusing Paul Martin of undermining Jean Charest and wanting a PQ victory in the next provincial election in Quebec, so he could continue to pose as the defender of Canada.[35] Hoping to repeat the child-porn dynamic of 2004, Martin called for an apology, but Stephen just shrugged it off.[36] It was all good theatre, and it made Harper look like a leading man on the Quebec stage, rather than a member of the supporting cast as in 2004.

On 22 December, Stephen also pushed back against the Liberals' other identity politics assault, the charge of being in the pocket of the Americans. He stopped in Winnipeg that day to unveil our platform on the North, including a deepwater port in the Arctic, three new ice-breaking submarines, and several other military investments:

> The single most important duty of the federal government is to protect and defend our national sovereignty. There are new and disturbing reports of American nuclear submarines passing through Canadian waters without obtaining the permission of – or even notifying – the Canadian government. You don't defend national sovereignty with flags, cheap election rhetoric, and advertising campaigns. You need forces on the ground, ships in the sea, and proper surveillance. That will be the Conservative approach.[37]

He had turned the tables on the Liberals by making himself the defender of Canada against US intrusion, doing it the Conservative way, with the "hard power" of military assets rather than the "soft power" of rhetoric. After 22 December, anti-Americanism ceased to be a major factor in the campaign. It continued to motivate the far left, as it always does, but it was no longer central to the main line of public discussion.

These Arctic announcements had originally been scheduled for Comox, BC, in the week between Christmas and New Year's, when they would have drawn much less attention. We didn't change the content, but we gave them more impact by moving them ahead to 22 December, when the whole media contingent was still with the Leader's Tour. For a lunatic half-hour, we even discussed sending the tour to Iqaluit for the announcement, but that bright idea could not stand up to the realities of winter travel in Canada.

On 26 December, Mike Klander, vice-president of the Ontario wing of the federal Liberal Party, resigned his position over offensive comments he had put on his blog. He had called NDP Leader Jack Layton an "asshole" and posted pictures of Layton's wife, NDP candidate Olivia Chow, and a chow-chow dog, with the caption "separated at birth."[38] Klander had no formal role in the Liberal campaign, but he was at least a peripheral member of "the Board"; and as an official of the Liberal Party, he had a certain official status, so opponents could plausibly cite his blog as typical of Liberal arrogance.

More seriously, Boxing Day also saw the death of Jane Creba in Toronto. A fifteen-year-old girl from a middle-class family, she was shopping with her mother and sister on Yonge Street when she was gunned down in a firefight between rival gangs. Paul Martin and Stephen Harper showed starkly different reactions to this heart-rending tragedy. Martin, looking for "root causes," came close to sympathizing with the killers: "I think more than anything else, they demonstrate what are in fact the consequences of exclusion. I was in Toronto not long ago and met with a number of members of communities in the Jane and Finch area ... and the young people talked to me about the void in their lives, and what hopelessness and exclusion can bring." Harper, in contrast, spoke about the importance of justice: "There is nothing else you can do to deal with crime other than to make sure people who commit crimes are severely dealt with, and that we don't run a revolving-door justice system. The problem is this is the first government in our history that seems unable to enforce our gun laws, and I think obviously this is just the consequence of 12 years of lax criminal justice law enforcement."[39] Our internal polling had already established criminal justice as the issue area where we had the strongest lead over the Liberals, and Jane Creba's tragic death helped to make our position more salient to voters.

28 December brought the mother of all turning points, when the NDP disclosed that the RCMP had responded positively to their request for an investigation of Ralph Goodale, the finance minister. Had he or someone on his staff tipped off stock-market insiders prior to his announcement on 23 November 2005 that the government would not change the rules for taxation of income trusts? The shares of some Canadian income trusts had risen sharply in price just prior to the announcement, and rumours had circulated for weeks that insiders had been tipped off.[40] Jason Kenney, who ironically had begun his political career working for Goodale, tried to make a campaign issue of it, but so far without much success, so this announcement was like manna from heaven.

The Liberals had been parrying charges of corruption, admitting that a few Quebec Liberals had been dishonest, but not Paul Martin, who had been "exonerated" by the Gomery Commission.[41]

But now Martin's finance minister would be subject to a criminal investigation over another form of financial manipulation. So much for the Liberals' defence that whatever had happened in Quebec in the last century was over and done with. Michael Marzolini calls the announcement of the income-trust investigation "the lightening [*sic*] rod that typified and collected together all the existing perceptions of Liberal scandals and entitlements of the previous few years." SES, the only pollster to stay in the field during the holidays, had already recorded some movement to the Conservatives, which accelerated after the income-trust announcement.[42] The income trust announcement worked against the Liberals the way our child-porn misstep had worked against us in 2004.

There was no end to the follow-up stories. Should Goodale resign as finance minister while the investigation was going on? (He chose not to.) What exactly had happened on the stock market? (It was very complicated, with lots of room for would-be analysts to offer interpretations.) Should the Ontario Securities Commission also investigate? What about US authorities? Many of these income trusts were also listed on the New York Stock Exchange, and the US Securities and Exchange Commission announced its own investigation in early January.[43]

This was *the* turning point of the campaign. Before Christmas we were running about six points behind the Liberals, whereas all major pollsters showed us tied with the Liberals when polling resumed in the New Year. Unfortunately, only SES was polling between Christmas and New Year's Day, and that was with a very short interview schedule, so we lack an accurate portrait of how public opinion changed in this crucial period.

It was unprecedented for the RCMP to announce an investigation of the finance minister during a campaign. Were the Liberals just unlucky? There's a bit of truth in that explanation, but only a bit. Rather than bad luck, it was more a case of chickens coming home to roost. Goodale had handled the issue badly from the start, announcing the possibility of tax changes for income trusts in September, which caused an immediate plunge in stock market value, then rescinding the possibility on the eve of the election in a blatant attempt to sweep the issue off the table. Moreover, we now know that at least some Liberals were talking more than they should have before Goodale made his 23 November announcement. Scott Brison, for example, sent an email to a CIBC employee saying, "I think you will be happier very soon, this week probably."[44] The Liberals handled the whole thing carelessly, and they deserved to get burned, even if no one could have predicted that the RCMP would light the fire in the middle of the campaign.

THE AIR WAR

Before Christmas, both the Conservative and Liberal campaigns ran only positive "brand" ads outside Quebec (we ran a negative ad against the BQ from the start in Quebec). Ours were the clunky "Harper in the window" ads, showing him responding to simple questions about policy from ordinary-looking people. The Liberals had a series called "Thirty Million Reasons to Vote Liberal," featuring young Liberal activists who were supposed to be ordinary Canadians. The Liberal ads were much slicker than our intentionally homely ones, but our polling consistently showed that ours were more effective in communicating policy ideas. In our last set of data before Christmas (20 December), 66 percent of respondents in Ontario and BC could recall seeing a Conservative ad, compared to 54 percent for Liberal ads; and of those who remembered seeing any ads, more could recall what the Conservative ads were about. Though panned by the critics, our ads were doing their job, "punching through" to tell people where we stood.

Early in the campaign we had received a printout of hundreds of pages from the Liberal Intranet, a resource bank of texts and visuals intended for the use of local campaigns. One of the visuals was a photo of Stephen Harper and Gilles Duceppe, sitting close together with Harper whispering to Duceppe, looking like co-conspirators. The Liberals clearly meant to use it to reinforce their allegation that Harper was in cahoots with the separatists. Fortunately someone on our team recognized that the photo was cropped from a picture of all four party leaders seated together at a Holocaust memorial held in Ottawa in the spring of 2005.

Campaign Co-Chair John Reynolds wrote a letter to all local Conservative campaigns, including the picture as proof that the

Liberals had already gone negative against us, so we would have to retaliate. The letter was sent to all local Conservative campaigns. One reason the strategy worked so well was that it linked back to a 24 November headline in the *Globe and Mail* – "Liberals plan negative campaign"[45] – and to Martin's post-debate comments about Harper not being fit to be prime minister.[46] People were already seeing a negative Liberal campaign, even though the party hadn't released any negative ads yet.

We started running our fact-based ads on a large scale on 2 January. The first featured Paul Martin on a TV monitor, saying in a loop, "The Liberal Party is not corrupt," plus former Liberal Cabinet Minister and Royal Mint of Canada President David Dingwall, who had been forced out of his job by Paul Martin, saying, "I'm entitled to my entitlements." The second had a scowling Martin coloured red. "Paul Martin allowed over $330 million to be spent on the sponsorship program. You paid for it," a narrator said. It used the sinister picture of Martin that we had acquired the previous spring.

One of the main trends in January, documented in all public polls as well as our internal polling, was the gradual erosion of Martin's leadership image and the correlated improvement in Harper's standing. I like to think our ads had something to do with that trend, though it is difficult to prove because many things were happening at the same time. In any case, our ads made us feel great. After fifteen years of being smeared by the Liberals as redneck racists, we were hitting back, and hitting back hard.

For reasons that maybe some day will be publicly explained, the Liberals waited dangerously long – until 10 January, after the second round of leaders' debates – to release their negative ads. Advertising takes time to work, and yet the Liberals were only allowing their negative ads two weeks to have an effect. The ads, moreover, went absurdly over the top and almost instantly became the subject of widespread ridicule. Chris Cobb described their general format in the *National Post*:

> The ads use a similar format: gloomy or military-style music played over a blurry image of Mr. Harper, accompanied by a female voice that reads bleak text about the Conservative

leader's opinions on, for example, the war on Iraq and his plans for the military.

One ad says Mr. Harper has a right-wing agenda similar to former Ontario premier Mike Harris, another says he is planning to put troops on Canadian streets. One accuses him of "insulting" Atlantic Canadians and another says he hasn't released a full list of donors to his leadership campaign.

The script for the donor ad was typical:

Who paid for Stephen Harper's rise to the head of the party? We don't know. He refuses to reveal his donors. What do you suppose he's hiding? We do know he's very popular with right-wingers in the U.S. They have money. Maybe they helped him. We just don't know. He just won't say.[47]

Frank magazine would later parody this script in a farcical cover, showing Stephen with the apocalyptic numerals 666 stamped on his forehead: "Is Stephen Harper the Antichrist? We just don't know. He refuses to talk about it. Now why would he do that?"[48] In fact, in autumn 2002 we put on the Canadian Alliance website the names of 54 of the 64 donors who gave more than the tax-credit limit of $1,075 to Harper in the Canadian Alliance leadership campaign.[49] At the time these people made their contributions, there had been no legal requirement or expectation of disclosure, so I personally called all of them and asked if they would allow us to reveal their names. Most were happy to oblige, but ten requested that their privacy be respected. As for the 2004 campaign for the Conservative leadership, the names of all donors who gave $200 or more to any of the three campaigns were posted on the party's website for two years after the conclusion of the campaign. The suggestion that there was any infusion of US money in either Harper leadership campaign is a false and absurd allegation of illegal behaviour. It is an offence to accept donations from outside Canada, unless they are made by Canadian citizens.

The ad that repeated Harper's words about the "culture of defeat" may have hurt us in the Atlantic region. SES found that Conservative support in Atlantic Canada declined after the ad received heavy play. Stephen had apologized for that remark at the beginning of the campaign, but few people were paying attention then. Probably he should have apologized again later in the campaign.[50]

The worst development for the Grits was that they had to pull one of their ads, briefly posted on their website, before they could ever air it (although they never pulled the French version). Here is journalist Bruce Cheadle's description of the ad:

> The military spot, which plays off a Conservative promise to boost the militia, states that Harper wants to increase the military presence in cities. "Canadian cities. Soldiers with guns. In our cities. In Canada. We did not make this up," says the woman's voice-over.[51]

Military support groups denounced the ad as a slur upon the Canadian Forces, and the Liberals had to retreat, compounding the damage with conflicting statements about whether the ad had ever been approved, and if so by whom, and whether it had really been intended to run. Our ad team quickly released a spot to highlight the confusion, showing Paul Martin saying, "I approved the ad, there is no doubt about that."[52]

Meanwhile, we were pushing on with our series of Martin-focused ads without receiving any noticeable criticism. "Can We Believe Him?" released on 10 January, highlighted Martin's use of the private Medisys clinic in Montreal and Canadian Steamship Lines' practice of reflagging Canadian ships, i.e., flying them under foreign flags to take advance of more relaxed labour codes and environmental regulations in other countries. We had tried to use these themes in 2004 without success, but now they were working for us with great effect, undermining the credibility of the negative ads that the Liberals launched after such a long delay.

BUILDING A LEAD

Tied with the Liberals when full-scale campaigning resumed on 2 January 2006, we quickly built up a substantial lead in the polls. Harper made an inspired move by pulling together his

"Five Priorities" at an Ottawa rally on 2 January. It was like a re-launch of the campaign. He had already announced the Account-ability Act, GST cuts, the Patient Wait Times Guarantee, the crackdown on crime, and the Child Care Allowance; now he put them together as a sort of mini-platform with an easily remem-bered name – the "Five Priorities."[53] To heighten the contrast with Martin, we put out a list of fifty-sex priorities that Martin at one time or another had declared, together with a quote from Martin himself: "If you have 40 priorities, you don't have any."[54] After 2 January, Stephen went back to the game plan of making a new policy announcement each morning. There was still a great deal in the platform that had not yet been released.

We also rethought our campaign rhetoric in early 2006. The material that we had been putting out, including the leader's speeches, was often quite explicitly critical of the Liberals and their policies. We thought that was in the spirit of the parliamen-tary system, in which parties are supposed to present voters with alternatives. But a special research project helped us understand that might not be the best way to bring voters over to the Conser-vative side. We could not hope to win without attracting the sup-port of some people who had previously voted Liberal, and attacking their previous commitment to the Liberals might stiffen their resistance to considering the Conservative alternative. After the New Year, we started to make our communications more pos-itive, emphasizing that Canadians needed and deserved new poli-cies, but not explicitly attacking the Liberal Party.

It was all right to criticize Martin, but not to criticize Liberals as such. I think our change in rhetoric contributed to the more favourable evaluation of Harper that developed during January. For example, SES reported on 11 January, just after the second pair of debates, that 30 percent of respondents thought Harper would make the best prime minister, compared to 27 percent who favoured Martin. On 1 December , in contrast, 29 percent had favoured Martin as against 21 percent for Harper.[55]

For their part, the Liberals started rolling out more of their own policies, but communications difficulties diminished their impact. For instance, the announcement on 5 January 2006 of their advanced-education position was marred by the premature release of the policy from the Liberal war room before the reporters travelling with Paul Martin saw it. CTV's Bob Fife re-fused to cover the release, focusing instead on the Liberals' orga-nizational and strategic problems.[56] Reporters on the leader's tour feel that their employers are paying dearly for access and don't like to be upstaged. In general, the mood on the Liberal bus wasn't good, to judge not only from published stories but also from tidbits of information that our own communications people picked up. That every one of Martin's subsequent policy an-nouncements was also leaked made the mood even darker.[57]

Also interfering with the Liberals' attempt to get back to policy was another corruption story. On 6 January, the *Globe and Mail* reported that Heritage Canada had asked the RCMP to investigate a $4.8 million grant made to Option Canada, a federalist group active in the 1995 referendum.[58] On the morning of 9 January, Quebec journalists Normand Lester and Robin Philpot held a press conference to release their book, *Les Secrets d'Option Can-ada*, improbably based on discarded documents found in a dump-ster. They charged Option Canada with illegally spending hundreds of thousands of dollars in the referendum.[59] Our cam-paign can't take any credit for it, but it was an effective destabi-lizer to launch against Paul Martin as the second round of leaders' debates was scheduled to begin that evening.

To judge from their actions, the Liberals hoped to turn things around with a three-part plan: (1) win the debates on 9–10 Janu-ary by having Martin promise to renounce the Notwithstanding Clause; (2) release a suite of negative ads immediately after the debates; (3) follow up quickly with their platform. It was a logi-cal plan, but none of the elements worked properly. Martin an-nounced in the English leaders' debate that he would amend section 33 of the Canadian Charter of Rights and Freedoms to renounce federal use of the Notwithstanding Clause, hoping to highlight the Liberals' contention that Harper would have to use that clause to repeal the gay-marriage legislation. The announce-ment fell flat, however, because nothing had prepared the way for it. Suddenly coming out of nowhere, it smacked of improvi-sation and even desperation. Ipsos-Reid had Harper beating Martin 34–32 in the second English debate, compared to Martin beating Harper 34–30 in the first English debate.[60] Martin hadn't done all that badly, but he needed a win to reverse his downward momentum, and he didn't get it.

As already recounted, the Liberals' first suite of attack ads was too over the top to be effective and actually backfired when they had to withdraw one. Nor did their platform launch save them. In fact, a leak turned it into the high point of our campaign. We were able to beat the Liberals to the punch, releasing their platform before Martin could do it, emphasizing the absence of the Notwithstanding Clause in the platform even though he had emphasized it in the second debate, and in general putting our own spin on it.

At that point, we felt invincible. Everything the Liberals had tried was failing. When I called my wife to say, "It doesn't get any better than this," I hadn't thought through all the implications of peaking on 11 January. What was going to happen in the next twelve days before the vote on 23 January? In fact, within two days we were caught up in a sequence of bad luck and self-inflicted errors. In virtually no time at all, we went from celebrating success to grimly holding on. It was another lesson about the changeability of campaigns.

HANGING ON

There was a glitch on 12 January, when it was revealed that Derek Zeisman, our candidate in the Southern Interior riding of British Columbia, faced smuggling charges for bringing a new car filled with liquor into Canada from the United States. These were not criminal charges, so they had not shown up during the criminal check we perform on all candidates, and Zeisman had not disclosed these activities on his candidate questionnaire. It was too late to take Zeisman's name off the ballot, but Stephen quickly announced that, even if elected, he would not be allowed to sit in the Conservative caucus. His rapid action prevented the story from becoming too negative for us, and the next day the Liberals had a similar problem when David Oliver, their candidate in Abbotsford, BC, was accused of attempting to bribe his NDP opponent to withdraw.[61]

Our troubles really started on Friday, January 13 (!), when we held a major campaign event to release the full text of our platform, including the fiscal framework. There was to be a major speech by Harper, preceded by an early-morning briefing session with tour reporters on "the numbers," i.e., on how to interpret our revenue and expenditure projections. Finance Critic Monte Solberg, Chief of Staff Ian Brodie, and Policy Adviser Mark Cameron were to conduct the briefing.

A lot was riding on our explanation of the fiscal framework because of the way the Liberals had used the myth of the "$50 Billion Black Hole" in the 2004 campaign. We had a contract with the Conference Board of Canada for an independent review of our projections, and we had a letter on file from their Deputy Chief Economist Paul Darby stating that our budgets would balance: "In summary," wrote Darby, "we found that the Conservative Party's economic platform is affordable in each fiscal year from 2005–2006 through 2020–2011. In each year there is enough fiscal room to pay down at least $3 billion a year in debt, as in the fiscal plan."[62] No other party had made a similar attempt to get external validation of its projections.

Given the importance of the Friday morning briefing, it was a bad sign that on Thursday afternoon the members of the writing team were still arguing about the right way to present the estimates. The essential problem was that our budgetary plan required a Conservative Government to save $22.5 billion over five years compared to current Department of Finance spending projections. Conceptually, this could be done by reducing the rate of growth in spending and would not require actual cuts to 2005–06 overall spending levels, though of course there might be an impact on particular programs. But our policy people were afraid of producing headlines such as, "Harper pledges to slash spending." In our final release, we described these savings as "Moderating spending on grants and contributions and in government departments and agencies," which was accurate and deliberately unexciting.

I was not at the lock-up, so I didn't see exactly what went wrong, but somehow confusion arose among Monte Solberg, Ian Brodie, and Mark Cameron about the totals. I was watching CTV in the war room when Bob Fife, CTV's senior political correspondent, came out of the lock-up and said, "I have to say there was a lot of confusion, a lot of voodoo economics this morning as we tried to figure out where the Conservative platform was going in terms of cost. For a long period of time they could not add up the figures."[63] It was a heart-stopping moment that led to three hours of high-pressure work in the war room, going over the day's release to make sure the numbers did add up. On the ground with the tour, Marjorie LeBreton saved the day by sitting down with Fife and answering his questions. An hour later, he came out again to tell the camera that it was all just a "glitch."

Of course, the Liberals were all over this immediately. Paul Martin said later in the day, "It reminds me of the kind of documents I first looked at when I became finance minister in 1993, and looked at the kind of documents that the Conservatives actually circulated."[64] But Martin had long ago squandered his credibility with the media as a successful finance minister through his exaggerated critique of our 2004 platform and his repeated spending sprees – the 2004 campaign, the spring 2005 accord with the New Democrats, and the pre-writ announcements in autumn 2005. Our fiscal plan would hold up in the media as long as impartial third parties did not denounce it.

That proviso, however, was soon to be sorely tested. 15 January was, we thought, going to be a slow Sunday afternoon. Yaroslav Baran, who had been running on fumes for weeks, had taken the day off, and Tim Powers was filling in as operations director in the war room. Suddenly a Canadian Press story by Dennis Bueckert was on the wire, alleging that the Conference Board's Paul Darby had withdrawn, or at least qualified, his support for our fiscal plan.[65] Darby reportedly had said that the plan he had analyzed had contained no expenditures for the Patient Wait Times Guarantee and nothing to rectify the fiscal imbalance. Indeed, these had not been included in the plan because they were not areas in which the federal government could act alone. Both would involve negotiations with the provinces; and before those negotiations were concluded, it could not be known exactly what the policies would be, what proportion of federal versus provincial expenditures would be involved, and when action would commence – essential information to have before estimating costs. Our fiscal plan had an "unallocated surplus" of $22.7 billion over five years to cover these and other contingencies, so we felt confident of being able to pay for whatever might finally arise under the heading of these two commitments.

Bueckert's story completely blindsided us. We were not aware that Darby had done an interview with CBC Newsworld on

Friday, 13 January, and it was certainly not part of our plan to have him do so. Economists should never be exposed to the media during a campaign (I guess I have to make an exception for Harper!) because the explanations and qualifications they feel compelled to make get immediately distorted in the overheated atmosphere of partisanship. And Bueckert hadn't followed the usual practice of giving the Conservative war room a chance to offer a comment for inclusion in the story.

Trying to control my temper, I spent hours on the phone with Darby; with OLO economist Jim Frank, who had been Darby's colleague at the Conference Board of Canada and had recruited him for this project; and with Yvette Diepenbrock, the Conference Board's communications director. The goal was to get the Conference Board to issue a statement reaffirming Darby's original letter of validation. Darby and Diepenbrock were cooperative, so we put together a draft fairly quickly (see figure 8.2). Getting it out, however, was another matter. The communications director felt she couldn't release it without approval from her president, Anne Golden; but it was Sunday, and Golden couldn't be reached.

As the hours wore on and we didn't seem to be able to get action, while we were getting killed in the media, our communications group lost control of the crisis management. One person shouted at the Conference Board communications director over the phone and another sent a field organizer to knock on Anne Golden's door in Toronto. Yvette Diepenbrock stopped responding to my phone calls and emails, and we lost all chance of getting the Conference Board to do anything. In the end, all we could do was to issue our own statement that Darby had "reaffirmed" his original analysis.[66] It wasn't nearly as useful as a Conference Board statement would have been to deflect Paul Martin's attack: "Mr. Darby told the press that the platform he endorsed was not the same platform that Stephen Harper released."[67] For the future, we'll have to tighten our management of communications crises so that people from other units don't hijack the damage-control process.

There was an air of absurdity about this. We were being attacked by the Liberals for allegedly inadequate external validation of our fiscal plan, whereas the Liberals had no external validation at all. Nonetheless, it was a serious blow. We had

Figure 8.2

DRAFT

CONFERENCE BOARD AFFIRMS
CONSERVATIVE PARTY'S FISCAL PLAN

OTTAWA, January 15, 2006 ... The Conference Board of Canada (CBoC) affirms that the Conservative Party's economic platform, released on January 13, 2006, is affordable in each fiscal year from 2005–2006 through 2010–2011. In each year there is enough fiscal room to pay down at least $3 billion a year in debt, as in the fiscal plan.

Over the five-year forecast horizon to 2010–2011, the CBoC economic and fiscal outlook suggest that there remains $15.7 billion in unallocated fiscal room, over and above the $3 billion annual debt payment, which provides a further cushion to ensure deficits do not occur due to adverse economic events.

The Conference Board's original assessment of the affordability of the Conservative Party's economic platform remains unchanged.

built up a solid lead of about ten points over the Liberals, and we had drawn widespread praise not only for our method of releasing our platform but also for the contents. Even those who disagreed with various policies, such as our cut to the GST rather than to personal income tax, agreed that the platform was politically intelligent. But now it was being said not only that our platform was unaffordable, but that we had deceived the economist we had hired to do an external review. We fought back as best we could, pointing out the Liberals' own history of bad numbers and challenging them to get an external review of their own fiscal plan, but the situation was difficult, bordering on dangerous.

What was particularly alarming was that we had no obvious way to change the channel. Our platform had been fully released as of Friday, 13 January, so we no longer had the ability to control the daily news agenda through an early-morning announcement of new policy. That left little for the tour in the final week except large rallies to show momentum, which excite partisans but bore reporters. Another problem was that the media were no longer interested in the war room's attacks on the Liberals. We had been successful over the campaign with themes such as beer and popcorn, income trusts, and Option Canada, and we had more ammunition to fire, but the media didn't care. What they really wanted was horse-race stories about whether we would win a majority government and speculations about how Harper would govern if we did win. Yet we were determined not to speak about these topics, remembering how much damage had been caused in 2004 by talk about transition teams, majority governments, and the influence of Brian Mulroney.

Fortunately, Buzz Hargrove did for us what we could not do for ourselves – he changed the channel away from the alleged deficiencies of our fiscal plan. On Wednesday, 18 January, he appeared in Strathroy, Ontario, campaigning with Paul Martin. First he attacked Stephen Harper as a separatist whose "view of the country is a separatist view that doesn't have a strong federal government." A Harper Government, he said, "will make it easier for the separatists to win in Quebec – surely that's pretty close to being a separatist." Then he urged NDP voters to vote Liberal in ridings where that was the best way to defeat the Conservatives. When asked about Quebec voters, Hargrove seemed to advocate voting for the BQ: "I would urge them to stop Stephen Harper in any way they can."[68] This was priceless – the most powerful union boss in the country questioning the patriotism of the leader of the Opposition and encouraging Quebecers to vote for a separatist party, with no contradiction from the prime minister of Canada standing right beside him. We dined out on that for the next twenty-four hours, and Martin was forced to issue a disclaimer: "Quebecers should vote Liberal. Voting for the Bloc will not stop Stephen Harper."[69]

This welcome diversion from the problems of our fiscal plan also undercut the attempt the Liberals were making to encourage NDP partisans to vote strategically. The Liberals had won in 2004 by "scaring the shit out of the Dippers" (if I may quote myself), and now they were trying to do it again, this time with the help of Canada's most prominent labour leader. But Hargrove's reckless comments blunted the thrust of what they were trying to do.

Also, the situation was different this time because the NDP leadership had learned its lesson in 2004 and was determined to prevent a repetition in 2006. Alan Whitehorn has summarized the NDP strategy:

> NDP planners had to find a way to counteract Liberal Party appeals to NDP voters to engage in strategic voting. One possible solution was to inoculate NDP supporters by making the Liberal Party seem so unappealing to social democrats that the gulf between the Liberal Party and the NDP would widen. To accomplish this, NDP ads targeted the Liberals and were more negative. The other side of the strategy was to lessen the fear of the Conservative Party and its Alberta-based leader. In order to achieve this, the NDP had to resist the inevitable temptation to portray the Conservatives as extremely right-wing and their leader as a scary man with a hidden agenda. Instead, the Conservative Party would be characterized as simply being wrong on policies and not congruent with most Canadians' values.[70]

The NDP carried out this strategy fairly consistently. They ran several ads against the Liberals but none solely against the Conservatives (they did run some that criticized both parties), and Layton went after Martin much more than Harper in the leaders' debates.[71] Toward the end, Layton made his own appeals to voters not to waste their votes on the Liberals but to support the NDP.[72] The strategy, however, led to open dissent on the part of James Laxer and Buzz Hargrove, who thought warding off a Conservative Government was more important than increasing the NDP's electoral success.[73] Hargrove's open campaigning with Martin was just a current and highly visible manifestation of the ancient controversy within the NDP about whether it should pursue its policy objectives by influencing Liberal Governments or by replacing the Liberal Party and forming NDP Governments.[74] The drama continued post-election with the NDP's expulsion of Hargrove, followed by the vote of his union, the Canadian Auto Workers, to sever their ties with the party. Implications for future elections remain to be seen.

Even though Hargrove broke the momentum the Liberals were building, we were still far from home. Stephen, trying to mitigate fears of what a majority Conservative Government might do, spoke on 17 January about the obstacles that our political system puts up in the face of major changes:

> There will be a bureaucracy appointed by the Liberals. So even with a majority, it's impossible to have absolute power for the Conservatives.
>
> The reality is that we will have for some time to come a Liberal senate, a Liberal civil service, at least senior levels have been appointed by the Liberals, and courts that have been appointed by the Liberals. So these are obviously checks on the power of a Conservative government, as I said that's why I say in the true sense of the word there's no, certainly no absolute power for a Conservative government and no real true majority. We will have checks on us and limits on our ability to operate that a Liberal government would not face.[75]

What Stephen said is true, but it was the wrong time, and he was the wrong person to say it. The Liberals immediately took comments that were perfectly valid as political science and twisted them into evidence that Harper lacked respect for the civil service and courts and intended to politicize them with Conservative appointments.

In an attempt to clarify his comments, he compounded the damage the next day with further remarks:

> We have no alternative but to accept the checks; they're part of our system. Judges are named; judges can't be removed by governments except under extraordinary circumstances.
>
> Obviously, the civil service has worked for many decades much more closely with Liberal governments than others. I actually think that the vast majority of civil servants would welcome a government that would provide some direction for the civil service and for the country. I think they've been lacking that the past few years.[76]

Again, good political science, but not part of the original plan for campaign communications.

Stephen improvised again that evening when Kevin Newman asked him about abortion. He was perhaps a bit off guard because the interview took place outside his boyhood home and had begun more with personal than with political questions. Then Newman suddenly brought up same-sex marriage and went on to abortion:

> Newman: On the issue of abortion, will you pledge that there will be no legislation on abortion, there will never be a free vote in Parliament on that issue?
>
> Harper: Never is a long time. What I'm saying is I have no desire to see that issue debated in the near future. We're saying very clearly in our platform we're not going to support or initiate abortion legislation and frankly I don't want this Parliament to have an abortion debate.
>
> Newman: So to be clear, you support a woman's right to choose?
>
> Harper: I've always said my views on the abortion issue are complex, I don't fall into any of the neat polar extremes on this issue.
>
> Newman: Explain them then if they are complex.
>
> Harper: No, I don't need to because I'm not proceeding with an abortion agenda.[77]

Complex views that you won't explain? Ouch! Even worse was the line, "Never is a long time," because it recalled Harper's statement in the 2004 campaign that he would not proceed with abortion legislation in his first term of office.

The unanimous view in the war room was that we had to get off the courts, the civil service, the Senate, and abortion, and back onto the bread-and-butter issues of the "Five Priorities" that had worked so well with the electorate. It was a crucial moment because our support had softened by two or three points in recent days as a result of the confusion over our fiscal plan as well as from Stephen's public musings. The Liberals were now in full cry over Harper's hidden agenda of social conservatism, precisely the area where we were most vulnerable. As in 2004, they were appealing to NDP supporters, indeed to "all progressive voters," to

vote Liberal to stop the dangerous Conservatives. We feared a repeat of 2004, when our support slipped away in the final days.
But things got resolved in a conference call with the tour on
Thursday night. After the catharsis of that meeting, Stephen got
back on message for the vital closing days of the campaign.

The door, however, had been opened for a final wave of attacks. Liberal outrider organizations – feminists, gay-rights activists, law professors, aboriginal leaders, environmentalists –
came at us in human waves, claiming that Harper would roll
back abortion rights, use the notwithstanding clause to quash
gay marriage, and repudiate the Kelowna Agreement and the
Kyoto Accord. The Conservative Party simply can't compare
with the Liberals in the depth and breadth of these external link-
ages; Real Women and Campaign Life can't compete with Egale
Canada and the National Action Committee on the Status of
Women in terms of public funding and media clout. (We did
score one minor coup when the Congress of Aboriginal Peoples
broke ranks with other aboriginal organizations to support us
instead of the Liberals.)[78] If the Conservatives can stay in power
for any length of time, it should be a high priority to de-fund the
support groups that the Liberals have cultivated so long with
grants, subsidies, and access to the government.

As part of their desperate final offensive, the Liberals also went
after our candidates who had social conservative connections.
They particularly targeted Darrel Reid, formerly the Canadian
president of Focus on the Family; David Sweet, former president
of Promise Keepers Canada; Harold Albrecht, a Protestant cler-
gyman who had a record of public statements on same-sex marriage; and Rondo Thomas, Vice-President of Student Affairs and
Dean of Biblical Studies at Charles McVety's Canada Christian
College. The Liberals' highly effective opposition research had
come up not only with printed texts but also audio and video re-
cordings of statements. This wasn't as bad as in 2004, when the
candidates who came under fire were incumbents and even caucus critics; but it was bad enough because it coincided in time
with Harper's statement about abortion.

We found two ways of dealing with these attacks. One, drawing on Keith Beardsley's quotes database, was to put out a barrage of old quotations from Liberal MPs on abortion, same-sex

marriage, and immigration. We had done this in 2004, too, but it seemed to work better this time, perhaps because those under attack were new candidates, not well-known MPs and caucus critics. Because Yaroslav Baran had developed good relations with working reporters, he would often know that something was coming, so we could respond quickly or even pre-empt the Liberals' attack. The key was to get our information into the first filing of the story, so that it would be reported not just that Conservative Candidate X took a Biblical view of marriage, but that thirty-two members of the Liberal caucus had also voted against same-sex marriage in Parliament. We didn't have to win this battle in the media, all we had to do was to fight the Liberals to a draw by getting the story to state that the views they were attacking were also held by many within their own party.

The other thing we could do was to keep the national media away from the candidate who was under attack, particularly when the Leader's Tour was travelling in or near his constituency. It's better to say nothing than to say something ill-considered or inflammatory. Doug Finley and Jenni Byrne successfully kept controversial candidates out of the limelight, but the strategy does have an obvious downside. If a candidate suddenly becomes unavailable, journalists report that as the story, and then opponents will accuse you of hiding candidates, which easily equates to having a hidden agenda. Ideally, we would have given a candidate the right talking points, rehearsed him thoroughly, and sent him out to explain what he had said in the past; but experience has shown that socially conservative attitudes on topics such as marriage and abortion don't play well in the national media in Canada. It's a Canadian reality that a conservative party must learn to work around.

Trying to take advantage of Harper's interview with Kevin Newman, the Liberals released an abortion ad on Thursday, 19 January. Harper's recent comments on abortion made it much more credible and effective than their previous negative ads had been, and we were worried about its possible effect. The advertising team had a formatted response ad ready that would show the words of our platform regarding abortion, and we debated whether we should use it. Some felt we should, while others thought a reply would just draw more attention to the

Liberals' attack. Also, by the time we could have plugged in the appropriate words and gotten it approved by the Broadcast Committee, there would have been hardly any time left to air it, because the media buy has to terminate by midnight of the day before polling day.[79] In the end, we decided against action, and we managed to survive. In the future, we must think more seriously about last-minute attack ads. The Liberals used them against us in both 2004 and 2006, leaving us without time for an adequate response. In view of the difficulties in replying, we may have to come up with a pre-emptive strategy, such as releasing our own last-minute ads, or perhaps attacking the Liberals for their plans to attack us.

While all this was going on, we were getting though the final week one hour at a time. It was palpable that the flow of the campaign had turned against us. Our platform was already out, our leader had stumbled a couple of times, the Liberals were making us pay for those errors with their new abortion ad, Paul Martin was on a frenzied desperation tour, and Liberal outrider groups were swarming like angry bees. Except for the Buzz Hargrove episode, we had been reduced to playing defence and trying to hold on to the ten-point lead that public pollsters were reporting. Polling suggested that our support was softening, particularly in Ontario. And indeed it did soften; we beat the Liberals by six points in the final result, not by ten. We would have done better if the vote had been held a week earlier, and we were glad to escape with a win, even if it was not quite as big as what had once seemed possible.

One thing that helped hold us up even as we started to sag was the support of newspaper editorial pages. By the day before the election, we were able to report that the following newspapers had endorsed us:[80]

Globe and Mail
National Post
The Economist
Vancouver Sun
Vancouver Province
Calgary Herald
Winnipeg Free Press

London Free Press
Ottawa Citizen
Ottawa Sun
Windsor Star
Montreal Gazette
La Presse
Le Soleil
Winnipeg Sun
Brandon Sun
Edmonton Journal
Calgary Sun
Toronto Sun
Edmonton Sun
Moncton Times and Transcript

Who would have predicted at the beginning of the campaign that we would end up with support from the *Globe and Mail* as well as major dailies in Quebec? Maybe they were fed up with Martin and the Liberals rather than truly enthusiastic about the Conservatives, but it was still an achievement to get their support.

TURNING OUT THE VOTE

Unlike the big changes we made from 2004 in advertising and communications, the story in ground campaigning emphasized continuity. Direct Voter Contact is like a snowball rolling down hill. Once you get it started, it keeps getting bigger and bigger as lists are extended within ridings and new ridings are brought into the program. Once again we had an elaborate, centrally supervised program of DVC. It was even bigger than in 2004, including sixty-seven targeted ridings as opposed to sixty-seven in the earlier election. It was bigger because we thought our prospects were better and we had more winnable ridings, especially in Ontario.

Unfortunately, we had to omit Quebec, because setting up the program there had faced many challenges. RMG had Francophone callers in Miramichi, New Brunswick, but their accent was Acadian, not Québécois, while our Quebec people insisted that calling had to be done by callers with a Québécois accent. In early spring 2005, I commissioned an initial experiment to see if voter identification could work in Quebec. We used VoiceLink technology, i.e., a recorded script allowing the respondent to verbally answer "Oui" or "Non" to several questions. With a well-recorded script in a native accent, the experience can be, if not perfectly lifelike, at least reasonably realistic. We dialed the better Conservative polls in four Quebec City ridings and were quite encouraged when we identified about two thousand respondents who said they were interested in joining the party. The next step would have been to approach these people locally, but our minimal ground organization in Quebec was never able to make use of the data.

I also got Josée Verner to go along with a live-calling experiment in her Quebec City riding of Louis-St Laurent. RMG located a telemarketing company in Montreal that was willing to try its hand at voter identification and trained them how to do it. The learning curve was steeper than anyone expected, but eventually they got up to levels of productivity approaching what RMG achieves in the rest of Canada. The experiment was over, and we were feeling good about the progress that had been made when we learned that all the calling had been done in the wrong riding! Someone in our organization, confusing Louis-St Laurent with Louis-Hébert, had sent the wrong data file to RMG. I gave up at that point, concluding that there were too many pitfalls in trying to create a DVC program for Quebec from the outside.

When the election was suddenly precipitated in fall 2005 by the NDP's change of heart, nothing further had been accomplished; so we went into the election without a DVC program in Quebec, even though Doug Finley and I had both wanted to have one. Once it became clear that we had some real chances of victory in Quebec, the targeted-seats unit scrambled to send out literature to voters in our strongest polls in marginal Quebec ridings. That may have helped swing some races, but it's a far cry from a true DVC program. Bringing DVC into Quebec has to be one of the highest priorities for the future.

In spite of our Quebec limitations, we enjoyed the same kind of overall advantage in ground warfare in close races that we had enjoyed in 2004. This time we won 60 percent of races (eighteen of thirty) in which the margin was five percentage points or less, and 53 percent (nine of seventeen) in which the margin was two points or less. Also as in 2004, all the other parties lost more of these close races than they won. However, our advantage was not quite as marked as in 2004, when we had won 64 percent of the first category and 75 percent of the second. There were more close races in 2004: thirty-nine in the five-point category, and twenty in the two-point category. Inspection of the results, particularly in Saskatchewan and Ontario, will show that a number of races we barely won in 2004 became more comfortable victories in 2006. The DVC program, when repeated over more than one election, builds up large lists of supporters and helps to make competitive seats more secure.

Overall, though, the stories of the two campaigns are somewhat different. In 2004, weaknesses in the air war (communications and advertising) allowed our support to sag in the final week, but we managed to claw out enough local victories in the ground war to achieve a respectable result. DVC was our "most valuable player" in 2004. In 2006, our air war was much better, so that we drove our support higher and kept it there, with only a little sag at the end. Our ground effort gave us a few more seats to strengthen Harper's minority government, but it probably did not change the fundamental result. Communications and advertising were the "most valuable players" in 2006. But in planning a campaign you want to be as strong as possible in both the air and the ground war, because success in one can compensate for deficiencies in the other.

For a visual analogy, think of the party's 308 candidates and their campaign teams as rowboats trying to land as far up on the beach as possible. The air war of paid and unpaid media is the "tide that lifts all boats." The higher the tide, the farther the whole flotilla of boats will be swept up onto the beach. But each of the 308 crews should also be rowing as hard as it can to drive its own boat. That rowing is the ground war of voter identification, persuasion, and GOTV. A successful ground war can propel an individual boat even farther up the beach than the tide would carry it. Each party has its own armada of boats, and victory is determined by getting more of your boats higher on the beach than the other parties do, so it is critical both to raise your tide as high as possible and to have the crews in the boats rowing as hard as possible.

In 2004, there were ten Conservative seats whose margin of victory was built up in the advance polls. Seeing that result, we put even more emphasis on advance voting in 2006. We wanted to get as many votes as possible "in the bank," so that the support couldn't slip away on us.

Results of the initiative were mixed. On the one hand, due at least partly to our pushing, more people than ever took advantage of the advance polls – 10.5 percent, more than one in ten of all voters, up from 9.2 percent in 2004. There were also far more special votes, i.e., mail-in ballots, in 2006 – 3.0 percent of all votes, compared to 1.2 percent in 2004. But only five of our seats were affected (as compared to ten in 2004), even though the advance polls were held when the Conservatives were at their highest in the polls. Specifically, we won four seats in Ontario, plus the Manitoba riding of Winnipeg South, "because of" the advance polls, which is to say that the surplus of votes that the Conservative candidate received over the Liberal candidate in the advance polls was smaller than the deficit of the Conservative candidate behind the Liberal candidate on election day.[81]

Overall, we made obvious progress in 2006. As compared to 2004, we advanced our vote share in every region in the country and our share of seats in every region except British Columbia. Decisive for the result were the gains we made in Central Canada – sixteen additional seats in Ontario, going from twenty-four in 2004 to forty in 2006; and ten new seats in Quebec. We added two seats in Atlantic Canada, not as much as we had hoped, but at least it was movement in the right direction. We maintained and even increased our dominant position in the prairies, adding two seats in Alberta and one in Manitoba. We lost a seat in Saskatchewan, but anecdotal evidence suggests the presence of voting irregularities. We might have challenged the result in court, but party officials decided it wasn't worth the cost because in a minority Parliament we would probably be into another election before the case could be decided. Our only real disappointment was in British Columbia, where we increased our popular vote from 36.3 percent to 37.3 percent but lost five seats, dropping from twenty-two to seventeen of thirty-six. Three of these losses were to the NDP and two to the Liberals; two were in Vancouver, two in the Interior, and one on Vancouver Island; three were of new candidates, and two of incumbents. It is clear that we have some widespread problems in British Columbia, but the pattern of results defies easy explanation.

UNFINISHED BUSINESS

The Conservative Party now has an experienced, well-funded campaign machine that can compete with anyone in Canada. Except in Quebec, it leads the other parties in ground campaigning, and it has caught up to the Liberals in communications and advertising. Indeed, most observers thought the Conservatives surpassed the Liberals in these areas in 2006, though the Liberals have so much experience and talent to draw upon in rebuilding, and their "brand" is so deeply entrenched in Canadians' minds, that we can hardly afford to be complacent. Our candidate recruitment also improved considerably over 2004. We haven't yet matched what the Liberals have been able to do in recruiting "star" candidates, but our recruiting should improve now that the Conservatives have the advantage of being in government.

Yet there is still plenty of work for Conservative campaign management to do, above all in bringing the Quebec organization up to the level of the rest of the country. A high priority is to introduce a modern DVC program. We were lucky in 2006 to win ten seats, including three very close races, without it, but we cannot count on being lucky every election. We simply must create the kind of machinery that we have built elsewhere to fight hotly contested ground wars.

We also have to develop a war-room communications group that functions in both languages. In 2004 and 2006, the war room worked almost entirely in English. Everything was translated and released in both languages, but the flow of communications really didn't address Quebec issues because we lacked Quebec personnel. There was a secondary communications group in Montreal to serve the Quebec media, but it was not integrated functionally with the Ottawa operation and could not execute the same kinds of tactics. In the second half of the campaign, Philippe

Gervais and Michel Lalonde started to put out releases targeted at the BQ that were similar to what we were doing against the Liberals – a worthwhile start but on a very small scale. Next time, we will have to have a full-scale communications effort against the BQ if we are going to continue to improve in Quebec.

Finally, we have to solve the conundrum of fighting a two-front war in BC – against the Liberals in parts of Vancouver and Victoria, and the NDP elsewhere. We made an effort in 2006, with a BC platform and a special BC ad, but the results weren't what we hoped. The ad, I think, misfired. Targeting "Downtown Jack" Layton, it showed a moustache hopping all over the screen. It was based on a certain theory of our problem in BC, namely that populist voters who used to support the Reform Party have gone back to the NDP because the Conservative brand is too "establishment" for them. The ad was supposed to persuade these voters that "Downtown Jack" from Toronto wasn't their kind of guy. But it didn't work; indeed, our support in BC fell during the time that the ad ran.

BC politics are very diverse. Vancouver resembles Toronto; some of the Interior is like Alberta in the extent of Conservative domination; but other parts of the Interior and Vancouver Island, with their Conservative-NDP competition, are like parts of rural Sakatchewan. What works well in one region of BC will not necessarily work in another. Just as we had to get more people from Quebec into our organization to make a breakthrough in that province, we may have to get more, and more highly placed, strategists from British Columbia to help us run a more effective provincial campaign.

Finally, there is the never-ending task of keeping up with the developments of the information age. The internet facilitates new approaches to advertising that may someday make massive media buys obsolete. US parties are far ahead of us in developing national web-based systems for managing volunteers, using them to make voter ID and persuasion calls or even knock on doors in other counties and states. Such systems would be useful for the Conservative Party of Canada because many of our ridings in Alberta and parts of BC and Ontario have large memberships and numbers of volunteers, far more than are really needed in such ridings. Many other constituencies in Saskatchewan, Manitoba, and elsewhere have smaller memberships and fewer volunteers, yet face tighter races. Better-off ridings have often sent money, and occasionally volunteers, to help their poorer cousins, but such help has been a patchwork of ad hoc initiatives. It would be consistent with the trend toward nationalization of campaigns to use the internet to guide the deployment of resources to where they are more badly needed. We have often talked about developing such a system, but there has never been time up till now because of facing one campaign after another. It should be a high priority for the party under a stable Conservative Government when one might expect four years between elections.

9

The Ten Commandments
of Conservative Campaigning

In the last five years, Canadian conservatives have made more progress than anyone expected, but the work is far from done. Canada is not yet a conservative or Conservative country; neither the philosophy of conservatism nor the party brand comes close to commanding majority support. Conservatives are able to win an election at least partly because liberals, social democrats, anti-American nationalists, environmentalists, feminists, and Quebec separatists are divided in their party allegiance among the Liberals, New Democrats, BQ, and Greens.

Some have argued recently that Canadian conservatives have to build for the long term, trying to affect public opinion so that conservatism becomes an entrenched public philosophy. Tasha Kheiriddin and Adam Daifallah wrote a book to that effect, and Preston Manning has organized the granting program of the Manning Centre for Building Democracy along the same lines.[1] Such efforts are essential, and I support them wholeheartedly, but in the meantime political life continues. Winning elections and controlling the government as often as possible is the most effective way of shifting the public philosophy. Who would deny that Canada's present climate of opinion has been fostered by the Liberal Party's long-term dominance of federal institutions? If you control the government, you choose judges, appoint the senior civil service, fund or de-fund advocacy groups, and do many other things that gradually influence the climate of opinion.

How then does the Conservative Party of Canada continue to win elections and form more governments, after making its breakthrough in 2006? The first thing is to keep the strategic situation in mind. The Conservatives win if the other four parties are at each other's throats; they lose if they line up together, particularly if NDP and Green voters swing to the Liberals. That means we must avoid being painted as the Great Satan of Canadian politics, as happened to the Reform Party, the Canadian Alliance, and to some extent the Conservatives in 2004. If chronically fearful moderate or left-wing voters become convinced that Conservatives are a threat to civilization as they think they know it, they are likely to vote for the Liberals rather than the NDP or Greens, because they may think only a Liberal Government can keep the Conservatives out of power.

In pursuit of this objective, a Conservative Government must align itself tactically in Parliament with different parties or segments of parties over different issues. Harper played this game successfully in his first year in office, getting the BQ to support his budget and the softwood lumber agreement with the United States; the BQ and the NDP to support the Accountability Act (the Liberals supported it in the House but delayed it in the Senate); one faction of the Liberals to support extension of Canada's mission in Afghanistan; and all three opposition parties to support his motion "That this House recognize that the Québécois form a nation within a united Canada."[2] When the writ is dropped, it is crucial for Conservatives to be able to say that many of their policies have at least some degree of support from one or more other parties.

However, once the writ is dropped it is equally important for the Conservatives to have platform positions that polarize against all the other parties – to represent the only conservative alternative against the welter of other parties. Let the Liberals, NDP, Greens, and BQ fight among themselves to speak for "progressive" voters. That strategic configuration is the best prospect for the Conservative Party to win elections based on support from a plurality of voters, since majority voter support seems unlikely to be available. Indeed, if Conservatives have played the parliamentary game skillfully by tacking back and forth among the other parties, it should be easier to polarize against them all during the campaign, because they will be nourishing resentments against each other left over from the last session of Parliament. Did I hear someone say *divide et impera*?

In this multiparty environment of cross-cutting cleavages, skill
in campaigning is likely to be crucial. Conservatives will probably never go into an election with victory already secured. In this
respect, the federal environment is far different from that in my
home province of Alberta. The conservative philosophy and
Conservative brand are so strong in Alberta that the provincial
Progressive Conservative Party can cruise to victory. Under
Ralph Klein, they let their party membership run down and depended almost entirely on big corporate donations. In 2004,
they ran an atrocious campaign with no message, no direct voter
contact, and virtually no advertising. They went down fourteen
points of vote share, lost thirteen seats, and yet won a comfortable majority in the legislature. As a newly constructed party
with a still tentative base of support, federal Conservatives have
no such room for error. They must go into every election thinking that they are just one campaign away from obliteration.

Fighting four campaigns for Stephen Harper in less than five
years has taught vital lessons about what works and what doesn't
for Conservatives. This chapter sets some of these lessons down in
the form of "Ten Commandments." There are many other essential principles of campaigning that apply to everyone in politics,
but experience shows these "Ten Commandments" to be of particular relevance to the Conservative Party of Canada at this point
in its short history, navigating in a fluid, multiparty environment.
Of course, now that there is a Conservative Government, its success in future elections will be heavily affected by its record in office. Success in the "stagecraft" of campaigning has taken Harper
and the Conservatives to the next stage of politics – developing the
"statecraft" of governing. Yet the stagecraft of campaigning remains indispensable. Just think of how Paul Martin's Liberals,
starting with all the advantages of a majority government in
power for eleven years, lost power in two campaigns. So let me
summarize what I think Canadian Conservatives should have
learned in the last five years about winning elections.

These Ten Commandments are meant to apply to conservative
campaigning no matter who the leader is. Stephen Harper led
Conservatives to victory, but he will not be leader forever. Conservatives have to institutionalize the rules of success, so they can
apply them under all circumstances.

I UNITY. *The Conservative Party contains libertarians, social conservatives, populists, Red Tories, Quebec nationalists, and Canadian nationalists, plus many people who don't care much about any of these "isms." They all need each other. They can never win unless they try to understand each other and reach compromises that they can all live with.*

As a way of gaining the leadership of the Canadian Alliance, Harper began with an appeal to the old Reform base. But even while using Joe Clark as a bogeyman, Stephen was careful to leave open the possibility of cooperation with the Progressive Conservatives; and he pursued that option with dogged determination once Clark was replaced by a new leader more open to discussions. To achieve unity, Harper granted liberal terms to the PCs – indeed virtually everything they demanded, including a method of selecting the new leader that was inimical to his own chances. After winning the leadership, he made a point of putting former PCs in important and highly visible positions – Peter MacKay as deputy leader, Irving Gerstein as chairman of the Conservative Fund, Michael Fortier as co-chairman of two election campaigns, Jim Prentice as chairman of the operations committee of Cabinet. At the same time, he has also been generous to former opponents coming from the Reform and Alliance parties, giving important cabinet positions to Stockwell Day, who opposed him for leadership of the Alliance, as well as to Chuck Strahl, who publicly contemplated opposing him for leadership of the Conservative Party. Beyond that, he has made an effort to bring in people from provincial politics, such as Tony Clement from the Ontario Progressive Conservatives, even though Tony had also opposed him in the Conservative leadership race.

Throughout, he has tried to act according to what he said at the 2005 Montreal convention: "This is the party of Jason Kenney and Jim Prentice; of Belinda Stronach [there are exceptions to every rule!] and Stockwell Day; of Peter Mackay and John Reynolds; of Preston Manning and Brian Mulroney."[3] I am sure historians will judge Harper's handling of the merger to be a remarkable achievement. Given the previous animosity between factions, the degree of amicable cooperation that has been achieved is nothing short of miraculous.

Similar things could be said about campaigning. The team that carried Harper to the leadership of the Canadian Alliance and then the Conservative Party was too narrow to win a national election. It was strong in policy development, grassroots fund-raising, financial administration, direct voter contact, and local campaigning; but it didn't have enough depth in advertising and media management, areas where there were some very experienced PC operatives. Unfortunately, the Liberals forced us so quickly into the general election of 2004 that we could only skim the surface of the PC talent pool, and our campaign was weaker because of that. But we were able to learn from experience and recruit the people we needed for the more successful 2005–06 campaign. Looking back on it, I don't see how we could ever have won without the contribution of the former PCs on our campaign team, such as Mike Coates organizing debate preparation; Perry Miele leading our advertising effort; and William Stairs, Sandra Buckler, and Marjorie LeBreton helping to deal with the media.

Of course, I could say the same about many people coming from the Reform/Alliance side. We could never have won in 2006 without Doug Finley's organizational ability, Debbie Campbell's management of the tour, Ken Boessenkool's scripting, and Patrick Muttart's strategy. The point is that everyone worked together without asking or caring where the other guy came from; all that mattered was where we were going. Whether or not the schismatic period of conservative politics was necessary in some larger historical sense, it should have taught us the lesson that we will not win any elections unless we are all on the same side, fighting the other parties instead of each other. In Hugh Segal's colourful words, the Conservative Party has to embrace "paleo-conservatives like myself, Red Tories, social conservatives, historical conservatives, and even the more flinty-eyed neoconservatives [maybe that's me]."[4]

2 MODERATION. *Canada is not yet a conservative or Conservative country. We can't win if we veer too far to the right of the median voter.*

One of the most interesting and important parts of game theory is the median voter theorem. It shows mathematically that under certain more or less plausible assumptions about elections (that there are only two parties in the system and it is hard for new parties to enter, parties assume positions along a continuum as a way of signalling their intentions to voters, and voters vote for the party closest to their own ideal point), the two parties will converge on the position of the median voter. A party that stations itself away from that midpoint yields more than half the potential votes to the other party and thus will lose the election.

Of course, the real world of Canadian politics is not that simple. Four parties are represented in the House of Commons, not just two, and history shows it is possible for new parties to break into the system if large numbers of voters become dissatisfied with existing parties. Nevertheless, the model does have something to teach us about strategy in the current situation. The purpose of the merger between the Canadian Alliance and the Progressive Conservatives was to create a party capable of contesting with the Liberals for government. Outside Quebec, there is a two-party fight between the Liberals and the Conservatives along a left-right dimension of ideas, with the NDP making the situation more complicated but not changing the fundamental character of the contest for government. To the extent that the threat from the NDP pulls the Liberals left of centre, the Conservatives can satisfy their core supporters by moving a bit to the right, but they cannot afford to get too far away from the median without conceding too much space to the Liberals.

The median voter analysis also applies in Quebec, but in a different way. Although ideological differentiation exists in Quebec, the main dimension of conflict is not left-right but rather a continuum of positions about separation, nationalism, provincial autonomy, and federalism. The BQ represents the separatist side of the debate, while the Liberals and Conservatives are now contending to represent the federalist side. In an attempt to get closer to the median voter in Quebec, Harper has advocated dealing with the fiscal imbalance, letting Quebec be represented at UNESCO, and recognizing the Québécois as "a nation within a United Canada." His "open federalism" positions the Conservatives between the Liberals and the BQ and thereby draws votes from both.

3 INCLUSION. *The traditional Conservative base of Anglophone Protestants is too narrow to win modern Canadian elections. While preserving that base, we have to appeal to Francophones,*

Roman Catholics (44 percent in the 2001 Census of Canada),
and other racial and religious minorities. The key to the long-
term success of the Liberals has been their cultivation of minor-
ity groups. We have to take away that advantage before we can
become the dominant political force in the country.

For most of the twentieth century, the cornerstone of Liberal
support was the Francophone vote, both inside and outside of
Quebec. Conservatives could win the government only when they
could temporarily detach the French vote from the Liberals, as
happened for periods of time under Robert Borden, John Diefenbaker, and (to a lesser degree) R.B. Bennett. Starting in 1984, the
Liberals lost much of the French vote in Quebec, first to
Mulroney's Conservatives, then to the Bloc Québécois; but they
were able to make up for the loss of Quebec seats by cultivating
ethnic voters in other provinces – Mediterraneans (Italians,
Greeks, Portuguese), Asians (Chinese, Indians), Africans and Car-
ibbeans, and native people in some parts of the country, though
the NDP has also made a strong effort with that constituency.

From the beginning, Harper has recognized that the Conservatives must extend their support beyond their core of Protestant Anglophones. As leader of the party, he gave a high priority
to Quebec initiatives, which finally paid dividends with ten seats
in 2006, most in largely French ridings. Obviously, Conservatives want to win even more seats in Quebec, but a Mulroney-
style sweep is probably not in the cards. Mulroney achieved that
great but short-lived success by inflating nationalist expectations beyond what he could deliver, and Harper is very aware of
such dangers.

It follows, then, that Conservatives will not win a majority
government simply by adding seats in Quebec, though that will
be part of the formula. They must also win additional seats elsewhere, and that means doing better with ethnic voters. The suburbs of Toronto, Vancouver, and to a lesser extent of other cities
are now filling up with people who, based on their social values
and capitalist work ethic, should be natural Conservative voters,
but who are still emotionally tied to the Liberal Party. Conservatives must break the Liberal hegemony over Italian, Chinese,
South Asian, and other ethnic voters. That doesn't mean getting

all of their votes, but it does mean getting a bigger share, in order to win the suburban ridings that a conservative party would ordinarily expect to win.

Harper has recognized the need and has done all he can to move the Conservative Party in that direction, starting with his anti-same-sex-marriage advertising campaign of early 2005. He insisted that the 2005–06 platform contain specific measures, such as an apology for the Chinese head tax, lower landing fees for immigrants, and better recognition of their credentials; and he has worked hard to fulfill these promises as quickly as possible after forming government. He also devotes a substantial amount of time to attending events in ethnic communities. In all of this, he is following the example of Brian Mulroney, who engineered a historic Conservative breakthrough in Quebec and who also started to welcome ethnics into the Conservative voting coalition.

To match Harper's initiatives, the Conservative Party must also learn to master another kind of politics. The party is well-versed in campaigning at the individual level (door-knocking, voter ID, GOTV, grassroots fundraising), and it has made great progress at campaigning in the media (advertising, communications management). Compared to the Liberals, however, it remains weak in cultivating relationships with clientele groups. Ethnic politics is clientelistic in nature, because people coming to Canada from different cultures and whose English is imperfect naturally band together in ethnic communities. When they participate in politics, it is often through community leaders acting as intermediaries with the larger world of Canadian society. Some Conservatives MPs have learned how to manage this environment in their own ridings, but the national campaign team is still learning how to do so. It is less a matter of a five-week campaign than of maintaining long-term relationships that can be mobilized at campaign time.

If the Conservative Party can expand its bridgehead in Quebec and develop enough ethnic support to win suburban ridings in Toronto and Vancouver, it will become Canada's majority party for the next generation. If not, it will constantly be contending for a narrow minority government and will be prevented from fully implementing the platforms on which it runs.

4 INCREMENTALISM. *We have to be willing to make progress in small, practical steps. Sweeping visions have a place in intellectual discussion, but they are toxic in practical politics.*

Incrementalism has marked Harper's leadership throughout. He has proposed numerous modifications to the tax code, but no grand reform, such as a flat tax. He proposes to reform the Senate one step at a time, starting with the baby step of reducing senators' terms from life to eight years. He also proposes to abolish the long-gun registry incrementally, starting with an amnesty for rifle owners.

Incrementalism is the twin of moderation. Small conservative reforms are less likely to scare voters than grand conservative schemes, particularly in a country like Canada, where conservatism is not the dominant public philosophy. In any case, incrementalism is the intrinsically right approach for a conservative party. Modern conservatism has its origins in Edmund Burke's critique of the sweeping radicalism of the French Revolution. "We must all obey the great law of change," he wrote. "It is the most powerful law of nature, and the means perhaps of its conservation. All we can do, and that human wisdom can do, is to provide that the change shall proceed by insensible degrees."[5] Proceeding by "insensible degrees" is wise because the knowledge of individual decision-makers is so limited. "We are afraid to put men to live and trade each on his own private stock of reason," said Burke, "because we suspect that this stock in each man is small, and that the individuals would do better to avail themselves of the general bank and capital of nations and ages."[6]

Incrementalism has its critics, to be sure. Sir Roger Douglas, New Zealand's reforming minister of finance, used to say that you can't jump over an abyss by taking small steps. Drastic measures may be required in emergencies, and Douglas did face an emergency over the value of the New Zealand dollar. But in normal times it is better to go slowly and cautiously. This is particularly true when, as in Canada today, there is no general consensus on the direction of reform and the party in power is only the largest of a number of minorities. Under such conditions, pushing for radical reform is more likely to lead to stalemate than to decisive action. The Liberals learned this long ago, which is why they have usually proceeded incrementally when in power. They only invoke the need for solving things all at once (e.g., Senate reform) when they don't want to do anything.

5 POLICY. *We have to develop well-thought-out policies and communicate them effectively. Since conservatism is not yet the dominant public philosophy, our policies may sometimes run against conventional wisdom. The onus is on us to help Canadians to understand what they are voting for.*

Although the Reform Party was populist in spirit, it tended to be rationalistic in its approach to policy-making. It too often deduced policies from general principles, as if political reasoning were syllogistic. But politics is less about logic than it is about getting support. Policies must be formulated so that they can be communicated to the general public and win support of voters who spend little time studying and thinking about public policy.

The Conservative campaign struggled with this in the general election of 2004. The platform was solid and media commentators liked it, but the campaign was less effective in communicating it to the public. We didn't use advertising to communicate the contents of the platform, and we did few photo ops. But things started to get better in summer 2005, after the campaign team was reorganized. By the time we went to the polls, we had the GST cut, the Child Care Allowance, and the Patient Wait Times Guarantee, plus numerous lesser policies that lent themselves well to visual illustration, such as the tax credits for children's athletic activities, students' books, and workers' tools.

A political campaign is an extended exercise in rhetoric, mobilizing *ethos* (character), *pathos* (emotion), and *logos* (reason) to persuade millions of people to vote for the candidates of your party. People don't vote just for good ideas; they vote for potential rulers whose character they can trust and who inspire passions of loyalty and support. Conservative statecraft has to be more than the logical deduction of policies from philosophical premises if it is going to succeed. It has to be an artistic combination of sound policy with the deft communication of conservative values, such as integrity, reliability, and fortitude.

6 SELF-DISCIPLINE. *The media are unforgiving of conservative errors, so we have to exercise strict discipline at all levels:*

- *there must be a complete plan for the campaign, so the leader is not forced to improvise;*
- *staff must avoid the limelight and let the communications department deal with the media;*
- *candidates must talk about the platform, not their personal beliefs, and (except for designated spokesmen) concentrate on local rather than national media;*
- *members and supporters must be careful and dignified in all their communications, even email and website postings.*

The media can be savage with any party that lacks discipline, but they are particularly suspicious of conservatives. There is no point complaining about it; the situation is the same everywhere in the democratic world. But it means that conservative parties must put special emphasis on self-discipline if they expect to win elections.

Senior Conservative staff have been pretty good about avoiding the limelight under Harper's leadership. If they were ever tempted to open their mouths, they had only to look at the damage that David Herle, Scott Reid, and John Duffy did to the Liberal cause in 2004 and again in 2005–06 when one or more of them took centre stage. The self-restraint of senior staff has generally served as the model for others in the Conservative organization.

Conservative candidates got a brutal lesson in 2004 from what happened to Scott Reid, Rob Merrifield, and Randy White, and they largely stayed out of trouble in 2005–06. Those who did become the centre of controversy did so because of things they had said years ago, long before they had ever thought of becoming Conservative candidates. Actually, there is plenty of room for candidates to go off message. On most topics, the media will make it a one-day story, and voters may appreciate candidates who show independence of mind. But because of the history of Reform and the Alliance, and the way the Liberals campaigned against those parties, there is no room for error on hot-button social issues such as bilingualism, abortion, gay rights, and medicare.

Ground-level campaign workers and ordinary members also have an important responsibility. Even if reporters can't get candidates off message, they will try to collect inflammatory comments from those who attend rallies or who are doing neighbourhood canvassing. Unfortunately, the Reform Party's populism encouraged excited members to make thoughtless remarks in the name of the grassroots. But Conservatives may have turned the corner in this regard. The 3,600 delegates to the Montreal convention showed great self-discipline; speeches from the floor were moderate in tone, and there was little attempt to be outrageous in front of the cameras in the corridors.

7 TOUGHNESS. *We cannot win by being Boy Scouts. We have to conduct thorough opposition research and make use of the results; run hard-hitting, fact-based negative ads; and do whatever is legally possible to jam our opponents' communications and disrupt their operations.*

Shortly after I went to work for Preston Manning in 1991, I tried to set up a program of opposition research; but it ran afoul of the Boy Scout mentality of many Reformers, and I was forced to discontinue it before it ever really got started.[7] Fortunately, we've come a long way since then. The Alliance was quite good with Access to Information and other types of documentary research, and things got even better after the merger with the PCs, who had Keith Beardsley's large database of quotes.

We still have a long way to go, however, before we catch up to the Liberals, who have shown an unsurpassed ability to collect ground-level information by ferreting out transcripts of old radio interviews (Darrel Reid), recording candidates at events (Rondo Thomas), searching obscure websites (Harper's address to the Council for National Policy), collecting private material from third parties (Randy White), or discovering a candidate's legal problems (Derek Zeisman). The Conservative Party conducts good opposition research in Ottawa, but it must develop a national intelligence network to match what the Liberals have done.

The Conservatives were ambivalent about playing hardball in 2004. Because we feared that negative ads might feed into the "scary" image that the Liberals had pinned on Harper, we made whimsical ads such as "Carousel" and "Cookie Jar." In 2006, however, Conservative advertising went for the jugular with an unflattering picture of Paul Martin, and it paid off. Ken Boessenkool appointed a task force that came up with at least a few potential destabilizers in 2004 (the Liberal campaign jet, Martin's use of the Medisys clinic), but didn't succeed in getting much mileage out of them. In 2005–06, with Jason Kenney in the war room, Conservatives scored repeatedly and heavily against the Liberals (their campaign jet, beer and popcorn rejoinder, income trust investigation, Tony Valeri's land dealings, etc.).

Another point for consideration is how Conservatives should respond when other parties play hardball. Stephen Harper set exactly the right tone during the last campaign in a squabble with Paul Martin about who was in bed with the separatists. When the media asked him if he wanted an apology, he said simply, "I don't go around demanding apologies. I can take a punch."[8] People expect conservatives to be tough. They believe in the values of self-help, individual responsibility, criminal justice, economic realism, and national interest. They look ridiculous if they go around snivelling and complaining about fairness every time an opponent takes a shot at them. Political campaigning is a civilized form of civil war. The point is to win the war, not to complain that people are fighting. Leave the whining to the utopians who fantasize about conflict-free societies.

8 GRASSROOTS POLITICS. *Victories are earned one voter at a time. Door-knocking, voter ID, and GOTV are the Holy Trinity that wins close races. We must extend the lead that we have opened up over the other parties in ground-level campaigning and grassroots fundraising.*

Grassroots politics has been a strong point of all the Harper campaigns. His team found 9,600 donors in the first leadership race and eighteen thousand in the second. Corporate and high-end giving was a useful supplement in the second contest, but the grassroots membership basically funded both campaigns. We then transferred that model to the Conservative Party, which continues to lead all other national parties by a wide margin in terms of fundraising. In 2005, the Conservative Party received $17,847,451 in personal contributions from 106,818 donors; the Liberals received $8,344,162 from 23,878 donors.[9] In other words, compared to the Liberals, Conservatives received more than twice as much money from more than four times as many donors. Precisely comparable data for 2006 were not yet available at the time of writing, but the trend was much the same in that year.[10] Under Irving Gerstein's direction, the grassroots model of fundraising has built the Conservative Party into a financial powerhouse that has fought election after election without going into debt. It is a huge advantage against a Liberal Party that is just starting to drag itself into the modern age of fundraising triggered by Jean Chrétien's Bill C-24 prohibiting corporate contributions and limiting individual donations.

We have also been strong in identifying our supporters and getting them to the polls. Winning close races and urging supporters to vote early saved our ship in 2004, when the tide ran out on us in the final few days. They also contributed to making the outcome clear enough in 2006 that there was no doubt that we had won the election and would form a minority government.

Much, however, remains to be done. Our grassroots model of fundraising and campaigning scarcely exists in Quebec, and without it our seats in that province will always be insecure. We have to transfer it into Quebec as quickly as possible, recognizing that cultural differences will complicate the process. It also needs to be said that our ground-level campaigning is spotty around the country, even in certain Western ridings where we are fundamentally strong. Some ridings are well organized, have lots of members and volunteers, have local phone banks and carry out comprehensive door-knocking protocols, while others struggle to put on the most minimal campaign. Training for volunteers has been rather haphazard in recent years because of the hectic pace of events, but Doug Finley is addressing that problem by establishing a Conservative Campaign Academy. For the future, we also need to learn how to use the internet to manage volunteers and direct their efforts around the country as needed.

Of course, all political parties need to raise money, identify supporters, and mobilize volunteers, so they all make use of the same methods, to varying degrees. But grassroots politics is particularly critical to the Conservative Party of Canada. As a conservative party, it stresses individual choice and responsibility in a competitive marketplace. That gives it a special responsibility to deal with voters as individuals, to find out what their concerns are, and to give them a stake in the political process by making it easy for them to donate time and money. Moreover, the Conservative Party draws heavily on the legacy of Preston Manning. His vision of the Reform Party as a neopopulist revival did not lead to forming a government, but it triggered an ongoing organizational revolution of political parties in Canada. Both federal and provincial parties are under continuing pressure to modernize their organizations, including fundraising practices, membership lists, leadership races, and candidate nomination procedures. As Manning's heirs, Conservatives have to be in the forefront of creating a political party that is easy for individuals to join, encourages donation and volunteerism, and is committed to winning elections one voter at a time.

9 TECHNOLOGY. *We are living in the biggest, fastest-moving communications revolution in human history. Each election campaign features new technologies. We must continue to be at the forefront in adapting new technologies to politics.*

Harper's first leadership campaign made a good start with the simple database and predictive dialer technology that we could afford at the time. Then, as the Canadian Alliance, we took a leap of faith and built CIMS, a combination of hardware and software that has enabled us to make remarkable progress in voter contact and grassroots fundraising. In the 2004 election, we learned how to use the Blackberry to keep in constant touch with the media, and with experience we did even better in that regard in 2005–06. In that most recent election, we also made a start on working with bloggers to amplify and diversify our message.

The pace of technological innovation is so rapid that no one can predict what we will be doing twenty or even ten years from now. In the short run, however, we need to make better use of the internet. We are still using our party and campaign websites mainly to archive information. If we can become more interactive, we can do better internet fundraising (still a minor part of our efforts). Even more exciting, we need to learn how to use the internet to recruit and manage volunteers and to deploy campaign workers around the country where they are most needed. Right now, we are the grassroots party of Canadian politics. We have to keep using technology to mobilize the grassroots in ways that no one has ever dreamed of.

Technology can help fulfill Preston Manning's dream of a populist, participatory political party. Also, this is the natural course
of evolution for a conservative party. As students of Hayek, we
believe in the market as a process of discovery. It is only logical
for us to be in the forefront of applying to politics the technological marvels produced by human ingenuity in a market economy.

10 PERSISTENCE. *Campaigning is a tough business, and mistakes are frequent. We have to correct our errors, learn from experience, and keep pushing ahead.*
The list of major mistakes that Harper's Team has made is
long and daunting. To mention only the most important:

- an unworkable organization at the beginning of the Canadian
  Alliance campaign;
- an inadequate plan for sales and processing of sales in the Canadian Alliance campaign;
- waste of several months in the Perth-Middlesex by-election;
- lack of response to negative ads, inadequate communication of
  the platform, and absence of an indigenous Quebec campaign
  in 2004;
- failure to envision endgame scenarios in 2004, resulting in a
  major slump at the end of the campaign.

But we studied our mistakes, learned from experience, and corrected them.
Indeed, the greatest triumph of Harper's Team came after the
disappointment of the 2004 election. Stephen spoke once about
quitting but did not. I tried to quit, but Stephen persuaded me to
stay. Ken Boessenkool went into the private sector in Calgary
but continued to play a key role as a volunteer. In the end we all
got down to figuring out how to do better the next time. There
were no sacred cows, no quick answers or single-factor explanations. We had to review everything we'd done, looking for possible improvements. Answers came slowly after much thought and
discussion, and we would still have been encumbered with problems if we had succeeded in forcing an election in the spring of
2005. But we ultimately got where we needed to go.

Politics is a tough business because you are competing against opponents who have their own moves to make. Everyone makes mistakes all the time because of imperfect information. No one in any party can succeed without persistence. Nonetheless, this advice is particularly relevant to the Conservative Party of Canada because Conservatives have never really recovered from the death of Sir John A. Macdonald in 1891. After he passed from the scene, no Conservative leader has ever able to duplicate his formula for holding together a long-term national coalition. Some – Borden, Bennett, Diefenbaker, Mulroney – had temporary successes, but these always ended not just in defeat but in disaster, leaving the party worse off than before.

Stephen Harper is now engaged in trying to do what no Conservative leader has been able to do for over a hundred years – build a viable, long-term coalition that can win victories and survive defeats without immolating itself on a bonfire of mutual recriminations. Of course there will be mistakes. No one has the secret of success in this endeavour. We have to work it out as we go along. We need not only persistence but a high degree of humility and tolerance on all sides. The Anglos have to learn about the specific character of politics in Quebec, while the Quebec Conservatives have to adopt modern methods of grassroots campaigning from the rest of the country. All of us have to learn how to bring ethnic voters into the Conservative coalition. We also have to admit that the Liberals have sometimes been better than us at opposition research, negative advertising, and putting out a coordinated message using all media simultaneously. We have to study their successes and co-opt their methods.

Stephen Harper's electoral victory in the 2006 election was just the beginning. There will be many more missed opportunities, mistakes, and false starts along the path to making the Conservative Party the natural governing party of Canada; but the goal is attainable if we keep learning from experience.

Getting Closer, 2008

In the national election of 14 October 2008, the Conservatives increased their share of the popular vote from 36.3 percent to 37.7 percent and won 143 seats, coming tantalizingly close to a majority government. The Liberals' popular vote fell from 30.2 percent to 26.3 percent – their worst performance since Confederation – and their seat total fell to seventy-seven. Thus, in spite of not quite reaching a majority, this election was another forward step in the Conservatives' long march toward replacing the Liberals as the dominant party in national politics.

This chapter is unlike the others in this book because it was written from the outside, not the inside. I went back to teaching at the University of Calgary after I resigned as campaign manager in June 2005. I worked in the war room in the election of 2005–06, but that was only a temporary engagement. Given the uncertainties of minority government, I could not do my job as a teacher while standing by for campaign duties at a moment's notice. In any case, my decision to publish *Harper's Team* meant that I could never go back and work in the secretive environment of Harper's team. So this chapter is written from an outside perspective, though with the insight that comes from having helped design the campaign machine.

POLITICAL MANAGEMENT

After winning the 2006 election, Stephen Harper moved into 24 Sussex Drive determined to last as long as he could as prime

minister. He had told me once that time was on his side. The best
way to shed the labels of being "scary" and having a "hidden
agenda," which the Liberals had used against him in both 2004
and 2006, was to govern moderately and responsibly. It was particularly important for him to implement campaign promises so
that voters could see that the platform was his agenda, that he
was not hiding anything.

This desire to stay in power and legislate rather than rush into
another election put a premium on survival in office – no small
challenge for a minority government holding only 124 of
308 seats in the House of Commons and vastly outnumbered in
the Senate. But it was a congenial challenge for Stephen, who
once said to me, "I think about strategy twenty-four hours a
day." In addition to his native strategic ability, he also had a couple of objective advantages. Paul Martin had resigned as leader,
so the Liberals would not want an election until after choosing
their new leader on 2 December 2006. In effect, that gave
Harper more than a year of clear sailing, because the new Liberal leader would need time to get ready for an election campaign. Also, although he commanded only 124 seats plus the
more or less predictable support of Quebec City independent
André Arthur, Stephen could pass legislation with the support of
any one of the three opposition parties. Once the Conservatives
helped Peter Milliken win re-election as speaker, even the
twenty-nine NDP votes plus the Conservatives plus Arthur would
constitute a majority in the House. The situation was tailor-
made for Harper the strategist, allowing him to tack back and
forth among the parties, passing bills with varying coalitions of
support, never becoming too dependent on any one ally.

Following this course through the first half of 2007, he was
able to pass two budgets and implement a fair number of campaign promises, including four of the Five Priorities – the Accountability Act, the Child Care Allowance, the one-percent GST
cut, and some criminal justice legislation – as well as a number
of other initiatives, including fixed election dates, an amnesty
for long-gun owners who did not register their weapons, a
home-ownership program for Indians living on reserve, and set-
tlement of the softwood-lumber dispute with the United States.
But not everything could be passed because the Liberals used

their control of the Senate to frustrate Senate reform and hold up some criminal justice initiatives.

Stephen decided to play harder ball in the second half of 2007, once it had become apparent what a mistake the Liberals had made in choosing Stéphane Dion as their leader. With the Liberals obviously afraid of an election, and Dion seemingly unable to get a campaign organized, Harper prorogued Parliament and came back with a new throne speech on 17 October 2007. This time, he announced, major government initiatives would be treated as matters of confidence, in contrast to his first eighteen months in office, when the only confidence votes were on budgetary matters.[1]

Under the first strategy, Harper had been playing for time, allowing himself to stay in office even if some of his bills could not be passed. Now, his message to the opposition was belligerent, not conciliatory – defeat us, and you'll have to face an election.[2] Dion and the Liberals responded by abstaining or offering only token opposition on most major bills through the first half of 2008, allowing the Conservatives to implement more campaign promises, such as an additional one-percentage-point reduction to the GST, a schedule of corporate income tax cuts extending through 2012, a small reduction in Employment Insurance premiums, and further criminal justice measures. There were also some new policies, such as immigration reform, that had not been previewed in the platform. When Parliament adjourned in June 2008, it seemed as if the Conservative Government would probably survive until the new fixed election date of 19 October 2009. Harper's minority government had lasted longer than any in Canadian history, except for Mackenzie King's two nominal minorities of 1920 and 1926, which were essentially de facto majority governments because of the predictable support of Progressive Liberals.[3] It could also point to a legislative record of achievement derived from the 2006 platform.

Of course, not everything was based on the platform. Stephen's biggest tactical triumph came in autumn 2007, when he pounced on a House of Commons resolution by Gilles Duceppe to recognize Quebec as a nation. Rewording the resolution to read that "the Québécois form a nation within a united Canada," Harper pulled off a coup by getting all parties, including the

out-manoeuvred BQ, to support it.[4] He also departed from platform commitments when he removed the tax exemption for income trusts and when he unveiled a new equalization formula
that fell short of his campaign promise to allow provinces to exempt 100 percent of natural resource revenues from the transfer
calculation.[5] Under heavy pressure, he went beyond the platform
to embrace the view that global warming was caused by greenhouse gas emissions and that the Canadian Government should
take action to reduce those emissions, a position he had resisted
in the past. He also made a dramatic apology to First Nations
over residential schools, something not mentioned in the 2006
platform. I didn't particularly like either the new greenhouse gas
policy or the residential schools apology, but they were in line
with the incrementalist course I had recommended in the first
edition of this book and which Harper openly professed in the
second week of the 2008 campaign.[6]

However, the advantages of staying in power were coming to an
end. The Conservatives had now implemented the most important
and most workable items from the platform, leaving questions
about what their agenda would be for another year in power.
Also, the opposition, afraid to defeat the government's legislation,
was trying to use House of Commons committees to investigate
alleged Conservative scandals, including Brian Mulroney's relationship with Karl-Heinz Schreiber, the Chuck Cadman affair (BC
journalist Tom Zytaruk had claimed that the Conservatives offered to buy Cadman a million dollars worth of life insurance in
spring 2005 if he would vote to defeat the Liberal Government of
Paul Martin),[7] and the so-called "in and out" financial plan, under which the Conservative national campaign had transferred
over a million dollars to local campaigns in the 2006 election, so
they could pay for additional advertising. None of these "scandals" had demonstrably hurt the Tories in the polls, but the publicity they created was nothing that any government would seek.

Also on the radar in summer 2008 was a highly uncertain economic picture: international financial markets trying to cope
with the aftermath of the United States mortgage crisis; oil prices
bouncing up and down; threats to Canadian manufacturing ex-
ports from the slowdown in the US economy. Some combination
of these might well lead to recession in Canada and increasing

unemployment if the government waited until October 2009 to go to the polls.

Stephen decided to see the governor general on 7 September to ask for an election to be held on 14 October 2008. This departed from the spirit but not the letter of the fixed-election-date legislation. The Act set the date of the next election as 19 October 2009, but also contained the following clause: "Nothing in this section affects the powers of the Governor General, including the power to dissolve Parliament at the Governor General's discretion."[8] Provincial fixed-date legislation in British Columbia, Ontario, and Newfoundland contains similar wording, which is required because it is impossible to change the power of the head of state to dissolve the legislature without a constitutional amendment. The net effect of the legislation is to prevent prime ministers from going beyond a four-year term of office while allowing them to request an earlier election if they wish.

In making use of this escape clause, Harper had to bear criticism for going against his earlier statements in support of fixed election dates. In itself, the issue quickly disappeared as soon as the writ was dropped; but it bolstered the larger narrative of the opposition parties that Harper was a promise-breaker who couldn't be trusted (income trusts, resource revenues in equalization, etc.). In the long run, maybe the furor over broken promises will lead to a more adult understanding of what politicians' commitments mean in an ever-changing world (e.g., Stéphane Dion rejected a carbon tax when he ran for Liberal leader in 2006 but then made it the cornerstone of his national election platform in 2008). However, in the short run there was also a price to be paid for broken promises, as Newfoundland Premier Danny Williams's ABC (Anyone But Conservative) campaign, launched over Harper's broken promise regarding the equalization formula, cost the Conservatives all three of their seats in the province. The ABC campaign was a pyrrhic victory for Danny Williams. While it punished the Conservatives by depriving them of three seats, those seats weren't enough to affect the overall outcome, and Newfoundland was left with no representation in the government cabinet and caucus. But in any case it was a lesson that breaking promises, no matter how necessary it may seem, can cause political retribution.

THE PRE-WRIT CAMPAIGN

Periods of minority government are periods of perpetual pre-writ campaigning. Parties have to remain campaign-ready because they can never be sure when the government might be defeated or the prime minister might request an election. In awareness of this, Harper kept all the major people and organizations from the 2006 campaign team geared up to prepare the next campaign, whenever that might come. That included campaign manager Doug Finley and communications strategist Patrick Muttart; advertising guru Perry Miele and the creative teams he had built up in Toronto and Montreal; the Responsive Marketing Group to handle fundraising and direct voter contact; Air Canada and Greyhound for the leader's tour; and Mike Coates to spearhead preparations for the leaders' debates.

In this ongoing state of pre-writ uncertainty, it was a big advantage for the Conservatives to have more money than their opponents. In the two and a half years from 1 January 2006 to 30 June 2008, the Conservative grassroots fundraising machine brought in $44.5 million while the Liberals raised $17.1 million.[9] Here are some ways in which the Conservatives leveraged their financial advantage in preparing for the next election.

The "Fear Factory"

Early in 2007, the Conservative rented state-of-the-art premises in Ottawa for a "war room," i.e., the command and control centre of a national campaign. Dubbed the "Fear Factory" by a Liberal wag,[10] the war room was quickly leased, furnished, and wired, including a TV studio so the party could stage its own press conferences. It was kept continually available until the election was finally called on 7 September 2008. The cost was considerable – hundreds of thousands of dollars a year – but it was a great convenience not to have to scramble for space and furnishings on short notice. As a signal to the other parties that they were in for a fight if they toppled the government, the normally secretive Conservatives allowed the media a tour of the "Fear Factory" so they could write stories about it.[11]

Direct Voter Contact (DVC)

As explained in preceding chapters, the Conservative approach to campaigning emphasizes voter identification and GOTV programs in targeted swing ridings. Ongoing grassroots fundraising helps create a base for writ-period DVC because it builds supporter lists and keeps contact information up to date. The prospecting side of the program means that DVC can more or less pay for itself while building the list of supporters and donors. The Conservatives had not been able to use their DVC program in Quebec in the past, but they did start grassroots fundraising in *la belle province* after the 2006 election, thus laying the groundwork for DVC in designated Quebec swing ridings in 2008. RMG set up a call centre in Quebec to undertake an ongoing DVC program of the type that has worked so well in the rest of Canada.

By-Elections

An effective DVC program is particularly useful in by-elections because turnout is always low. If you can use DVC to get your supporters to come to the polls while others are staying home, you can pull off upset victories. The Conservatives did this in four by-elections in the pre-writ period, winning two new ridings and coming close in two others where they had been given little chance.

On 17 September 2007, the Conservatives gained a sweeping victory in the rural Quebec riding of Roberval – Lac-St-Jean, getting 60 percent of the vote compared to 27 percent for the runner up Bloc Québécois, even though the BQ had won this riding in 2006. The Conservative candidate in St-Hyacinthe – Bagot also did much better than expected, getting 37 percent of the vote to 42 percent for the victorious BQ candidate. On the same day, Stéphane Dion's handpicked candidate in the formerly safe Liberal seat of Outremont was crushingly defeated by the NDP's Thomas Mulcair. In that race, the Conservatives made little effort, knowing that the NDP had a much better chance to defeat the Liberal candidate. All in all, it was a good day for the Conservatives, while the BQ and NDP also had something to cheer about; but it was an awful day for Stéphane Dion and the Liberals.

The Conservatives repeated their by-election success on 17 March 2008, taking back the northern Saskatchewan riding of Desnethé – Mississippi – Churchill River, which they had won in 2004 but lost in 2006, and coming second by only 151 votes to the Liberals in Vancouver Quadra. Both races had significance far beyond their own borders. In the heavily native Saskatchewan riding, the Conservative candidate, a status Indian and former RCMP officer, handily beat a former provincial NDP cabinet minister who had been recruited by Ralph Goodale, Stéphane Dion's lieutentant in Saskatchewan. Quadra had been a Liberal seat ever since John Turner represented that riding in the 1980s. The Liberals tried to take solace in holding two safe seats – Toronto Centre and Willowdale – but the Conservatives had made little effort there, preferring to concentrate their forces where it could make a difference. All in all, the Conservatives' by-election performance, based on aggressive DVC, paid big dividends in keeping the Liberals off balance.

A Jet for the Leader's Tour

The centrepiece of a campaign for a national party is the leader's tour. Having a jet plane to move the leader, his staff, and accompanying media representatives is essential because Canada is such a big country. The Conservatives, who previously leased their campaign jet from Air Canada, quickly made a deal with Air Canada after the 2006 election to get a jet whenever they might need it. Such deals are expensive, involving a retainer of hundreds of thousands of dollars a year, but they are necessary if you want a plane on short notice. Having a campaign jet in place allowed the Conservatives to play brinksmanship games in Parliament without worrying about being defeated.

In contrast, the Liberals, whether from organizational problems or financial difficulties, did not lock up a jet until the last minute, when Air Inuit leased them a thirty-year-old Boeing 737, which the Conservatives claimed was 20 percent less fuel-efficient than their own Airbus C-319. Moreover, the Liberal jet was not ready until day 4 of the campaign[12] and then suffered a mechanical breakdown that caused it to be grounded in Montreal on 16 September.[13] The Liberals may have saved money by not leasing a jet in advance, but they paid a high price in terms of bad publicity throughout the campaign.

Advertising

The Conservative Party's most striking display of financial muscle occurred in advertising. Historically, Canadian political parties have made little use of paid advertising outside the writ period, but the Conservatives unleashed several waves of advertising against Stéphane Dion, starting soon after he became Liberal leader in December 2006 and continuing to the eve of the 2008 election.

On 28 January 2007, the Conservatives rolled out a suite of three ads ridiculing Dion and paid for them to run on Canadian TV networks during the Super Bowl. Conservative spokesmen also gave the ads more resonance in unpaid media by pursuing the theme that the weak leader Dion was a "flip-flopper" who kept changing his positions.[14] Although most people, when asked by pollsters, denied being influenced by the ads, the campaign almost certainly contributed to the dismal leadership rankings that Dion quickly started to gather in polls.[15] By early April 2007, Dion was seen as the best leader by only 17 percent of respondents in a Nanos poll, compared to 42 percent for Stephen Harper.[16]

The most effective of the three ads – entitled "What Kind of Leader Is Stéphane Dion?" – used footage from the debates held among the candidates in the Liberal leadership race. It showed Michael Ignatieff at his most professorial, wagging a long finger and saying, "Stéphane, we didn't get it done" (referring to the Liberals' commitment to cut greenhouse gas emissions under the Kyoto Protocol), and Dion replying in high-pitched, heavily accented English, "This is unfair! You don't know what you speak about. Do you think it's easy to make priorities?" Just by letting the two Liberals speak, the ad brilliantly showcased the divisions within the party as well as Dion's prickly personality and his difficulty in communicating in English.

On 29 May 2007, the Conservatives launched another flurry
of radio and TV ads targeted at Dion, this time over the Liberal-
dominated Senate's hold-up of the government's bill to limit sen-
atorial terms to eight years. The theme was "Stéphane Dion is
(once again) not a leader."[17] These ads could hardly have depressed Dion's leadership numbers lower than they already were,
but they may have helped keep them low.

The third cycle of Conservative ads was a pre-emptive strike
against Stéphane Dion's "Green Shift," which he was planning
to unveil in June 2008. The Tories beat him to the punch with
radio and TV ads labelling it "Dion's tax trick" and "Dion's tax
on everything."[18] Running all summer, mostly on radio in battleground ridings, the ads contributed to the Green Shift's loss of
popularity during the summer. Supported by a majority of respondents when it was unveiled in June, the Green Shift was opposed by a majority in an Ipsos-Reid poll when the writ was
dropped in September 2008.[19]

Finally, ten days before the election was called, the Conservatives launched a new series of six positive ads about Stephen
Harper. Designed to rub the sharp edges off the prime minister's
personality, they showed him dressed in a casual blue sweater, talking about sentimental topics such as his family, immigrants, and
veterans.[20] The ads fit the Conservative campaign strategy of por-
traying Harper as the safe choice and Dion as risky. They contributed to the surge in polling numbers with which the Conservative
campaign began; five polls released between 7 and 10 September
2008 reported an average Conservative lead over the Liberals of
12.8 percentage points.[21] A Harris-Decima poll taken during the
first week of the campaign showed that far more people had seen
Conservative ads than those of the other parties, a result that certainly owed something to the jump that the Conservatives got on
the other parties through their pre-writ campaign.[22]

Estimating the effect of political advertising is notoriously difficult because so many things are happening at the same time.
But every time the Conservative ran a series of ads in the extended pre-writ period, the trend in public opinion as measured
in polls was consistent with the obvious purpose of the ads – to
drive Stéphane Dion's leadership ratings down and keep them
down, to make voters skeptical of the Green Shift, and to make

them feel better about supporting Stephen Harper. Indeed, when Dion announced his retirement as Liberal leader a week after the election, he blamed Conservative pre-writ advertising for his electoral defeat. Voters, he whined, "have seen the propaganda of the Conservatives and that's the way they saw me."[23] That analysis is simplistic and self-serving; negative ads don't work unless they highlight something real in the target's character and behaviour. But even if the ads themselves didn't defeat Dion, they certainly drew voters' attention to his weaknesses.

THE 2008 CAMPAIGN: THEMATICS, MECHANICS, AND DYNAMICS

Thematics

The 2008 campaign was quite different from the 2006 campaign in terms of *thematics*, because of differences in the strategic situation. In 2005–06, the Conservatives were the official opposition, trailing the Liberals in the polls not only in top-line voting support but also in voters' confidence in their ability to handle crucial issues such as the economy, taxes, and relations with the United States – almost all issues, in fact. Moreover, Stephen Harper was far less trusted as a leader than Paul Martin at the outset of that campaign. But all these factors were reversed in 2008. On the eve of the election, the Conservatives were in government, leading in the polls, and regarded as better able to manage most issues, while Stephen Harper was far ahead of Stéphane Dion in leadership rankings.

In 2006, the Conservatives had to run from behind, drawing attention to their platform to build voters' confidence in their ability to manage issues. This led to the communications strategy of announcing a new platform plank early in the morning every day, in order to get out in front in the news cycle. In contrast, 2008 was a classic frontrunner campaign for the Conservatives. Running on their record of achievement in office, they depicted themselves as the safe choice against the risk of Stéphane Dion's "tax on everything." The Conservative positive ads proclaimed, "We're better off with Harper," while the negative ads said, "Stéphane Dion – not worth the risk."[24]

Campaign iconography was deliberately reassuring. In the positive ads as well as in many campaign appearances, Stephen wore a navy blue sweater vest with a light blue shirt that matched his china-blue eyes. He spoke in the ads about emotional topics such as his family, veterans, and the North. He gave an interview to the *Globe and Mail* about his love of music,[25] and even played the piano and sang in a campaign appearance.[26] This, by Stephen's standards, was an extraordinary act of self-disclosure. To put it in perspective, I had known Stephen since 1991 and worked with him very closely for many of the intervening years, but I didn't even learn until 2004, when I was reading the draft of William Johnson's biography of Harper, that he played the piano.[27]

As might be expected, the thematics for the Quebec campaign were somewhat different. While the English campaign was all about the contrast between Harper's strong and Dion's weak leadership, the Quebec campaign was less personalized. The slogan was, "Le Québec prend des forces," or "Quebec is getting stronger." Harper initially appeared in only one ad; and when he did appear, it was in conversation with his Quebec cabinet ministers. Most of the other ads were "streeters," showing ordinary Quebecers saying that the Bloc Québécois couldn't deliver anything for Quebec and that they looked to the Conservatives for results. It was basically a replay of the 2006 strategy of arguing that the BQ was useless. Unlike 2006, however, there were also some negative ads directed at Dion, reflecting the Conservatives' hopes at the beginning of the campaign that they might make progress in areas around Montreal where the Liberals were still a significant opponent.

Although the Conservatives were running mainly on their record, both in Quebec and in the rest of Canada, they did unveil some new policies. But these were not as numerous as in 2006, and much smaller in scope. There was nothing like the GST cut, which affected everyone, or the Child Care Allowance, which was for all parents of children under six. This time the policies were smaller in their reach, such as allowing self-employed people to opt into the maternity and parental benefits of Employment Insurance. All announcements were cast in modest terms. For example, Harper said about the EI initiative, "Allowing self-employed Canadians to access maternity and parental benefits is another step in our plan to provide sensible, balanced and affordable tax relief and benefits."[28] The platform document estimated the cost of all promises at only $8.67 billion over four years.[29] Needless to say, these micro-policies were calibrated for political target groups, especially family-oriented women.

With the benefit of hindsight, one can see two important problems with the thematics. First, it turned out to be a mistake to try to rerun the 2006 Quebec campaign in 2008, because it did not respect the BQ's ability to learn from experience. In the event, the BQ ran on a different and unexpected theme in 2008 – preventing the Conservatives from winning a majority government – which the Conservatives were not prepared to rebut.

The second mistake was that, although the 2008 campaign had a detailed platform, it had nothing similar to the 2006 campaign's "Five Priorities" to make the platform intelligible to voters. In 2008, Harper followed the procedure that had worked so well in 2006, announcing one plank a day before releasing the whole platform about a week before election day. But in 2008 there was a lot of grumbling from the media that the Conservatives had no platform, which wasn't strictly true but reflected the fact that, without something like the "Five Priorities," no one could remember and make sense of the platform's dozens of boutique policies.

Mechanics

In terms of mechanics, it was 2006 all over again. The Leader's Tour was much the same, relying on morning message events and evening rallies, with occasional special interviews for the media thrown in. As in 2006, the tour ran on time as it went from one target area to another, trying to push candidates in winnable ridings over the top. Message events were carefully planned and controlled, and rallies were well attended. Inevitably, some reporters complained about the "bubble" in which the prime minister travelled; but the reality is that, if you don't create a bubble, the leader will be caught in unscripted moments that the media will report as evidence of incompetence.

Advertising was in most respects similar to 2005–06:

- separate campaigns in Quebec and the rest of Canada, with the Quebec campaign constructed mainly against the Bloc and the Canada-wide campaign directed mainly at the Liberals (though some anti-Dion ads were also produced for Quebec);
- heavy reliance on Harper as talking head in the English ads but not in the French (except at the end);
- a balance of positive and negative ads, though in this shorter election, the negative ads ran from the beginning, rather than being introduced half-way through, as in 2005–06;
- concentration of the ad buy in media markets serving targeted ridings.

The main difference was the enormously greater importance of pre-writ advertising in 2008.

Campaign headquarters were physically bigger and better than the last time, but it is unclear whether the investment in having a TV studio on site was worth the cost. A few news conferences were held there early in the campaign, but interest seemed to wane thereafter. Organization was about the same as in 2006, with specialized units for managing tour logistics, scripting the leader's daily appearances, maintaining liaison with candidates, and supporting targeted ridings.

There was once again a rapid response team, functioning much as before, responding to attacks and attacking the other parties, working at the warp speed required by campaigning in the age of the internet and the speeded-up news cycle. However, in contrast to 2006, the 2008 rapid response effort was concerned less with offence than with playing defence, responding to Liberal attacks and candidate problems. The rapid response team had, in fact, stockpiled good ammunition against Dion, but he seemed so woeful that the media were not interested in learning much more. For example, the Conservatives early in the campaign released the fact that Dion had not complied with the Elections Canada timetable for reporting his efforts to repay his leadership debts,[30] but there was virtually no media take-up. It seemed too trivial to journalists already convinced that Dion was hopeless.

The whole campaign was backstopped by the same kind of DVC program that the Conservatives had used in the past to get an edge in close races in targeted ridings. The main difference compared to the past was that the program was now able to operate in Quebec as well as in English Canada. In the end, however, that didn't confer much of an advantage in 2008 because, when the Conservatives sagged in Quebec in the second half of the campaign, support in ridings thought to be winnable dropped below the point where DVC can produce a victory.

Dynamics

In 2008, campaign dynamics were markedly different from 2004 and 2005–06. In the earlier two campaigns, the Conservatives started about six percentage points behind the Liberals and had to claw their way into the lead, using a commanding performance in the leaders' debate (2004), a smooth tour based on dribbling out the platform (2006), and attacks on Paul Martin (both campaigns). By contrast, the Conservatives were in the lead when the writ was dropped in 2008, having polled ahead of the Liberals consistently since January 2006. The lead, moreover, was accentuated by the Conservatives' ability to advertise heavily in the ten days before the election began, while no other party was on the air. Thus, when polls started to come out three or four days after the writ was dropped, most of them showed double-digit leads, with the Conservatives close to or even above 40 percent and the Liberals in the mid-20s.

From the very beginning, then, it seemed that the Conservatives were almost certain to win, which allowed three other questions to come to the fore: (1) could they win a majority of seats; (2) who would finish second, the Liberals or the NDP; and (3) could the other parties somehow get together to stop the Conservatives from winning a majority of seats?

In fact, the BQ sounded this note from the very beginning, correctly claiming that, by holding onto its seats in Quebec, it was the only party that could prevent a Conservative majority. This was a new departure for the Bloc, for it was now aligning itself on a right-left ideological dimension rather than promoting Quebec's independence. Although dismissed by commentators at the outset as an admission of defeat, this proved to be a canny move for the Bloc, allowing it to play off Conservative positions adopted mainly for their effect elsewhere in Canada. In the end, the Bloc made the Conservatives pay in Quebec for being conservative elsewhere.

The key opportunity for the Bloc came from exploiting the "culture cuts" – some small reductions to federally funded arts programs that had been announced before the campaign ever began. These cuts were not part of the campaign platform, which indeed purported to be arts-friendly, promising to "maintain financial supports for arts and culture at or above existing levels, while continuing to improve the effectiveness of allocations where possible."[31] The spending reductions had come earlier in the summer from the Treasury Board, prompted by publicity about how the Conservatives had allowed spending on arts and culture to balloon above what the Liberals had ever approved. As a cabinet minister later told me, the cuts represented a "red-meat moment," designed to keep the Conservative base happy. They were then announced to the media by the PMO, reflecting a deliberate decision to use them as campaign fodder; and the campaign went ahead with them even though it was obvious by the end of August that they would be a big issue is Quebec.[32]

It surprises me that the arts cuts weren't held up until after the election because they violated the "small target" strategy outlined to Patrick Muttart and me by Brian Loughnane, Federal Director of the Australian Liberal Party, in March 2005. Loughnane explained that the Australian Liberals had learned from experience not to irritate vociferous special-interest groups at election time because they are implacable enemies when aroused. It's common sense, really: make yourself a small target so you can concentrate on getting out your own message rather than fending off attacks from all quarters.

Although they generated criticism from luminaries such as Margaret Atwood, the cuts did no discernible political damage in most of Canada, but they worked differently in Quebec, where arts and culture easily become issues of national identity. Once the Bloc started to draw attention to the cuts, Quebec's writers, musicians, and actors started denouncing them with extraordinary vigour. There were letters to the editor, appearances on TV and radio, rallies, and, most effective of all, a video posted on YouTube which portrayed francophone artists being dismissed by square-headed anglophone bureaucrats and politicians. Quebec Premier Jean Charest also piled on, taking a nationalistic position on this as well as other issues. The criticism was way over the top for piddling reductions in federal spending that would have almost no impact in the bigger picture of arts funding, but the Conservative campaign was caught flat-footed because the issue didn't fit into their plan of attacking the BQ as ineffective. It was also a problem that the Conservative organization does not have an acknowledged, high-profile Quebec lieutenant who can put out fires like this.

Harper made things worse when he said in Saskatoon: "I think when ordinary working people come home, turn on the TV and see a gala of a bunch of people, you know, at a rich gala all subsidized by taxpayers claiming their subsidies aren't high enough when they know those subsidies have actually gone up – I'm not sure that's something that resonates with ordinary people."[33] This wasn't the smartest thing to say, not least because Stephen's wife, Laureen, as well as many of his cabinet ministers, are often seen at arts galas. Harper knew right away his words would play badly in Quebec and refused to repeat himself in French, but the damage was done.

And the damage was considerable. In the first two weeks of the campaign, the Conservatives and Bloc were running neck and neck in Quebec, both in the low 30 percent range. At that rate, the Conservatives were on track to win perhaps fifteen additional seats, which might well have given them a majority on election night. But, once the culture issue exploded, BQ numbers went up to about 40 percent, while the Conservatives went down to about 20 percent or even lower in some polls. For a while it looked as if the Tories might lose half the eleven seats they held going into the election.

The arts issue catalyzed the freefall because artists can get to the microphone so easily and because of the national-identity implications in Quebec, but other issues were also involved, most importantly, Harper's call to strengthen the Young Offender's Act. The Bloc attacked the proposal for stiffer sentences for fourteen- and fifteen-year-old teens convicted of serious violent

offences, even though the platform explicitly allowed provinces
to override this with their own definition of threshold age.[34] For
Gilles Duceppe, sterner treatment of young offenders, like the
arts cuts, was an offence against "Quebec values" and showed
that Harper was an ideological clone of George W. Bush. In a
particularly gross distortion, he said incarcerating young offenders would be like giving "fresh meat" to older prisoners, even
though the Conservative platform did not propose mixing young
offenders with the general prison population. But, as unfounded
as the criticism was, it had an impact because the Conservative
campaign seemed to have no effective response.

The Conservatives lost their chance at a majority through
these Quebec misadventures; without fifteen additional Quebec
seats, there was almost no chance of getting to the magic number of 155. But, bad as that was, what happened on 2 October
was much worse. On that day, the Toronto Stock Exchange index dropped more than eight hundred points,[35] even though the
United States Congress had just approved President Bush's bail-
out package – a nice introduction to the English-language leaders' debate scheduled for that evening. In the debate, Stephen
followed his frontrunner strategy – keep calm and look states-
manlike while the other four gang up on you, and in particular
don't get mad at Elizabeth May because a display of temper
might drive away the female voters you've been courting.[36] Instant polling showed that he "won" the debate but performed
below expectations, while Dion performed above expectations
depressed by years of Conservative attack ads.[37] Dion also put
forward a five-point plan to deal with the economic crisis,
which Stephen dismissed as hysterical improvisation. Indeed,
there wasn't much substance to Dion's plan, which consisted
mainly of promises to consult experts and other political leaders, but at least he had acknowledged the seriousness of events.
Stephen's mantra, on the other hand, was to keep calm because
the fundamentals were strong. It was uncomfortably reminis-
cent of Trudeau's disastrous 1972 "The Land Is Strong" campaign,[38] especially when Harper's platform, released a few days
later, was entitled "The True North Strong and Free."

Even though Stephen "won" the English debate, Conservative
polling numbers nosedived in the following days as the Dow

Jones, TSX, and other stock market indexes around the world continued to fall, while Stephen said not much of anything. Opponents had a field day claiming he lacked empathy. By the middle of the final week, the Conservative double-digit lead had shrunk to four percentage points in published tracking polls. Stephen appeared to have frozen as he did in the final week of the 2004 campaign, refusing to depart from the original plan when conditions suddenly changed. But it was not that simple. He had to be extremely careful about what he said in public because the Department of Finance was already involved in negotiations with the banks leading to the $25 billion "asset swap" announced later in the week.[39] In the pressure cooker of an election campaign, one wrong word from the prime minister could have killed the deal and caused a jarring decline in bank stocks as well as a run on the dollar.

But Stephen rebounded and pulled it together. On 8 October, he showed that he understood the impact of the financial crisis by referring to his mother:

> We're getting this criticism that I somehow don't understand the stock market or I don't understand what people are feeling about the stock market …
>
> I use my mother as an obvious example because, you know, she's the person closest to me who's most worried about the stock market these days.
>
> And believe me, I get quicker updates from her on the stock market than I do from the Department of Finance.[40]

It was a bit hokey, but far better than what he had said the day before, while the TSX fell another four hundred points: "I think there's probably some great buying opportunities emerging in the stock market as a consequence of all this panic."[41] Good advice, to be sure, but not what most people want to hear when their pensions are evaporating!

The "great buying opportunities" comment will go down in the annals of campaign clunkers; but, even though the opposition immediately pounced on it, it didn't seem to matter much. The important thing was that Harper was out in public talking about the crisis, saying something other than "the fundamentals are strong." Voters who were already convinced that he was the best leader on offer in this race didn't expect miracles from him; they just needed to be reassured that he understood what was going on and that he appreciated the impact on ordinary people.

Then a number of things happened in the final few days to give the Conservative campaign a boost. Perhaps the biggest windfall was Stéphane Dion's disastrous interview with CTV host Steve Maher in Halifax on Thursday, 9 October. Maher asked Dion, with reference to the financial crisis, "If you were prime minister now, what would you have done that Mr. Harper has not done?"[42] Seemingly unable to understand the question, Dion asked three times to restart the interview and never did give a coherent answer; CTV executives then upset Liberal expectations that the false starts would not be shown and aired the entire interview. Posted on YouTube, the video was widely seen and discussed. Indeed, Harper goosed the publicity by personally drawing the video to the attention of journalists travelling with his leader's tour. It was risky for the prime minister to intervene this way rather than letting a surrogate carry out the attack, but it ensured maximum publicity. The Liberals protested that the question was convoluted (too many verb tenses), that Dion's hearing impediment was at fault, and that CTV had broken its word not to broadcast the repeats; but most viewers seemed to see the interview as evidence that Dion could not understand a simple English question and had no actual policy.

On Friday, 10 October, Statistics Canada reported that 107,000 new jobs had been created in September, the largest one-month gain since reporting of this statistic began in 1976.[43] The same day, the World Economic Forum released a survey rating Canada's banks as the soundest in the world.[44] Both announcements lent credence to Harper's repeated statements that Canadian fundamentals were strong. Simultaneously, the federal government carried out a $25 billion "asset swap" with Canadian banks, increasing their liquidity by buying mortgages from them for CMHC to hold.[45] In normal times, this non-bailout bailout might have been perceived as evidence that the banks were not so sound after all, but in context it seemed to show that the Conservative Government was taking constructive action.

Stephen also helped himself by campaigning vigorously over the weekend. On 12 October, he went to Quebec to appear at a

"Western festival" at Saint-Tite, trying to undo some of the damage from the Bloc's negative campaign. His remarks were folksy. He was not, he said, "the devil in a cowboy hat." Further, "Our platform isn't a right-wing platform. Our platform is a platform based on families who work hard to succeed, a platform based on economic development, a platform based on providing stability at a time of economic uncertainty."[46] On Monday, 13 October, the final day of the campaign, he made a coast-to-coast flight from Prince Edward Island to British Columbia, touching down in contested ridings along the way. Then he got another break as international markets went strongly upward on election day, including the TSX, which gained 890 points, its best single-day gain ever.

The hard push at the end represented a welcome progression in Stephen's campaigning ability. In 2004 he had frozen over the child pornography fiasco, and we could not get him to make necessary last-minute adjustments in tour and messaging. In 2006 when he got into trouble with unscripted remarks, we got him back on script and he coasted to the finish line without taking new initiatives. But in 2008, after a period of hesitation at the beginning of the last week, he waded back into the fray, campaigning hard and responding creatively to difficulties. It was by far the best endgame of the three Harper campaigns.

Harper's closing effort was rewarded with a surge in the final polls. The low point came with his "buying opportunities" comments; the next morning the Conservatives were only four points ahead of the Liberals in the Harris-Decima tracking poll. But Conservative numbers started to go up after Stephen referred to his mother, and by the weekend the published polls were converging around a lead of seven or eight points over the Liberals. But tracking polls cannot fully capture rapid change because of their three-day roll. The ongoing surge showed most clearly in Nik Nanos' one-day numbers for Sunday night, giving the Conservatives a lead of 10.4 points over the Liberals with an overnight sample of 423.[47] In fact, the Conservatives' margin on election night proved to be 11.4. As in 2004, there was a last-minute shift that no pollster could fully measure, but this time it was in favour of the Conservatives, not against them.

The strong endgame was also assisted by a shift in advertising in the final week. The last-minute French advertising showed three Harper-in-a-sweater ads designed to counteract Gilles Duceppe's scorching personal attacks, plus a final ad on the futility of the Bloc. The closing English ad showed a little girl seated at the kitchen table while her mother pondered the bad financial news and concluded that "Dion scares me ... He's just not worth the risk." Serious in tone and designed to appeal to the family-oriented women who were the main demographic target of the whole Conservative campaign, it was quite a shift from the comic, sometimes cartoonish quality of the early anti-Dion ads. The Conservatives played it heavily in targeted ridings during the final days of the campaign.[48]

RESULTS

The 2008 election results showed encouraging gains for the Conservatives as compared to the outcome of the 2006 election (see table 10.1). The Conservatives won an additional 1.4 percent of the popular and nineteen more seats, while the Liberals went down by 3.9 percent of the popular vote and twenty-seven seats. The Conservatives' gains were broadly distributed, including new seats in British Columbia, Saskatchewan (repeating a by-election win), Manitoba, Ontario, Quebec (another by-election win), New Brunswick, Nova Scotia, and Prince Edward Island.

Drilling down further makes it apparent that the strategy of courting ethnic voters in metropolitan areas paid off. The Conservatives won six new seats in the so-called 905 belt of suburbs around Toronto and regained three suburban seats in the Vancouver area; and even where they did not win in the 905 belt and in Vancouver, the Conservatives were competitive. For example, Ruby Dhalla's margin of victory in Brampton-Springdale, which had been eight thousand in the 2006 election, fell to one thousand this time; and Ujjal Dosanjh, who had a margin of nine thousand votes in Vancouver South in 2006, won by only twenty votes after a judicial recount. A precise analysis of the ethnic vote remains to be done, but it is obvious that the Conservatives could not have achieved these results without getting more ethnic support than in the past.

In other ways, too, the Conservative coalition is becoming broader. Peter Kent won the heavily Jewish riding of Thornhill

Table 10.1

Canadian General Election Results, 2006 and 2008

Party	2006		2008	
	Popular Vote (%)	*Seats*	*Popular Vote (%)*	*Seats*
Cons.	36.3	124	37.7	143
Lib.	30.2	103	26.3	77
NPD	17.5	29	18.2	37
BQ	10.5	51	10.0	49
Green	4.5	0	6.8	0
Other	1.0	1	1.2	2

just outside Toronto. The Conservatives won Nunavut with an Inuit candidate, Desnethé – Mississippi – Churchill River with a status Indian candidate, and two ridings in Winnipeg with Metis candidates. The Conservatives are also appealing now to franco-phones outside Quebec, winning three ridings in eastern Ontario with large francophone populations as well as St. Boniface in Manitoba and Miramichi in New Brunswick. All this helps make the Conservatives a party that, even if it does not win every elec-tion, will always be in the running.

Yet amidst this good news for the Conservatives, it is apparent that they still face major problems in Canada's three largest cities. They won some suburban seats around Vancouver and Toronto, but nothing at all in the inner cities, and they won neither subur-ban nor central seats in Montreal. Conservative parties in the modern world do better in rural or suburban areas than in inner cities, so Vancouver, Toronto, and Montreal will never become bastions of Conservative strength; but the party needs to win some seats there to establish better contact with the intellectual and artistic communities that thrive in big cities. Further progress with ethnic voters should eventually yield at least a few metro seats. Victories in Vancouver may be the most attainable, since the Conservatives are already competitive, even if not yet victori-ous, in some of the inner ridings in that city. Montreal seats will be the most difficult to achieve, because the Liberals are deeply entrenched on the West Island as the protector of English-language rights and the BQ is very strong among Montreal francophones. Between these extremes, seats in Toronto will require a lot of further work, but at least a few victories should eventually become possible in middle-class areas that are suburban in character even though legally part of Toronto. The biggest obstacle is probably the *Toronto Star,* which is so Liberal that it was the only metropolitan daily in Canada to endorse Dion in the 2008 election. The largest newspaper in the country, the *Star* is widely read by the sort of middle-class voters who in other cities vote Conservative, and its ceaseless proselytizing for the Liberals is a serious hindrance to Conservative growth in Toronto.

The Conservatives did not win a majority of seats in this election, even though they beat the Liberals by 11.4 percentage points, a margin that in past elections had always produced a majority for the victorious party.[49] That the Conservatives failed to get a majority is due to their anemic result in Quebec, winning only ten seats, the same as in 2004. This result was based on getting 21.7 percent of the popular vote, as compared to 38.1 percent for the BQ. Had the two parties each gotten about 30 percent of the vote, as the polls were indicating in the first two weeks of the campaign, the Conservatives would probably have won about twenty-five seats instead of ten, and might have earned their majority.

The simple analysis is that Harper made a mistake and lost his majority over the culture cuts; but, while not wrong, the simple analysis is a little simplistic. The cuts became a big deal because the BQ, which has been entrenched in the province since 1993, decided to make an issue of them. Previous national leaders, such as Pierre Trudeau and Brian Mulroney, who made Quebec a major part of their national coalition did not have to face anything like the BQ. Also, it is fair to ask how deep Quebeckers' support for the Conservatives was if they could withdraw it over such a small issue after all the benefits that the Conservative Government had conferred on Quebec, including a seat at UNESCO, recognition of the Québécois as a nation within a united Canada, and revision of the equalization formula to address the so-called "fiscal imbalance."

The 2008 result leads to questions about the "Three Sisters" formula for restoring the Conservative voting coalition. It looks

as if the Quebec sister will be hard to attract and keep in the
fold. Particularly entering a recession of unknown duration,
there will be no more money to buy loyalty in Quebec. If Quebec
voters get upset about $45 million in arts cuts, whose impact on
Quebec might have been $20 million at most, how will they
react if the government has to cut $4 or 5 billion out of federal
expenditures in order to keep the budget in balance? Another
challenge for political management in Quebec is the endless
feuding between federal Conservatives who support the provincial Liberals and those who support the ADQ. In any case, neither Liberal leader Jean Charest nor ADQ leader Mario Dumont
is a reliable partner for Harper, since both provincial leaders are
inevitably motivated by provincial concerns that do not necessarily align with federal priorities.

The most basic problem with positing soft nationalists in
Quebec as the essential "Third Sister" in a national Conservative
coalition is an underlying clash of objectives. Many Conservative
voters in Quebec are not conservative in any real sense; they just
see a Conservative Government as a source of benefits – symbolic recognition, legal jurisdiction, transfer payments – to their
province. Their desires can be met to some extent by a general
policy of devolving responsibilities to all provinces, but that can
only go so far if the federal government is to maintain its constitutional responsibilities. And at that point Quebec provincial
leaders are likely to say, "Reopen the constitution"[50] – the kiss
of death in the rest of Canada.

Wooing the "Fourth Sister" – ethnic voters – seems easy by
comparison. Middle-class Asian families in the suburbs of
Vancouver and Toronto make few demands. They want to feel
accepted, and they have understandable concerns about aspects
of immigration policy; but beyond that they are mainly interested in the issues that motivate all conservatives – a favourable
business climate, lower taxes, safe streets, and family-friendly
policies. They aren't particularly attracted by the fashionable
causes of the left, such as environmentalism, feminism, gay
rights, and animal liberation. Many are strongly religious and
socially conservative. They would be natural supporters of the
Conservative Party except for the Liberals' historic success in
courting ethnic communities. If the Conservatives can build

upon their success in 2008 to bring ever larger segments of ethnic communities over to their side, they can build their majority without having to cater to francophones in Quebec.

A supporting factor in this calculus is that the proportion of Quebec seats in the House will continue to decline over time. Quebec now has slightly fewer than 25 percent of the seats – 75 of 308. After the next decennial census and reapportionment, that will sink to about 22 percent – 75 of, say, 340. Almost all the new seats will be in areas where the Conservatives are dominant or at least competitive – Calgary and Edmonton, and the suburbs of Vancouver and Toronto. Harper might even hasten such a reapportionment, as he tried unsuccessfully to do in the last Parliament.[51]

None of this is to argue that the Conservatives should abandon Quebec. Any government will always want to have ministers from Quebec in the cabinet, and that requires winning seats in the province. But after this election, Quebec no longer provides the unique and indispensable path to majority government. The Conservatives can afford to deal with Quebec as they would with any other province, treating it fairly but not obsessively.

FINAL THOUGHTS

Harper's team is now the biggest, best-funded, best-organized political machine in Canada. It has, in fact, created a new model of Canadian political campaigning – the "permanent campaign." We used to think of political campaigns as episodes, spasms of energy every four or five years. About a year before an election was expected, a party would appoint a campaign committee and a manager to get ready. Obviously planning and preparation was required, and there might be a brief period of pre-writ advertising before the election was called; but the campaign itself was basically a five-week phenomenon.

Harper's team, in contrast, never rests. A campaign manager reporting directly to the leader, not to a committee, is always in place. Voter identification linked to fundraising goes on 363 days a year (Christmas and Easter excepted). With the cash flow from such aggressive fundraising, the party can afford to spend millions on advertising, even years in advance of the writ, and to fund other activities such as the Conservative Campaign University, which trains candidates and workers, especially in the use of the potent Direct Voter Contact program and the CIMS database. Activities funded by the House of Commons can also be channelled to political purposes – travel to targeted ridings and ethnic communities, mail outs with a response card for voter identification, public opinion research to find policies that will resonate with target demographic groups. All parties do some of these things some of the time, but the Conservatives are unique in the scale on which they operate and the degree to which everything is coordinated. They have produced a campaign equivalent of Colin Powell's doctrine of "overwhelming force" – apply all possible resources to the battleground ridings where the election will be won or lost.

But the most formidable machine can sometimes be beaten, or may beat itself even if no opponent can do so. This election showed a couple of tendencies that Harper's team will have to guard against in the future.

One is arrogance. Voters can turn against you if they perceive that you don't show basic human respect for your opponents. Two episodes during the campaign were illustrative in this regard. First was the "pooping puffin" incident, which involved a picture of Stéphane Dion on the Conservative website. A puffin would periodically fly across the screen and leave a little deposit on the hapless Dion's shoulder. The pooping puffin was an insider reference to a bizarre statement by Dion's rival Michael Ignatieff, who said when he visited Newfoundland for a Liberal caucus meeting that the puffin would be a good mascot for the Liberal party: "They put their excrement in one place. They hide their excrement ... They flap their wings very hard and they work like hell."[52] The website was funny in the way that *Frank* magazine was funny, but it was not appropriate for a campaign because it played with an opponent's body image, thereby showing disrespect for the person. Conservative advertising was already getting close to the edge by using a lot of unflattering sound bites and photos of Dion, but those could be defended as simply reproductions of the public record. The pooping puffin took another disrespectful step, and the campaign was right to yank the little bird immediately when the Liberals complained.

No campaign is free of mistakes, and this one did no permanent harm; but it illustrates a tendency toward arrogance that could be damaging in a more serious context.

The other episode also occurred in the first week, when war room spinner Ryan Sparrow gave information to CTV about a man who had criticized Harper's commitment to end the military mission in Afghanistan in 2011. When Jim Davis, whose son had been killed in Afghanistan in 2006, said that Harper's commitment to withdraw might mean his son's death was in vain, Sparrow emailed CTV reporter Tom Clark that Davis was a Liberal activist who had worked for Michael Ignatieff in the leadership race. Harper quickly apologized, Sparrow apologized and left the war room, and swift damage control minimized the harm to the campaign. But I am also the father of a soldier, and I saw Sparrow's assault on Jim Davis as a derogation from basic human values. A father's grief doesn't make him an expert on foreign policy, but it surely entitles him to respect above the partisan fray.

Lack of agility can also be a failing of large, well-organized machines. Harper's team tries to plan everything, having learned from bitter experience in 2004 what can go wrong when there is no adequate plan for the endgame. Adherence to the plan is almost always the right course of action, but occasionally conditions change so dramatically that a departure is justified. The Conservatives seemed slow to react twice in this campaign – first when the culture cuts became a major issue in Quebec, and second when financial markets collapsed. Although they never did find an adequate response to what the BQ made of the arts cuts, Stephen improvised effectively in the final days to save a victory that suddenly seemed in jeopardy. Campaign planners reviewing those episodes might reflect on the delicate balance between disciplined adherence to the plan (generally desirable) and the need for spontaneity (sometimes unavoidable).

Finally, don't forget the importance of policy. In this Conservative campaign, policy was mainly inferred from Harper's record in government. The platform was modest, and there was nothing like the "Five Priorities" to lend a sense of vision. The advertising and iconography was largely devoid of policy – Harper in a sweater, slogans such as "You're better off with Harper" and "Le

Québec prend des forces." Against an incompetent Liberal leader running on the unpopular Green Shift, this worked well enough. Combined with Conservative negative advertising, it turned the election into a referendum on Stéphane Dion, who was ultimately deemed too risky by many voters.

But in the long run it probably won't be good enough to depict Stephen Harper as your kindly next-door neighbour. Voters can see his combination of razor-sharp intellect, cunning strategic sense, and ruthless determination. They won't support him for the long haul unless they understand and approve of the direction in which he wants to lead the country. This campaign was exceptional because of Dion's vulnerability and incompetence; but in the longer term, facing stronger opponents, Conservative campaigns will have to give voters more positive reasons to support Harper.

The Politics of Survival

In his victory address on the night of 14 October 2008, Stephen invoked the ancient words from Ecclesiastes, "To every thing there is a season ..."[1] He seemed to imply that the time for political conflict had ended with the campaign and that the new Parliament would be more harmonious than the "dysfunctional" old Parliament to which he had referred when he asked for an early election. But things quickly moved in the opposite direction because of the ever-worsening global recession.

During the campaign, Harper, like the other party leaders, had promised to keep the government away from deficit spending, but that stance seemed steadily less persuasive as the economic news got worse. When Parliament opened on 19 November, the Speech from the Throne hinted at controlled deficits combined with cuts to wasteful spending, promising that the government would "ensure sound budgeting so that Canada does not return to ongoing, unsustainable structural deficits while putting all federal expenditures under the microscope of responsible spending."[2] But on 22 November, at an Asia-Pacific Economic Co-operation meeting in Lima, Peru, Harper raised the stakes, saying, "The financial crisis has become an economic crisis, and the world is entering an economic period unlike, and potentially as dangerous, as anything we have faced since 1929." For the first time he spoke of introducing a so-called stimulus package, though he promised to guard against long-term deficits.[3]

Those remarks seemed to set the stage for Finance Minister Jim Flaherty to present a Keynesian-style fiscal update on 27 November, but Harper must have had further thoughts after his stimulus-friendly remarks in Peru, for he authorized Flaherty to present projections showing that Canada would stay out of deficit not only in fiscal 2008–09 but in all following years. Finance Department officials had offered him a range of scenarios, and he had picked one of the more optimistic ones. Moreover, the specific proposals in the fiscal update were all cost-cutting measures, the exact opposite of a stimulus package:

- eliminate the taxpayer subsidy for politicians and their parties;
- reduce the cost and ensure the effectiveness of government operations;
- ensure sustainable federal public sector wage rates and modernize the pay equity regime, applying also to MPs, senators, Cabinet ministers and senior public servants;
- put equalization on a sustainable growth path.[4]

The whole statement was politically maladroit, but by far the worst suggestion was to eliminate the annual $1.95 per vote subsidy that had been introduced by the Liberals' Bill C-24, effective 2004. The Conservatives would lose the most money, because they had gotten the most votes in 2008; but they could survive without the subsidy, whereas it would be a death sentence for the Liberals, given the sorry state of their grassroots fundraising. Not only was the proposal bound to inflame the opposition parties, it made Harper appear to be playing political games at a time of national crisis. It was probably his single worst mistake not just as prime minister but in his career as a party leader. It would stick to him personally, because it was obvious that a proposal like this must have come from the PMO, not from the PCO or the Department of Finance.

As I pointed out in chapter 9, since the Conservative Party has no natural coalition partner, the key to its success in a minority situation is to "align itself tactically in Parliament with different parties or segments of parties over different issues."[5] Polarize against all other parties during the election campaign, but play "divide and conquer" while Parliament is in session. But Harper's subsidy stratagem had precisely the opposite effect. The government almost immediately withdrew it along with other aspects of the fiscal update; but it impelled the Liberals, who saw it as a financial death threat, to throw in their lot with the NDP and the BQ, who had already had some behind-the-scenes discussions about forming a coalition.[6]

The opposition coalition was announced on 1 December 2008. Following the model of the Liberal-NDP Ontario Accord of 1985, in which Bob Rae had been a participant, there was a written Accord between the Liberals and the NDP, under which the Liberals would get eighteen seats in a coalition cabinet, including prime minister and minister of finance, while the NDP would get six. This accord would expire 30 June 2011. There was also a side agreement, including a "Policy Accord,"[7] with the BQ, according to which the latter would get no cabinet seats but would agree not to defeat the coalition government for eighteen months.[8]

Planning to bring a non-confidence motion to a vote on 8 December, Stéphane Dion notified the governor general that he would be willing to form a government if asked. All members of the Liberal and NDP caucuses signed the accord to signal that the arrangement would be stable. No one could say for sure what the governor general might do if the coalition defeated the Conservatives on a confidence vote. It was only two and a half months since the election, and the government had not yet passed a budget. Based on past precedents, this might be one of those rare cases where the governor general could ignore a defeated prime minister's request for an election and invite the leader of the opposition coalition to form a government. But that was far from certain because Dion had denied during the campaign that he would form a coalition with the NDP, and there was no precedent for a minority government relying on the support of the Bloc Québécois, a party devoted to the separation of Quebec from Canada.

The coalition concept was unpopular except in Quebec, so Conservative support in national polls shot up to the mid-40s.[9] If Stephen had been able to count on having another quick election, he might have accepted defeat in the House and then tried to win a majority government by running against the coalition and the threat of separatism. But what if the governor general decided not to grant his election request? Or what if voters blamed him for provoking such a quick election? It was just too risky, so Stephen decided to play for survival.

He counterattacked vigorously, disavowing the fiscal statement and promising to bring down a budget containing a major stimulus package on 27 January 2009, a month earlier than previously anticipated. He denounced the coalition as an opportunistic seizure of power, a virtual coup d'état supported by separatists. He asked for free television time to address the nation, as Paul Martin had done in spring 2005. Most significantly, he asked Governor General Michaëlle Jean to prorogue Parliament until 26 January, thus preventing the possibility of a non-confidence vote before the government had a chance to bring down its budget. After a two-hour private meeting, she agreed.

With more bad economic news coming almost every day and forecasts steadily worsening, Harper now became a convert to the doctrine of fiscal stimulus:

> We know right now that because of the unprecedented nature of the turmoil in global markets, we're seeing a lot of money sitting on the sidelines. We know many people are afraid to spend. We know that businesses are afraid to invest. We know that even in bond markets, people are worried about capital losses. In that downward spiral of economic activity, with money sitting on the sidelines, this is the time for government to come in, to borrow money at low rates and make sure that money goes to productive usage in the economy immediately – to sustain confidence and in some cases to make some good investments that will strengthen the economy down the road. That's what we're going to do.[10]

Harper seemed to have become a Keynesian, though his reasoning was a little different from the classical Keynesian notion that fiscal stimulus is necessary to combat unemployment because wages are sticky on the downside, so that in a recession employers have to lay off some workers altogether rather than lowering wages for all. Fiscal stimulus in that scenario fools economic actors about the value of money, thereby inducing them to consume or invest where they would otherwise hold back.

Whatever Stephen's new economic views, they hardly mattered; the political challenge was to get the Liberals to vote for the budget, thus detaching them from the NDP and BQ and breaking up the opposition coalition. That strategy seemed more viable once Michael Ignatieff replaced Stéphane Dion as Liberal leader. Dion had already promised to resign after the election, but he was supposed to stay on as Leader until a convention could be held in May 2009 to select a replacement. Dion, however, sealed his fate on 3 December, when he bungled his televised follow-up to Harper's address to the nation. His office was late sending over the recorded version of Dion's message, and the recording itself looked amateurish. It soon came out that Dion had been working on the text and hadn't left enough time to do a professional job of recording; then, when the equipment didn't work properly, the recording had been made with a cellphone camera.

This fiasco led to calls for Dion's immediate resignation, which he finally offered on 8 December, the day on which he had hoped to defeat Harper and be invited to become prime minister. Dominic Leblanc, one of the Liberal leadership candidates, immediately pulled out of the race and endorsed Michael Ignatieff. With a good deal more reluctance, the other candidate, Bob Rae, did the same on 9 December, and Ignatieff was declared interim leader on 10 December with the approval of caucus and the national executive of the Liberal Party.

Ignatieff, like Paul Martin, had become Liberal leader by pushing his rivals out of the race and getting the support of party elites – in his case, members of the caucus and national executive, in Martin's case the members of constituency executives. It was a favourable outcome for the party because Ignatieff is a much stronger leader than Dion, and installing him immediately avoided the necessity for him and the other candidates to run up leadership debts that might ultimately become the responsibility of the Liberal Party, which is still struggling to bring its fundraising into the modern age.

Almost as soon as he became leader, Ignatieff began hinting that he might depart from Dion's bargain with Jack Layton and Gilles Duceppe. He said he would wait to see Jim Flaherty's budget before deciding whether to vote for it, whereas Layton and Duceppe were ready to defeat it sight unseen. "A coalition if necessary, but not necessarily a coalition," became Ignatieff's mantra.[11] Harper, therefore, continued with his strategy of crafting a budget that would get Ignatieff's support. There was a veritable blitz of consultative efforts in December and January – appointment of a high-level citizens committee to advise the minister of Finance; consultative sessions by Flaherty and other ministers across the country; private meetings of party leaders with Harper and finance critics with Flaherty; even a first ministers meeting. The Liberals preferred to play dog in the manger and refrained from making specific demands, but there was enough highly visible consultation for the budget to look something like a national consensus.

The government also resorted to an unusual communications strategy for the budget. The Canadian tradition is to maintain rigid secrecy until the budget is presented in the House of Commons, although Paul Martin sometimes authorized strategic leaks. But in the several days leading up to 27 January, the Conservative Government revealed an unprecedented amount of information, beginning with the aggregate size of the projected deficit – $34 billion in 2009–10 and $85 billion over five years before returning to balanced budgets. By 27 January, the only important details not known concerned the size and shape of the tax cuts.

The 2009 budget was a marked departure from Harper and Flaherty's previous budgets, or indeed from any budgetary model inspired by conservative thinking. There would have been a deficit in the range of $10–15 billion in any event because of revenue shortfalls caused by the recession, but this budget more than doubled the inevitable deficit with a rash of spending plans in the name of stimulus: funding for "shovel-ready" infrastructure projects; special aid for impacted industries, such as forestry; a new regional development agency for Southern Ontario; social housing renovation and construction; and tax credits for private home renovations.

Right-wing voices usually friendly to the Conservatives, such as the Fraser Institute and the *National Post*, condemned the budget. Other conservatives, myself included, said the budget was wasteful and would be ineffectual but added that it was a political necessity under the circumstances. Having provoked the opposition coalition into existence with its misguided fiscal update, the government could not survive unless it danced to Ignatieff's tune with the goal of getting the Liberals out of the coalition.

Everything unrolled as predicted once the budget was presented on 27 January. Ignatieff announced the next day that the Liberals would support it if the Conservatives would accept his face-saving amendment requiring the government to report to Parliament three times during 2009 on the progress of budget implementation, to demonstrate that money was being shovelled out the door in timely fashion to shovel-ready projects. Of course, Ignatieff found much in the budget to criticize; but in the end he and the Liberals supported it, just as Dion and the Liberals had voted for Conservative legislation dozens of times in the previous Parliament. The coalition was finally put out of its misery as the NDP launched anti-Ignatieff radio ads the very same day. Gilles Duceppe also quickly piled on, having realized that the Liberals, given Ignatieff's popularity in Quebec, had now become a greater threat to the Bloc than the Conservatives.

No one can foretell the future, but a number of trends seem to be evident. Whereas Dion had pushed the Liberals to the left, even to the point of making a coalition with the NDP and the BQ, Ignatieff is moving back to the centre, adopting positions similar to Harper's on a number of key issues, such as supporting the budget, endorsing the further development of the Alberta oil sands, and refusing to bail out the Vancouver Olympics with federal money. He is following the old opposition strategy of matching the government on almost all issues, waiting for an opportunity to polarize around a government mistake or some external development. The logical course for the Liberals is to wait until the recession seems to have reached its trough, declare that Harper's stimulus has failed, and seek to defeat the government when public opinion is at its most negative. The "red zone" would seem to open up in autumn 2009 and continue for months or years afterwards, depending on whether the shape of the recession turns out to be a V (sharp, quick rebound), a U (prolonged stagnation), or a W (double dip). However, there is one problem with this otherwise promising strategy. If things do get bad and polling suggests the Liberals could win, will the NDP and BQ join them in forcing an election? A Liberal wave probably means that both parties would lose seats, though one or the other (or both) might have the opportunity to extract concessions by propping up a Liberal minority government.

What about the Conservatives? For the time being, they still retain their financial advantage over the opposition parties. The Conservatives had their best year ever in 2008, raising about $21 million in contributions, whereas the Liberals and NDP were both under $6 million.[12] The Liberals claim they will turn things around by imitating Barack Obama's internet methods of raising money, but the success of that venture remains to be seen. Canadians are not Americans, and Ignatieff is not Obama.

In other respects, though, the Conservatives have suffered real damage. Harper's reputation has been particularly hard-hit. Before the fall fiasco, he wasn't exactly loved by the public, but he was widely respected by political observers as a competent manager and a shrewd strategist. But after his misadventure with the political subsidy issue, many are saying that his strategic sense has been overrated. This is a dangerous development, for if you are not to be loved you must at least be respected.

After a long string of policy pirouettes, Stephen's credibility is also getting tattered. Here are just a few of the reversals he has made since first getting elected in 2006:

- after promising to cut out corporate subsidies in the 2004 platform, he has become an enthusiastic dispenser of such subsidies, even setting up a new regional development agency for Southern Ontario;
- after promising in the 2005–06 campaign to maintain the special tax treatment of income trusts, he reversed that position without warning on Halloween 2006;
- after promising not to count resource revenue in equalization calculations, he decided to accept the recommendation of the expert panel chaired by Al O'Brien to count 50 percent of resource revenues;
- after introducing fixed-election-date legislation, he asked the governor general for an early election;
- after running on balanced budgets in the 2008 campaign, he took Canada back to deficit spending in the 2009 budget.

Each of these reversals may be defensible in its own right, and indeed I have defended some of them in print. But taken together, along with other less publicized reversals, they have created a widespread impression that Harper stands for nothing in particular, except winning and keeping power. This is a major loss for a political leader who was once seen as a man of conviction. How long will voters continue to support someone who is thought to be mainly a cunning tactician, especially if a run of mistakes makes him seem not even particularly cunning?

Whenever the next election comes, the campaign task for the Conservatives will be harder because of what the politics of survival has done to Harper's image. Also, he no longer has the automatic advantage that he enjoyed over the ineffectual Stéphane Dion. Michael Ignatieff has his flaws and weak points, but he should be a far tougher opponent than Dion. In short, the most important thing for Harper in getting ready for the next election is to repair the damage to his reputation. Here are some ideas that may be helpful:

- Good government can be good politics. Forget the tricky tactical moves, such as cutting off your opponents' supply of money, and concentrate on government.
- Reconnect with the Conservative base. These are the people who give the money that is required to run Harper's Team, with its effective but expensive campaign doctrine of intensive pre-writ advertising and systematic voter identification. Many donors will not be happy with the 2009 budget; they have to be reassured about the leader's conservatism.
- Reassuring the base means pushing conservative policy items in Parliament. The necessity of constructing a Liberal budget for political survival doesn't imply the necessity of junking the whole conservative agenda.
- While being conservative in substance, be transpartisan in style. Observe how President Obama has deliberately reached out to Republicans, appointing them to his cabinet and inviting them to social occasions at the White House. Practice the politics of conciliation, and leave the attacks to surrogates.

To end on a personal note, I went through many ups and downs with Stephen. He has never made it easy for himself. But he has powers of recuperation, and those who now predict his demise because the economy is down and because he made some tactical errors shouldn't start writing his epitaph. Just as Stephen found a way to survive against the threat of the coalition, he will find a way to lead Harper's Team into the field again.

APPENDIX

Political Terminology and Acronyms

ADVANCE PERSON   Campaign staffer sent ahead to check out the arrangements – e.g., room capacity, amplifying equipment, lighting – before a political event takes place.

AUTODIALER   Computer programmed to dial telephone numbers from a database and leave a recorded message.

BRAND AD   Advertisement that emphasize what a party or candidate believes or stands for.

CAMPAIGN SCRIPT   Daily plan for campaign communications, including leader's speeches, press releases, etc.

DESTABILIZER   Release of information designed to throw opponents off balance by revealing or emphasizing something they would prefer not to talk about.

DIAL GROUP   Small pollster's group in which each participant holds a dial or other computer control that can record an instantaneous numerical evaluation of lines in a speech, words in an ad, etc.

DVC   Direct voter contact: program of contacting voters directly through door-knocking, direct mail, email, and telephone.

FOCUS GROUP   Small group used by pollsters for qualitative research, i.e., discussion of perceptions of leaders, ad storyboards, etc.

GOTV   Get Out the Vote: program of using direct mail, phone calls, email, and personal contact to encourage your supporters to vote.

GROSS RATING POINTS   Standardized measure of how deeply an ad is penetrating into the market, affected both by amount of time bought and size of audience for the shows on which spots are purchased.

LEADER'S TOUR   Program of travel organized by the national campaign, in which the leader travels around the country with journalists.

NEGATIVE AD   Advertisement highlighting an opponent's weakness.

OLO   Office of the Leader of the Opposition: staff of several dozen serving the Opposition leader's needs for research, communications advice, travel planning, etc.

OPPOSITION RESEARCH   Collection of information about opposing parties and candidates, often used to create destabilizers and negative ads.

PMO   Prime Minister's Office: staff of several dozen organizing the prime minister's political activities (as opposed to governmental activities, which are organized through the Privy Council Office).

PREDICTIVE DIALER   Computer that automatically dials telephone numbers from a database, allowing a live caller to contact people more efficiently.

SPINNER   Employee whose job is to explain party or leader's positions to the media.

SWOT ANALYSIS   Standardized way of beginning a political campaign, analyzing Strengths, Weaknesses, Opportunities, Threats facing the candidate.

TALKING POINTS   Short, bulleted summaries of positions given to those who speak publicly on behalf of a party or candidate

TOMBSTONE DATA   Name, address, and telephone number.

VOTER ID   Voter identification: phase of DVC in which supporters of a party or candidate are located and their information
entered in a database.

WAGONMASTER   On the Leader's Tour, the staff member responsible for coordinating everything relating to the physical
side of the tour – luggage, schedule, equipment, etc.

Notes

INTRODUCTION

1 Paul Wells, *Right Side Up: The Fall of Paul Martin and the Rise of Stephen Harper's New Conservatism* (Toronto: Douglas Gibson Books, 2006), 76.

2 James Surowiecki, *The Wisdom of Crowds: Why the Many Are Smarter than the Few and How Collective Wisdom Shapes Business, Economies, Societies, and Nations* (New York: Doubleday, 2004).

3 Aristotle, *Rhetoric*, 1356a.

4 Jon H. Pammett and Christopher Dornan, "From One Minority to Another," in Jon H. Pammett and Christoper Dornan, eds, *The Canadian Federal Election of 2006* (Toronto: Dundurn, 2006), 19.

5 Wells, *Right Side Up.*

6 The most recent is Pammett and Dornan, *Canadian Federal Election of 2006.* Various editors have published books in this series for every federal election from 1984 onward. The standard title prior to 2006 was on the model of *The Canadian General Election of 2004.*

7 Stephen Clarkson, *The Big Red Machine: How the Liberal Party Dominates* (Vancouver: UBC Press, 2005).

8 Richard Johnston et al., *Letting the People Decide: Dynamics of a Canadian Election* (Montreal: McGill-Queen's University Press, 1992), was particularly insightful on the 1988 election.

9 John Duffy, *Fights of Our Lives: Elections, Leadership, and the Making of Canada* (Toronto: HarperCollins, 2002). An older book, still very useful for learning about campaigns from 1867 through 1968, is Murray Beck, *The Pendulum of Power: Canada's Federal Elections* (Scarborough: Prentice-Hall of Canada, 1968).

10 John Laschinger and Geoffrey Stevens, *Leaders and Lesser Mortals* (Toronto: Key Porter, 1992).

11 Quintus Tullius Cicero, *A Short Guide to Electioneering* (London Association of Classical Teachers, 1970), LACTOR no. 3, para. 52.

12 William Johnson, *Stephen Harper and the Future of Canada* (Toronto: McClelland and Stewart, 2005; 2nd edition 2006); Lloyd Mackey, *The Pilgrimage of Stephen* Harper (Toronto: ECW Press, 2005); Hugh Segal, *The Long Road Back: The Conservative Journey, 1993–2006* (Toronto: HarperCollins, 2006); Bob Plamondon, *Full Circle: Death and Resurrection in Canadian Conservative Politics* (Toronto: Key Porter, 2006); Don Martin, *Belinda: The Political and Private Life of Belinda Stronach* (Toronto: Key Porter, 2006); Wells, *Right Side Up*; Chantal Hébert, *French Kiss: Stephen Harper's Blind Date with Quebec* (Toronto: Alfred A. Knopf Canada, 2007). I had the opportunity of commenting on the manuscript of Johnson's book, so it corresponds to the facts as I am aware of them. The other books all contain some factual errors, but I have not tried to correct them here except in a few cases of exceptional importance. Where my account differs from that of one of the books cited here, the reader can assume that I have read the other book, am aware that it tells a different story, but believe that my own version is correct.

CHAPTER ONE

1 F.A. Hayek, *The Constitution of Liberty* (Chicago: University of Chicago Press, 1960); *Law, Legislation and Liberty*, 3 vols (Chicago: University of Chicago Press, 1973–79).

2 John Stuart Mill, *On Liberty* [1859] (Indianapolis: Liberal Arts Press, 1956), 68.

3 Edmund Burke, *Reflections on the Revolution in France* [1790] (Indianapolis: Liberal Arts Press, 1955), 99.

4 Stephen Joseph Harper, *The Political Business Cycle and Fiscal Policy in Canada* (MA thesis in Economics, University of Calgary, 1991).

5 Tom Flanagan, *Waiting for the Wave: The Reform Party and Preston Manning* (Toronto: Stoddart, 1995).

6 House of Commons Debates, online Hansard, 21 October 1996, 5454–5.

7 Claire Hoy, *Stockwell Day: His Life and Politics* (Toronto: Stoddart, 2000), 108.

8 Speech to the Mortgage Loans Association of Alberta, 1998, quoted in Wells, *Right Side Up*, 18.

9 Stephen Harper and Tom Flanagan, "Our Benign Dictatorship," *The Next City*, January 1997, 35–40, 54–7. We published a revised and expanded version under the title "Conservative Politics in Canada: Past, Present, and Future," in William Gairdner, ed., *After Liberalism* (Toronto: Stoddart, 1998), 168–92.

10 Jeffrey Simpson, *The Friendly Dictatorship* (Toronto: McClelland and Stewart, 2001).

11 Harper and Flanagan, "Our Benign Dictatorship," 40.

12 Ibid.

13 Preston Manning, *Think Big* (Toronto: McClelland and Stewart, 2002), 271–99.

14 Flanagan and Harper, "Conservative Politics in Canada," 175–7.

15 Posted at www.ccicinc.org/politicalaffairs/060103.html, reprinted in *Report Magazine*, June 2003.

16 Bob Plamondon, *Full Circle: Death and Resurrection in Canadian Conservative Politics* (Toronto: Key Porter Books, 2006), 186–7.

17 Tom Flanagan, "Stockwell Could Carry the Day," *Globe and Mail*, 13 March 2000.

18 Tom Flanagan, "Taking Stock: Making Choices," *National Post*, 29 November 2000.

19 Stephen Clarkson, "The Liberal Threepeat: The Multi-System Party in the Multi-Party System," in Jon H. Pammett and Christopher Dornan, eds, *The Canadian General Election of 2000* (Toronto: Dundurn Group, 2001), 30.

20 Stephen Harper, "Separation, Alberta-Style: It Is Time to Seek a New Relationship with Canada," *National Post*, 8 December 2000.

21 Stephen Harper, Tom Flanagan, Ted Morton, Rainer Knopff, Andrew Crooks, and Ken Boessenkool, "Open Letter to Ralph Klein," *National Post*, 24 January 2001.

22 Ibid.

23 Preston Manning, "Haultain's Determined Efforts Couldn't 'Avert' Unequal Birth," *Calgary Herald*, 5 June 2005.

24 Quoted in William Johnson, *Stephen Harper and the Future of Canada* (Toronto: McClelland and Stewart, 2005), 288.

25 Deborah Grey, *Never Retreat, Never Explain, Never Apologize* (Toronto: Key Porter, 2004), 190–213.
26 Manning, *Think Big*, 394–7.
27 Johnson, *Stephen Harper*, 290, quoting Ken Boessenkool.
28 Plamondon, *Full Circle*, 218.
29 Sheldon Alberts, "Harper Mounts Campaign to Lead the Right: Behind the Scenes: Unlikely to Declare until Alliance Collapses," *National Post*, 30 June 2001.
30 Stephen Harper, "Beliefs," *National Post*, 3 July 2001.
31 Link Byfield, "Now Is the Time for Stephen Harper to Come to the Aid of the Party," *Report Newsmagazine*, 30 July 2001, 8.
32 *Calgary Herald*, "On the Prowl: If Harper Seeks Leadership of the Alliance, Everything Changes," 15 August 2001.
33 Barry Cooper and David Bercuson, "Lack of Leadership," *Windsor Star*, 29 August 2001.
34 Michael Taube, "The Right Knight? The Alliance's Best Choice Probably Won't Run," *Toronto Star*, 8 August 2001.
35 Jeffrey Simpson, "Message to Stephen Harper: Don't Do It!" *Globe and Mail*, 20 July 2001.
36 Warren Kinsella, "A Strike against Harper," *Windsor Star*, 21 August 2001.

CHAPTER TWO

1 *Winnipeg Free Press*, "Leadership Search," 30 August 2001.
2 Gerry Warner, "Alliance Party Big Wheels Roll into Cranbrook," *Cranbrook Daily Townsman*, 21 September 2001.
3 Steve Mertl, "Alliance Forum in BC Offers Split Vision of Party's Future," *Prince Albert Daily Herald*, 15 October 2001.
4 Sheldon Alberts, "Harper Will Try to Beat Day Out of the Gate: May Enter Race Next Week," *National Post*, 30 November 2001.
5 *Draft Stephen Harper Newsletter*, vol. 1, no. 6.
6 Sheldon Alberts, "Forget Unification with Tories under Clark, Harper Says," *National Post*, 4 December 2001; Norma Greenaway and Joe Paraskevas. "Harper Aims to Lead Alliance," *Calgary Herald*, 4 December 2001.
7 Kelly Cryderman, "Harper's Stand Worries MLAs: Provincial PCs Wish Him Good Luck, but Are Puzzled," *Edmonton Journal*,

5 December 2001; *Regina Leader Post*, "Harper's Stance Not Seen as Helpful," 5 December 2001.

8 Sheldon Alberts, "Ablonczy Begins Race on the Attack: Day Steps Down," *National Post*, 13 December 2001.

9 *Ottawa Citizen*, "A Strong Start to the Alliance Race," 13 December 2001.

10 Norm Ovenden, "Day Waiting to Reveal Next Move," *Calgary Herald*, 13 December 2001.

11 Edward Greenspon, "The Queer Politics of Dr. Hill," *Globe and Mail*, 20 December 2001.

12 Stephen Harper, "Appeasing the Tories Has to Stop," *National Post*, 21 December 2001.

13 Don Martin, "Day Returns to Haunt Alliance Leadership Race," *Nelson Daily News*, 9 January 2002.

14 Andrew Coyne, "Why Day Should Run," *National Post*, 9 January 2002.

15 *Guelph Daily Mercury*, "Quebec Tories Throw Support behind Day," 7 January 2002.

16 Stephen Harper, "A Vision of Federalism for All Canadians," *National Post*, 19 January 2002.

17 *Timmins Daily Press*, "Alliance Debate More like a Series of Speeches," 21 January 2002.

18 Cindy E. Harnett, "Harper Decries PC Union," *Victoria Times Colonist*, 24 January 2002.

19 Ibid.

20 Stephen Harper, "Canada's Soldiers Deserve Much Better," *Calgary Herald*, 2 February 2002.

21 Peter Hadekel, "Harper Brings Ideas to the Debate," *The Montreal Gazette*, 26 January 2002.

22 Richard Dooley, "Ablonczy Preaches Alliance-Tory Union," *Halifax Daily News*, 5 February 2002.

23 Stephen Harper, "Get the State Out of the Economy," *National Post*, 8 February 2002.

24 Sheldon Alberts, "Day Slips into Bible College for Rally: Absent from His Itinerary," *National Post*, 12 February 2002.

25 Michael Taube, "Alliance Remains Alive ... for Now; But Quick Fixes Are Needed if Party Is to Be Saved from Self-Destruction," *Hamilton Spectator*, 21 February 2002.

26 *Ottawa Citizen*, "Leading the Alliance: One Candidate Blends Competence with the Right Ideas," 2 March 2002.

27 Chantal Hébert, "The Smart Money Is on Day," *Kitchener Record*, 1 March 2002.

28 Chantal Hébert, "The Sun Might Set on Day," *Charlottetown Guardian*, 20 March 2002.

29 Laschinger and Stevens, *Leaders and Lesser Mortals*, 170–1.

30 Warren Kinsella, "Martin's Man Stoops to a Nazi Smear; Mike Robinson Owes Stephen Harper an Apology," *National Post*, 22 May 2004.

31 Paul Wells, "Alliance Race Weighted with Albertans," *National Post*, 17 December 2001.

32 Sheldon Alberts, "Harper Camp Rips Day as Lightweight," *National Post*, 9 January 2002.

33 Elizabeth Thompson, "Back off, Alliance Tells Anti-Abortion Coalition," *The Montreal Gazette*, 9 February 2002.

34 Brian Laghi and Richard Mackie, "Alliance Puts Brakes on Campaign Life," *Globe and Mail*, 9 February 2002.

35 Norma Greenaway, "Leadership Race Too Close to Call," *Calgary Herald*, 20 March 2002; *Halifax Daily News*, "Alliance Camps Biting Their Nails," 20 March 2002.

36 Don Martin, "Will Alliance Live to See Another Day?" *Tribune*, 19 March 2002; Louise Elliott, "Day on Brink of Remarkable Comeback: Spurned Alliance Leader a Good Bet to Win His Job Back," *Halifax Daily News*, 17 March 2002.

37 TeleResearch Inc., A Leader Preference Survey of Canadian Alliance Party Members across Ontario, Manitoba, Saskatchewan, Alberta and British Columbia, March 2002.

38 Chris Cobb, "A Politician of Conviction Rather than of Consensus," *Vancouver Sun*, 21 March 2002.

39 Larry Johnsrude, "Triumph of Substance over Style," *Edmonton Journal*, 21 March 2002.

40 Lorne Gunter, "Harper Didn't Win, Day Lost," *Kingston Whig-Standard*, 23 March 2002.

41 *The Montreal Gazette*, "At Least It's a Start," 21 March 2002.

42 Norma Greenaway, "Harper's Uphill Struggle," *Halifax Daily News*, 21 March 2002.

43 Andrew Coyne, "Manning with a Mean Streak: The New Alliance Leader Shares Traits with Former Mentor," *National Post*, 21 March 2002.

44 Chantal Hébert, "Harper Fits Bill for Ontario Faithful," *Toronto Star*, 22 March 2002.

45 Tom Flanagan, "Database Party: The 2002 Leadership Campaign for the Canadian Alliance," *Canadian Parliamentary Review* 26 (Spring 2003): 11.

CHAPTER THREE

1 Sheldon Alberts, "'We Took Out the Trash Last Night': Manning Rival: Ex-Leader's Riding Rejects His Unity Bid," *National Post*, 23 November 2001.

2 Sean McKinsley, email to author, 28 December 2001.

3 Tom Flanagan, email to Sean McKinsley, 2 January 2002.

4 *North Bay Nugget*, "'Stockaholic' Refuses to Step Aside," 28 March 2002.

5 Louise Elliott, "Calgary Candidate Steps Aside to Allow Leader Shot at Seat," *Truro Daily News*, 30 March 2002.

6 Sean McKinsley gave me a CD containing the data.

7 Tom Flanagan, "The Uneasy Case for Uniting the Right," Fraser Institute, Public Policy Sources, no. 53 (2002), 21.

8 Tom Flanagan, "Nault Shows Courage in Taking on Indian Act," *National Post*, 18 June 2002.

9 Jeffrey Simpson, "He Makes Harper Think Uncharitable Thoughts," *Globe and Mail*, 7 May 2002.

10 Richard Roik, "'Defeatists' Hurt Alliance Gains," *New Brunswick Telegraph Journal*, 29 May 2002.

11 *Cape Breton Post*, "Resolution Condemning Harper Unanimously Endorsed," 31 May 2002.

12 Jane Armstrong, "Defeatism Comments Taken out of Context, Harper Says," *Globe and Mail*, 1 December 2005.

13 Nigel Hannaford, "How a Pancake Became a Political Statement," *Calgary Herald*, 13 July 2002.

14 Norma Greenaway, "Debate Heats up on Harper's Low Profile: Savvy or Missed Opportunity," *Ottawa Citizen*, 22 July 2002.

15 Sheldon Alberts, "Harper Apologizes to Ipsos-Reid," *National Post*, 24 September 2002.

16 Peter O'Neil, "Harper Apologizes for Robinson Remark," *Ottawa Citizen*, 24 October 2002.

17 Dick Morris, *Power Plays: Win or Lose – How History's Great Political Leaders Play the Game* (New York: HarperCollins, 2002), 95–126.

18 Quoted in Plamondon, *Full Circle*, 383.

19 en.wikipedia.org/wiki/Sister_Souljah_moment.

20 Mackey, *Pilgrimage of Stephen Harper*, 155.

21 Richard E. Neustadt, *Presidential Power: The Politics of Leadership* (New York: John Wiley, 1960), 157.

22 Wells, *Right Side Up*, 103–9.

23 L. Ian MacDonald, "A Conversation with the Prime Minister," *Policy Options* (February 2007), 6.

24 Government of Canada, House of Commons, Hansard, 17 May 2003, 1415.

25 Hansard, 20 March 2003, online edition, 40.

26 Stephen Harper, "Canada Should Stand with Its Allies," *Ottawa Citizen*, 22 March 2003.

27 Chantal Hébert. "Iraq Claims First Canadian Casualty: Harper," *Toronto Star*, 19 March 2003.

28 Don Martin. "Harper Plays Solo on the War Drums," *National Post*, 20 March 2003.

29 Gloria Galloway. "PM's Iraq Call Backed by 66%, Poll Reveals," *Globe and Mail*, 22 March 2003.

30 Ipsos-Reid website, archive.

31 Quoted in Norma Greenaway. "We'd Be There for You, U.S. Ambassador Says," *Vancouver Sun*, 26 March 2003.

32 Peter O'Neil, with files from Joan Bryden, "Think-Tank Critical of PM's Stance," *Vancouver Sun*, 25 March 2003.

33 Quoted in Robert Fife. "Mulroney Slams PM's View on War," *National Post*, 24 March 2003.

34 *National Post*, "Cherry Rant Finds Way into MP's Debate," 26 March 2003.

35 Speech, "Reviving Canadian Leadership in the World," Calgary, 5 October 2006.

36 *National Post*, "Ontario MP Resigns, Cites Personal Reasons," 12 October 2002.

37 *Cape Breton Post*, "Revote Ordered by Grits in Federal Nomination," 14 January 2003.

38 *Kitchener Record*, "Liberals Will Take Second Crack at Electing Local Candidate," 20 January 2003.

39 *North Bay Nugget*, "Hearing for Liberals to Find Out if Recount Is Needed," 11 January 2003.

40 Bill Curry, "Liberal Riding Nominee Did Not Reveal NDP Membership," *National Post*, 27 December 2002.

41 Rana F. Abbas, "Libs Pick Innes as Candidate for Perth-Middlesex Riding," *Hill Times*, 10 February 2003.

42 Stacey Ash, "Riding without an MP," *Kitchener Record*, 15 March 2003.

43 *Victoria Times-Colonist*, "Christian Heritage Party Leader to Seek Ontario Seat," 16 April 2003.

44 Sheldon Alberts, with files from Bill Curry, "Liberals Hold Slim Lead over Tories," *National Post*, 10 May 2003.

45 Read by Brandon-Souris MP Rick Borotsik in the House of Commons, Hansard, 2 May 2003, 1110.

46 Government of Canada, House of Commons, Hansard, 6 May 2003, 1410.

47 *Sault Star*, "Alliance Byelection Signs Vandalized," 6 May 2003.

48 Frank Doyle, email to Jenni Byrne (6 May 2003), forwarded to author 6 May 2003.

49 Brian Laghi, "Buy Ads or Suffer Bad Press, Editor Tells Candidate," *Globe and Mail*, 8 May 2003.

CHAPTER FOUR

1 *Calgary Herald*, 13 June 2003. Plamondon, *Full Circle*, 287, makes it appear as if Peter MacKay initiated the merger talks, but the public record shows clearly that Harper began the process with this speech in Calgary.

2 *National Post*, 17 June 2003.

3 CTV website, 19 June 2003; Plamondon, *Full Circle*, 287.

4 Plamondon, *Full Circle*, 290.

5 Don Martin, "United Only by Their Embarrassment," *National Post*, 30 September 2003.

6 Johnson, *Stephen Harper*, 330; Plamondon, *Full Circle*, 296.

7 Bill Curry, "MacKay Opens Door to Cooperation with Alliance," *Ottawa Citizen*, 15 August 2003; Bill Curry, "Orchard in Regular Contact with Tory Leader MacKay," *Ottawa Citizen*, 21 August 2003.

8 Wells, *Right Side Up*, 65.

9 Sean Gordon, "Alliance, Tory Talks Becoming a Farce," *Ottawa Citizen*, 9 October 2003.

10 Plamondon, *Full Circle*, 297.

11 Item no. 14 of Harper's fourteen-point proposal, printed in Plamondon, *Full Circle*, 300.

12 Item no. 11 of Harper's fourteen-point proposal, printed in Plamondon, *Full Circle*, 300.

13 Plamondon, *Full Circle*, 317–18.

14 Hugh Segal, *The Long Road Back: The Conservative Journey, 1993–2006* (Toronto: HarperCollins, 2006), 161.

15 Agreement in Principle, s. 5.

16 Plamondon, *Full Circle*, 341.

17 Sean Gordon, "Tory Unity Backlash Emerging," *National Post*, 17 October 2003.

18 Now section 2.1.1 of the party's constitution, 2005.

19 www.redtory.ca.

20 Plamondon, *Full Circle*, 190–1, citing the *Toronto Star*, 14 September 1998.

21 Jim Brown, "Defections Rock New Tories," *Kingston Whig-Standard*, 9 December 2003.

22 CTV website, archive.

23 Plamondon, *Full Circle*, 359.

24 Martin, *Belinda*, 120.

25 CBC website, 3 November 2003.

26 CBC website, 13 January 2004.

27 Martin, *Belinda*, 117.

28 According to Don Martin, she raised $250,000 for MacKay (*Belinda*, 114).

29 Martin, *Belinda*, 133.

30 Martin, *Belinda*, 120–3; Jaime Watt to Tom Flanagan, email, 10 October 2006.

31 Martin, *Belinda*, 123.

32 Plamondon, *Full Circle*, 246.

33 Martin, *Belinda*, 136.

34 Plamondon, *Full Circle*, 347.

35 "Harper Thanks Leadership Donors," Conservative Party media release, 20 May 2004.

36 Eric Hughes, CFO Harper Campaign, email message to the author, 12 June 2006.

37 Agreement-in-Principle, 15 October 2003, s. 4.
38 Sean Gordon, "Race Is on for Tory leadership," *Ottawa Citizen*, 27 December 2003.
39 Peter O'Neil and Sean Gordon, "Conservatives Ponder Bulk Memberships," *Ottawa Citizen*, 30 January 2004.
40 Agreement in Principle, s. 5.
41 Sean Gordon, "Harper Has the Numbers," *Edmonton Journal*, 13 March 2004.
42 Laschinger and Stevens, *Leaders and Lesser Mortals*, 34.
43 Ibid, 95.
44 Comment from Mike Coates, 12 January 2004.
45 Sean Gordon, "Harper Launches Bid to Lead Canadian Conservatives," *Daily News* (Prince Rupert), 13 January 2004.
46 Johnson, *Stephen Harper and the Future of Canada*, 341–2.
47 Martin, *Belinda*, 149, 269.
48 Martin, *Belinda*, 160–1.
49 Plamondon, *Full Circle*, 347.
50 CBC website, 11 March 2004.
51 Graeme Hamilton, "In Quebec, 2 Liberals Select 14 Delegates," *National Post*, 19 October 2006.

CHAPTER FIVE

1 Peter Woolstencroft, "Some Battles Won, War Lost: The Campaign of the Progressive Conservative Party," in Jon H. Pammett and Christopher Dornan, eds, *The Canadian General Election of 2000* (Toronto: Dundurn Group, 2001), 99.
2 Terence Corcoran, "Harper's Moderate Formula," *National Post*, 15 May 2004.
3 *Demanding Better: Conservative Party Platform 2004*, 32.
4 Ibid., 14.
5 Ibid., 8.
6 Ibid., 16.
7 Ibid., 27.
8 Ibid., 29.
9 Ibid., 34.
10 Ibid., 43.

CHAPTER SIX

1 "Martin, Harper, Come Out Fighting," *Calgary Herald*, 24 May 2006.
2 Clarkson, *Big Red Machine*, 219.
3 www.cbc.ca/story/election/national/news/2004/05/23/harper040523.html.
4 www.ctv.ca/servlet/ArticleNews/mini/CTVNews/1085436338100_52?s_name=election2004&no_ads=.
5 www.ctv.ca/servlet/ArticleNews/mini/CTVNews/1086462494983_17?s_name=election2004&no_ads=.
6 Johnson, *Stephen Harper*, 360–1.
7 Jill Mahoney, "Tory Critic Wants New Abortion Rules," *Globe and Mail*, 1 June 2004.
8 Don Martin, "A Bungled Attempt to Score Points on Abortion," *National Post*, 3 June 2004.
9 Elizabeth Goodyear-Grant, Antonia Maioni, and Stuart Soroka, "The Role of the Media: A Campaign Saved by a Horserace," *Policy Options*, September 2004, 89, figures 4 and 5.
10 Ibid.
11 "Gallant Compares Abortion to Terrorism," *Calgary Herald*, 8 June 2004.
12 Peter O'Neill and Bill Curry, "Harper Rejects Changing Abortion Law: Polls Put Tories in First Place," *Calgary Herald*, 10 June 2004.
13 Ibid.
14 Brian Caldwell, "Area Tory Widely Chastised; Remark about Gays Criticized," *The Record* (Kitchener), 11 June 2004.
15 Jane Taber, "Confident Harper Talks Majority," *Globe and Mail*, 11 June 2004.
16 Clarkson, *Big Red Machine*, 248.
17 Wells, *Right Side Up*, 119.
18 Paul Attalah, "Television and the Canadian Federal Election of 2004," in Jon H. Pammett and Christopher Dornan, eds, *Canadian General Election of 2004* (Toronto: Dundurn, 2006), 271.
19 Keith Mcarthur, "Liberal Attack Ads Answered Anger with Fear," *Globe and Mail*, 29 June 2004.
20 Internal polling, three-day roll.
21 Goodyear-Grant, Maioni, and Soroka, "The Role of the Media," 90.

22 "Conservatives Closing in on Majority: Polls Find Tories Pulling Away from Liberals," *Edmonton Journal*, 17 June 2004.

23 Tony L. Hill, "Advance Polling and Partisan Mobilization in National Elections in Canada, 1979–2004," Association for Canadian Studies in the United States, St Louis, 16–20 November 2005. See also Barry J. Kay and Chris Cattle, "Advance Polls and the 'Late Switch' in the 2004 Election," *Canadian Parliamentary Review*, Autumn 2005), 18–23.

24 Peter Loewen, "Early Birds and Worms: Advance Voting in Canada," unpublished ms., August 2006.

25 Johnson, *Stephen Harper*, 366.

26 Clarkson, *Big Red Machine*, 254.

27 Michael Marzolini, "Public Opinion and the 2006 Election," in Pammett and Dornan, *Canadian Federal Election of 2006*, 257.

28 Tony Seskus and David Heyman, "PM Calls Alberta Tories a Threat: Martin Says Klein-Harper Hurt Medicare," *Calgary Herald*, 18 June 2004.

29 Clarkson, *Big Red Machine*, 21; "Alliance Supports Two-Tier Health Care," *Globe and Mail*, 31 October 2000.

30 Francine Dube, "Top B.C. Court Strikes Down Child-Porn Law," *National Post*, 16 January 1999.

31 *Demanding Better*, 37.

32 Marlene Habib, "Child Porn Made Me Kill Holly, Man Says," *Kingston Whig-Standard*, 18 June 2004.

33 Yaroslav Baran to Tom Flanagan, email, 5 July 2004.

34 Wells, *Right Side Up*, 126.

35 Johnson, *Stephen Harper*, 367–8.

36 Goodyear-Grant, Maioni, and Soroka, "The Role of the Media," 89, figure 5.

37 Johnson, *Stephen Harper*, 369.

38 Tonda MacCharles, "Harper's Plan, Playing It Safe with the Media; Leader Prefers Partisan Rallies, Risks Are Fewer as Race Winds Down," *Toronto Star*, 25 June 2004.

39 George Mathewson, "National Media Upset over Eleventh Hour Silence," *Observer* (Sarnia), 25 June 2004.

40 Alexis Fosse Mackintosh, interview with Derrick O'Keefe, *Seven Oaks*, 10 August 2004, www.sevenoaksmag.com/questions/25.html.

41 www.lifesite.net/ldn/2004/aug/04081802.html.

42 Quoted in Johnson, *Stephen Harper*, 370.

43 Ibid., 371.

44 Johnson, *Stephen Harper*, 372.

45 *Demanding Better*, 21.

46 Ibid., 43.

47 Michael Marzolini, "Public Opinion Polling and the 2004 Election," in Pammett and Dornan, *Canadian General Election of 2004*, 293–5.

48 André Turcotte, "Canadians Speak Out," in Pammett and Fornan, *Canadian General Election of 2004*, 328, table 6. There seems to be something wrong with the column totals reported in this table. However, we found similar results in a post-election poll commissioned for the leader.

49 www.ctv.ca/servlet/ArticleNews/mini/CTVNews/ 1086792682317_82201882?s_name=election2004&no_ads.

50 Paul Attalah, "Television and the Canadian Federal Election of 2004," in Pammett and Dornan, *Canadian General Election of 2004*, 269–70.

CHAPTER SEVEN

1 David Heyman and Sean Gordon, "Calgary MPs urge Harper to Stay On: Leader Says He'll Consider Political Future," *Calgary Herald*, 30 June 2004.

2 André Blais, "Accounting for the Electoral Success of the Liberal Party in Canada: Presidential Address to the Canadian Political Science Association," *Canadian Journal of Political Science* 38 (2005), 821–40.

3 Martin, *Belinda*, 167.

4 "Budget Gets Quick Endorsement from Harper, Assuring It Will Pass," *Daily News* (Halifax), 24 February 2005; Campbell Clark, "Budget's Approval Rests in Harper's Hands," *Globe and Mail*, 25 February 2005.

5 "Goodale Budget Passes Commons with Help from the Tories," *National Post*, 10 March 2005.

6 Martin, *Belinda*, 169.

7 Quoted in Johnson, *Stephen Harper and the Future of Canada*, 396.

8 Conservative Party of Canada constitution, amended 19 March 2005, ss. 8.6.5 and 8.6.7. www.conservative.ca.

9 Ibid., ss. 9.2, 9.3, and 10.5.

10 Segal, *Long Road Back*, 98.

11 *National Post*, 19 March 2005.

12 *Ottawa Citizen*, 19 March 2005.

13 The famous chair-kicking incident arose later in the day, when MacKay's staff sent Harper a demand that he say positive things about MacKay in his speech.

14 21 March 2005.

15 Miro Cernetig, "Gomery Bans Reporting on Key Figures' Testimony," *Toronto Star*, 30 March 2005.

16 www.captainsquartersblog.com/mt/archives/004220.php; Rondi Adamson, "Of Blogs, Borders and Bans," *Calgary Herald*, 14 April 2005.

17 Don Martin, "Canada's Watergate," *National Post*, 8 April 2005.

18 Les Whittington, "Liberals Plummet to Second in Ontario; Party at 33% Compared to 40% for Conservatives; Gomery Inquiry 'Lit the Fuse' of Voters' Anger, Pollster Says," *Toronto Star*, 11 April 2005.

19 Tom Flanagan to Perry Miele, 14 April 2005.

20 Glen McGregor, "Tory Motion Calls on Liberals to Resign: Sponsorship Affair," *National Post*, 21 April 2005.

21 Anne Dawson, "Showdown in Ottawa: Martin Pledges Winter Election, Opposition May Not Wait," *Edmonton Journal*, 22 April 2005.

22 Grant Robertson and Anne Dawson, "Martin's Big Deal," *National Post*, 27 April 2005.

23 Mark McNeil, "Harper Driven by Power Lust," *Hamilton Spectator*, 28 April 2005; "PM Blasts Tory Deal: National Unity at Stake in Next Election, Martin Says," *Windsor Star*, 28 April 2005.

24 Colin Perkel, "Harper Vows Conservatives Will Bring Down 'Corrupt' Gov't," *Whitehorse Star*, 27 April 2005.

25 Brian Laghi, "Stronach Sees Risk in Forcing Fast Election," *Globe and Mail*, 3 May 2005.

26 Martin, *Belinda*, 177–8.

27 Plamondon, *Full Circle*, 391–3; Martin, *Belinda*, 192–7.

28 Martin, *Belinda*, 187.

29 Tonda MacCharles, "Stronach, Party Fighting; Her Campaign Owes $350,000," *Toronto Star*, 24 March 2004.

30 Siri Agrell, "$379,000 Remains Owing for Leadership Bid," *National Post*, 18 May 2005.

31 "Independent MP Parrish Latest Scare for Liberals in Key Vote," *Whitehorse Star*, 19 May 2005.

32 Shannon Proudfoot, "An Unlikely Politician: 'Authentic, Dignified, Gentle,'" *Ottawa Citizen*, 10 July 2005.

33 Anne Dawson and Allan Woods, "Drama on the Hill," *National Post*, 19 May 2005.

34 Grant Robertson, Anne Dawson, Jack Aubrey, and Allan Woods, "Grewal Tapes Irregular: Expert," *Calgary Herald*, 3 June 2005.

35 Campbell Clark, "Harper Backs Grewal as Ethics Probe Starts," *Globe and Mail*, 4 June 2005.

36 Plamondon, *Full Circle*, 394.

37 Plamondon, *Full Circle*, 395.

38 Mark Kennedy and Allan Woods, "Liberal Support Plummets, Poll Finds," *Ottawa Citizen*, 14 May 2005.

39 Alexander Panetta, "Troubled Liberals Lead Tories by 14 Points," *The Montreal Gazette*, 9 June 2005.

40 Johnson, *Stephen Harper and the Future of Canada*, 2nd ed., 430–8.

41 Gloria Galloway, "Harper Rolling Out an Image Makeover," *Globe and Mail*, 16 June 2005.

42 Don Martin, "The Wit and Wisdom of a Candid John Crosbie," *National Post*, 18 August 2005.

43 Brian Laghi, "Majority Want Harper Replaced, Poll Says," *Globe and Mail*, 16 July 2005.

44 "The Liberal Mole: A Look at Liberal Advertising Planning," 8 January 2006, stevejanke.com/archives/150317.php.

45 Wells, *Right Side Up*, 213–14.

46 Wells, *Right Side Up*, 177–9.

47 *Stand up for Canada*, Conservative Party of Canada, Federal Election Platform, 2006, 14.

48 Ibid., 26.

49 Ibid., 27.

50 Ibid., 15.

51 Ibid., 15.

52 Ibid., 15.

53 Ibid., 28.

54 Ibid., 28.

55 Ibid., 28.

56 Ibid., 29.

57 Ibid., 33.

58 *Demanding Better*, 22.

CHAPTER EIGHT

1 Anne Dawson, "Martin Talks Leave Layton Sour," *Ottawa Citizen*, 26 October 2005.

2 Jamey Heath, *Dead Centre: Hope, Possibility and Unity for Canadian Progressives* (Toronto: John Wiley and Sons Canada, 2007), 110–13.

3 Allan Woods, "Harper Leaves Death Blow to Layton," *National Post*, 8 November 2005.

4 CP, 29 June 2004.

5 *Regina Leader-Post* 29 June 2004.

6 Susan Riley, "Harper's Curious Launch," *Ottawa Citizen*, 30 November 2005.

7 Ibid.

8 Wells, *Right Side Up*, 177.

9 Don Martin, "Harper's Team Stumbles Along through the East," *Calgary Herald*, 1 December 2005.

10 Carolyn Stewart-Olsen to Yaroslav Baran, 1 December 2005.

11 Ray Novak to Ian Brodie, Doug Finley, and Tom Flanagan, 20 December 2005.

12 Wells, *Right Side Up*, 182–3.

13 Christopher Waddell and Christopher Dornan, "The Media and the Campaign," in Pammett and Dornan, *Canadian Federal Election of 2006*, 222.

14 Stephen Clarkson, "How the Big Red Machine Became the Little Red Machine," in Pammett and Dornan, *Canadian Federal Election of 2006*, 37.

15 Wells, *Right Side Up*, 187–8.

16 www.ctv.ca/servlet/ArticleNews/story/CTVNews/20051206/federal_elexn_update_051207?s_name=election2006&no_ads=.

17 www.cbcwatch.ca/?q=node/view/1599; Wells, *Right Side Up*, 189–90.

18 www.stephentaylor.ca/archives/000490.html.

19 Anne Dawson and Allan Woods, "Martin Ticks Off One President, Welcomes Another," *Edmonton Journal*, 10 December 2005.

20 www.ctv.ca/servlet/ArticleNews/story/CTVNews/20051209/
clinton_climate_051209/20051209?s_name=election2006.

21 www.ctv.ca/servlet/ArticleNews/story/CTVNews/20051213/
wilkins_canada_051213/20051213?s_name=election2006.

22 Campbell Clark and Gloria Galloway, "Martin Cranks Up Nationalist Rhetoric," *Globe and Mail*, 15 December 2005.

23 Wells, *Right Side Up*, 198–9.

24 John Ward, "Canada Called 'Welfare State' by Harper in 1997
Speech," *Calgary Herald*, 15 December 2005.

25 Johnson, *Stephen Harper and the Future of Canada*, 2nd ed., 452.

26 thestar.blogs.com/azerb/2005/12/commentapalooza_1.html.

27 "From the Campaign Trail," *The Montreal Gazette*, 19 December
2005; Jack Aubry, "Harper Wins by a Nose in English," *The Montreal Gazette*, 11 January 2006; Yaroslav Baran to Tom Flanagan,
19 October 2006.

28 Michael Marzolini, "Public Opinion and the 2006 Election," in
Pammett and Dornan, *Canadian Federal Election of 2006*, 266.

29 Chantal Hébert, *French Kiss*, 56.

30 Johnson, *Stephen Harper and the Future of Canada*, 2nd ed., 453.

31 L. Ian Macdonald, "Stephen Harper's Quebec Gambit," *National
Post*, 22 December 2005.

32 Eric Bélanger and Richard Nadeau, "The Bloc Québécois: A Sour-
Tasting Victory," in Pammett and Dornan, *Canadian Federal Election of 2006*, 129.

33 Stephen Clarkson, "How the Big Red Machine Became the Little
Red Machine," in Pammett and Dornan, *Canadian Federal Election of 2006*, 42.

34 "Harper Willing to Debate Duceppe in French," *Calgary Herald*,
21 December 2005.

35 Norma Greenaway and Anne Dawson, "Liberals Need PQ: Tories:
Harper Says Martin Wants to be Fighting Separatism," *National
Post*, 21 December 2005.

36 Norma Greenaway and Anne Dawson, "Harper Says He Will Not
Apologize," *National Post*, 22 December 2005.

37 "Harper Pledges Larger Arctic Military Presence," 22 December
2005, www.ctv.ca/servlet/ArticleNews/story/CTVNews/20051222/
harper_north051222/20051222?s_name=election2006.

38 Bill Curry, "Liberal Resigns over Vulgar Blog," *Globe and Mail*,
27 December 2005.

39 Both quotations are in "Party Leaders Speak out on T.O. Shootings," 27 December 2005, www.ctv.ca/servlet/ArticleNews/story/CTVNews/20051227/ELXN_leaders_guns_051227/20051227?s_name=election2006.

40 Steven Chase, Andy Hoffman, and Jeff Sallot, "RCMP Launch Trust Probe," *Globe and Mail*, 29 December 2005.

41 Jane Taber, "PM's 16-Hour Head Start Dampens Crisis from Within," *Globe and Mail*, 2 November 2005.

42 Michael Marzolini, "Public Opinion and the 2006 Election," in Pammett and Dornan, *Canadian Federal Election of 2006*, 272.

43 Joan Bryden, "Income Trust Complaints Draw US Response," *Calgary Herald*, 7 January 2006.

44 Sandra Cordon, "Brison Denies Tipping Off Banker," *Toronto Star*, 8 March 2006.

45 Wells, *Right Side Up*, 159.

46 Mark Kennedy, "Harper Not Fit for Office," *Edmonton Journal*, 18 December 2005.

47 Chris Cobb, "Liberals Launch Attack," *National Post*, 11 January 2006.

48 *Frank*, vol. 2, no. 5, 1 February 2006.

49 www.cbc.ca/news/background/cdngovernment/political-contributions.html.

50 Michael Marzolini, "Public Opinion and the 2006 Campaign," in Pammett and Dornan, *Canadian Federal Election of 2006*, 275.

51 Bruce Cheadle, "Liberals Take Heat after Ad Pulled from Web," *Brantford Expositor*, 11 January 2006.

52 Stephen Clarkson, "How the Big Red Machine Became the Little Red Machine," in Pammett and Dornan, *Canadian Federal Election of 2006*, 51.

53 Norma Greenaway, "Harper Focuses Conservative Campaign on Five Big Ideas," *Edmonton Journal*, 3 January 2006.

54 "Politician Paul Martin: All Things to All People," Conservative release, 2 January 2006, www.conservative.ca/EN/2459/37451?PHPSESSID=3949270c4c2e0ae4c298de0ce6e039e4; Wells, *Right Side Up*, 211.

55 Johnson, *Stephen Harper and the Future of Canada*, 2nd ed., 458.

56 Stephen Clarkson, "How the Big Red Machine Became the Little Red Machine," in Pammet and Dornan, *Canadian Federal Election of 2006*, 38; Waddell and Dornan, "The Media and the Campaign," 245–6.

57 Wells, *Right Side Up*, 220.
58 Jane Taber and Daniel Leblanc, "Mounties Probe $4.8 Million Pay-
   ment," *Globe and Mail*, 6 January 2006.
59 Normand Lester and Robin Philpot, *Les Secrets d'Option Canada*
   (Montreal: Editions des Intouchables, 2006).
60 Jack Aubry, "Harper Wins by a Nose in English," *The Montreal
   Gazette*, 11 January 2006.
61 davidakin.blogware.com/blog/_archives/2006/1/13/1674463.html.
62 Paul Darby to Stephen Harper, 22 December 2005, attached to
   "Harper Releases Plan Rooted in Canadian Values," released
   13 January 2006.
63 bondpapers.blogspot.com/2006/01/unfit-to-govern-costing-
   confusion-on.html.
64 "Tory Platform Preserves Social Programs; Liberals Dismiss Budget
   Figures as 'Hocus-Pocus,'" *Daily Mercury* (Guelph), 14 January 2006.
65 Dennis Bueckert, "Tories Didn't Tell All, Economist Says," *Edmonton Journal*, 16 January 2006.
66 "Conference Board of Canada Reaffirms Analysis of Conservative
   Platform," Conservative release, 15 January 2006.
67 Dennis Bueckert, "Tories Didn't Tell All, Economist Says," *Edmonton Journal*, 16 January 2006.
68 Mark Kennedy and Allan Woods, "Hargrove Outburst Derails
   PM," *The Montreal Gazette*, 19 January 2006.
69 "Martin Thrown off Message by Hargrove Comments," 19 January 2006, www.ctv.ca/servlet/ArticleNews/story/CTVNews/
   20060117/
   elxn_liberals_martin_060118?s_name=election2006&no_ads.
70 Alan Whitehorn, "The NDP and the Enigma of Strategic Voting,"
   in Pammet and Dornan, *Canadian Federal Election of 2006*, 96–7.
71 Ibid., 107–8, 112.
72 Wells, *Right Side Up*, 234–5; Heath, *Dead Centre*, 146.
73 Ibid., 119.
74 Heath, *Dead Centre, passim*.
75 Quoted in Liberal release, 17 January 2006.
76 "Senate, Courts Would Keep Tories in Check: Harper," 18 January
   2006, www.ctv.ca/servlet/ArticleNews/story/CTVNews/20060117/
   elxn_harper_campaign_060118/
   20060118?s_name=election2006&no_ads.

77 "My Views on Abortion Are Complex," *National Post*, 19 January 2006.

78 "Conservatives Get Endorsement," *Kamloops This Week*, 18 January 2006.

79 *Canada Elections Act*, s. 323(1: "No person shall knowingly transmit election advertising to the public in an electoral district on polling day before the close of all polling stations in the electoral district."

80 "Reynolds and Fortier Welcome Newspaper Endorsements," Conservative release, 22 January 2006, www.conservative.ca/EN/1091/40211.

81 Tony Hill to author, email, 28 September 2006.

CHAPTER NINE

1   Tasha Kheiriddin and Adam Daifallah, *Rescuing Canada's Right: Blueprint for a Conservative Revolution* (Toronto: Wiley Canada, 2005); Manning Centre website, www.manning centre.ca.

2   Statement of the Prime Minister to the House of Commons, PMO release, 23 November 2006.

3   Quoted in Johnson, *Stephen Harper and the Future of Canada*, 396.

4   Segal, *Long Road Back*, 200.

5   Edmund Burke, "Speech on the Reform of Representation," cited in Russell Kirk, *The Conservative Mind* (Chicago: Henry Regnery, 1960), 41.

6   Edmund Burke, *Reflections on the Revolution in France* (Indianapolis: Liberal Arts Press, 1955), 99.

7   Tom Flanagan, *Waiting for the Wave: The Reform Party and Preston Manning* (Toronto: Stoddard, 1995), 94–5.

8   Les Whittington, *Toronto Star*, 22 December 2005.

9   Elections Canada website, checked 14 September 2006.

10 On 2 February 2007, the Elections Canada website had posted the quarterly returns for all of 2006 but not the annual returns. A quarterly return gives the number of contributors in that quarter, whereas an annual return gives the number of contributors in that year. The two numbers can be quite different because many people make contributions in more than one quarter.

CHAPTER TEN

1 Chantal Hébert, "Humbled Opposition Forced to Swallow Harper Crime Bill," *The Record* (Kitchener), 19 October 2007.

2 Peter H. Russell, *Two Cheers for Minority Government: The Evolution of Canadian Parliamentary Democracy* (Toronto: Emond Montgomery, 2008), 57.

3 Ibid., 62.

4 L. Ian MacDonald, "'Nation Resolution Marks the Beginning of the Bloc's Decline," *The Montreal Gazette*, 17 September 2008.

5 *Stand Up For Canada*, 38.

6 John Ivison, "On Gas, Gaffes, and 'Mr. Mean,'" (interview with Stephen Harper), *National Post*, 13 September 2008.

7 Tom Zytaruk, *Like a Rock: The Chuck Cadman Story* (Vancouver: Harbour Publishing, 2008).

8 *Canada Elections Act*, s. 56(1).

9 Elections Canada website, www.elections.ca/scripts/webpep/fin/welcome.aspx?lang=e. The Liberal total of $10 million in 2006 was artificially inflated by including the registration fees for their leadership convention. Most of this would have gone to cover costs, leaving little profit.

10 "Fear Factory" is a heavy-metal rock group, www.fearfactory.com; "Fear Factor" is an NBC TV show about overcoming scary challenges, www.nbc.com/Fear_Factor.

11 "Conservatives Show Off Election War Room," *Daily Mercury* (Guelph), 3 April 2007.

12 Peter Kuitenbrouwer, "Fuel Use of Liberal Campaign Jet under Attack," *National Post* , 8 September 2008.

13 Campbell Clark and Josh Wingrove, "Liberals Left in Dark as Plane Grounded in Montreal," *Globe and Mail*, 17 September 2008.

14 Donald Gutstein, "The Real Blitz That Buried Dion," *The Tyee*, 28 October 2008, thetyee.ca/Mediacheck/2008/10/28/Dion.

15 Canadian Press, "Anti-Dion Ads Producing Laughs, Not Votes; Poll Shows Majority Believe Conservative TV Advertisements Attacking Liberal Leader Are Unfair," *Daily Mercury* (Guelph, Ontario), 8 February 2007.

16 www.ctv.ca/servlet/ArticleNews/story/CTVNews/20070410/ses_poll_070410.

17 www.conservative.ca/EN/1091/80381.

18 www.ctv.ca/servlet/ArticleNews/story/CTVNews/20080609/
    carbon_plan_080609.
19 Juliet O'Neill, "Green Shift Support Declining, Poll Shows Liber-
    als' Carbon Tax Proposal Not Enough to Beat Tories: Pollster,"
    Ottawa Citizen, 2 September 2008.
20 www.conservative.ca, viewed 10 September 2008.
21 Fleishman Hilliard poll tracker, election08.fleishman.ca, viewed 10
    September 2008.
22 Joan Bryden, "Tory TV Ads a Success, Poll Shows: Barrage of
    Sweater-Clad Harper Ads Help Tories Win Air War," Canadian
    Press, 13 September 2008.
23 Bruce Campion-Smith and Les Whittington, "Dion Resigns but
    Will Remain as Leader for Now," *Toronto Star*, 20 October 2008.
24 "Strong Foundation" and "Gamble 1," www.conservative.ca,
    viewed 17 September 2008.
25 James Bradshaw, "Harper Plays Populist Tune on Arts Cuts,"
    Globe and Mail, 12 September 2008.
26 "PM Played the Piano and Sang a Few Songs for the Journalists
    Covering the Conservative Tour," www.flickr.com/photos/
    pmharper/2854635404.
27 Johnson, *Stephen Harper*, 11.
28 "Extending Maternity and Parental Benefits," Conservative cam-
    paign release, 15 September 2008.
29 *The True North Strong and Free: Stephen Harper's Plan for Cana-
    dians*, 41.
30 Conservative campaign release, "Just the Facts: Will Stéphane Dion
    Answer the $230,000 Question?" 10 September 2008.
31 *The True North Strong and Free*, 27.
32 Chantal Hébert, "Tories' Arts Cuts Spark Ire in Quebec," *Toronto
    Star*, 29 August 2008; *Maclean's*, "Election 2008: The Inside
    Story," 27 October 2008, 34.
33 Bruce Cheadle, "Harper Skewers Gala Crowd, Defends Arts Cuts,"
    Canadian Press, 23 September 2008.
34 *The True North Strong and Free*, 36.
35 www.cbc.ca/money/story/2008/10/02/markets-drop.html.
36 *Maclean's*, "Election 2008: The Inside Story," 27 October 2008, 38.
37 Ipsos News Centre, "Post-Debate Summary: English-Language
    Leaders' Debate," 2 October 2008, www.ipsos-na.com/news/
    pressrelease.cfm?id=4106.

38 Clarkson, *Big Red Machine*, 26.

39 Eoin Callan and Paul Vieira, "Politics Factored into Bank Aid Deal," *National Post*, 24 October 2008.

40 www.ctv.ca/servlet/ArticleNews/story/CTVNews/20081006/ election2008_harper_081008/20081008.

41 Andrew Mayeda, Juliet O'Neill, and Glenn Johnson, "Opposition Attack Harper's Comments on Stock Bargains," *National Post*, 7 October 2008.

42 Link on Stephen Taylor's blog to YouTube video, 9 October 2008, www.stephentaylor.ca/page/2.

43 David Akin, "Canada Sets Record for Creating Jobs," *National Post*, 10 October 2008.

44 "Canada Rated World's Soundest Bank System," *Financial Post*, 10 October 2008.

45 Canadian Press, "Bank Deal Is Asset Swap," *Winnipeg Sun*, 10 October 2008.

46 Andrew Mayeda, "Harper Makes Final Push for Quebec Votes," *National Post*, 12 October 2008.

47 www.nanosresearch.com/main.asp.

48 *Maclean's*, "Election 2008: The Inside Story," 27 October 2008, 49.

49 Tom Flanagan, "The Mathematics of a Majority Government," *Globe and Mail*, 28 September 2007.

50 Les Perreaux, "Opponents Issue Battle Election Cries, Slam Charest," *Globe and Mail*, 27 October 2008.

51 Bill C-22: An Act to amend the Constitution Act, 1867 (Democratic representation), www.parl.gc.ca/common/Bills_ls.asp?lang=E&ls= c22&source=library_prb&Parl=39&Ses=2.

52 CBC News, "Ignatieff Champions Puffin as Symbol of Liberal Party," www.cbc.ca/news/yourview/2007/08/ ignatieff_champions_puffin_as.html.

CHAPTER ELEVEN

1 Ecclesiastes, 3:1.

2 Throne speech summary, posted at www.sft-ddt.gc.ca/eng/media. asp?id=1383.

3 Steve Rennie, "Harper Compares Economic Crisis to 1929; APEC Pledges to Shun Trade Barriers," Canadian Press, 22 November

2008, g8live.org/2008/11/22/harper-compares-economic-crisis-to-1929-apec-pledges-to-shun-trade-barriers.

4 Department of Finance Summary, www.fin.gc.ca/n08/08-095-eng.asp.

5 Flanagan, *Harper's Team*, 275.

6 CTV, "NDP, Bloc in Coalition Talks before Fiscal Update: Tape," 30 November 2008, www.ctv.ca/servlet/ArticleNews/story/CTVNews/20081130/conservative_budget_081130/20081130?hub=TopStories.

7 "A Policy Accord to Address the Present Economic Crisis," www.liberal.ca/pdf/docs/081201_Policy_Frame_en_signed.pdf.

8 CBC, "Details of Proposed Liberal-NDP Coalition emerge," 1 December 2008, www.cbc.ca/canada/ottawa/story/2008/11/30/canada-coalition.html?ref=rss&loomia_si=to:a16:g2:r1:c0.150258:b19907567.

9 Norma Greenaway, "Poll Exclusive: Big 'No' to Coalition," *Vancouver Province*, 10 December 2008.

10 "Q&A: Prime Minister Stephen Harper speaks with The Post's John Ivison," *National Post*, 15 January 2009.

11 Andy Blatchford, "Ignatieff Won't Rule Out Election: Coalition, Liberals Await Tuesday's Budget," *Hamilton Spectator*, 21 January 2009.

12 Andrew Mayeda, "Conservatives Raise $21M in 2008, New Fund-raising Record," *National Post*, 2 February 2009.

Index